Asian Social Science Series
Editors: Chan Kwok Bun, Syed Farid Alata

The Making of
SINGAPORE
SOCIOLOGY
Society and State

Tong Chee Kiong & **Lian Kwen Fee** (eds.)

Academic Publishers

B R I L L
TIMES ACADEMIC PRESS

First published 2002
by Times International Publishing
under the imprint **Times Academic Press**
Times Media Academic Publishing
Times Centre, 1 New Industrial Road,
Singapore 536196
Fax: (65) 62854871
E-mail: tap@tpl.com.sg
Online Book Store:
http://www.timesone.com.sg/tap

Printed by Loi Printing Pte Ltd, Singapore

Published by Times Academic Press
in association with Brill Academic
Publishers.
Exclusive distribution outside
ASEAN (Brunei Darussalam,
Cambodia, Indonesia, Laos,
Malaysia, Myanmar, Philippines,
Singapore, Thailand and Vietnam)
by Brill Academic Publishers.

Brill Academic Publishers
PO Box 9000, 2300 PA Leiden
The Netherlands
tel: +31 715353566
fax: +31 715317532
email: cs@brill.nl

For US and Canadian customers:
Brill Academic Publishers
112 Water Street Suite 400
Boston MA 02109
tel: 1 800 9624406
fax: 617 2632324
email: cs@brillusa.com

National Library Board (Singapore) Cataloguing in Publication Data

The Making of Singapore Sociology / Tong Chee Kiong and Lian Kwen Fee (eds.). –
Singapore : Times Academic Press in association with Brill Academic Publishers, 2002.

p. cm. – (Asian Social Science Series ; vol. 2)

ISBN: 981-210-198-5

1. Sociology – Singapore. 2. Singapore – Social conditions.
I. Tong, Chee Kiong. II. Lian, Kwen Fee, 1950- III. Series: Asian social science series ;
vol. 2

HN700.67
306.095957 — dc21   SLS2002028832

CONTENTS

Preface

The first attempt to bring together a collection of work on the sociology of Singapore society was in an edited volume by Riaz Hassan, *Singapore: Society In Transition*, published in 1976 by Oxford University Press. In 1976 the development of sociology in the island state, which had only a decade earlier gained independence, was still in its infancy. The contributions in this volume reflected a small but engaging range of issues that concerned social scientists at that time. Thirty-two years after sociology was established as a discipline at the University of Singapore, sufficient local research had accumulated to warrant producing another collection of previously published essays in *Understanding Singapore Society* (1997) edited by Ong Jin Hui, Tong Chee Kiong and Tan Ern-Ser. This volume made available to students a broad range of work carried out in the period on Singapore society, which may not have been so easily accessible. It was also intended as a sourcebook for graduate students and researchers. On the initiative of Ong Jin Hui, *The Making of Singapore Sociology* was conceived, as a timely effort to take stock of sociological research. This volume reviews significant developments in selected fields, indicates the empirical work that has been done, and assesses its contributions in the light of relevant theoretical questions. We would like to thank Adeline Loi for providing unstinting administrative and clerical support, and seeing this book to its completion.

Tong Chee Kiong
Lian Kwen Fee

Introduction

Constructing and Deconstructing Singapore Society

Lian Kwen Fee & Tong Chee Kiong

The construction of nation-states in Southeast Asia has been an unplanned and hurried process. Formed as a consequence of post-War decolonization, these states have been created out of territories under colonial administration. As Hobsbawm (1990,171) comments, their boundaries were drawn without any reference to, and sometimes without the knowledge of, their inhabitants. Having inherited the state, the local political elite was immediately confronted with the challenge of creating a collective identity. Singapore is no exception to this experience. Granted limited self-government by the British in 1959, it was incorporated into the Malaysian Federation in 1963 and reluctantly gained independence on expulsion from Malaysia in 1965. Its leaders found themselves in possession of a state but without a nation. Since then, the Peoples' Action Party leaders and Singaporeans themselves have struggled to come to terms with their cultural/national identity. Despite all the efforts that have been put into creating this national identity — and with it hopefully a collective self-assurance — in the last two decades, this deep-seated *angst* has remained very much in the consciousness of many older Singaporeans.

To understand this psychological ambivalence that some Singaporeans continue to hold with regard to their political identity and sense of community, it is necessary to highlight several developments in the political history of Singapore. The first generation PAP leadership was a group of politically conscious Malayans who were totally convinced that Singapore could not survive except in a union with Malaya (later Malaysia) and who were committed to unification for both economic and sentimental reasons. Between 1949 when the non-partisan Malayan Forum was formed by these leaders (which

1

included Abdul Razak who later became the second Prime Minister of Malaysia) for the purpose of forging a "Malayan" consciousness and until the 1965 separation, the PAP devoted much of its political energy toward achieving this union. They were largely successful in convincing the island population to support such a merger. When they were expelled, it came as a rude shock. So emotional was the experience that the Singapore government referred to Malaya, soon after separation, as "one people in two countries" (Turnbull 1977, 297). While the newly independent government redirected its energy toward managing the problem of its economic viability, it was also left with the task of forging its collective identity as a nation — made acutely difficult because it had lost its past in one stroke of the pen.

Over the next 15 years after separation, the PAP government set about urgently solving the problems of economic survival. The past was best forgotten as this could only be a hindrance to such a task. Singaporeans were called upon to absorb the full impact of a global culture that was essentially instrumental, technically-oriented, consumption-conscious, and utilitarian. The overwhelming success of its economic policies was evident by the mid-1970s. Between the mid-sixties and the mid-seventies Singapore's economic growth was among the world's highest. Near full employment was achieved by 1970 and real per capita income doubled in the 1970s. A consumer-utilitarian culture was firmly entrenched in Singapore by the late seventies. It was only in the early 1980s that government representatives expressed disquiet over the pace at which Singapore's heritage was being obliterated in the rush for development dollars.

The Singapore psyche emerged out of these political developments in the period of decolonization, and this has a direct bearing on how Singapore sociology has unfolded. The "Singapore identity" is best described as one of ambivalence for two reasons. First, there are four, what Wolf (1988, 755) refers to as, cultural world orders superimposed on one society — namely Confucian-Chinese, Islamic-Malay, Hindu-Indian, and Christian, Anglo-Saxon — out of which a common community has to be constructed. Second, its separation from Malaysia has engendered mixed responses to its national consciousness. Does it deny the past or acknowledge it? In the early period of independence, it did indulge in self-denial by de-emphasizing the importance of history in primary schools. It has promoted an awareness of the origins of Singapore in recent years. For much of the development of Singapore sociology the question of identity, both national and ethnic, have dominated the interests of local scholars, second only to the instrumental problems of development and modernization.

It is against this political backdrop — a society reluctantly dragged into nationhood and forced to stand on its own feet economically — that the social sciences in general, and sociology in particular, were established. It should therefore be unsurprising that if sociology is about making sense of the societies that sociologists live in, the development of sociology in Singapore reflects local concerns framed against the exigencies of building a society that could be economically viable, yet possessing a measure of self-confidence which accompanies a people who may yet come to share a common collective identity. It is a mere coincidence, though not insignificant, that sociology was formally established as a teaching and research discipline in the same year that Singapore was expelled from Malaysia in 1965. It is certainly not a coincidence that the path that sociology in Singapore has taken was dominated by a concern with the institutional and material problems of a new, migrant, and heterogeneous society as well as the social cohesion of such a society.

Singapore's geopolitical position in Southeast Asia, its territorial compactness and resource limitations, and the sensitivities of its ethnic heterogeneity, combined with a government determined to face these difficulties by committing itself to impose what it deemed to be a social model best for its citizenry, have given Singapore the reputation of being a society that comes closest to being a social laboratory. For this reason, Ong et al. (1997) comment, sociological research and frames of reference can easily infringe on the territory of government. For this reason too, the making of Singapore sociology has been a self-conscious exercise, because Singapore society has not evolved from unconscious long-term processes, it was created in a conscious and pragmatic manner.

The early practice of sociology in Singapore was not, however, informed by the problematic of the "nation-state" referred to earlier. This was to come later. The early work of the sociology of Singapore was influenced by modernization theory and its application within the sociology of development. It was the problematic of "development" rather than that of the "nation-state" that came to the forefront of the work of the early sociologists. The sociology of Singapore may be described under two general themes, modernization and modernity, which constitute the two parts of the volume.

Modernization

In his contribution to a volume on *Modernization in South-East Asia* (Evers 1973, 81-93), the Deputy Prime Minister at the time Goh Keng Swee — who is a trained economist and took a strong interest in the development of the social sciences in Singapore — argued that for developing societies in Southeast Asia to "take off", it should concentrate on what he describes as the leading sector of the economy, the manufacturing industry. The expansion of this sector would introduce new technology, new social attitudes, raise levels of existing skills, provide employment for the large numbers of unemployed or underemployed citizens. However, he continues, such an economic breakthrough could only occur if political institutions of sufficient strength and durability were established. In particular he singled out the quality of government and education as the two most important institutions. In his view of modernization, the economic and social transformation of a society would occur most effectively in the city. To a large extent the issues that sociologists addressed in the seventies and eighties came within the parameters of what Goh conceived as modernization; and reflected the concerns of the dominant analytic paradigm of American sociology of the sixties, modernization theory.

The sociology of development in Singapore, as Khondker in Chapter 1 comments, reveals a gradual shift from the modernization studies of the 1970s to a more political-economic turn, as a consequence of the influence of dependency and world systems theories, in the 1980s. Echoing the tenor of American modernization literature, local sociologists focused their attention on the institutions and agents that facilitate or impede change: the role of the elite and the middle class, the impact of industrialization on family, marriage and fertility, housing and relocation in a rapidly changing urban environment. These were issues that reflected the programmatic aspect of modernization, and as the author notes, preoccupations that should be appreciated in a period when Singapore experienced impressive economic growth and prosperity. Amidst the dominant interest in the modernization agenda, there were, subsequently, several forays into a more global approach that emphasized external linkages and the international division of labour, bringing attention to the iniquities of much acclaimed economic progress. However, as the East Asian dragon economies including Singapore gained wide attention and admiration for their performance, the question was inevitably asked as to what they had in common to explain their rise. In the late 1980s, there has been a return to the role of culture/values in development under the cover of neo-modernization theories; attention was drawn to the relationship between Confucian values and the East Asian economies. This predictably spawned a plethora of studies attempting to uncover the "magic" of Confucianism, exposing it to the criticism of being culturalist and reductionist in offering explanations for the success of not only such economies in general but right down to a wide range of micro studies on Chinese business and enterprise. We would do well to remind ourselves that any attempt to replicate Weber's thesis that the Protestant ethic is the spirit of capitalism is doomed to fail if we ignore historical contingencies. It is timely that Levy (1992,17) reminds us to make the distinction of "first-comers" from "latecomers" to modernization. He notes:

> In the interim, there developed a demonstration effect of something capable of replacing this-worldly religious asceticism — the religious motivation to ceaseless this-worldly striving to which Weber attached so much importance in the first phase of modernization. The replacement was the demonstration effect of an exponentially increasing curve of material productivity. That is generally regarded as "material betterment." By the end of the nineteenth century, the possibility of limitless material betterment was held out to everyone.

Simply put, there were enough people in Singapore, the majority of whom had a strong migrant background and aspirations, hungry and pragmatic enough to seize the opportunities that came their way with the help of timely interventions from a strong government. Khondker quotes from Huff, "The Singapore model is unlikely to be replicated elsewhere, not only because the Republic is a city state, but also because of the unacceptability in many other polities of a very heavy foreign economic presence, and because of difficulties in effecting the same degree of government control as in Singapore." In the search for general explanations, we sometimes forget the invisible hand of historical contingency.

The sociology of development in Singapore, Khondker concludes, has been a derivative and borrowed discourse, in contrast to the theoretical insights generated on Latin America, Africa, and South Asia. Calling for more innovative and comparative-historical work, he also acknowledges that the sociology of development and change in the future should take into account the impact of globalization and the knowledge society on Singapore.

Urban studies in Singapore, Ho notes (Chapter 2), have been traditionally dominated by economic geographers and historians. They focused on the role of the port city in entrepot trade and its ability to derive maximum benefit through the interplay of trade, communication, and transportation. In the urbanization literature of the so-called Third World, Singapore, because of its status as a city-state, has been regarded as atypical of cities. Created by colonization and trade, it is a heterogenetic centre responsible for diffusing new ideas and tastes, in contrast to the orthogenetic role of older cities of Southeast Asia in maintaining tradition, culture and heritage.

Sociological studies contributed to understanding the social organization of the city: the ethnic division in urban communities and occupations, the consequences of high density living and urban relocation precipitated by the establishment of HDB estates, and urban subcultures centred around youth, consumption and deviance. The more recent developments have paid some attention to urban politics and governance. As a collective consumption good, housing has been unknowingly politicized to such an extent that it has become a significant source of political legitimacy for the ruling party. The growth of a sizeable middle class has not, however, contributed to civil society largely because as the chief beneficiaries of state-led development, they eschew political participation that is easily construed as oppositional. In the 1990s, the government's initiative in economic restructuring in response to regionalization and globalization prompted researchers to look at Singapore as a global city in a comparative perspective. Such restructuring has led to the relocation of manufacturing to regional industrial parks and the location of capital/technology-intensive and service-based activity in the city. The resultant movements of people will have an impact on the social organization of the family and gender relations.

Pioneering work on the study of the family was carried out, when Singapore was still a British colony in the late 1940s, by British anthropologists who were commissioned to write reports on family life, social customs and religious practices of local communities. Freedman's ethnographic study of the Chinese family and Djamour's on the Malay family yielded much information and occasionally provided sociological insights; both are often referred to as the earliest benchmark of local research on the family. Systematic research on the family began in the mid-1960s in what Quah (Chapter 3) describes as a period of consolidation, the result of the establishment of social science in the university and the availability of international funding. Much of this research looked at family fertility, size and procreation decisions, driven by a particular agenda. The problem of unchecked population growth, which both international development agencies and domestic governments had singled out as the most serious hindrance to effective economic growth in developing countries, was one major focus of social science research in the seventies in Singapore. Data were needed for economic and family planning purposes. In the mid-seventies more sociologically-inclined research was carried out. In studies of inter-ethnic marriages, religion rather than ethnic affiliation was a significant influence. Muslims and Christians were more likely to marry across ethnic boundaries. Well-known theories in the sociology of the family such as the "isolated" nuclear family in industrial society and the kinship networks in an urbanized society were revisited. Work of this nature had the potential to contribute to middle-range theory. Certainly the opportunity to examine change in family structure and process in a highly urbanized and rapidly industrializing society presented itself. However the momentum, we contend, was lost as research in the 1980s reverted to policy-driven issues such as family formation, fertility, and marriage decisions. This is directly attributed to government concern in 1983 that Singaporeans were engaging in a "lop-sided procreation pattern"; namely that women with low educational qualifications were producing more children than those with tertiary education, precipitating the debate on eugenics for the rest of the decade.

As an island-nation, created by fiat and with no resources except its strategic location and people, the PAP government quickly set about devising economic strategies that would ensure its survival. Critical to its plan was and continues to be education and manpower training. No issue has dominated the lives of Singaporeans more than credentialism and has been more relevant to the social fabric of Singapore society. However, the contributions of sociology to understanding this most important influence have not been commensurate. Chang (Chapter 4), drawing on classical sociology, identifies three theoretical approaches that have been used to varying degrees in research on education in Singapore. The functionalist view, exemplified in Durkheim's work, argues that modern education is directed toward developing the individuals for the purpose of meeting the needs of society. This view readily struck a chord with government sentiments and much of the research gravitated toward the economic benefits of education, its impact on the occupational structure and social mobility, and the effectiveness of the educational system. A Marxist approach draws attention to the influence of education on social inequalities, and one of the more important concepts used to understand social reproduction is cultural capital. Some work was done on language differences and income levels. English was regarded as economically advantageous relative to Chinese. While Chang lauds local contributions on bilingualism and education to the international literature, it is sorely lacking in two areas where research in developed societies has been impressive: ability tracking and school climate. In a society where streaming has played such a major role in people's lives, the contribution of social science has been disappointing.

Studies of labour and work in Singapore fall in three areas (Chapter 5). First, there is a steady stream of data collected by state agencies on labour regulation, market and organization that are useful for secondary analysis. Second, more scholarly work has come from economics and management. One in particular, partial toward political economy, traces the corporatist mode of labour regulation adopted in Singapore by examining the historical evolution of industrial relations and political developments since the end of the Japanese Occupation. This and some recent work draw attention to the relationship between the labour process and wider social relations such as state policies, employer initiatives and market imperatives. Such studies, Hing comments, point to a positive development in the field. Third, sociological contributions have been uneven. One attempt at examining the relationship between the division of labour and patterns of inequality display only a rudimentary knowledge of class formation and class processes. Another attempt, an ethnographic study of the everyday lives of women in a factory, could lead the way for more innovative work on the culture and discourse of the workplace in Singapore. The important question of how class processes are gendered and/or ethnicized may then be addressed.

Research interests in medical sociology, Straughan outlines in Chapter 6, have a strong applied orientation and fall in two areas. Research on preventive health behaviour, such as cancer screening, heart disease, contraception, and condom use to prevent sexually transmitted diseases are illustrative of the concerns of an advanced industrial society. These studies produced useful results in ethnic and gender variations in health behaviour. The other concentration of work is in the health care system itself. Some examples of this are the dual utilization of modern and traditional medicine, the medical and nursing professions. The author identifies several issues that sociologists could well pay attention to in the near future: the rising cost of medical care and state intervention in the organisation of health, lifestyle and preventive behaviour, alternative forms of healing, and the uncharted social consequences of increasing use of medical technology.

In Chapter 7, Ko highlights two issues that have dominated research on social stratification. Reflecting the interest of scholars internationally at a time when many developing societies were experiencing rapid economic growth, social scientists in Singapore in the 1970s ask themselves whether this would increase or reduce income inequality. Contrary to prevailing wisdom consistent results revealed greater equity amongst Singaporeans. Two alternative explanations were offered. The presence of a high proportion of self-employed workers in the service and commercial sectors of the local economy had the overall effect of reducing income inequality. The other explanation offered was the redistributive policies adopted by a government, committed to Fabian ideals, in public housing, education, public health, and transportation. The other issue that concerned social scientists in the 1970s was over the question of whether a significant middle class had emerged as a consequence of outstanding economic growth between the mid-1960s and mid-1970s, reflecting the agenda of modernization theorists who considered the middle class a critical agency to the development of a modern society.

The absence of a distinctive class structure in Singapore may be attributed to the fact that it is a new society, with a strong and recent migrant background and unprecedented levels of social mobility in the last three decades. Together with an interventionist government with regard to domestic policies, for example close to 80% of the population are accommodated in more or less uniform state housing, class differences are not readily discernible. Studies in the seventies cited by Ko point out that one's social origins have a negligible effect on educational and occupational attainment. In contrast, the income disparity between Malays and non-Malays has increased in the 1960s and 1970s of high economic growth. Various reasons have been offered, including low female labour participation, low educational attainment, employment problems of Malay youths, and even an attempt at a culturalist explanation. Similarly, the disparity between female and male incomes has been explained by looking at educational attainment, family origins and segmented labour market theory. None of these studies offer a satisfactory explanation. The reason, Ko asserts, is that existing theoretical approaches to the study of social inequality are preoccupied with individual attributes rather than with normative structures, a concern of the classical approaches of Marx and Weber. There is a need to overcome the individualistic bias and address normative structures in the educational system and labour market such as streaming, social networks, and industrial sectors. Ko sees future research in such a structuralist approach as well as cross-national research for comparative purposes.

Modernity

Singapore was the product of Western modernity, which bequeathed to the rest of the world three critical structures: capitalism, industrialism, and the nation-state. The last, the nation-state, is responsible for the creation of a single world (Giddens, quoted in Hall et al. 1992, 72); for as societies evolve into nation-states, they are drawn into participation in an increasingly unitary inter-state system, a process we now call globalization and the associated phenomenon of modernity. The globalizing condition did not begin with the inauguration of the nation-state in Singapore 1965. The process, to be more accurate regionalization, began much earlier with the founding of Singapore as a British trading outpost in 1819. It was strategically located as a confluence of trade, services, migrations, and capital flows — first for its immediate hinterland in the 19th century, Malaya, with which it shares a common past including its Malay, Chinese, and Indian origins; then growing into a regional centre for Southeast, South, and East Asia in the 20th century; and now making the transition to a city of the world in the 21st century.

The current preoccupation with the concept of modernity is attributed to a shift from economy to culture (Luhmann 1998, 2). The culture of modernity may be regarded in two senses. First, it refers to the experience of a modern lifestyle   consumption conscious and utilitarian-oriented — that transcends time and space in a way not seen previously. It has homogenizing and fragmenting consequences. Second, it refers to the culture of the nation-state and deals with how national histories, origins and myths are maintained through popular culture, for the purpose of identity-construction and maintenance. Because of history and location, the Singaporean inhabits a complex cultural universe consisting of the two mentioned, global-regional and national. To this may be added a third, communal-ethnic. Together they constitute the three sources of cultural knowledge that individuals and communities have to contend with and arbitrate. While the twin processes of globalization and modernity "diminishes the grip of local circumstances over people's lives" (Hall et al. 1992, 66), it is not a zero-sum game. The global and the local requires mediation, resulting in a new articulation (ibid, 304). The nation-state too attempts to mediate between the global and local constituencies as sources of cultural knowledge for its citizens.

If social scientists were asked to identify the most critical influences of the social landscape of Singapore, it surely must come down to two: ethnicity and government. In Chapter 8, Lian and Rajah underline the role of the state in essentializing ethnicity, which has structured not only the commonsense understanding of such differences but also in the way in which generations of scholars have come to make sense of ethnic relations in this part of the world. Ascriptive ethnicity was used as an instrument of the colonial authority to govern the local population by assigning ethnic groups presumed economic and social roles. The PAP government adapted this practice by espousing multiracialism as its national ideology, bestowing equal status to the cultures and identities of the four founding races. The vigour and consistency with which it has applied the CMIO (Chinese, Malay, Indian, Others) categorization of the population across a range of social policies has affected the everyday lives of most Singaporeans to the extent that local sensibilities about group differences are significantly defined by the state. Recent work has begun questioning such essentialist conceptions by deconstructing the all-inclusive labels of Chinese, Malays, and Indians. In this regard the authors call for more work to be done on how ethnic boundaries are crossed, for example through intermarriages and increased migration. In the face of migration and transnationalization, the authors suggest, essentialist understanding of "Chineseness", "Malayness" and "Indianness" will undergo a process of relativization. The issues raised here are relevant to the following three chapters on the Chinese, Malays, and Indians.

"Locating the Chinese", in an era that has spanned colonization, the expansion of capitalism, the emergence of new nation-states and now transnationalization, is the underlying theme of the next chapter (9). Given that the history of the Chinese overseas is the history of migration and settlement, locating them methodologically is necessary to a sociological interpretation of the Chinese. Hence, the Chinese in Singapore may be viewed from the standpoint of

Singapore society (Chinese identity in a colonial and post-colonial multiethnic society), Chinese studies (comparative study of social organisation), Southeast Asian studies (comparative treatment of the Chinese in Southeast Asian societies), Overseas Chinese (the *huaqiao* and *huaren* dichotomy), East Asian studies (Confucianist society as a cultural world order), and Diaspora studies.

Kwok also outlines a number of topics appropriate to a historical sociology. In the 19th century and the first half of the 20th century, a sociology of the Chinese in Singapore should include looking at: the Straits-born Chinese (*Babas*) versus the China-born Chinese who came mostly as coolies, the social organization of the Chinese including the role of secret societies and autonomous traditional associations, community leaders and intellectual movements. The process of "Malayanization" in the pre-War decades has hardly been explored, a period when Malayan Chinese and English literature together with the "Nanyang" school of painting flourished. The Japanese Occupation and its impact on the Chinese educated can be studied from the sociology of memory. Decolonization precipitated a political battle between a nascent Malayan nationalism led by the English-educated and *huaqiao* patriotism that captured the aspiration of the Chinese-educated, as both sought to assert a political identity on an island they have come to regard as their home. In post-independence Singapore it is the state that has come to be the major protagonist in shaping the identity of the Chinese.

The overseas Chinese (including those in Singapore) have had to confront modernity headlong with an intensity that their counterparts in China or the other ethnic groups here did not have to face. This is because, the author argues, overseas Chinese society such as Singapore evolved under conditions of modernity in contrast to China, where modernity struggled to come to terms with a pre-existing traditional social order. Hence the overseas Chinese, quoting from Goh Keng Swee in 1967, "had to make their own adjustments to the modern world unimpeded by traditionalist institutions." The consequence is that they have had to assume multiple identities in order to cope with a shifting condition that we have now come to describe as globalization and transnationalization.

The Malays, on the other hand, have had to come to terms with modernization and modernity. Alatas (Chapter 10), in a reflexive essay, attempts to answer the question, what is the sociology of Malay studies in Singapore? He identifies several areas that have contributed to the sociology of Malay society. The majority status of the Malays while Singapore was part of Malaysia has undoubtedly influenced how they perceived their identity on the island. Separation has reconfigured Malay identity. Whereas in the past most Arabs would have considered themselves Malays, the author relates the strong Arab reaction when they were portrayed as part of the Malay community in a recent television programme. Clearly, when traditional intergroup rivalry between the Chinese and Malays have diminished because they have largely been depoliticized or channelled into economic and educational pursuits by skilful government, intraethnic distinctions within the "Malay" community have become more strident. Complex distinctions are now being forged in the interests of maintaining social boundaries among themselves.

Three other areas are highlighted as potential for the advancement of sociological research. The author recommends a relational approach to understand the class position of the Malays, in place of the distributional approach that has dominated work on stratification. A relational approach would draw attention to the hierarchy of political-economic relations responsible for income differentials that exist between the ethnic groups, thereby situating the explanation for relative Malay economic disadvantage in the social structure of Singapore. In the sociology of ethnic relations, empirical research has been directed at intermarriages and political integration. Finally, Malay "underdevelopment" has been a traditional interest of scholars in the region. The emphasis has been on the non-economic causes of Malay economic "backwardness", much interest gravitating to explanations of cultural determinism.

Theoretical work in ethnic and racial studies, Arumugam (Chapter 11) comments, view ethnicity as historical, socially constructed, situational, negotiable, dialectical and political. However, there are few examples in the sociology of Indians in Singapore that illustrate such developments. The Indians here, like everywhere else they have settled in Southeast Asia, are the most understudied of all the ethnic minorities. Being the most visible and disadvantaged of the minority groups in Malaysia and Singapore, their experience of discrimination has been poorly documented sociologically. Citing studies of Indians in the US, the author suggests that the interplay between structural constraints and resistance through individual agency and negotiation is a useful line of inquiry for scholars interested in this group. Not surprisingly, Indians had not perceived themselves as "Indians" before colonialism and independence. The "Other" was regarded in terms of culture and caste, and this brings us to the next point.

South Indians were drawn voluntarily to this region as indentured labour for the plantations and public works; yet the record of exploitation of Indian labour in Singapore and Malaysia in sociological or anthropological literature has been sparse. Furthermore, the author notes, the coolie system represented a dramatic rupture of traditional social, religious and caste structure. On the voyage here and in the new settlements, these structures were rendered obsolete and adjustments were made in living arrangements, marriage across castes, ritual pollution and religious practices. The Indian experience in Singapore and Malaysia encapsulated both rupture and continuity, and cries out for sociological and anthropological investigations. The Indian diaspora of recent years may be distinguished from Indian migration in the early 19th century. The former, referred to as "border", are those with technological skills to market and regard Singapore as a springboard to more attractive opportunities elsewhere. The second type, "exclusivism", includes those permanently settled in Singapore and no longer regard India as its home.

A combination of its migrant background, multiethnic and multicultural composition, and strong market orientation has produced an exceptional pattern of multilanguage use, both spoken and written, in Singapore. The situation has been described as "polyglossia", where several languages and varieties of a language exist side by side. The politics of nationbuilding and education are also the politics of language use. In Chapter 12, Leong describes the language pattern of Singaporeans, asking the pertinent question, who speaks what to whom and for how long? No firm conclusions can be drawn about code-switching. Linguistic divisions also reflect issues of social inequality in society. There is some evidence to suggest that higher income is related to use of

English. The practice of streaming in primary schools, partly based on language competence, may compound inequality but more research will be required. In concluding, Leong proposes a materialist account that shifts in language use can be attributed to economic and instrumental motives, citing Mandarin as an example.

Changes in the religious affiliations of Singaporeans act as a barometer for social change. The census of 1931 showed that those who claim adherence to Chinese religion constituted over 97% of the population. In 1990, this had dropped to about 52%. Over the same period, Christianity registered a growth from nearly 3% to close to 13% in 1990. Noting that much of the early studies of Chinese religion were anthropological/ethnographic accounts of ritual practices and spirit-medium cults, Tong (Chapter 13) cites attempts at understanding changes in religious practices by relating them to the urban/migrant character of Chinese communities in Singapore. In particular, Freedman distinguishes between two kinds of ancestor worship, the domestic cult and the cult of descent group — the former being universal while the latter occurs only where lineages are present. The urban/migrant character of Chinese communities in Singapore is conducive to the practice of the domestic cult. The author notes that while research on Chinese religion has been strong in its empirical contributions, sociological attempts (like Freedman's) at examining how religious institutions and practices have evolved in tandem with Chinese society and culture in a migrant setting are wanting. Similarly, Hindu religious practices have been transformed over the years when the South Indian population migrated to Malaya. Two of the most celebrated events in the local Hindu religious calendar, *Thaipuisam* and *Timithi* (fire-walking) have assumed an importance in Indian migrant society, not experienced in India. Local research suggests that these are occasions when traditional caste, age, and gender categories are temporarily suspended, and may be seen as expressions of a greater Indian-Hindu identity — the significance of which, in our view, stems from the minority status of South Indian Tamils in Singapore and Malaysia. In contrast, the practice of Islam in Singapore has been poorly documented, making it difficult to develop sociological interpretations. Most local studies of Islam have been undertaken as part of a larger project on Islam in Southeast Asia. Perhaps in coming to terms with modernization and

Westernization, there has been a significant increase in Christian conversion among younger, English-educated, and socially mobile Singaporeans. To make sense of this, Tong considers this as the "intellectualization" of religion in Singapore.

Much of the research work done on crime and deviance, Narayanan states in Chapter 14, centre around three distinct areas: Chinese secret societies, drug abuse, and crime prevention. Renewed activity of secret societies after the Second World War, and an increase in drug abuse and crime among the youth in the 1970s, which the government credited to the decadent influence of excessive Westernization, directed research interests to these areas. Most of the work focused on criminally-deviant behaviour, resulting in a preoccupation with identifying deviant motivations in both academic and state-sponsored research. Because of its alignment with the political elite's strongly Hobbesian view of its citizens, social control theory assumed prominence in the local literature on crime and deviance. Control theory was more concerned with the issue of conformity rather than deviance and for this reason regarded the family as having a critical influence, especially in delinquency and adolescent behaviour. Local research inevitably gravitated toward examining the role of the family in juvenile and adult criminal offending. The New Criminology, which places the study of crime and deviance squarely within the conflicts and contradictions inherent in capitalist society, has not drawn much local interest, partly because practitioners in the criminal justice system are not convinced of any possible association between class and crime, and partly because of the strong tendency in Singapore society toward ethnic categorization of perceived social problems. Social control explanations, Narayanan concludes, are likely to become more important as increasing public awareness is drawn by the media to the "problem" of teen gang activities and youth crime.

References

Evers, H.D. (ed) (1973) *Modernization in South-East Asia,* Singapore: Oxford University Press.

Hall, S., Held, D. and McGrew, T. (eds) (1992) *Modernity and Its Futures,* Cambridge: Polity Press.

Hobsbawn, E. (1990) *Nations and Nationalism since 1780,* Cambridge: Cambridge University Press.

Levy, M.J. (1992) "Confucianism and Modernization", *Society,* 29(4): 15-18.

Luhmann, N. (1998) *Writing Science,* Stanford: Stanford University Press.

Ong, J. H., Tong, C. K. and Tan, E. S. (eds) (1997) *Understanding Singapore Society,* Singapore: Times Academic Press.

Turnbull, C.M. (1977) *A History of Singapore 1819-1975,* Kuala Lumpur: Oxford University Press.

Wolf, E. (1988) "Inventing Society", *American Ethnologist,* 15(4): 752-61.

PART I

MODERNIZATION

1

The Sociology of Development in Singapore

Habibul Haque Khondker

The rapid economic growth of East and Southeast Asia and its consequences in the last quarter of the 20th century will be remembered by future historians as one of the milestones of the 20th century. Intellectual disciplines and fields that seek to explain and understand this drama perforce occupy a great deal of importance. As the turbulent century — and with it the millennium — comes to a close, it is time to take stock of the achievements and failures of our various intellectual endeavours. In this chapter, I assess the progress of work in Singapore on the sociology of development, an academic discipline that followed the trail of momentous socio-economic development in this island-state with a population of nearly four million people. I dwell on the twin developments — of Singapore's socio-economic journey and the sociology of development — since 1965, a year that marked both the independence of Singapore as well as the inception of sociology in Singapore.

The importance of the field of sociology of development in Singapore can be directly attributed to the fact that Singapore, "a 20th century Venice" (Regnier 1991, 262), has had a remarkable record of economic development that entailed rapid changes in all aspects of its social and cultural institutions. The growth of the social sciences in general and sociology of development in particular need to be situated in the context of these dramatic changes. I would like to approach this subject in terms of the following questions: What are the main theoretical perspectives that underpinned research in the area of the sociology of development? Is it possible to discern an evolution of theoretical concerns in some coherent manner? What might explain these changes? What has been the relationship between the sociology of development, an academic concern, and the process of socioeconomic development itself? Since it is putatively recognized that the Singapore state has played a central role in socioeconomic development, could there be some bearing of this dirigisme on the development (or underdevelopment) of the sociology of development? Does the sociology of development in Singapore reveal certain unique characteristics, or is it a derivative discourse, a replay of the debates and discussions of development in the core countries, that is, the United States or Europe? If it is a derivative discourse, then what might account for the relative infertility of the theoretical insights and innovations in Singapore's sociology of development compared to say, Latin America's, Africa's and South Asia's, or even East Asia's?

A discussion of the sociology of development compels us to recount the history of Singapore's remarkable socio-economic development despite the fact that Singapore, along with the rest of Asia, found herself in economic difficulties in recent years. Yet, the difficulties should not be allowed to weigh too much or to erase or deflect the stories of economic success. Besides, this is not just an account of Singapore's economic success, her subsequent economic woes and re-emergence as an important economic power in this region. The main task here is to evaluate the discourses of sociology of development in the context of socioeconomic transformation.

What is the sociology of development? A conceptual difference can be made between studies on social change in general and the sociology of development in particular. The study of social change, given the vastness of the subject matter, is almost synonymous with sociology itself. The sociology of development looks at, broadly, the social embeddedness of economic development. It deals with the consequences of economic changes on society and culture. It is concerned with the dialectical relations between structure and culture. It is, therefore, unavoidable to skirt the "sociocentrism" which entails an examination of the role of culture and social institutions in economic development. Economic institutions exist in society, not the other way around. Overlapping fields of inquiry such as development studies, economic sociology, and industrial sociology also address the general relationship between the economic and the sociocultural institutions of society.

A review of the literature on the sociology of development reveals a gradual theoretical shift from the modernization studies of the 1970s to a more politico-economic turn in the 1980s and 1990s. Paralleling this trajectory, a similar transition took place in Singapore. The theoretical developments can be recounted in a schematic manner. First arose the Modernization theory, where debates took place as to whether culture was an impediment to economic development or, conversely, a facilitator, and the consequences of modernization and industrialization on culture. In the literature produced in the 1980s, the influence of Dependency and World-systems theories couched in a politico-economic framework was quite visible. Studies of the role of the MNCs and the labour process were pursued both by overseas as well as local researchers. Yet the paradigmatic shift has not taken place in an unproblematic way. In the 1980s a renewed interest emerged on the issue of the role of culture in economic development. The culturalist discourse led to broad and sometimes sweeping discussion of "Asian values" and their impact on social, political and economic institutions.

Sociologists of social change and development often couch their discussions in terms of differentiation, a master process in society. The undertone of evolutionism is unmistakable in this. Modernization literature was solidly grounded in the theoretical assumptions of evolutionism and functionalism. The notion is firmly ensconced in abstract formulations with which we can talk about society irrespective of time and place. The politico-economic approach, which was the basis of dependency/world-systems approaches, deals with recognizable societies in time and space. I define "political-economy" to mean the social configuration made up of interactions of economic, political, social and cultural forces. The politico-economic approach sheds light on the tensions which are built into this configuration without privileging one set of factors (political or economic) over the other but deals with the totality as such. Such a conceptualization is more in line with the classical view of political economy.

In the late 1980s and 1990s there appears to be a return to culture, under the cover of Neo-modernization theories. Apart from the putative failure of the dependency theories, the state elites played a role in advancing the discussion of a cultural fault line between the "East" and the "West". This period also witnessed a post-modern turn and a shift towards cultural studies, sociology of consumption and other assorted fields which made "modernity" rather than modernization their problematique.

Studies on globalization and regionalization also characterized the 1990s. A considerable amount of research on these areas reflected the new realities as Singapore began to engage more consciously in the process of regionalization which was an aspect of globalization. Studies on civil society, the rise of the middle class, the growth of a new class of consumers and their impact on politics also signalled the changes in the 1990s. In this chapter, I explore, in summary form, the mileposts of these contributions.

This chapter is organized in four sections. Following the introductory section where I sketch out some of the conceptual and theoretical questions concerning the sociology of development in Singapore, I provide a brief background of the remarkable economic development in Singapore as well as a summary of the explanations of this impressive feat. I then summarize the contributions of the social scientific literature — mainly, though not exclusively, sociological — that have emerged on this subject. In the concluding section, I discuss the challenges that confront the students of social change and development in Singapore and identify certain key areas that need systematic exploration.

A Brief History of Economic Development in Singapore

In a letter to Colonel Aldenbrooke on 10 June 1819, Raffles outlined his game plan on Singapore: "...Our objective is not territory, but trade; a great commercial emporium, and a fulcrum, ...One free port in these seas must eventually destroy the spell of Dutch monopoly;"

(Alatas 1971, 40). True to Raffles' objective, Singapore in the next 150 years became a "commercial emporium", an economic showcase. It is one of the top two ports commanding the seas connecting important trade routes.

Singapore's dramatic economic development has attracted international attention in recent years. Reputable international journals have regularly featured articles on Singapore as well as comments by leaders of Singapore. Apart from praise, Singapore has also attracted a good deal of criticism in the Western media for its alleged high-handed, authoritarian government. However, on balance, the favourable perceptions outweigh the unfavourable ones. Clearly, Singapore's influence has been highly disproportionate to its size. A tiny city-state (640 square kilometres in size), with about four million people, Singapore has emerged as a major player in the region.

Singapore's paramount leader, Lee Kuan Yew, has been a much sought after speaker at various international fora. His advice has been regularly sought both by governments as well as MNCs. Owing to his sagacity and vision, Lee Kuan Yew has been described as the "architect of the new century" (*The Straits Times* 13 November 1996). In an article in *New Perspectives Quarterly,* Nathan Gardels, its editor, wrote,

> Fashionable though it may be to vilify Singapore as just one more historically outmoded dictatorship, a case can be made that it ought to be extolled as a model for the future when the center of gravity of human civilization shifts to Asia. Probably no place on the planet is as prepared to enter the 21st century as this orderly, high-tech, middle-class, multicultural, tolerant — but post-liberal — city-state (Gardels 1996, 58)

A small city-state, with limited resources but unlimited resolve, made it to the ranks of the developed economy in about three decades. According to the World Bank GNP per capita ranking, Singapore was considered a high-income economy or developed country, ranking 4th among about 133 countries for which such ranking is prepared. Only Switzerland, Japan and Norway were ahead of Singapore in terms of per capita GNP of US$32,940 in 1997. In Quality of Life indicators such as life expectancy at birth, Singapore is closer to industrialized developed countries like Europe and the US than to its Asian neighbours with the exceptions of Japan and Hong Kong. Singapore's female life expectancy at birth was 79 which compared favourably with that of 82 for both the US and Switzerland (*World Development Report* 1997/8).

Although Singapore's ranking has slid a little according to Human Development Index (HDI) of UNDP (*Human Development Report* 1998) which, using a wide range of economic and non-economic criteria supposedly measures quality of life. Singapore's 28th position — compared to Hong Kong's 25th and South Korea's 30th — is, in part, attributable to the relatively high illiteracy rate among sections of its older population. Singapore's adult illiteracy rate stood at 89.9% in 1992 compared to Hong Kong's 91.2%, South Korea's 97.4% or Bahamas' 98% (*Human Development Report* 1995). Few would contest the fact that the quality of life in Singapore is very high and Singapore's development is the envy of many nations and a source of amazement in many parts of the developing world.

Much of this remarkable development can be attributed to Singapore's ability to integrate into the global system under the guidance of a group of enlightened and pragmatic leaders. A single-minded leadership on one hand, and a hard-working and determined populace on the other must share the credit for this remarkable economic feat. The government as well as the people of Singapore showed a great deal of pragmatism and an outward orientation that made such a globally oriented development possible. I argue that since independence in 1965, Singapore sought to integrate its economy with the world system to its own advantage. With hindsight, this strategy of economic development was made possible thanks to a highly autonomous state in Singapore. Singapore's development trajectory has taken a more explicitly global posture in recent years, especially, since the later part of the 1980s following a mild recession. This shift in focus shows not only the pragmatism of the governing elite but also the contingencies that forced the leadership to look for new opportunities.

In recent years, Singapore faced the challenge of an economic crisis, part of a larger regional and global crisis. Surely, the crisis set off by the financial crisis in Thailand in the summer of 1997 caught everyone off-guard. Even in the early nineties, the economy of this island-state was going through a boom with a 9.8% growth rate in GDP for 1993 (*The Straits Times* 1 January 1994). After the 9.2% GDP growth in the third quarter of 1993 which was incidentally slightly lower than the second quarter growth of 10% (*Economic Survey of Singapore*, Third Quarter, 1993), the economic growth rate of 7.5 to 8% for 1993 forecast in August 1993 was revised to about 9%. GDP growth rate, however, showed a downward trend as it declined from 9.0% in 1990 to 8.7% in 1995, 6.9% in 1996 and 7.8% in 1997 (*Economic Survey of Singapore* 1997). In sectoral terms, the growth had been broad-based (*Economic Bulletin* December 1993). In 1992 the GDP stood at $64.4 billion (*Asia Pacific Economic Outlook* 1993, 25) with one of the highest per capita income in the world. The robustness of the economy is underpinned by various factors, which includes one of the world's highest savings rates. Gross National Savings in 1991 stood at 47.3% (*Asian Development Outlook* 1992, 86, table 2.3). In 1997 Gross National Savings stood at 51.2% of the GNP compared to 9.4% in 1970 (*Economic Survey of Singapore* 1997). As of mid-February 1999, Singapore's foreign reserve stood at a whopping US$75.9 billion (*Economist* 20 February 1999), which rose from S$1.2 billion in 1963 and S$22.7 billion in 1983 (Lim 1988, 17).

It is interesting to recollect that in 1986 when Singapore was in the middle of an economic recession, Goh Chok Tong, the then Deputy Prime Minister, was discussing whether and by which means Singapore could achieve the status of a developed country by 1999 (Goh 1986). In terms of per capita income, Singapore joined the ranks of developed countries by 1999. However, rather than celebrating the achievement, a number of scholars on Singapore's development hold the view that in terms of technology, skill, education, and other indicators Singapore is yet to achieve the status of a developed country (Low et al. 1999, 21).

Singapore has been presented as a model of economic development. The idea of lessons from the Singapore experience was mooted in the wider international context. In a speech before African business leaders, Senior Minister Lee Kuan Yew presented seven lessons that benefited Singapore and could be emulated in the

African context. According to Mr Lee the seven goals Africa can draw from Singapore's experience were:

1. Clean government
2. National Solidarity
3. Family Planning
4. Pragmatism, not dogma
5. Attracting investments
6. Education for everyone
7. Going for results
   (*The Straits Times* 9 November 1993, 27)

However, the idea of a Singapore model is not new. As early as 1978, Mr Lee, then Prime Minister, talked about Singapore's experience in a speech at the 26th Congress of the International Chamber of Commerce in Florida (Lee 1978). It is interesting to note that there has been very little change in Mr Lee's original notions on the correct strategies of development. Notions such as "clean government", "going for results", "pragmatism, not dogma" were clearly contained in his earlier thoughts. In the 1978 speech, his pragmatic ideas came through very clearly in his anti-xenophobic position and in his emphatic need for learning from others. He gave the example of how in setting up Neptune Orient Shipping Line, the national shipping company in 1968, Singapore hired a Pakistani who had years of experience and held senior positions in the Pakistan Shipping Corporation.

The other example of this pragmatic and outcome-oriented decision was to invite a United Nations Industrial Survey Mission to visit Singapore in 1960 under the leadership of Albert Winsemius. It is following the recommendation of this mission that the Economic Development Board (EDB) was set up and Mr Winsemius was retained as an advisor. Hon Sui Sen was made the first chairman of EDB. In justifying the establishment of EDB, Goh Keng Swee underscored the "positive role" of the government (EDB 1991). The role of EDB, the rough equivalent of MITI in Japan, and was staffed by some of the ablest of Singaporeans, can hardly be overemphasized in the economic development of Singapore.

Another interesting aspect of this consistency can be seen in the acceptance of certain fundamentals of development from very early on. In the late 1950s, economist Lim Tay Boh wrote, "... it is urgent for the Singapore Government to plan a programme of industrial development which will increase employment opportunities to absorb the rapidly growing population" (1960, 13). The continuation of free trade, an open economy, and the adverse effects of nationalism, especially in economic matters, were all pointed out in the late 1950s.

Now whether the Singapore model — or for that matter the Japanese or Korean one — is extrapolatable or not is a debatable question. In my judgment, it is not. Each country aspiring towards economic development must have its own "tryst with its own destiny" in view of its own historical specificities and its location in the world system. Besides, Cline (1982) argued that the export-led growth model of the four East Asian countries is unlikely to be generalized because of the finite capacity of the international market. According to Huff, "the Singapore model is unlikely to be replicated elsewhere, not only because the Republic is a city state, but also because of the unacceptability in many other polities of a very heavy foreign economic presence, and because of difficulties in effecting the same degree of government control as in Singapore" (Huff 1995, 753).

However, it is important to note that certain aspects of Singapore's experience are not only relevant and important for developing countries but also for the developed, industrialized world. The key lesson is the role of the state in economic development, a developmental state flexible enough to change its strategies and macro-policy adjustments and ready to learn from "mistakes", yet tough enough to adopt "politically incorrect", unpopular policies to meet long-term "economically correct" objectives. Development in the Singapore context was the creation of comparative advantages where there were none. This was evident not only in the successful infrastructural development but also in the investment of human resources development.

What is distinctive of Singapore's economic development is its rapidity; the unfavourable initial conditions; relative evenness in income-distribution; and a calibrated role of the state in an open economy. Much of this high rate of economic development has been achieved in a span of less than 30 years. Incredible as it may be, those who visited Singapore in the late 1960s and early 1970s can vouch for the relatively squalid conditions they encountered in the Garden State of today. In 1960 Singapore had one of the highest population growth rates in the world at about 4.6% per annum. The unemployment rate stood at over 10%. Two decades later, unemployment fell to 3% and three decades later, there is concern about the declining population growth rate. The population control programme has been a little bit more successful than the leaders wanted. However, the growing unemployment because of the economic crisis poses some problems. The unemployment rate stood at 2% in 1996 and 1.8% in 1997. In June 1998 the figure was a mere 2.3% although it rose to 4.5% in September 1998 (*Economic Survey of Singapore* 1998, 16).

Singapore has been transformed from a largely entrepot economy into a highly industrialised economy. In 1960, the manufacturing sector accounted for 8.8% of the GDP, in 1990 it stood at 34.3%. In 1988, 71.8% of total exports were manufactured goods compared to 21.1% in 1960 (Lim 1991, 197). Diversification has been one of the top policy concerns of the leaders of Singapore. The recent emphasis on building technological and innovative capacities is in line with that policy goal.

The evenness of economic development is borne out by the fact that absolute poverty is virtually non-existent in Singapore. In 1953-54, about 19%, almost one in five, households lived in absolute poverty. In 1982, the figure plummeted to a mere 0.3% (Lim, 1988). Although, as Islam and Kirkpatrick (1986) suggest, inequality may have increased in the 1980s, Singapore does not have an underclass. Despite the methodological limitations of the poverty studies (Rao 1988), it can be stated that absolute poverty and hunger, though part of everyday reality in many parts of the world, developed and developing, is a matter of the past in Singapore.

What accounts for this remarkable success? According to Dennis Gayle,

> Singapore is an economic success because accepted cultural traditions have permitted strong socio-political institutions to encourage entrepreneurial acumen and to attract foreign direct investment. The paramount goals of the government have been rapid industrialization and the

maintenance of internal security. Subsidiary objectives have included the provision of sound socioeconomic infrastructure and the achievement of industrial stability. The state systematically sought to generate a societal value system which was premised upon sustained hard work, capital accumulation, cooperative work habits, and willingness to innovate (Gayle 1986, 100).

The above explanation includes two important points: the role of government and the role of culture in economic development. The same writer characterizes Singapore as a case of a "market socialist" city-state, a characterization many of the key architects of modern Singapore would not disagree with. At a speech before the Singapore Manufacturers' Association in 1969, the then Finance Minister Goh Keng Swee announced that "... the PAP Government are good socialists notwithstanding our genial relations with the capitalists" (Goh 1972, 210). Dr Goh went on to suggest that in so far as socialism was defined as the state ownership of the means of production, the socialist state of Singapore was ahead of the achievements of most other socialist governments in the world.

Whether Singapore's success can be explained solely in terms of an effective government and a conducive cultural heritage is a matter of some debate. There is a widely shared view that much of the credit for Singapore's phenomenal economic development should be given to the leadership. This perception has also been nurtured by the ruling elites in Singapore in their various pronouncements. The only exception to this seems to be Brigadier General George Yeo, Minister for Information and Culture, who once gave due credit to the factor of luck for Singapore's development. The academic support for the leadership theory comes from, *inter alia* Milne and Mauzy. As they state: "Singapore has been unusually fortunate in that from its founding it has been led by an extraordinarily dedicated, competent, and far-sighted group of leaders. Lee Kuan Yew, his inner circle of colleagues — Goh Keng Swee, S. Rajaratnam, and Toh Chin Chye — and other PAP ministers. To a far greater extent than in most states, these leaders have moulded and shaped Singapore in their image" (Milne and Mauzy 1990, 103). The intellectual calibre of the leadership in Singapore, their penchant for efficiency and outcome, and their very low level of tolerance for corruption as contributing factors to Singapore's success is by now well known.

But there are inherent problems in "great men theory". To paraphrase Marx, leaders make history but not under the circumstances chosen by themselves. Sometimes in historical discussion — depending on political correctness of a view — too much credit is given to the leaders. For example, in Singapore's history it appears that the role of Sir Stamford Raffles is exaggerated. According to Turnbull, six months after the founding of Singapore, Raffles left the island in June 1819 and did not return for more than three years. Communications with Bencoolen, his headquarters, "were so poor that Singapore developed on her own" (Turnbull 1989, 12). Turnbull goes on to state that: "Singapore's convenient location, free trade policy, and comparative orderliness were responsible for much of her early success". Other historians have even been unkind to Raffles. Carl Trocki has documented the importance of opium in Singapore's historical development implicating the role of Raffles in promoting this trade, with Singapore as its base. In his words,

> The overwhelming importance of the drug (opium) to the financial security of the British Empire in Asia made it a major variable in the historical development of the entire region. Singapore would have been a different place without opium. As a source of excise revenue, it made it possible to run Singapore as a free port. Opium paid for free trade; without it, Raffles' 'broad and liberal principles' would have been only so many words (Trocki 1990, 223).

The location of Singapore on a strategic sea route, which was appreciated among others by Scot seafarer Alexander Hamilton as early as in 1727 as a factor in her development, has been contested. A leading Singaporean economist posed the problem thus, "If strategic location was that important, why was Singapore so underdeveloped before Sir Stamford Raffles founded it in 1819?" (Lim 1988, xiv) A short answer to the question is: strategic location, like many other individual factors in economic development, was necessary but not a sufficient condition for Singapore's development. Then there is this difference between potential and the realization of potential. For example, Saudi Arabia became a rich country only after its petroleum resources were explored and marketed. Being endowed with a huge amount of petroleum was not in itself enough for her to be rich. In the 1920s, petroleum was not explored, the potential was not realized until the 1930s. In realising that potential other conditions had to be met: technology, interest of the MNCs and the local rulers, and most important, the demand for petroleum in the international market and the sharp price increase in the early 1970s due to both economic and extra-economic factors. The opening of the Suez Canal in 1869 gave a boost to Singapore's position as the "premier staging-post in South-East Asia" (Regnier 1991,18).

The above discussion illustrates not only some of the basic problems of the historiography of Singapore but problems of interpretations of social change that have contemporary relevance. The controversy over the master cause of development in Singapore came to its peak in the debate over culture in the late 1980s. I was in the audience at a forum entitled "The Role of Culture in Industrial Asia — The Relationship Between Confucian Ethics and Modernization" at the Singapore Conference Hall on 6 January 1987. What struck me most in that forum was a debate that ensued between the "Western" and the "Asian" scholars on the relative importance of Confucianism for explaining East Asian development.

The debate on the relative importance of culture vis-à-vis social structure has not ended. As the Asian economic crisis unfolded in mid-1997, Asian cultural values that allegedly fostered nepotism, secrecy, and other negative practices were attacked. At the Davos (Switzerland) conference where the political as well as the business leaders gather annually to discuss the global economic situation, the role of culture was discussed not just in economic development but also in the management of the crisis. "Several delegates said Confucian attitudes had helped bring on the crisis and would help resolve it. The Confucian attachment to harmonious human relations had discouraged change and promoted 'crony capitalism'. The Confucian commitment to learning from the misfortunes and the successes of friends would encourage reform" (Dale in *International Herald Tribune* 23 February 1999, 11).

I now turn to an examination of the social scientific literature on socio-economic development in contemporary Singapore.

The Sociology of Development in Singapore

A complete survey of the literature on social change and development in Singapore, a society that has undergone momentous changes in the past three decades, entails a major undertaking which cannot be done here because of the limitation of space. The enormity of Singapore' economic development has been matched by the productivity of the first generation of social scientists, especially sociologists. Singapore has undergone its development under the tutelage of a leadership self-conscious of its achievement; a group of intellectuals whose accounts in addition to a fund of official reports provide a rich data source. A caveat is in order at the very outset: I have been selective in my treatment of this expansive literature. In choosing the representative works, I have tried to give a sense of the breadth, culling the theoretical frameworks of these various contributions.

What I would like to do in the following is to explicate the development of a sociological literature on development in Singapore in terms of shifting theoretical or paradigmatic emphases in sociology. Not surprisingly, the economists have produced a good part of the studies on Singapore' development. It would be useful to take into account those aspects of economic literature that verge on the territory of Sociology. I am using the word "territory" in the sense in which Emmanuel Le Roy Ladurie (1979) used it to claim a space for the historians. The point is that although I strongly espouse the view of a uni-disciplinary, historical social scientific approach *a la* Immanuel Wallerstein, there is still some justification and need for specialization. There are fields of Economics which are of great interest to Sociology, for example, studies of inequality, income distribution, labour and welfare economics, economic history, and institutional economics, to name a few. On the other hand, a discussion of exchange rate or monetary policy may be important in itself, insofar as economic development is concerned but would not be of immediate concern to sociology. Needless to say, such tasks should be left to number-crunching economists rather than to post-modern sociologists.

The sociological discussions of development in the initial phase concentrated mainly on the consequences of rapid development. This is interesting in the sense that the early sociological discourse in Singapore followed the established pattern set in Western Sociology where sociologists traditionally studied the consequences of modernization, ie, the impact of industrialization and urbanization on culture and social institutions. It is only in recent years that sociologists have participated in the mainstream of the debate on development, which also marks a paradigmatic shift in Sociology as such.

The early sociological works on Singapore's development can be categorized as belonging to the Modernization perspective, in which the most notable representatives included Syed Hussein Alatas (1970, 1971, 1977a, 1977b), Hans-Dieter Evers (1980), Peter Chen (1977, 1983), Riaz Hassan (1977, 1983), Eddie Kuo (1979), Aline Wong (1981, 1983), and John Clammer (1985), among others. "Modernization" according to Alatas

> is the process by which modern scientific knowledge concerning all aspects of human life is introduced at varying degree, first in the Western civilization, and later diffused to the non-western world by different methods and groups with the ultimate purpose of achieving a better and more satisfactory life in the broadest sense of the term, as accepted by the society concerned (Alatas 1970, 66).

The above definition of modernization echoes the understanding of modernization provided by Western scholars such as Eisenstadt (1966). This view emphasized the programmatic aspect of modernization which provided the point of departure for many local sociologists. In his other writings, however, Alatas developed a more critical stance which was best reflected in his treatise on "captive mind" (Alatas 1977a) and in demolishing the myth of the "lazy native" (Alatas 1977b).

The focus of the contributions of the above-mentioned social scientists was on the impact of rapid industrialization and economic modernization on various social institutions and practices or, broadly, the relationship between culture and industrialization. The latter theme was best illustrated in a collection entitled *Culture and Industrialization*, edited by Rolf Vente and Peter Chen (1980) which included essays focusing on culture as an impediment to modernization and industrialization, as well as the consequences of induced social change on culture. Many of these studies followed American modernization literature quite faithfully and profitably. The theoretical and conceptual frameworks of some of the important contributions of Peter Chen were grounded in the modernization school of the American academia. For example, Chen's discussion on the role of elites in modernization closely follows that of Eisenstadt (1966). In this regard, other areas of research in the field of social change also showed a close connection with American sociology. Most of the sociologists in this era were trained in the US in the 1970s.

The impact of industrialization and modernization on family and marriage was the concern of several writings of Kuo and Wong (1979). The works of Chang, Ong and Chen (1980) explored the relationship between fertility change and economic modernization. Riaz Hassan (1977) and Peter Chen and Hans Evers, (1978) examined the consequence of urbanization, especially high-rise living conditions on a wide range of what some of these writers called "pathological" behaviours including suicide. Writers such as Chan Heng Chee (1976) and Chiew Seen Kong (1978) considered the question of national identity in the face of changes in society and public policy. In a study, Chiew (1978) showed how depluralization contributed to the attainment of national integration as reflected in structural, attitudinal and communicative integration. Peter Chen attempted the analysis of various public policies, elites and their role in social change in light of the parameters of the modernization paradigm.

Sociological research throughout the 1970s also took a great deal of interest in aspects of policy and planning. One writer has viewed Peter Chen as a major representative of this school of thought where social scientists were seen to be "arguing for the planners" (Preston 1987, 111). In this school, Chen's work tended "to fuse scholarly social science with policy science" (Preston 1987, 12). The important aspect of this tradition of sociological research at that time was that by producing socially relevant knowledge, it could help legitimize sociology as a "useful" discipline. This was in consonance with an environment permeated by utilitarianism.

Riaz Hassan's (1977) examination of the impact of housing on families, especially the discussion of the impact of living in flats, had policy implications. Although he observed that relocation had not resulted in social disorganization and that social ties with primary groups continued, he emphasized the need for community organizations. His conclusion that the low-income families experienced more hardship due to relocation was based on economic variables such as higher rental and public utility cost. He was, however, also sensitive to the cultural dimensions of the relocation experience. His point about the valuation of and the practical use of privacy by the poor (Hassan 1977, 142), though counterintuitive, is consistent with the importance given to notion of "loss of face" in Chinese culture. On the whole, the subject of culture as a phenomenon in itself also received systematic treatment in the writings of another group of writers best represented in the writings of Benjamin (1976) and Clammer (1985). There was also a methodological divide in these two traditions. The modernization approach represented in the works of Peter Chen, Hassan, Kuo et al. had a clear empirical mooring. In the preface to his study on suicide in Singapore, Hassan passionately defends the importance of empirical evidence and chides the prospective critics for raising the bogey of "mindless empiricism" (1983). The studies on the role of elites in social development (Chen 1977), Wong on public housing (which culminated in Wong and Yeh 1985) or Kuo and Wong's (1979) study on family and marriage, and Quah's (1988) study on motherhood are examples of systematic use of empirical techniques. Commenting on the methodological directions, Evers wrote, "A major part of this research was the social survey type stimulated both by the development of appropriate techniques in the United States and by the growing demand for survey-based data from government institutions and international organizations" (Evers 1980, ix).

The writings of Clammer (1985) dealt with the broad issues of cultural transformation and conflict. It is interesting to note that against the tide of the received position, he emphasized similarities rather than differences between the "Eastern" and the "Western" culture. Benjamin's writings were more conceptual and historically grounded. His essays on the logic of multiculturalism (1976) and nation-state (1988) are good illustrations.

It is important to recognize the politico-economic context in which the modernization literature in Singapore was produced. A rapid economic growth and prosperity provided the backdrop against which the modernization literature came to fruition. Looking at these works from the vantage point of today and treating them as dressed-up apologia or insufficiently uncritical would be both patronising and erroneous.

The shift from the Modernization paradigm to a more world-systemic level discussion culminated in the work of Manuel Castells (1988). But this theoretical shift was already in the making for quite some time. Writers such as Pang and Lim (1977), Tan (1979), Chow and Tyabji (1980), Deyo (1981), Heyzer (1983), and Wong (1981, 1983) set in motion a more global focus, emphasizing the external linkages, the international division of labour, and even a politico-economic approach in the study of the socioeconomic development of Singapore. In justifying this shift, Heyzer pointed out that, "for a long while, academic analysis of the 'new nations' concentrated on problems of national integration, of modernization, of development as perceived by ruling groups, giving little place to the difficulties experienced by the less privileged in the system that is being established" (Heyzer 1983, 105). In her own discussion, Heyzer utilizes the conceptual categories of Samir Amin and Cardoso and provides an alternative view. Wong's (1983) earlier works were also sensitive to the impact of the international division of labour in particular on female workers in the electronics industries in Singapore.

The most laudable aspect of Castells' contribution is that it provides a world-systemic framework, giving due credit to the government for its central role in steering economic development in Singapore without being apologetic. This position is in sharp contrast to both the existent traditions of academic apologists as well as what I would call "liberal critics" of the Singapore system as represented in some – not all – of the writings of Rodan, for example. To use a phrase like "liberal critics" (here pun is intended: not only do these critics come from a liberal position, they are quite liberal in their criticisms and conservative in their praise) is surely to invite criticism. Summarizing the evolution of political processes in Singapore in a competent manner, Rodan attempts to account for the advent of the "authoritarian regime". He goes on to state "...the PAP's own political objectives could be presented as economic imperatives" (Rodan 1993, 82). As I see it, turning this statement on its head makes an equally plausible argument: "The economic objectives could be presented as the PAP's political imperatives". Rodan's point that "the authoritarian regime was fundamentally in place before the EOI programme took root..." ignores the argument that ensuring social and political stability was a precondition for the success of an export-oriented industrialization (EOI) strategy. Singapore moved to an export-oriented industrialization strategy from the end of 1966 as a deliberate policy to lessen its reliance on the staple port economy (Huff 1994, 34).

As Deyo points out: "In Singapore, the institutionalization of corporatist labour relations has been an especially important aspect of development planning by virtue of the fact that apart from its strategic geographical location and excellent natural harbour, Singapore's only significant development resource has been its abundant, urbanized, and economically ambitious labour force" (Deyo 1981, 41). Pang et al. (1989) suggest that in the 1960s, labour discipline was a central issue as labour unrest was deterring foreign investment and creation of employment through industrialization. The logic of industrial discipline, a prerequisite for economic growth, created a corporatist, "authoritarian" state.

Rodan's analysis of the political and social processes in Singapore is an important contribution, albeit viewed from the vantage point of a liberal critic. His categorization of Singapore as an "authoritarian regime" is somewhat sweeping, especially if it is done without some qualifications. Brazil from 1964 to 1985 was an authoritarian regime, as was Chile under Pinochet from 1973 to 1989. Obviously, Singapore cannot be grouped with these two Latin American countries without certain qualifications. It is important to recognize the point that there are varieties of authoritarian regimes and states just as there are varieties of democratic regimes and states. According to Castells, "...although clearly authoritarian, Singapore is not a dictatorship but a *hegemonic state*, in the Gramscian sense, as suggested by John Clammer. Namely, it is based not simply on coercion, but also on consensus" (1986, 78). I recount vividly John Clammer's remark: "Singapore is a terrible place for the opposition politicians. There are no unemployment, no homelessness, no deprivations, in fact no major issues to fight the government. It is very difficult to organize people around such abstract issues as freedom" (remarks made by Clammer in 1987). Even if one agrees that Clammer was exaggerating, there is a point in his remark. Castells' discussion of the interplay of political and economic forces provides a more plausible explanation with reference to concrete world-systemic circumstances. So I turn to him.

It would be appropriate at this point to provide a summary of the main arguments of Manuel Castells. Castells' starting point is that Singapore's independence was marked by political instability and international isolation. The key factor in Singapore's development, capital, was mobilized both by local effort as well as by creating favourable conditions for the flow of international capital. The government played a central role in capital accumulation by ensuring high national savings as well as by creating favourable conditions for the inflow of international capital. It is important to remember that Singapore embarked on a road to economic development during an expansionary phase of the world economy in 1966-72, (Castells 1988, 8), when capital was more easily accessible. The role of the government in this regard included maintaining social and political stability, infrastructure building, maintaining industrial discipline, and ensuring the supply of low-cost and high quality labour supply.

The centrality of the role of state in directing the Singapore economy to development is captured by the notion that Singapore is an open but not a laissez-faire economy (Castells 1988). Strong government-guided policies made possible Singapore's successful participation and competition in the world economy. "Singapore", in Castells' words, "is the quintessential Developmental State" (1988, 4). What Streeten has recently said on Korea seems to be equally, or perhaps more, apt for Singapore: government interventions have been "market-friendly" and markets have been "people-friendly" (Streeten 1993, 1286). Unfortunately, many writers hold a simplistic state-market dichotomy: it is either the "invisible hands of the market", that is the laissez-faire model or the "visible hands of the state", that is the statist model. It is important to recognize the difference between the enabling and the constraining role of the state vis-à-vis the market.

In discussing the possibilities of transformation of the status of a country in the world system, Wallerstein (1981) argues that the world system often presents with certain opportunities which some peripheral societies can take advantage of in upgrading their status. These are seizing the chance, development by invitation, and self-reliance. The Singapore state, no doubt, has been able to seize such an opportunity leading to her transformation from a peripheral status to a semi-periphery. In view of the presence of capital and high technology-intensive development and the attendant information revolution, Singapore can be termed as a semi-core rather than a semi-periphery. This transition is part of a global shift, a sea-change in terms of the relocation of the global economic centre of gravity from the Anglo-American context to the Asia-Pacific region.

The shifts in the nature of Singapore's political economy have been mirrored in new research areas of the sociologists. The works of Eddie Kuo (1985), Lim and Kuo (1999) on information society, Hing and Chiew (1989, 1991) on automation are some of the representative works. The shift in the nature of technology and its contribution to the relocation possibilities of the transnational industries is an important point. Castells pointed out that the technological shift towards information-based industries also contributed to Singapore's growth. It is in keeping with this shift that research projects on the sociology of science and technology are being conducted.

The other trend in the contemporary thinking about and contributions to the studies on social change in Singapore as revealed in the writings of Chua (1989), Tong (1992), Leong (1989), Kwok (1993) and PuruShotam (1992) have a clear cultural leaning. Chua's (1989) reflexive essay on social change in Singapore is a good representative of this tradition. It is at once an exercise in nostalgia, a sensitive and somewhat Simmelian treatment of the everyday life and its transformation in Singapore in the face of modernity, bureaucratization and the imposition of the regimen of schedule. Free from statistical charts and the tradition of "grand narrative", these authors posit a counter-narrative informed by a variety of contemporary sociological perspectives. Chua's (1995) works on political sociology bridge the concerns of culture with those of politics. For him, communitarianism was an ideological response to liberalism. Tamney's work on cultural values of Singapore deals with the interplay of western modernity, especially the notion of individualism with Asian cultural values (Tamney 1995). Tong (1992) follows a more down to earth sociological approach in his study of religious affiliation linking conversion to social structural changes and the intellectualization of religion. The study on the coexistence of traditional practices in modern Singapore (Tong, Ho and Lin 1992) refutes the simplistic modern-tradition dichotomy which was popular with first generation modernization writers. Many of these works can be classified as in the vein of the neo-Modernization approach. Tamney (1995) pays special attention to the process of differentiation.

PuruShotam's (1992) study of Singapore Indian traders makes a contribution to the sparse historical studies of social change. Mak's (1981) study on secret societies remains an important contribution to historical sociology. Chan and Chiang's *Stepping Out* (1993), a study of Chinese business is another important step in the right direction. Leong's (1989) essays are at once critical and reflective, though focused on the theme of culture and communication. The subject of space, urban living, consumption (Chua 1999) and other problems of modernity engage the interest of the new generation of sociologists. Rodan's (1996) point about the autonomy of consumers more in terms of cultural products rather than political objectives is highly insightful and foreshadows many other works on this subject. Kwok's (1993) concern with the question of civil society is reflective of broader changes in the politico-cultural milieu in Singapore. As the sociological works try to capture changes in the constitution of society, their works themselves are reflective of changes that they seek to grapple with. In the 1990s, much public discussion took place on the issues of civil society, citizenship and the need for creating a "cultivated society". In an essay Kwok and Ali (1998) stressed the importance of intellectual life in creating a cultivated citizen.

A number of writers in the latter half of the decade of the 1990s began to apply globalisation approaches to Singapore. These studies focused on the economic and cultural linkages of Singapore to the world system and presented Singapore as a global city (Murray and Perera 1995, Chiu, Ho and Lui 1997, Perry, Kong and Yeoh 1997). In this context, it may be pointed out that the social scientists are trailing the cerebral politicians by about two and a half decades. The idea of Singapore as a global city was mooted as early as in 1972 by S. Rajaratnam, the then Foreign Minister. "The Global Cities", Rajaratnam contended, "unlike earlier cities, are linked intimately with one another. Because they are more alike they reach out to one another through the tentacles of technology. Linked together they form a chain of cities which today shape and direct, in varying degrees of importance, a world system of economics" (Rajaratnam 1972, 19).

A Note on Future Research

To summarize the trajectories of sociological research traditions on the subject of social change and modernization in Singapore, it can be said that the intellectual journey began in the late 1960s with studies on "modernization" and via research on the political economy in the 1980s, we have come to the present preoccupation with "modernity" and globality in the 1990s. To a large extent, the sociology of development in Singapore has been a derivative and borrowed discourse. Sociologists of social change in Singapore need to do more innovative and comparative-historical work. It is worth hypothesizing that the relative absence of historical sociology may be attributable to the fact that in some sense Singapore is an ahistorical society. At the time of celebrating 150 years of Singapore in 1969, Goh Keng Swee noted: "One of the more notable character traits of the Singaporean is the unconcern for the history of his country" (Goh 1972, 163). Singapore is the first "new nation" in this region. The orientation of the entire society lies in the future. It is a futuristic society reluctantly living in the present. And perhaps, this explains why the past remains understudied or worse, only selectively studied. This is a handicap in examining social change. If we want to know where we are going, we need to know how far we have come.

It is important to note that in recent years, an official initiative has been taken to underscore the importance of history in Singapore.

Since the official discourse has been highly nationalistic, how much can be achieved in terms of promoting genuine historical imagination and sensitivity is an open question. From a sociological point of view, it is important to undertake more comparative-historical studies for a deeper understanding of Singapore's development in the context of changes in Southeast Asia.

Secondly, we live in a globalized economic and cultural milieu. We need to understand the location of Singapore in both spatial and temporal dimensions. Future comparative studies using a world system or global framework have great potential. In embarking on these projects, social sciences in Singapore need not free themselves completely from the umbilical cord of official agenda and the borrowed paradigms, but need to exercise some autonomy in charting new directions and theoretical innovation. One of the lessons that Singapore can learn profitably from the advanced countries of Europe and North America is the autonomous role of the intellectual elites and the systems of knowledge production. More research in the area of the role of intellectual autonomy in the production of scientific knowledge and technological innovations are in order in Singapore.

There has been much talk about the indigenization of knowledge in recent years. "But", as King observes, "to date it appears that local scholars have mainly been reacting to and criticizing the concepts formulated by outsiders rather than creating their own" (King 1994, 171). It is important to bear in mind that as a consequence of globalisation, many of the features of development are becoming homologous. As such a common set of concepts would yield valuable results. This is not to deny the fact that there are idiosyncrasies of the local culture which justify the case for indigenization. Interestingly, the call for indigenization itself has become a global phenomenon.

The social scientific focus on the region by locating Singapore within it may be of value. The sociology of development in Singapore has to walk on two legs: one venturing out of Singapore in the region, the other a systematic exploration of the local/national issues. The field of science and technology, the so-called "knowledge society", the civilizing process that encompasses the formation and cultivation of civil society are to be given priorities by the researchers. While maintaining necessary linkages between the official policies and research agenda, it is time sociology sets its own imprint on the research agenda and charts its own course.

References

Alatas, S. H. (1970) "Religion and Modernization in Southeast Asia", *Archive of European Sociology*, Xl.

Alatas, S. H. (1971) *Thomas Stamford Raffles: Schemer or Reformer?* Singapore: Angus and Robertson.

Alatas, S. H. (1977a) *Intellectuals in Developing Societies*, London: F. Cass.

Alatas, S. H. (1977b) *The Myth of the Lazy Native*, London: F. Cass.

Asian Development Bank (1992) *Asian Development Outlook*.

Asia Pacific Economic Outlook, 4th Quarter, 1993.

Benjamin, G. (1976) "The Cultural Logic of Singapore's Multiracialism", in R. Hassan (ed) *Singapore: Society in Transition*, Kuala Lumpur: Oxford University Press.

Benjamin, G. (1988) "The Unseen Presence: A Theory of the Nation State and its Mystifications", National University of Singapore: Dept. of Sociology, Working Paper No. 91.

Castells, M. (1988) "The Developmental City-State in an Open World Economy: The Singapore Experience", BRIE Working Paper, Berkeley: University of California.

Chan, H. C. (1976) "The Political System and Political Change", in R. Hassan (ed) *Singapore: Society in Transition*, Singapore: Oxford University Press.

Chan, K. B. and Chiang, C. (1993) *Stepping Out: The Making of Chinese Entrepreneurs*, Singapore: Prentice-Hall.

Chang, C. T., Ong, J. H., and Chen, P. S. J. (eds) (1980) *Culture and Fertility in Singapore*, Singapore: ISEAS.

Chen, P. S. J. (1977) "The Role of Professional and Intellectual Elites in Singapore", in K.E. Shaw, P. S. J. Chen, S.Y. Lee and G. G. Thomson (eds) *Elites and National Development in Singapore,* Tokyo: Institute of Developing Economies.

Chen, P. S. J. and H. D. Evers (eds) (1978) *Studies in ASEAN Sociology: Urban Society and Social Change,* Singapore: Chopmen.

Chen, P. S. J. (ed) (1983) *Singapore Development Policies and Trends,* Singapore: Oxford University Press.

Chiew, S. K. (1978) "National Integration: the Case of Singapore", in P. S. J. Chen and H.D. Evers (eds) *Studies in ASEAN Sociology,* Singapore: Chopmen

Chiu, S., Ho, K.C. and Lui, T.L. (1997) *City States in the Global Economy,* Boulder, USA: West View Press.

Chow, K. B. and Tyabji, A. (1980) *External Linkages and Economic Development: The Singapore Experience,* Singapore: Chopmen.

Chua, B. H. (1989) "The Business of Living in Singapore", in K. S. Sandhu and P. Wheatley (eds) *Management of Success: The Moulding of Modern Singapore,* Singapore: Institute of Southeast Asian Studies.

Chua, B. H. (1995) *Communitarian Ideology and Democracy in Singapore,* London: Routledge.

Chua, B. H. (1999) "The Attendant Consumer Society of a Developed Singapore", in Linda Low (ed) *Singapore: Towards a Developed Status,* Singapore: Oxford University Press.

Clammer, J. (1985) *Singapore: Ideology Society Culture,* Singapore: Chopmen.

Cline, W. R. (1982) "Can the East Asian Model be Generalized?", *World Development,* 10(2).

Dale, R. "Many See a Stronger Asia Emerging", *International Herald Tribune,* 23 February 1999.

Deyo, F. C. (1981) *Dependent Development and Industrial Order,* New York: Praeger.

Economic Bulletin, December 1993.

Economic Development Board (1991) *Thirty Years of Economic Development,* Singapore.

Economic Survey of Singapore, Third Quarter, 1993.

Economic Survey of Singapore, Third Quarter, 1997.

Economic Survey of Singapore, Third Quarter, 1998.

Economist, 20 February 1999.

Eisenstadt, S.N. (1966) *Modernization: Protest and Change,* Englewood Cliffs, NJ: Prentice-Hall.

Evers, H. D. (ed) (1980) *Sociology of Southeast Asia: Readings in Social Change and Development,* Kuala Lumpur: Oxford University Press.

Gardels, N. (1996) "Singapore: Post-Liberal City of the Future", *New Perspectives Quarterly,* 13(2) (Spring).

Gayle, D. J. (1986) *The Small Developing State,* Hampshire, England: Gower.

Goh, C. T. (1986) *A Nation of Excellence* (text of a speech given to the Alumni International) Singapore: Ministry of Communications and Information.

Goh, K. S. (1972) *The Economics of Modernization and Other Essays,* Singapore: Asia Pacific Press.

Hassan, R. (1977) *Families in Flats,* Singapore: Singapore University Press.

Hassan, R. (1983) *A Way of Dying: Suicide in Singapore,* Kuala Lumpur: Oxford University Press.

Heyzer, N. (1983) "International Production and Social Change", in Peter Chen (ed) *Singapore Development Policies and Trends,* Singapore: Oxford University Press.

Hing, A. Y. and Chiew, S. K. (1989-90) *National Automation Survey,* Singapore: Singapore Industrial Automation Association.

Hing, A. Y. and Chiew, S. K. (1991-92) *National Automation Survey,* Singapore: Singapore Industrial Automation Association.

Huff, W. G. (1994) *The Economic Growth of Singapore,* Cambridge: Cambridge University Press.

Huff, W.G. (1995) "What is the Singapore Model of Economic Development?", *Cambridge Journal of Economics*, 19(6).

Islam, I. and Kirkpatrick, C. (1986) "Export-led Development, Labour Market Conditions and Income Distribution", *Cambridge Journal of Economics*, 10(2).

King, V. (1994) "The Sociology of Southeast Asia", *Bijdragen*, 155(1).

Krause, L. B., Koh, A. T. and Lee, T. Y. (1987) *The Singapore Economy Reconsidered*, Singapore: Institute of Southeast Asian Studies.

Kuo, E. and Wong, A. (1979) *The Contemporary Family in Singapore*, Singapore: Singapore University Press.

Kuo, E. and Huey, T. C. (1985) "Towards an Information Society: Changing Occupational Structure in Singapore," National University of Singapore, Dept. of Sociology, Working Paper No. 69.

Kwok, K. W. (1993) "The Moral Conditions of Democratic Society", *Commentary* (Singapore), 11(1).

Kwok, K. W. and Mariam Ali (1998) "Cultivating Citizenship and National Identity", in Mahizhnan A. and Lee Tsao Yuan (eds) *Singapore: Re-engineering Success*, Singapore: Oxford University Press.

Lee, K. Y. (1978) "Extrapolating from the Singapore Experience", Special Lecture at the 26th World Congress of the International Chamber of Commerce, Orlando, Florida USA.

Le Roy Ladurie, E. (1979) *The Territory of the Historian*, Sussex: Harvester Press.

Leong, W. T.(1989) "Culture and the State: Manufacturing Traditions for Tourism", *Critical Studies in Mass Communication*, (6)4.

Lim, C. Y. and Associates (1988) *Policy Options for the Singapore Economy*, Singapore: McGraw Hill.

Lim, C. Y. (1991) *Development and Underdevelopment*, Singapore: Longman.

Lim, T. B. (1960) *The Development of Singapore's Economy*, Singapore: Eastern Universities Press.

Low, L. and Kuo, E. (1999) "Towards an Information Society in a Developed Nation", in Linda Low (ed) *Singapore: Towards a Developed Status*, Singapore: Oxford University Press.

Mak, L. F. (1981) *The Sociology of Secret Societies*, Kuala Lumpur: Oxford University Press.

Milne, R. S. and Mauzy, D. K. (1990) *Singapore: The Legacy of Lee Kuan Yew*, Boulder: Westview Press.

Murray, G. and Pereira, A. (1995) *Singapore: The Global City-State*, Folkestone, Kent: China Library.

Pang, E. F. and Lim, L. (1977) *The Electronics Industry in Singapore: Structure, Technology, and Linkages*, Singapore: Chopmen.

Pang, E. F., Tan, C. H. and Cheng, S. M. (1989) "The Management of People" in K.S. Sandhu and P. Whitley (eds) *Management of Success: The Moulding of Modern Singapore*, Singapore: Institute of Southeast Asian Studies.

Perry, M., Kong, L. and Yeoh, B. (1997) *Singapore: A Developmental City State*, West Sussex: John Wiley.

Preston, P. (1987) *Rethinking Development*, London: Routledge.

PuruShotam, N. (1992) "The Singaporean Indian Trader: Traditions of a Modern Economic Sector" in K. C. Ban, C. K.Tong and A. Pakir (eds) *Imagining Singapore*, Singapore: Times Academic Press.

Quah, S. R. (1988) *Between Two Worlds: Modern Wives in a Traditional Setting*, Singapore: ISEAS.

Rajaratnam, S. (1972) "Singapore: Global City", in T. B. Wee (ed) *The Future of Singapore – the Global City*, Singapore: University Education Press.

Rao, B. (1988) "Income Distribution in East Asian Countries: Evidence Revisited", *Asia Pacific Economic Literature*, 2(1).

Regnier, P. (1991) *Singapore: City-State in Southeast Asia*, London: Hurst & Company.

Rodan, G. (1993) "Preserving the One-Party State in Contemporary Singapore", in K. Hewison, R. Robison and G. Rodan (eds) *Southeast Asia in the 1990s,* Singapore: Allen and Unwin.

Rodan, G. (1996) "Class Transformations and Political Tensions in Singapore's Development" in R. Robison and D.S.G. Gordon (eds) *The New Rich in Asia,* London: Routledge.

The Straits Times, various issues.

Streeten, P. (1993) "Markets and States: Against Minimalism", *World Development,* 28(3).

Tamney, J. (1995) *The Struggle Over Singapore's Soul,* Berlin: de Gruyter.

Tan, E. S. (1979) "A Re-Appraisal of Singapore's Development: the Ideology and Policy of the Ruling Elites", Academic Exercise, National University of Singapore, Dept. of Sociology.

Tong, C. K. (1992) "The Intellectualisation of Religion in Singapore", in K. C. Ban, C. K. Tong and A. Pakir (eds) *Imagining Singapore,* Singapore: Times Academic Press.

Tong, C. K., Ho, K. C. and Lin, T. K. (1992) "Traditional Chinese Customs in Modern Singapore", in Y. M. Cheong (ed) *Asian Traditions and Modernization,* Singapore: Times Academic Press.

Trocki, C. A. (1990) *Opium and Empire: Chinese Society in Colonial Singapore, 1800-1910,* Ithaca: Cornell University Press.

Turnbull, C.M. (1989) *A History of Singapore 1819-1988,* Singapore: Oxford University Press (2nd edition).

UNDP (1995) *Human Development Report.*

UNDP (1998) *Human Development Report.*

Vente, R. E. and Chen, P. S. J. (eds) (1980) *Culture and Industrialization: An Asian Dilemma,* Singapore: McGraw-Hill.

Wallerstein, I. (1981) "Dependence in an Interdependent World", in H. Munoz (ed) *From Dependency to Development,* Boulder: Westview Press.

Wong, A. K. (1981) "Planned Development, Social Stratification, and the Sexual Division of Labour in Singapore", *Signs,* 7(2).

Wong, A. K. (1983) "A Study of Female Workers in Transnational Electronics Firms in Singapore", (mimeo) A Research Report.

Wong, A. K. and Yeh, S. H.K. (eds) (1985) *Housing a Nation: 25 Years of Public Housing in Singapore,* Singapore: Maruzen for Housing Development Board.

World Bank (1997/98) *The World Development Report.*

2

Urban Studies in Singapore

Ho Kong Chong

Introduction

The literature on urbanization in Singapore is both interdisciplinary and broad-based, with contributions from geography, history, economics and political science, in addition to sociology. Urban studies in Singapore have also been characterized by a number of policy-driven initiatives that cumulatively provide a good statistical profile of the city over a period of time, especially in housing and urban demography. Yet, until recently, urban studies in Singapore suffer from a lack of comparative analyses and from being under-theorized. The relatively recent development of the social sciences in the university curriculum is one reason. Serious efforts during the colonial period were sparse and sporadic, given the absence of a developed institutional background. Most works were produced in the 1950s and originate mainly from geographers and historians (Hodder 1953, Bogaars 1955, 1956, Stahl 1959, Wheatley 1954, Wong 1960). These were focused on various facets of Singapore's development and have been highly descriptive, with a greater concern for data collection than with attempts to theorize. Compared to the colonial period, the literature in the post-colonial indigenous phase of development is characterized by greater variety. Scholarly contributions have come from new social science perspectives, as the establishment of new disciplines at the University of Singapore[1] produced an important

1   Political Science was introduced in 1961 and Sociology in 1965. See Kapur (1986) for a collection of bibliographic essays on various disciplines.

and systematic record of research reports, working papers and academic journals. I have referred to these papers in various parts of the essay to illustrate both policy directions and underlying theoretical perspectives. Another reason for the relative absence of comparative attempts is Singapore's "atypicalness". As a city-state, Singapore is not really bound by the pressures facing cities in large countries. This removes Singapore from being considered in the Third World urbanization literature, a fertile source of comparative urban research. The weak institutional ties between Malaysia, Indonesia and Singapore, and the relative absence of scholars who specialize in the study of cities in Southeast Asia also inhibits comparative research efforts.

A fair amount of urban studies in Singapore are related to the work of government. In the colonial period, this type of literature was largely the result of government-appointed commissions that were tasked to examine issues and problems rather than the systematic and regular collection of data. The Simpson Report on sanitation (1907), the two housing commission reports (1918, 1948), the British Military Administration [BMA] (1945) report assessing Singapore's entrepot trade, Allen's (1950) report on the major ports of Malaya, Fraser's (1949) report on the work of the housing agency, and the Department of Social Work's two social surveys ([DSW] 1947 and [Goh] 1956) are all examples of this genre. The significance of these social surveys will be discussed later. The independence of Singapore and the creation of various agencies with developmental roles resulted in the expansion and professionalisation of urban planning and created a demand for more regular and comprehensive data on housing, transportation and land use. The literature of the 1970s and 1980s have also been characterized by a number of works commissioned by statutory boards (e.g. HDB 1975 [edited by Yeh], HDB 1985 [edited by Wong and Yeh], NTUC 1982 [edited by Jayakumar], URA 1989, MRTC 1989), some of which are attempts to celebrate organizational achievements.

I have chosen to organize this chapter thematically, highlighting the conceptual developments in the literature within a developmental perspective. However, to the extent that the urban studies literature reflect issues and problems of the time, this review also documents the evolution of Singapore, from port city to a global hub for the Asia Pacific region.

Urban Structure and Function

Of the various strands of urban studies, the work of economic geographers and historians have a long and uninterrupted tradition. Their focus was an attempt to understand the development of Singapore as a colonial port city and to assess the economic significance of this function.

Collectively, this literature provides a comprehensive account of Singapore's development at two levels. The first strand is the story of the changing external economic and political environment of Southeast Asia and Singapore's role within this environment. The work of the IBRD (1955), Stahl (1959), Wong (1960), Chiang (1963), Van De Wal (1968), Turnbull (1972), Courtney (1972), Sardesai (1977), Dick (1990) and others demonstrated the competition between the Dutch and the British over the trade of Southeast Asia, and the gradual rise of Singapore as a trading hub, as British triumphed over Dutch interests.

Following these accounts, the founding of Singapore as a trading port by the British in 1819 was an outcome of several factors; the increasing importance of the China-India trade in tea, cotton and opium meant more frequent British marine traffic through the Archipelago seas; the gradual British involvement in the lucrative spice trade; the need to counter Dutch monopolistic practices in the region; and lastly, the realization that Penang, an existing port located about 550 miles north of Singapore, was sited too peripherally to take advantage of these trade developments (Wong 1960, 1,2,14, Courtney 1972, 67). The Singapore free port filled an economic niche that was neglected by the Dutch, whose economic policy in the mid-1800s was aimed at the exploitation of Indonesia's natural resources and an exclusive focus on Java at the expense of the Outer provinces. British efforts at capturing the trade in the region were also aided by a plentiful supply of cheap British manufactured goods to trade for local produce. As a result, the trade of the Outer Islands became focused increasingly on Singapore (Van Der Wal 1968, 194-195, Sardesai 1977, 37, Dick 1990, 300).

The second strand is an account of the increasing dominance of entrepot trade in the Singapore economy and the effects this had on the internal development of the city. This can be seen in a number of ways. Most directly, many studies showed how the growing entrepot trade resulted in the development of associated economic activities such as the merchant trade comprising European, Chinese and local traders (BMA 1945, Makepeace 1921, Wong 1960) and the banking system which grew out of this trade (Lee 1969). In particular, the early control of the regional trade via financing from Singapore is significant because this laid the economic foundation which ensured the flow of produce through the island, thus avoiding the decentralizing tendencies associated with direct shipping and state intervention in the channels of trade (BMA 1945, 18). The success of Singapore as a major port in the Malayan Archipelago was a major factor in Singapore becoming a fuel depot towards the end of the 19th century (Bogaars 1956,118).

Technological (in particular communications) and military consequences also flow from the entrepot function. As accounts by Melville (1921), Makepeace (1921), Wong (1960) and Chiang (1963) show, the flow of trade is also highly dependent on the flow of information in the form of trade reports, commercial intelligence, instructions between trade houses and their overseas headquarters, and goods orders between traders. Accordingly, the development of trade has been matched by a demand for a system of reliable and rapid communication of information, both externally in terms of Singapore's link to other major ports, and internally in terms of the development of communication links between the harbour and the shipping agents in the downtown area[2].

The development of Singapore as a coal depot and later as an oil depot increased the strategic significance of Singapore to the British. This was important to Singapore's development as a military base protecting British interests in the region (Makepeace et al. 1921, 101, Bogaars 1956, 136). Military installations, had by the 1950s, occupied one-tenth of the colony's land area (Humphrey 1985, 12-13).

2   The first telephone trail in Singapore was in 1878, just two years after the Graham Bell telephone was invented. By 1882, agency houses, banks, the two dock companies, and the P & O line monopolised usage of the telephone system (Makepeace: 1921:170,171). The Tanjong Pagar Dock Company ran its own system by 1900.

Thus, the interplay between trade, communication and transportation, provided the infrastructures that made Singapore into an important centre for British economic and political interests, which in turn guaranteed the survival and continued prosperity of Singapore. Reading the economic history of Singapore, one gets a good appreciation of not only first mover advantages in terms of competition between rival ports, but equally important is the development of complementary activities reinforcing what economic geographers call agglomeration economies.

One also appreciates the negative consequences of an entrepot economy, such as the vulnerability of the city to external shocks. For example, the development of rival port cities and the dissipation of inter-country trade, as in the rise of Hong Kong and its effect on the China-Singapore trade (Stahl 1951, 87, Turnbull 1972, 186) or of Saigon and the Indo-China-Singapore trade (Bogaars 1955,114-115, Buchanan 1972, 28). Other examples show how political disturbances and trade depressions in major trading countries affect the volume of trade (Chiang 1963, 76, Wong 1960, 165, Turnbull 1972, 186-187).

Another consequence is the absence of industrial development as a result of colonial economic policy. There was little indigenous manufacturing partly because the colonial state did not encourage its development, believing that such activities were for industrial nations and that Singapore should concentrate on doing what it did best (ie commerce) and not dissipate its energies by venturing into untested domains (Ho 1993, 48). This bias was reflected in a tariff structure which discouraged local manufacturing (Dixon 1991, 114).

One could also approach Singapore's urban development as McGee (1967) and O'Connor (1983) have done: as one type of urbanization in contrast to other types of earlier and existing urban development in the region. Thus, if we look at Singapore as a port city in the British colonial empire, it is a modern product in contrast to the sacred cities of Southeast Asia which were built as centres of civilizations, religious complexes, existing for the purpose of reflecting the magnificence of the kingdom and the status of the native god-kings (Reed 1976). Such cities were also centres of art, religion and political, administrative organization, supporting a non-agrarian elite, who survived on the tributes of the agrarian countryside. However, as a port city its function is similar to the older coastal trading settlements that proliferated along the trade routes of Southeast Asia. As a product of colonization and a city of commerce built from scratch, Singapore has always played a more functional role as a centre for the diffusion of new ideas of trade and commerce, fashion and taste and of inventions such as the telephone (see footnote 2) through its role as an entrepot. In this sense, Singapore is very much a heterogenetic centre (Redfield and Singer 1954), standing in marked contrast with older capital cities in the region which function as orthogenetic centres charged with the role of perpetuating the cultural heritage of the nation.

Social Organization and Urban Subcultures

The key contribution of sociology to Singapore urban studies has been an attempt at understanding the social structure of the city. The immigration histories of various ethnic groups, the British policy of dealing with ethnic communities separately and leaving them to look after the provision of public goods such as schools and medical facilities, the ethnic occupational divisions, along with an absence of mechanisms that allowed for social integration across communities contributed to ethnically-segregated communities. Hodder's (1953) attempt at marking the spatial boundaries of the various communities is one of the few social maps of the city of the period.

Singapore, after the Second World War, was characterized by high urban population density and poverty. The extent of these features can be deduced in two fairly detailed surveys done on Singapore's central area by the Department of Social Welfare (DSW) in 1947 and 1954. In both surveys, the term "space" is used to denote the most congested sleeping arrangement: "places like bunks in passage ways, the tiered bed-lofts common in Singapore, sleeping selves under or over staircases, sleeping arrangements in five-foot ways, kitchens and backyards, and other places used for sleeping without enclosures or partitions" (DSW 1947, 70). In 1947, the percentage of households using such spaces constituted 21% in ward 1 (the harbour area stretching to west Chinatown), 16% in ward 2 (the rest of Chinatown, including the business district, extending east to Middle Road) and 26% in ward 3 (comprising areas east of Middle Road, bounded by Serangoon Road and the Kallang River) (DSW

1947, 71). By 1954, when the second survey was done, the figures had increased to 38% for wards 1 and 2, while remaining unchanged at 25% for ward 3 (Goh 1956, 68-69).

These conditions are elaborated in Barrington Kaye's (1960) *Upper Nanking Street,* arguably the first urban sociology study attempted in Singapore. Upper Nanking Street in the 1950s was one of the most congested neighbourhoods in the heart of Chinatown. Kaye's interviews in particular provide an enduring account of the hardship faced by residents coping with cramped, spartan and often unsanitary living conditions, unemployment and ill health (see Kaye's chapter 12).

If the sociological studies of the 1950s were concerned with congestion and poverty in the city, the attention of studies in the 1960s and 1970s was on the quest for community. Rapid social change in the city-state as a result of industrialization, the introduction of public housing, and urban renewal programmes, caught the attention of sociologists. The result was a large collection of "relocation studies", works which essentially looked at how families coped with the transformation of their neighbourhoods. This comes closest to being called an urban research tradition within the Department of Sociology at the University of Singapore.

The massive exodus of families from the city into public housing estates, a mass education programme, the start of the industrialization process, and reshaping of state-society relations in the 1960s and 1970s meant that this was a period of great change for adults, children and families. Several edited collections captured both structural changes and their effects on the population (notably Ooi and Chiang 1969, Hassan 1976a, Chen and Evers 1978).

For an increasing segment of the population, the 1970s marked a new era in which a way of life was dramatically transformed. Nowhere was this more evident than in the move into public housing estates. The proliferation of relocation studies undertaken by staff and students in the Sociology Department left an important record of this experience. Tai (1988) and Ho (1993) have reviewed this large collection. Families moving into public housing estates were generally satisfied with the improved amenities offered by the HDB estates in the form of better access to schools, marketing and recreation. But these advantages were attained at the cost of higher prices in HDB estates and the loss of a sense of solidarity, mutual help and a warm social environment of older villages and *kampongs* (Chang 1975, Hassan 1976b, 343-345, Tai 1988, 9-10).

HDB neighbourhoods are also different from traditional neighbourhoods in other ways. They are characterized by social and economic heterogeneity as the policy of the HDB (via its allocation policy and in planning for flats of different sizes within the same precinct) was aimed at ethnic and social class integration within the estate. Unlike low-rise villages and *kampongs* where extended families can be accommodated via simple extensions to the existing premise, HDB flats do not offer this facility. Subsequent policy revisions encouraged the formation of extended family units by giving priority in flat allocations to extended families and by changing the design to incorporate extended families ("granny flats"). However, the effectiveness of encouraging extended family residential units is being eroded by the greater desire on the part of newly-formed families to live apart from their families of orientation. Consequently, the one family nucleus has increased from 71.5% in 1970, to 81% in 1980 and 84.6% in 1990 (Dept of Statistics 1992, 3-4).

The transition from older, traditional neighbourhoods to HDB estates and the accompanying adjustment process was largely over by the end of the 1970s. In 1980, close to 70% of the population were living in public housing. More importantly, for the younger generation who have grown up in HDB estates and know no alternatives, HDB neighbourhoods represent a familiar and intimate setting which does not require any adjustment. This does not mean that a sense of belonging to such estates has increased, as high residential mobility characterises HDB estates. The young get married and move out and the upwardly mobile choose larger premises with better amenities in newer HDB estates or they upgrade to private housing. One emergent problem of the 1990s is the overwhelming presence of the elderly left behind in older public housing estates.

Youth in Singapore have attracted the attention of the media and scholars for different reasons. Local media have periodically attacked youths for their seemingly excessive consumption and materialistic and "westernized" attitudes. Explaining this reaction has been the one entry point for the research on urban youth cultures. Leong's (1996) argument has been that adult discourses on youth reflect adult anxieties and fears for the new generation. Youth cultures, Leong suggests, are expressive and experimental, and these energies are important for creating a more vibrant society. Chua's (1998) analysis of youth consumerism provides a different level of analysis. While Leong points to domestic factors in arguing that youth consumption is an outcome of an affluent industrial society, Chua looks to external influences — Singapore's openness to the global economy. As a result, Chua (1998, 990) argues that youth culture in Singapore is very much driven by the access youths have to a globalized "image bank", consisting of stylised bits derived from both West and East mass media content on fashion, music, movies and television.

Kong's analysis of fringe music indicates yet another approach to youth culture. While Leong and Chua look at consumption, Kong examines music genres created by young people. This shift in focus allows Kong to study lyrics as youth reactions to the conditions and issues that confront them. In her analysis of *xinyao* (a musical style popular among the Mandarin-speaking Singaporean youths) for example, Kong shows how the essence of this movement revolves around coming to terms with the challenges of modern living. Some lyrics express a longing for a simpler past, while others represent a commentary on social issues like westernization:

> The words of the (winds of the) west
> The more they blow, the more they become untamed/arrogant
> The love of the East is sighing softly
> (From the song *An Eastern boy's tragedy* by Liang Wern Fook [cited by Kong 1996, 113])

The counterpart in English music also deals with youth attempts to relate to their social environment:

> Everybody tells us what to do
> Everyone forces shit down our throats
> They expect all their shit to be swallowed
> Quietly by us without a single choke
> (From the song *Its our lives* by Opposition Party [cited by Phua and Kong 1996, 225])

The difference between Mandarin and English styles in youth marginal music should be noted. While both genres are similar in that they represent youth responses to the social context, the expressive style, the anger, cynicism, vulgarity represented in the lyrics of English musical genre also reflect their Western musical genres in heavy metal and rap.

The study of delinquent youths represents yet another route in youth culture studies. Taking an interactionist stance popular in deviance studies, such youth studies have stressed process rather than responses. Thus, the argument is that delinquent youth subcultures are the result of the attitude and actions of agents of social control (eg law enforcement officers, teachers), and how these responses in turn work to alienate certain segments of youth: working class youths and academically poor performers (Tan 1992, Noordin 1992).

Examining youth culture studies as a collection, we see that much of the energies that go into the making of youth cultures in Singapore are indicative of the context that youth find themselves in, a context that is highly urban, affluent, fast changing, and open to external influences. These conditions operate to create greater choice (many lifestyles to choose from), increased opportunity (a certain level of tolerance for difference), and larger capacity (the financial means to do so). They encourage a diversity of subcultures among youths in Singapore.

The same conditions that feed youth culture are also responsible for crime and deviance. Cities have been acknowledged as centres of innovation and creativity, but they are also known for underground cultures. An odd blend exists in Singapore with some curious contradictions. The government for pragmatic reasons tolerates prostitution. While street walking is illegal, organized prostitution in the form of brothels in designated red light districts is allowed (Ong 1993). Ironically, because official policy is spatially based, the trade has flourished and concentrated in certain districts, resulting in places such as Geylang acquiring a trade-based reputation and a matching set of late night food outlets. Yet homosexuality is illegal even among consenting adults (Leong 1997). It is the criminalization of homosexuality that has, in part, led to a well-developed underground culture, with its own haunts, pick-up areas, codes, beliefs and identities (Low 1995, Au 1997).

Urban Politics and Governance

Research on the question of politics and governance in Singapore has developed in a number of directions, in terms of state-society relations and in terms of state management of the economy. To the extent that the economic success of Singapore was also due to popular support of state programmes, then attention must be focused on how this legitimacy was achieved. Following Castells (1977), who drew attention to the provision of collective consumption goods as a way of understanding state-society relations, Chua (1991, 1995) examined the provision of public housing in Singapore, and argued how this provision provided the basis of legitimacy and a building block of ideological hegemony for the state. Part of the legitimacy also stems from the economic opportunity for an increasing segment of the population, opportunities created by an expanding economy (Rodan 1989).

The rapid growth of East Asian economies has led to an expansion of the middle class (Hsiao 1993). The second approach has thus been directed at the question of whether the middle class in Singapore has created conditions for the rise of a civil society and increased participation in government, in which the middle class lends its professional expertise and leadership to various areas. The debate between Jones (1994) and Rodan (1996) focuses on the capacity of the middle class in bringing about further democratization. Hill and Lian (1995, chapter 9) have demonstrated that while there have indeed been a proliferation of non-government organizations in tandem with the growth of the middle class, the position taken by these groups has not been confrontational. Thus, while an infrastructure has been created to facilitate participation, the conservative orientation of the middle class, as the prime beneficiaries of development, and their traditional links with the state in terms of jobs and housing have not led to a more active independent voice, even though civic participation has increased.

As far as state involvement in the management of the economy is concerned, an interesting development has occurred with regard to state and capital relations. A strong entrepot economy had already developed under the laissez-faire policy promoted by the colonial government. But as neighbouring countries became independent and established their own national trade policies and ports, this function came under increasing threat. The new government, without strong ties with domestic merchant capital, and under pressure to create jobs for a burgeoning population, formed a new alliance with foreign industrial capital, a relationship that was responsible for much of the economic growth in the 1970s and 1980s. Mirza's (1986) work showed in good detail the extent of Singapore's dependence on multinational companies, while Chiu, Ho and Lui's (1997) comparative analysis of Hong Kong and Singapore indicated how the different state-capital models worked in the two city-states.

In the case of Singapore, the role of government in economic management was radically transformed from a laissez-faire position to that of a developmental state tasked with infrastructure provision, attracting and nurturing new industries, and actively using incentives to attract multinational companies. The success of this strategy for Singapore should however be evaluated against an external context of international capital movements. Timing was crucial, because multinational companies in the 1960s were pushed by high domestic wage costs to move away from their home bases (Froebel et al. 1980, Dicken 1986).

By the 1990s, the government had over two decades of managing an MNC-led economic development strategy. As Singapore prospered, the domestic cost pressures elaborated in the next section, pushed MNCs to restructure their operations by reallocating their labour and land-intensive operations to neighbouring countries. It also caused the government to reconsider its industrial strategy and develop a broader-based alliance with capital. In addition to its traditional relationship with MNCs, the 1990s saw a strategy to strengthen government-linked companies and turn them into national economic champions to compete in the global marketplace (Yeung 2000). Another alliance was forged with local entrepreneurs and venture capital to develop high technology companies through an emphasis on fostering local research and development (Wong 1999). At the time of writing, it may be too soon to gauge the effectiveness of these new alliances. But it is important to understand the nature of these new relationships and the inherent problems. Unlike the old alliance where the division of labour between state and capital involved essentially clear managerial roles for the two partners, it is unclear whether local industrial and technical entrepreneurs can fully develop under a developmental state regime. In the comparative analysis of the industrial developmental paths of Hong Kong and Singapore, Chiu, Ho and Lui (1997, 120-21) argue that while the lack of state involvement in Hong Kong meant that Hong Kong firms were agile and responded fast to market changes, they did not have the capacity to transform themselves into high-tech and capital-intensive enterprises. A reverse question may be asked of Singaporean firms: can local firms which have easy access to state funds develop the agility required to survive in highly competitive environments?

The Global City

The rapid growth that Singapore enjoyed in the 1970s created a number of problems for the city-state in the 1980s. The incorporation of rural Malaysian labour into Singapore factories occurred on a massive scale in the 1970s (Heyzer 1982). But this was only a temporary measure, and in the 1980s, labour was not only getting more expensive, but also in short supply, in spite of various government intervention strategies. The appreciating Singapore dollar, while keeping the cost of living down, reduced Singapore's competitiveness by making exports more expensive. The combination of these factors, together with the inflation of land cost, invariably forced labour-intensive firms to relocate to cheaper production sites. But industrial policies instituted in the 1980s also saw a selective attraction of investment in higher technology industries in electronics and pharmaceuticals (Ho 1993, 1995).

An outcome of economic restructuring is the attempt by Singapore to regionalise. As pointed out by a committee tasked to examine new economic directions: "our comparative advantage in exporting services is greater than our advantage in exporting goods" (MTI 1986, 11). The new niche represents a move away from production and envisions a greater managerial role in administrative, production control, and treasury activities within Singapore, and to provide service expertise in hotel management, air and sea port management, town and city planning to other countries (MTI 1986, 12).

Compared to the earlier phase of development where the strategies adopted by Singapore were not very different from the investment promotion policies adopted by other countries, the regionalization strategy is based on Singapore being a key city or hub in the region. Faced with a need to conserve limited supplies of land and labour and shift to increasingly higher revenue earning activities, the state strategy of managing growth has been directed at the technical and geographical division of labour such that Singapore ends up consolidating and attracting more of the core economic activities.

This is achieved in two ways. The regional industrial parks strategy represents an attempt to export Singaporean expertise in estate development and management, along with investment attraction to neighbouring countries. State-linked companies in Singapore contribute their expertise in terms of planning and project management in the building of industrial townships and estates as well as in the use of overseas investment promotion offices to attract investments. Consortium partners pool funds needed to bankroll the projects. At the host country, local partners source for land and labour and work to secure various approval and permits for the building of industrial parks. Thus, through the control of estate and investment promotion and fund management, influence is maintained in Singapore, as industrial projects move into the region. The research which has examined the earlier phases of such schemes, centred in the Indonesian islands of Batam and Bintan, and Southern Johor not only account for the nature of economic integration with Singapore, but identified socio-political problems associated with rapid labour movements into the region — slums, crime, unrest between newcomers and locals (Guinness 1992, Perry 1991, Parsonage 1992, Peachey et al. 1997).

In contrast to the regional industrial parks strategy, the operational headquarters scheme recognizes that there is already in place extensive economic involvement (either in terms of market penetration or in terms of production networks) by multinational companies in the region and works on trying to attract the regional control centres of these companies to Singapore (Dicken and Kirkpatrick 1991). Attempts to understand the presence of regional offices centre on the spatial-organizational dynamics of multinational corporations, the functions these offices play in the overall structure, and the changing attractiveness of places (Ho 1998, Yeung 1998, Perry et al. 1998).

Both the strategies of developing regional industrial parks and operational headquarters worked to move Singapore from a dependence on manufacturing to a services centre or a key economic node in the region and the global economy. Work has already started in examining the consequences of this new role of Singapore as a global city. In this regard, work by Yeoh and Khoo (1998) and Yeoh et al. (2000) is important in examining the migration flows created by these new economic strategies and its impact on Singaporean families and gender relations. The increasing openness of Singapore society to the rest of the world has also introduced a debate on the preservation of local values and identity in the midst of globalizing forces (Tan 1998). At the level of state ideological work, there is an ongoing initiative at convincing locals of the necessity of "foreign talent", to combat local fears of job loss and various forms of envy brought about by the influx of expatriate workers.

Future Directions in Urban Studies

For the next decade of urban studies, a major focus will relate to the issues which result from Singapore's status as a global city. Three broad types of studies — economics, culture and politics — should follow from this orientation. Within an economics and planning perspective, urban studies will examine Singapore's role in the regional and global economy in the face of greater economic integration in terms of trade, production, transportation links and migratory flows. Strategies of competition and collaborations between cities and sub-regions will become increasingly important as a focal area, along with questions regarding the vulnerabilities or resilience of such strategies to fluctuations in the global and regional economy. Hopefully, one subset of these studies will focus on comparisons with cities in a similar league: Hong Kong, Seoul, Taipei, Bangkok, etc. This type of analysis and the links with the global organization of production will add to significant insights into the future role of cities in the region. As suggested in the beginning of the essay, unlike many Southeast Asian cities, Singapore was created at the dawn of the modern commercial era. As the rest of the region industrializes and as globalization impacts on the region, will cities in this region become similar?

As Singapore globalizes, studies of social organization and urban cultures will occupy an even more important area for urban scholars. The notion of Singapore as a hub invokes a dynamic image of not only the flows of economic activities but also of the flows of people and cultural ideas and images. Thus, work on identities will dominate the attention of researchers. This will be the case in terms of Diaspora studies and the attempts of groups to forge alliances across space. Attention will also focus on age groups such as the elderly because of demographic trends, and youth because they will experience the full impact of cultural globalization. In the 1970s, the issue of community was a key focus in urban studies as the residential environment was rapidly transformed from urban villages to high-rise public housing. Thirty years later, the issue of neighbourhood communities will resurface as researchers respond to the question of whether these clusters are merely for convenience or whether there exist local bonds and sentiments in spite of competition from lifestyle and leisure communities. As Internet usage expands and as new products, services and forms of entertainment are introduced, Singaporeans will spend more time on the Web, and virtual communities will also receive their fair share of attention as users escape from present confines into their electronic networks.

Just before the Asian Crisis in 1997, work was well underway in studying consumption in Asia. A growing middle class was the product of three decades of impressive economic growth. Largely based in cities, the lifestyle of the urban middle class has not only given rise to a highly visible landscape of consumption, but urban scholars are also asking how the explosive growth in consumption has fundamentally changed the lifestyle and culture of the middle class (Chua 1999), along with an interest in how the infrastructure of consumption shapes different demands for new products.

With the separation from Malaysia in 1965, Singapore lost more than an economic hinterland. The countryside that Singapore shared with Malaya has disappeared as well. I have often wondered about the significance of this loss in terms of the implications for the cultural development of the city-state. The term "heartland", for example, has two conventional meanings. It has been used in geopolitics to refer to an agricultural or industrial area that can be considered as a buffer in the event of a military attack. In North America, this term has also referred to a geographically central region that is the locus of mainstream or traditional values. Without the experience of the countryside, the term "heartland" in Singapore has been appropriated in local politics and used to denote some imagined residential groupings in public housing estates. In reality, Singapore is simply too small (these are, after all, urban "estates" rather than "regions") to talk about any part of the island being a strategic buffer. Neither can public housing estates be thought of as a conservative heartland, given the heterogeneity of public housing estates in terms of income and ethnicity and because of high residential mobility. The term, "heartland", as it has been applied in Singapore therefore represents a corruption of the conventional understanding.

The informal sector and squatter housing are now absent in the city, without the countryside to fuel the rural-urban migration process. This was a major factor in its rapid transformation into a modern metropolis. Without a rural anchor and its associated craft industries and ethnic traditions, Singaporeans have been quick to embrace technology and modernity. Globalization will tend to accelerate this tendency precisely because the absence of a cultural heartland implies minimal resistance to these forces.

The politics of the global city is obviously a more complex process. Because Singapore is a city-state, the relationship between its foreign policy and local politics, economics and culture represents a set of issues that is largely missing in other cities. Singapore's role in the Earth Summit in 1991 and how this subsequently shaped government negotiations with local environmental groups is one example. The Singapore government's use of diplomatic relations with Asian neighbours to enhance its regionalization drive is another example. On the domestic front, researchers will spend their time understanding the various tensions and trade-offs involved in managing the politics of a more diverse constituency. Specifically, the politics of the global city, as this applies to Singapore, will involve balancing global economic aspirations with local political realities, especially with regard to securing the loyalties of the spatially immobile working class. In the global city, the task of building national identity will be increasingly difficult in the face of competing orientations (built on ethnicity, religion, lifestyles) and new migrants with their links to the old country. Managing class-based tensions that may be exacerbated by globalization represents yet another facet. If creativity and innovation are the new drivers of competitiveness in the global economy, then politics need to keep pace with economics in ensuring flexible intervention — knowing when to intervene and when to cut back in order to foster and sustain creativity and innovation.

References

Allen, D. F. (1950) *Report on the Major Ports of Malaya,* Kuala Lumpur, Malaysia: Government Press.

Au, W. P. (1997) *Gay Culture in Singapore,* unpublished paper presented in "Multiculturalism: On Paper and in Practice", organised by The Substation, Singapore, September.

Bogaars, G. (1955) "The Effect of the Opening of the Suez Canal on the Trade and Development of Singapore", *Journal of the Malayan Branch of the Royal Asiatic Society,* 28(169): 99-143.

Bogaars, G. (1956), *The Tanjong Pagar Dock Company, 1864-1905,* Memoirs of the Raffles Museum No. 3 Singapore.

British Military Administration, Dept. of Trade and Industry (1945), *Entrepot Trade of Singapore,* Singapore.

Buchanan, I. (1972) *Singapore in Southeast Asia,* London: Bell and Sons.

Castells, M. (1977) *The Urban Question,* London: Edward Arnold.

Chang, C.T. (1975) "A Sociological Study of Neighbourliness", in S. H. K. Yeh (ed) *Public Housing in Singapore,* Singapore: Singapore University Press.

Chen, P. J. S. and Evers, H. (eds) (1978) *Studies in ASEAN Sociology: Urban Society and Social Change,* Singapore: Chopmen Publishers.

Chiang H. D. (1963) "Straits Settlement Foreign Trade 1870-1915," *Memoirs (1978) of the Raffles Museum* No. 6.

Chiu, S. W. K., Ho, K. C. and Lui, T. L. (1997) *City-States in the Global Economy*, Boulder, Colorado: Westview.

Chua, B. H. (1991) "Not Depoliticized but Ideologically Successful: the Public Housing Programme in Singapore", *International Journal of Urban and Regional Research*, 15: 24-42.

Chua, B. H. (1995) *Communitarian Ideology and Democracy in Singapore*, London: Routledge.

Chua, B. H. (1998) "World Cities, Globalisation and the Spread of Consumerism: A View from Singapore", *Urban Studies*, 35 (5-6): 981-1000.

Chua, B. H. (1999) "The Attendant Consumer Society for a Developed Singapore", in L. Low (ed), *Singapore: Towards a Developed Status*, Singapore: Oxford University Press.

Courtney, P. P. (1972) *A Geography of Trade and Development in Malaya*, London: Bell and Sons.

Department of Social Welfare [DSW] (1947) *A Social Survey of Singapore: A Preliminary Study of Some Aspects of Social Conditions in the Municipal Area of Singapore*, Singapore.

Department of Statistics (1992), Census of Population *1990 Release No. 2 Household and Housing*, Singapore: Dept. of Statistics.

Dick, H.W. (1990) "Inter-island Trade, Economic Integration, and the Emergence of the National Economy", in A. Booth, W. J. O'Malley and A. Weidemann (eds) *Indonesian Economic History in the Dutch Colonial Era*, New Haven: Yale University Southeast Asia Series.

Dicken, P. (1986) *Global Shift: Industrial Change in a Turbulent World*, London: Harper & Row.

Dicken, P. and Kirkpatrick, C. (1991) "Services-led Development in ASEAN: Transnational Regional Headquarters in Singapore", *The Pacific Review*, 4: 174-84.

Dixon, C. (1991) *Southeast Asia in the World Economy*, Cambridge: Cambridge University Press.

Drakakis-Smith, D.W. and Yeung, Y. M. (1977) "Public Housing in the City States of Hong Kong and Singapore", Development Studies Centre Occasional Paper No. 8, Australian National University.

Fraser, J. M. (Comp) (1949*), The Work of the SIT 1927-1947*, Singapore: SIT.

Froebel, F., Heinrichs, J. and Kreye, O. (1980) *The New International Division of Labour*, Cambridge: Cambridge University Press.

Gamer, R. (1976) *The Politics of Urban Development in Singapore*, Ithaca: Cornell University Press.

Goh, K. S. (1956) *Urban Incomes and Housing: A Report on the Social Survey of Singapore, 1953-54*, Singapore: Government Printing Office.

Guinness, P. (1992) *On the Margins of Capitalism*, Kuala Lumpur: Oxford University Press.

Hassan, R. (ed) (1976a) *Singapore: Society in Transition*, Kuala Lumpur: Oxford University Press.

Hassan, R. (1976b) "Symptoms and Syndrome of the Developmental Process" in R. Hassan (ed) *Singapore: Society in Transition*, Kuala Lumpur: Oxford University Press.

Heyzer, N. (1982) "From Rural Subsistence to an Industrial Peripheral Workforce: An Examination of Female Malaysian Migrants and Capital Accumulation in Singapore", in L. Beneria (ed) *Women and Development: The Sexual Division of Labour in Rural Societies*, New York: Praeger.

Hill, M. and Lian, K. F. (1995) *The Politics of Nation Building and Citizenship in Singapore*, London: Routledge.

Ho, K. C. (1993) "Issues on Industrial and Urban Development in Local Literature: Public Housing in Singapore", in B. H. Lee and K.S.S. Oorjitham (eds) *Malaysia and Singapore: Experiences in Industrialisation and Urban Development*, Kuala Lumpur: University of Malaya Press.

Ho, K. C. (1993) "Industrial Restructuring and the Dynamics of City-State Adjustments", *Environment and Planning A,* 25: 47-62.

Ho, K. C. (1995) "Singapore: Manoeuvring in the Middle League", in G.L. Clark and W.B. Kim (eds) *Asian NIES and the Global Economy,* Baltimore: John Hopkins.

Ho, K. C. (1998) "Corporate Regional Functions in Asia Pacific", *Asia Pacific Viewpoint,* 39(2): 179-91.

Hodder, B. W. (1953) "Racial Groupings in Singapore", *Journal of Tropical Geography,* 1: 25-36.

Hsaio, M. (1993) *Discovery of the Middle Classes in East Asia,* Taipei: Academia Sinica.

Humphrey, J. W. (1985) "Geographic Analysis of Singapore's Population", Census Monograph No. 5, Singapore: Dept. of Statistics.

International Bank for Reconstruction and Development (IBRD) (1955) *The Economic Development of Malaya,* Singapore: Government Printer.

Jayakumar, S. (ed) (1982) *Our Heritage and Beyond,* Singapore: NTUC.

Jones, D.M. and Brown, D. (1994) "Singapore and the Myth of the Liberalising Middle Class", *The Pacific Review,* 7(1): 79-87.

Kapur, B. K. (1986) *Singapore Studies: Critical Surveys of the Humanities and Social Sciences,* Singapore: Singapore University Press.

Kayes, B. (1960) *Upper Nanking Street Singapore,* Singapore: University of Malaya Press.

Kong, L. (1996) "Making 'Music at the Margins'? A Social and Cultural Analysis of *Xinyao* in Singapore", *Asian Studies Review,* 19(3): 99-124.

Lee, S. Y. (1969) "Financial and Credit Institutions", in J.B. Ooi and H.D. Chiang (eds) *Modern Singapore,* Singapore: Singapore University Press.

Leong, W. T. (1996) "In Defence of Youth Culture", in S. Krishnan et al. (eds) *Looking at Culture,* Singapore: Artes Design and Communication.

Leong, W. T. L. (1997) "Singapore", in D. J. West and R. Green (eds) *Sociolegal Control of Homosexuality: A Multi-Nation Comparison*, New York: Plenum Press.

Low, K. H. (1995) "Recognizing Strangers: Gay Cruising in the City", Unpublished Academic Exercise, Dept. of Sociology, National University of Singapore.

McGee, T. G. (1967) *The Southeast Asian City*, London: Bell and Sons.

Makepeace, W. (1921) "The Machinery of Commerce", in W. Makepeace et al. (eds) *One Hundred Years of Singapore, Vol. 2*, London: John Murray.

Makepeace, W., Brooke, G. E. and Braddell, R. S. J. (1921) "The Mineral Oil Trade", in W. Makepeace et al. (eds) *One Hundred Years of Singapore, Vol. 2*, London: John Murray.

Mass Rapid Transit Authority [MRTC] (1989) *The MRT Story*, Singapore: MRTC.

Melville, T. A. (1921) "The Post Office and Its History", in W. Makepeace et al. (eds) *One Hundred Years of Singapore, Vol. 2*, London: John Murray.

Ministry of Trade and Industry [MTI], Report of the Economic Committee (1986) *The Singapore Economy: New Directions*, Singapore: MTI.

Mirza, H. (1986) *Multinationals and the Growth of the Singapore Economy*, London: Croom Helm.

Noordin, S. (1992) "Mat Rockers: An Insight into a Malay Youth Subculture", Unpublished Academic Exercise, Dept. of Sociology, National University of Singapore.

O'Connor, R. A. (1983) "A Theory of Indigenous Southeast Asian Urbanism", *ISEAS Research Notes and Discussion Paper No. 38*, Singapore: Institute of Southeast Asian Studies.

Ong, J. H. (1993) "Singapore", in N.J. Davis (ed) *Prostitution: An International Handbook on Trends, Problems and Policies*, Westport, Connecticut: Greenwood Press.

Ooi, J. B. and Chiang, H. D. (eds) (1969) *Modern Singapore*, Singapore: Singapore University Press.

Parsonage, J. (1992) "Southeast Asia's Growth Triangle: a Sub-regional Response to Global Transformation", *International Journal of Urban and Regional Research*, 16, 307-18.

Peachey, K., Perry, M. and Grundy-Warr, C. (1997) "The Riau Islands and Economic Cooperation in the Singapore-Indonesia Border Zone", *Boundary and Territory Briefing*, 2(3).

Perry, M. (1991) "The Singapore Growth Triangle: State, Capital and Labour at a New Frontier in the World Economy", *Singapore Journal of Tropical Geography*, 12, 138-51.

Perry M., Yeung, H. and Poon, J. (forthcoming) "Regional Office Mobility: The Case of Corporate Control in Singapore and Hong Kong", *Geoforum*, 29(3): 237-55.

Phua, S. C. and Kong L. (1996) "Ideology, Social Commentary and Resistance in Popular Music: A Case Study of Singapore", *Journal of Popular Culture*, 30(1): 215-31.

Redfield, R. and Singer, M. (1954) "The Cultural Role of Cities", *Economic Development and Cultural Change*, 3: 53-73.

Rodan, G. (1989) *The Political Economy of Singapore's Industrialisation*, London: Macmillan.

Rodan, G. (1996) "State-society Relations and Political Opposition in Singapore", in G. Rodan (ed) *Political Oppositions in Industrialising Asia*, London: Routledge.

Reed, R. R. (1976) "Indigenous Urbanism in Southeast Asia", in Y.K. Yeung and C.P. Lo (eds) *Changing Southeast Asia Cities: Readings in Urbanisation*, Singapore: Oxford University Press.

SarDesai, D. R. (1977) *British Trade and Expansion in Southeast Asia: 1830-1914*, New Delhi: Allied Publishers.

Sassen, S. (1991) *The Global City*, New Jersey: Princeton University Press.

Simpson, W. J. (1907) Report on the Sanitary Conditions of Singapore 1901-1906.

Singapore Housing Commission (1918) *Proceedings and Report of the Commission Appointed to Inquire into the Course of the Present Housing Difficulties in Singapore, and the Steps which should be taken to Remedy such Difficulties*, 2 volumes, Singapore. Singapore Housing Commission (1948) *Report of Housing Committee Singapore, 1947,* Singapore.

Stahl, K. M. (1951) *The Metropolitan Organization of Trade*, London: Faber and Faber Ltd.

Tai, C. L. (1988) *Housing Policy and High-Rise Living: A Study of Singapore's Public Housing,* Singapore: Chopmen Publishers.

Tan, G. (1992) "Experiencing Marginality: The Resistance Subculture of Marine Kids", Unpublished Academic Exercise, Dept. of Sociology, National University of Singapore.

Tan, K. Y. (1998) "Singapore in the International Economy: Going Global, Staying Singaporean", in A. Mahizhnan and T. Y. Lee (eds) *Singapore: Re-Engineering Success*, Singapore: Oxford/IPS.

Turnbull, C. M. (1972) *The Straits Settlements 1826-67*, Singapore: Oxford University Press.

Turnbull, C. M. (1977) *A History of Singapore: 1819-1975*, Kuala Lumpur: Oxford University Press.

Urban Renewal Authority (URA) (1989) *The Golden Shoe: Building Singapore's Financial District*, Singapore: URA.

Van de Wal, S. L. (1968) "The Netherlands as an Imperial Power in Southeast Asia in the 19th century and After", in J.S. Bromley and E.H. Kossmann (eds) *Britain and the Netherlands in Europe and Asia*, London: Macmillan.

Wheatley, P. (1954) "Land Use in the Vicinity of Singapore in the Eighteen-Thirties", *Malayan Journal of Tropical Geography*, 2: 63-66.

Wong, A. and Yeh, H. K. S. (1985) *Housing a Nation: 25 Years of Public Housing in Singapore,* Singapore: HDB.

Wong L. K. (1960) "The Trade of Singapore 1819 – 1869", *Journal of the Malayan Branch of the Royal Asiatic Society*, 33 (192 part 4): 1-315.

Wong, P. K. (1999) "From Leveraging Multination Corporations to Technopreneurship: The Changing Role of S&T Policy in Singapore", text of paper in the following url: http://www.fba.nus.edu.sg/cmit/fulltext.asp.

Yeh, S. H. K. (ed) (1975) *Public Housing in Singapore*, Singapore: Singapore University Press.

Yeoh, B. S. A. (1998) "Global Cities, Transnational Flows and Gender Dimensions: The View from Singapore", unpublished paper presented at the Conference on 'City, State, and Region in a Global Order', Hiroshima, December 1998.

Yeoh, B. S. A. and Khoo, L. (1998) "Home, Work and Community: International Skilled Migration and Expatriate Women in Singapore", *International Migration*, 36: 159-86.

Yeung, H. W. C. (1998) "Competing for Transnational Corporations? The Regional Operations of Foreign Firms in Hong Kong and Singapore", in I. Cook et al. (eds) *Dynamic Asia: Business, Trade and Economic Development in Pacific Asia*, Aldershot: Ashgate.

Yeung, H. W. C. (2000) "State Intervention and Neoliberalism in the Globalizing World Economy: Lessons from Singapore's Regionalization Programme", *The Pacific Review*, 13(1): 133-62.

3

Sociology of the Family*

Stella R. Quah

The development of family sociology in developing countries has been characterized, so far, by an emphasis on descriptive studies and testing of conceptual propositions rather than by substantial theoretical contributions. Far from being characteristic of family sociology, this is a typical predicament found in studies covering other areas of sociology and in other social science studies conducted in countries where research facilities and research funding are scarce.

The aim of this chapter is to provide an account of what has been accomplished in Singapore on the study of the family. As a developing country, Singapore shares, to some extent, the difficulty mentioned above. Thus, it is relevant to dedicate the second section of this chapter to identifying the most salient aspects of Singapore as the setting where sociologists work. Following a chronological sequence, the third section will deal with the historical background of family studies, covering the work of pioneer researchers before Singapore's independence in 1965. The fourth section will deal with the period of consolidation between 1965 and 1979. The fifth section will discuss the main changes in direction and emphasis in the development of family research in Singapore from 1980 onwards. A summary of the main features in the development of family sociology and a note on future trends will be provided in the concluding section.

The other point that needs to be clarified in this brief introduction is how the family will be defined. I will follow the definition of family prevalent in Singapore and that has been used in sociological research conducted locally. The concept of family in Singapore requires some elaboration. In Europe, North America, Australia and New Zealand, analysts and policy makers have recognized for some time already, the existence of a multiplicity of family forms (Rapoport and Rapoport 1982, Sussman and Steinmetz 1987, Moen 1989, Kamerman and Kahn 1989, Edgar 1990, Koopman-Boyden 1990). In contrast, the concept of family has undergone comparably minor variations in Singapore over the past ninety years. Yet, one needs to distinguish between ideal family and actual family forms. This conceptual distinction introduced by Levy (1949, 1965) based on his study of the family in China, is highly relevant to the case of Singapore.

Over the decades, the major ethnic communities in Singapore — Chinese, Malays and Indians — have continuously followed and transmitted to their children their image of the ideal family as dictated by their respective cultural traditions. My personal observations of everyday family life in Singapore, of official pronouncements by political and community leaders and more formal accounts and descriptions of cultural traditions (Doolittle 1986, Tan 1986, 1990, Winstedt 1981, Majlis Pusat 1990, Husin Ali 1981, Mani 1979) indicate that, notwithstanding the cultural differences among these three ethnic groups, they are all inclined to regard as their ideal family the extended family, understood as a tightly-knit group involving at least three generations where parents, their married children — all, some, or only one child — and their children's children and spouses live in the same household.

The actual family, however, is that which people can "afford" to have according to the specific circumstances of their lives. During the past nine decades the ideal family has remained a cultural icon of Asian tradition while the actual family has been reshaped by the changing tides of social, political and economic development. Today, the legal arrangements covering public housing, income tax deductions and health care suggest that there is a certain awareness of the actual presence of different types of families such as three-generation families, nuclear families and single-parent families born out of widowhood, separation or divorce. Yet, these are variations of one socially recognised legitimate family where parents are legally married and the children are born within such a legal union. Singapore has not yet recognised legally — or socially — other family forms not based on, or derived from, a legal marriage.

The Societal Context of Family Research

Every human community captivates the attention of sociologists, but Singapore is an especially attractive subject of study because of three attributes. The best known of Singapore's features is its particularly rapid pace of socioeconomic development during the past three decades. The second characteristic of Singapore is its status as a city-state or island republic. And its third key feature is the ethnic and cultural composition of its population. All these three features are very relevant to our understanding of the perception and importance of family and kinship networks, of the family's everyday life in the different ethnic and religious communities, and of the impact of social policies on the family. These three features are related and require some elaboration.

Singapore's rapid pace of economic development is a phenomenon that began after its relatively unassuming existence as a British colony for nearly 140 years until 1959, an agitated period of internal self-government, and a stint as a member of the Federation of Malaysia. In a peaceful but momentous transition in 1965, Singapore took charge of its own destiny as an independent republic. The basic structures of nation-building that had been set up during the first years of the 1960s took off in 1965 and have been consolidating and undergoing transformations ever since.

Being a former British colony is a very relevant aspect of Singapore's history in this discussion. Singapore experienced the British judicial and political systems and retained most of the properties of both systems after independence. The judicial system comprises the Supreme Court and the Subordinate courts. The English common law is followed in the Singapore legal system covering the non-Muslim population. Following the precedent set by the British crown during the colonial period, and cognizant of the heterogeneous composition of the population and of the differences in regulations ordering the lives of the Muslim community, the Singapore government recognized that the

Muslim Law Act and the Syariah Court should rule most family and religious affairs of Muslim Singaporeans. Thus, Singapore has two legal systems working concurrently, the Muslim law and the non-Muslim law.

The presence of this dual legal system is one important indication of the Singaporean approach to ethnic relations. As the country strives to minimize the probability of ethnic conflict — the painful experience of racial riots in the 1960s has not been forgotten — it is evident that the political and social importance of ethnic minorities is not measured by their numbers. Muslims are numerically a small minority. According to the 1990 census of population, the large majority of Singaporeans (77.7%) are of Chinese descent, while 14.1% are Malays, 7.1% are Indians, and 1.1% are people from a variety of other ethnic groups (Dept. of Statistics, 1991b, 4). More importantly, there is an interesting overlap between religion and ethnicity, as major world religions tend to follow ethnic boundaries. Indeed, 99.7% of Malays are Muslims; 68% of Chinese classify themselves as Buddhist or Taoist; and 53.2% of Indians follow Hinduism. The Indian community shows the greatest variation in religious affiliation. After Hinduism, the next largest religion is Islam: 26.3% of Singapore Indians are Muslims; and 12.8% of Indians are Christians (Dept. of Statistics 1991b, 12).

This is the multiethnic and multireligious setting shaping the everyday life of the 3,002,800 population (89% of them residents) in the small island of Singapore. But the rich cultural diversity of its population belies the diminutive physical size of the country. The total land area, including the main island and about 58 offshore islets, is only 626.4 square kilometres (Ministry of Communications and Information 1991, 1). Considering that Singapore is a city-state with very limited land, and an independent republic that needs to look after its own economic and political survival, it is not surprising that one of the major concerns of Singapore is to attain an optimum utilization of the nation's physical environment and human resources. The size and political status of Singapore are relevant to the discussion of family and family studies because this concern with the link between physical space and human resources influences families in at least two main ways: the management of population growth and the provision of housing. As it will be discussed later, the concern with population growth has led to policies directed to influence decisions on the number of children a married couple wants to have. Similarly, the housing options for families are restricted — mostly high-rise apartments — on account of the scarcity of land. The 1990 census indicates that 85.7% of Singapore resident households own and live in public housing high-rise apartments (Dept. of Statistics 1991b, i).

Its rapid pace of economic development is another evident feature of Singapore. Reporting on her research, the British anthropologist Judith Djamour wrote in 1959 that she spent two years in Singapore, from January 1949 to November 1950, doing fieldwork in Tanjong, "a fishing community on the south-west coast and an urban area" (Djamour 1959, 1). If Djamour had returned to Singapore in 1990, she would have found that the old fishing villages have been replaced by modern neighbourhoods of high-rise buildings. As part of the national economic development design geared towards industrialization and urban renewal, most villagers and their families had been relocated to new public housing apartments in the 1970s (Yeh 1970, 1973, Chew 1982). The rural south-west coast that Djamour visited is now part of the growing urban metropolis. Only 1.9% of the total land area was occupied by farms in 1990 (Ministry of Communications and Information 1991, 1).

More importantly, the nature of the labour force has been transformed by the exigencies of a modern industrial economy. Djamour would find rather few fishermen today. In 1947, 8.8% of the total male population were working as fishermen or farmers, but only 4.2% of the males were in these occupations in 1990. Among the Malays, who were the subjects of Djamour's study, 6% of Malay men were fishermen and farmers in 1947, but this proportion dropped to 0.5% in 1990. People working in professional and technical occupations made up only 2.7% of the labour force in 1947. The proportion of professional and technical workers reached 15.7% of the labour force in 1990 (Del Tufo 1949, 110, 519, Department of Statistics 1991b, 54).

A few additional indicators of rapid economic development will complete the picture. The indigenous gross national product per capita in 1977 was $5,712, it increased steadily to $12,584 in 1983, and to

$17,909 in 1989. Annual electricity consumption per person was 1,938 kwh in 1977; 3,054.7 kwh in 1983; and 4,724.6 kwh in 1989 (Ministry of Culture 1984, 46, Ministry of Communications and Information 1991, 32). According to an international study of quality of life indicators by the 1990 Population Crisis Committee comparing 100 countries, Singapore ranked 1st in housing standards (availability of utilities), 1st in noise level; 5th in food cost as percentage of income; 6th in public health (based on infant mortality); 7th in traffic flow; 20th in public safety (based on murder rate); 20th in communications (number of telephones); 40th in education (percentage of population with secondary education); and 42nd in living space (Economic Planning Committee 1991, 24).

These are, broadly, the most significant aspects of the social context of family research in Singapore. The details will become clear as the discussion progresses, but this outline prepares the way for the subsequent analysis.

Historical Background: the Pioneers

As it is commonly found in other Third World countries with a colonial past, the concern for the collection of facts about the institution of the family was brought to Singapore by British colonial administrators, scholars, and missionaries (Quah 1993a). The British Crown acquired the island of Singapore in 1819, and in 1826 Singapore became part of the British Straits Settlements together with the island of Penang and Malacca — a former Portuguese colony. The British colonial government showed less curiosity for the cultures of indigenous peoples in the Straits Settlements, compared to the keen interest in gathering systematic information displayed by the Spanish, Dutch, Portuguese and American colonial powers ruling over other Southeast Asian territories before the Second World War.

Still, getting acquainted with the local customs of the various communities living in Singapore was important for the colonial government. A major preoccupation of British colonial administrators was to maintain law and order while guaranteeing as far as possible to the local people — mainly the Chinese and Malay communities – the exercise of their respective customs, especially concerning family matters. This was not an easy task.

The colonial administrators had to learn the key local customs, and "the extent to which English law was to be modified to pay this respect to local usages was not clear" (Freedman 1950, 97). Perhaps as an outcome of this ambivalence, the British followed an unwritten laissez-faire approach throughout the second half of the nineteenth century so that "the codes by which Chinese regulated their family affairs...were beyond the reach of the [colonial] government" (Freedman 1950, 98).

Nevertheless, while there was no direct involvement of British colonial administrators in the study of family customs among the local peoples, two trends are identified. First, there were British scholars and missionaries who, on their own, observed and wrote about local customs and behaviour during the late 1800s and the early 1900s. Although these "pioneer researchers" were foreigners and did not have formal training in social sciences, their descriptions of local customs, daily life and physical settings, still offer data of great sociological interest (see for example Buckley 1902, Reith 1907).

The second trend was for the colonial government to tap the expertise of British scholars, both officially and unofficially. An early indication of this trend was the appointment of British scholars studying China and the Chinese language to the office of "Protector of Chinese" created in 1869 to supervise "the Chinese community on behalf of the government". The post of Protector was enhanced with statutory powers in 1877 (Freedman 1950, 98). In the handling of legal matters involving the Chinese, the colonial government also referred to the English translations of Chinese law under the Manchu dynasty and "call(ed) for the testimony of Chinese Consuls, Protectors of Chinese, and local Chinese of standing" (Freedman, 1950, 98-99).

Later on, during the first half of the 20th century, British scholars were commissioned to write specific reports on family life, social customs and religious practices of local communities. The best example of this mode of collaboration between the British colonial government and British academics is the "Colonial Research Studies", a series "intended for the publication of research studies by persons... engaged in research in the Colonial sphere financed from Government sources" [Explanatory note on the back cover of Freedman (1957)]. This early phase of social science research on the family — represented by the reports from the Colonial Research Studies series — was characterized by two important features. The first feature is a preference for descriptive studies over conceptual analyses. The second is a twofold feature: anthropology was introduced to Singapore earlier than sociology, and the earliest anthropologists had a tendency to dismiss disciplinary boundaries between anthropology and sociology. The latter has been an aspect of the British academic landscape for some time.

A good illustration of these two dimensions of pioneer social science research is the 20th Report in this series. It was published in 1957 under the title "Chinese Family and Marriage in Singapore" by Maurice Freedman, a Lecturer in Anthropology at the London School of Economics and Political Science. Freedman established the descriptive nature of his work as he indicated that his Report was

> ...to be read mainly by non-anthropologists. It follows that, from an anthropological point of view, a number of theoretical matters have been ignored or insufficiently discussed...and that the combination of analytical and minutely descriptive matter makes the book more heterogeneous than an anthropological monograph written according to prevailing [academic] standards. (1957, 5).

Freedman also dismissed, or was not aware of, any disciplinary differences between sociology and anthropology. His accentuation in the Foreword that his work was anthropological did not deter him from stating in his conclusion that his was "the first **sociological** exploration of the Chinese in Malaya" [emphasis mine] (1957, 229), and indicating in the description of his anthropological fieldwork that "my study might eventually need to be weighted in favour of urban sociology" (1957, 9). It is noteworthy that some British anthropologists currently working in Singapore still feel that there are no significant distinctions between the two disciplines.

Freedman's book on the Chinese family covered the historical roots of family organization in China before proceeding to the detailed description of the situation he observed in Singapore between January 1949 and December 1950 concerning four aspects of family life. These aspects were the structure and functions of the household; the kinship system, including the clan and clan associations; the structure, formation and disruption of marriage; and the aspect of death and death rituals. The book is the published version of the report he submitted to the Government of the Colony of Singapore — through the Colonial Social Science Council — in 1953. He arrived in Singapore with the official assignment to conduct a study of the Chinese family and was "informally attached to the Department of Social Welfare" of the Colony "which generously put an office at my disposal and made some clerical help available" (Freedman 1957, 7).

Doing research for his previous study of Chinese culture and British colonial law (Freedman 1950), Freedman had the opportunity to assess the dearth of information on the social and family life of the peoples residing in Singapore. He lamented,

> As far as Malaya is concerned, our ignorance of social organization among the Chinese was well-nigh all-embracing before the recent studies of Dr Victor Purcell...This absence of information is all the more surprising when we reflect that several generations of Chinese Protectors have passed since [the setting up of] the special agency for dealing with Chinese affairs in 1877. Documents have been piled up in offices; Protectors of Chinese and Secretaries for Chinese Affairs have amassed lifetimes of experience of Chinese problems; we have little access to either. When the Japanese took Singapore in 1942 they made a bonfire of the papers in the Chinese Secretariat, and now...the detailed history of a remarkable political institution has gone for good. (1957, 8).

Victor Purcell was a historian who studied the immigration of Chinese to Southeast Asia (1952). An earlier study was conducted by Braddell (1921) on Chinese marriage and the colonial Supreme Court, but this was an analysis of the legal aspects involved in the attempt to incorporate Chinese customary marriages and general Chinese custom into English law. Thus, Freedman may be considered as the first social scientist that conducted systematic research, albeit mostly descriptive, on the Chinese family in Singapore.

Maurice Freedman's wife, Judith Djamour, was the other pioneer anthropologist who contributed to the study of family in Singapore, but her focus was on the Malay family. Freedman reported that his wife, Djamour, "was commissioned to write a report on Malay family organization under the same auspices as myself" (1957, 9). The Colonial government engaged the husband and wife team and both arrived in Singapore together and conducted their respective anthropological fieldwork concurrently from 1949 to 1950. Djamour submitted her report entitled "The Family Structure of the Singapore Malays" to the Colonial Government through the Colonial Social Science Research Council. This report served as the basis for Djamour's Ph.D. dissertation submitted to the University of London and was subsequently published under the title *Malay Kinship and Marriage in Singapore* (Djamour 1959).

Just as Freedman's (1957) analysis of the Chinese family has become a classic reference in the study of the Singapore family, so it is with Djamour's (1959) book on the Malay family. However, the same limitation found in Freedman's (1957) work is also found in Djamour's (1959). As an ethnography of the Malay family, her study was primarily descriptive and did not include a conceptual analysis of the social phenomena she observed. She declared that when she went to the field "I had no specific major theory which I wanted to test" (1959, 1). Instead, she had two main objectives: on the one hand, she was interested in "the instability of Malay marriage and in the effects which [it] had on the divorced couples themselves, on their children, and on their respective kinsmen"; and on the other hand, having observed that Malays did not have effective community organizations and "no political representation as Malays," she wanted "to determine whether in contrast to the lack of corporate groupings there might not be special types of economic solidarity of an informal nature between a person and his close kinsmen" (1959, 1-2).

As in the case of Freedman's study (1957), Djamour had the advantage of the recent data from the "Social Survey" conducted in 1947 by the Singapore Social Welfare Department, and the detailed information collected by the 1947 population census (Del Tufo 1949) which helped her in her description of the "structure of the Singapore

Malay society" in the first chapter. The second chapter is a description of Malay kinship which included a section on "emotional relations" that today we may see as child socialization and parent-child relations. Chapter 3 described the Malay household composition and physical setting. The other three chapters dealt with marriage; matters pertaining to children such as childbirth, adoption and socialization; and divorce.

In her concluding chapter, Djamour turned to what, in my view, constitutes the only conceptual aspect of her book, the exploration of "social and economic solidarity" between a Malay individual and his or her kinsmen. Djamour did not define these concepts and did not review critically any pertinent social science literature. But, summarizing her observations, she reported that "there is in fact considerable solidarity (emotional as well as economic) between an individual and his close kinsmen" particularly between parents and children. The "strongest operative tie" among the Malays in this case is that "parents must be forever ready and willing to help their children in every way (even after they have married and settled in independent residences), and they expect little in return" (1959, 143-44).

Furthermore, her observations of the Malay community led Djamour to suggest, in more general terms, that "in all societies where marriage relationships are unstable, and whatever the economy, one may expect to find a high degree of emotional and economic solidarity between a woman and her close kinsmen" (1959, 142). However, it appears that her generalization would not apply to the Malay men. Predicting the future, she indicated that "if the majority of men are in stable employment…one effect…may be to lessen the need for economic solidarity among close kin" (1959, 147).

Djamour's study on the Malay family gained attention even before it was published as a book. Her Report to the Colonial Government was quoted extensively in a paper presented at an international conference organized by the International Union of Child Welfare by the Singapore Children's Society (1958). The members of the sub-committee of the Society in charge of writing that paper were not scholars. They were "Singaporeans of different communities, connected with social work in a professional or voluntary capacity"

(1958, 51). Djamour's Ph.D. thesis was also quoted as an authoritative source on Malay marriage in Singapore before the book appeared (Swift 1958).

In general, the work of Freedman (1957) and Djamour (1959) are the two most significant contributions to the study of family in Singapore before Singapore attained independence in 1965. There were other comparatively minor contributions on Chinese women by Topley (1954) and Wee (1954), and on the Chinese family by Comber (1954). Freedman pursued his topic of Chinese marriage (1962) followed by Stephen Yeh (1964) who wrote his Ph.D. dissertation also on Chinese marriage in Singapore.

The Period of Consolidation, 1965-1979

One of the main reasons for the scarce number of important social science studies on the family before 1965 was the absence of a genuinely local — as opposed to British — institutional framework to support the development of social science research in Singapore. The first — and still the only — Department of Sociology was established within the Faculty of Arts and Social Sciences of the University of Singapore in 1965, the same year that Singapore became a republic. The Department provided the first local organizational setting for systematic sociological and anthropological research conducted by resident scholars, both Singaporean and foreign. Between 1965 and 1970 there were a few mostly descriptive studies on the legal aspects of Muslim marriage (Ahmad 1965, Siraj 1965) in addition to the follow-up by Djamour (1966) on the Muslim matrimonial court; on housekeeping practices among rural Malays (Firth 1966); and intermarriage and assimilation (Edmonds 1968). But, understandably, these studies were conducted outside the framework of the Department of Sociology as the latter was still in its infancy.

The trend towards systematic family research in Singapore actually took off in the 1970s, propelled by the combination of two factors, the presence of an academic setting and the international availability of funds for family planning research. During the decades of the 1960s and 1970s, there was a world-wide inclination among social scientists towards research on population growth.

International foundations were ready to finance research projects on subjects such as contraceptive use, husband-wife communication concerning procreation decisions, and the value of children, among others. Inevitably, the availability of international funds also influenced social research in Singapore particularly during the 1970s. Besides the required research reports, spin-off publications were also generated by these research projects. Two examples of this type of work are Chen's (1974) paper on the social and psychological aspects of fertility, and Wong's (1977a) paper on the value of children.

In his 1974 paper, Chen provided a concise description of social research work on family planning involving Singapore as well as on the policies designed and implemented in Singapore to control population growth. Of the three "large-scale sample surveys" mentioned by Chen, two were sponsored by international bodies: The "Husband-Wife Communication Survey" conducted by Chen in Singapore was sponsored by ECAFE and the United Nations and involved three other countries, India, Iran and the Philippines. The other project was a national survey on "Birth Order and Family Size" conducted by D. Y. Yuan and Peter Chen and funded by the National Institute of Child Health and Human Development in the United States.

These two studies were conducted under the purview of the Department of Sociology. But the third major project was a survey on the knowledge, attitudes and practice of family planning in Singapore involving two government bodies, the Singapore Family Planning and Population Board and the National Statistical Commission. The authors participated as consultants. The findings from these and other family planning studies in Singapore followed trends found in other countries. Chen wrote that the practices, attitudes and values on family planning varied with people's socioeconomic, ethnic and religious background. Chen concluded that the family planning programme was "very successful in Singapore", but that there was a need to do more research on the "socio-psychological aspects of fertility behaviour" (Chen 1974, 23-24).

Such a research gap was already narrowing by then. Indeed, the pace of social research on family planning was so rapid that three years later, writing on the value of children, Aline Wong found that "there has been more social psychological research on fertility behaviour" in South and Southeast Asia "than in any other region of the developing world" (Wong 1977a, 4). After describing the main factors preceding the international interest in 'Value of Children' (VOC) studies, Wong summarized the principal findings from VOC studies in Third World countries including Singapore. She suggested that the preference for sons over daughters was found "to be linked to the cultural emphasis on continuity of the family name" as well as to "the economic benefits" of having sons in Asia (1977a, 8-9). The conceptual aspects discussed in Wong's paper followed the conceptual framework of the VOC studies as explained by Arnold, Bulatao and others (1975). Basically, they proposed that a set of socio-demographic factors together with five "psychological and social orientations", influence the parents' perception of the value of children which, in turn, affect their decisions on fertility and family planning (Arnold Bulatao et al. 1975, 1-14). Today, the findings from these VOC studies have been confirmed. Furthermore, international interest in research on family planning and on the perceived value of children provided social scientists in the Asian countries involved with the financial support and opportunity to test various methodological approaches to the analysis of family behaviour and to explore, albeit tentatively, interesting conceptual perspectives applicable to other aspects of social behaviour.

While research on family planning was popular in the 1970s, other significant aspects of family behaviour and attitudes were not overlooked by sociologists and anthropologists in Singapore. The themes of seven of the 67 working papers written from 1972 to 1979 by scholars at the Department of Sociology covered interethnic marriage (Hassan and Benjamin 1972, Kuo and Hassan 1974); the family and change, both economic (Kuo 1974a) and ideological (Wong 1974b); the role of women (Wong 1974a) and divorce (Kuo 1974b). There were also some journal articles and books produced during the 1970s on the family as an institution in a changing society (Kuo 1975, Kuo and Wong 1979); the main aspects of parenthood (Chen, Kuo and Chung 1979, Chung, Chen, Kuo and PuruShotam 1979), social policies affecting the family (Chen and Fawcett 1979); and problems faced by women (Wong 1975, 1977b).

In contrast to the preponderance of anthropological studies before 1965, and of the collaborative work between the few anthropologists and sociologists at the Department of Sociology during its early years (from 1965 to 1975), the evident trend since 1975 has been towards more sociological research. Some of the works mentioned above require further comments as they are good illustrations of the kind of sociological research on the family prevalent in the 1970s.

The first paper in the Sociology Working Paper Series published by the Department of Sociology of the former University of Singapore — the predecessor of the National University of Singapore — appeared in 1972, and dealt with inter-ethnic marriage in Singapore (Hassan and Benjamin 1972). As a follow-up of a previous study by Hassan, the authors discussed official statistics on intermarriage patterns in Singapore for various years between 1962 and 1969. They found that the rate of interethnic marriage in Singapore fell "somewhere into the middle of the range of world-wide figures" (1972, 5). The authors reported that more Chinese women married out compared to Chinese men and that Muslims "show such a degree of convergence as to suggest that non-ethnic factors outweigh the ethnic factors" (1972, 17). A positive feature of this paper is the authors' effort to qualify their findings indicating that they were not making "advanced claims", as their study was "only a tentative beginning" (1972, 17). Their caution in presenting and interpreting their findings is understandable: theirs was an exploratory study. A negative feature of the paper is that the authors did not consider religion as an important aspect of "outmarriages". Hassan and Benjamin focused on ethnicity but included Hindus and Muslims — two religious categories — in their analysis while omitting a discussion of other religious groups. Nevertheless, their finding on the inclination among Muslims to marry across ethnic boundaries was significant. Based on further research and more detailed data, we know today that religion plays a significant role in the decision to marry someone outside one's ethnic group and available figures show that Muslims and Christians are more likely than people of other religious persuasions to have ethnically mixed but religiously homogeneous marriages.

Pursuing further the interest in the cultural aspects of marriage, Eddie Kuo and Riaz Hassan (1974) analysed again the same official statistics on marriages used earlier by Hassan and Benjamin (1972), that is, marriage figures from December 1966 to January 1969. Kuo and Hassan confirmed the finding that Christianity and Islam acted as a "double melting pot" facilitating interethnic marriages (1974, 7) and that more inter-ethnic marriages were found among divorced people who remarried (1974, 13). In their conclusion, the authors discussed the possibility of applying two concepts, "rebelliousness" and "autonomy" to explain inter-ethnic marriage decisions among young and old people, respectively. But they found that the Singapore data did not substantiate their assumptions. They rightly pointed out three problems in their study: their findings were tentative because they were looking at secondary data; they did not have data on attitudes towards marriage; and the application of the two concepts of rebelliousness and autonomy was "thus at best conjectures" (1974, 14).

The year 1974 was particularly fruitful in terms of the number of sociological papers on the family. The study by Kuo and Hassan (1974) focused on the empirical testing of two concepts rather than any grand or even middle-range theory. But in his discussion of "Industrialization and Family Type" Eddie Kuo (1974a) dealt with the link between the family and socioeconomic change from a larger conceptual perspective. He took industrialization as an independent variable commonly used to explain the emergence of the nuclear family. Kuo reviewed the relevant literature, focusing on the concept of "isolation" of the nuclear family and on the notion that while the isolated nuclear family was the most suitable family structure in industrialized societies, the traditional extended family fitted best non-industrialized societies. Kuo also looked into the most important views of the day on the possible causal link between industrialization and family structure. He concluded that economic changes such as those manifested in industrialisation are not the only social forces shaping the family structure. Appropriately, Kuo emphasized that one must look at the situation as "a network of interrelationships" and that the assumed relationship between family structure and industrialization "is only analytical and probably too naive to result into any definite conclusion" (1974a,

33). I must add that his presentation of the nuclear family as an ideal type in industrialized societies was incomplete. This thesis has been controversial since Parsons introduced it nearly five decades ago despite its popularity in the 1950s and 1960s (Sussman 1959, Sussman and Burchinal 1962, Lenero-Otero 1977, Hareven 1987, Lee 1987).

The theme on the link between social change and the family was also pursued by Aline Wong (1974b). Although her paper was not on the Singapore family, it provided information relevant to our understanding of family matters among the local Chinese population. Wong addressed the possible effects that the ideological and political changes in the People's Republic of China had over the family. She described and analyzed the most important aspects of these changes such as the Marriage Law of 1950, the creation of the communes and the Cultural Revolution, upon family life including the concept of love, dating, marriage, family size and family structure. Considering the complexity and scope of political and socioeconomic changes that the PRC was experiencing, Wong's discussion of their effects on the family was a helpful contribution. Particularly useful was her presentation of a systematic list of contrasting features of the "traditional Chinese family" on one hand, and the "modern Chinese family" on the other hand (1974b, 29-31).

In another paper she contributed earlier the same year, Wong (1974a) focused her attention on "Women as a minority group in Singapore". She accurately referred in the introduction to the dearth of research on the status of Singaporean women and proceeded to present a brief but sensible analysis of some important aspects in women's lives such as legislation contained in the Women's Charter, the Muslim Ordinance and the Administration of Muslim Law Act, employment, education, career and the "dilemma of home versus career". An important feature of this paper is the reference to official statistics on labour force participation, employment, marriages, divorces, weekly earnings, school and university enrolment and other pertinent data on the status of women. Wong indicated that a large majority of women were housewives and that working women were "facing many conflicting demands and expectations from society" as they were "not fully accepted" in the "working world" of men and had the added problem of not being "fully accepted by other women either", all adding to the prospect of a "long road to equality" (1974a, 25-26). While significant improvements have been made since Wong wrote this paper, the basic problems faced by working women are still there and are now affecting more people as the number of working women and dual career couples has increased. Wong continued this theme on problems faced by women in Singapore in a book she edited (1975) on women and modernization and a paper on women's needs and socioeconomic development (1977b).

The last Sociology Working Paper on the family released in 1974 was Kuo's "Field Theory as a Conceptual Framework for Divorce Study" (1974b). This paper was a useful review of the literature on the application of field theory as a conceptual framework to explain marital dissolution. After describing the main concepts and premises of field theory, Kuo discussed its application to family conflict and, in particular, to marital conflict and to the main aspects leading to the decision to divorce. Based on Levinger's (1965) concepts of "attractions" and "barriers" to divorce, Kuo illustrated the interplay of "restraining forces against divorce" and "driving forces towards divorce" in a diagram on outcomes where four types of situations are possible, only one of which is the decision to divorce. Kuo proposed that the decision to divorce was "a function of" four sets of factors namely, cultural, social, family and personal factors. The bulk of his paper is dedicated to the discussion of concepts, but Kuo referred to the problems in methodology as he acknowledged the difficulties in ascertaining empirically the concepts involved in the field theory.

Notwithstanding the relevance and informative value of the studies discussed so far, the most substantial work on family sociology in the decade of the 1970s was the book edited by Eddie Kuo and Aline Wong on *"The Contemporary Family in Singapore"* (1979). The sociological themes covered in preceding studies were interesting but there was a need for a unifying effort to integrate the earlier piecemeal research for the benefit of researchers and students. Kuo and Wong recognized this need (1979, 13) and their book represented such an integrating effort. They put together twelve individually authored chapters dealing with three major areas of interest in family sociology namely, family relations and social change, marriage patterns in transition, and family policy. Four of these papers — Chapters 2, 3, 4, and 8 — compare Singapore data with data from other countries at the level of working hypotheses and, in some cases, middle-range theories.

Chapter 2 on "The urban kinship network in Singapore" was written especially for this book by Wong and Kuo. Their figures on urban kinship networks cast some doubt on the popular notion that most Singaporean families in the 1970s were isolated nuclear families. Chapter 3 on "Women's status and changing family values" is a reprint of a previous article by Wong published in 1976 in *Journal of Economic Development and Social Change in Asia and the Pacific*. Chapter 4 on "Daughters and Working Mothers" by Chee-Yin Boey is based on her original study of a small group of Chinese schoolgirls. Following the work of Hoffman (1960, 1963, 1974), Douvan's (1963) and Banducci's (1967) — among others — on the effect of mother's employment, Boey tested a few hypotheses on the possible impact of mothers' working status on their daughters' self-esteem and on their daughters' perception of female roles. Boey concluded that her data supported "the contention that...maternal employment helps liberalize the daughter from the traditional female role definition" and that daughters of working mothers showed "higher achievement motivation and academic performance than do those of non-working mothers" (1979, 85). Chapter 8 on "Ethnic inter-marriage in a multi-ethnic society" is a revised version of Kuo and Hassan's (1974) *Sociology Working Paper* No 32 discussed earlier.

Five other chapters were entirely dedicated to describe the local situation and did not attempt comparisons with sociological studies conducted elsewhere. These were: Chapter 5 on "Social Change and the Malay Family" by Tham Seong Chee; Chapter 6 on "Nuptiality patterns among women of childbearing age" by C.T. Chang; Chapter 9 on "Caste and marriage among the Singapore Indians" by A. Mani; Chapter 11 on "Marriage counselling as part of social welfare" by J. Ang; and Chapter 12 on "The family and the law in Singapore" by K. Wee. The latter two authors, Ang and Wee were the only non-sociologists contributing chapters to this book. Ang is a social worker and Wee is a lawyer.

One aspect of Kuo and Wong's (1979) book that deserves attention is the exploratory nature of five of the chapters. The data collected for Chapters 2 to 5 and Chapter 9 came from small non-representative samples of some subpopulations in Singapore. More specifically, Chapter 2 on urban kinship networks deals with 88 "working-class" and 80 "middle-class" married couples, mostly Chinese (1979, 19). Chapter 3 on women's status is based on data from 900 Chinese mothers (1979, 41). Chapter 4 on daughters of working mothers involved 152 female students in their third year of Secondary school (1979, 65). Chapter 5 on the Malay family was based on Tham's Ph.D. thesis and dealt with 60 Malay families and 45 Malay university undergraduate students interviewed by the author (1979, 88, 95, 102). And in Chapter 9 on Indian marriage, Mani reported that he obtained his data from "a purposive sample" of 200 "Indian Tamil Hindus" comprising 50 members from each of four castes, namely, Vellalars, Chettiars, Kammalans, and Adi-Dravidas (1979, 193). Because these five chapters were based on non-representative samples, their findings must be used with caution. In contrast, three other chapters are more likely to provide an accurate picture of the situation in the 1970s: they had a wider empirical base as they covered official population records. These chapters are: Chapter 6 on nuptiality patterns; Chapter 7 on divorce; and Chapter 8 on ethnic intermarriage.

In general, in addition to being an interesting reader for sociology students, Kuo and Wong's (1979) book also fulfilled a less tangible but important function. It represented the point of transition between two phases in the development of family sociology in Singapore namely, the period of consolidation from the mid-1960s to the late 1970s, and the subsequent trend towards systematic and comparative research that characterised the 1980s and continues into the 1990s.

In sum, this period of consolidation of family research was characterised by the influence of two factors: the availability of substantial research grants from international foundations and agencies for studies on population growth control and the Singapore government's interest in promoting family planning. These two factors shared the same focus: the impact of social policy on matters related to procreation. The family became the centre of researchers' attention. As most of the studies supported by international foundations and agencies were comparative (cross-national), researchers in Singapore had the opportunity to address their work to that of their counterparts in other countries not only in terms of empirical data but also in terms of conceptual analysis. As this type of studies emphasized the testing of middle-range theories rather than "grand" theorizing, it is not surprising that this was precisely the main feature of the period of consolidation of family research in Singapore.

Current Trends, 1980-1999

Compared to sociological work conducted before 1980, the past twelve years has seen an overall improvement in the quality of research on the family by resident sociologists. Indeed, three main positive trends may be discerned from the published family studies by resident sociologists during this period: (1) they show a keener awareness of the significance of valid and reliable empirical evidence; (2) they are more inclined towards the application of exhaustive data analysis techniques; and (3) they are more mindful of the importance of comparative research whether internally (among different communities in the country), regionally, or globally.

In contrast to these three improvement trends, a fourth feature of local sociological research on the family points to continuity rather than change: (4) Just as in the pioneer and consolidation phases of the local development of sociology of the family, the local sociological work after 1980 has been characterized by the testing of concepts and theoretical propositions advanced by other sociologists, mostly American and European. There have been no contributions from Singapore to the international body of sociological theory during the current period. This potentially unfavourable feature must be seen in the proper context. Empirical work ascertaining concepts and conceptual propositions is not only a legitimate but also a rather necessary area of endeavour in all sciences, social or otherwise. This is particularly true when the testing of conceptual propositions formulated in Western countries takes place in highly diverse social, cultural, economic and political settings such as those found in Singapore. Moreover, as I indicated earlier, sociology has been practiced in Singapore for a relatively brief period of time compared to its long history in Europe and North America. In 1905 when Max Weber produced *The Protestant Ethic and the Spirit of Capitalism* in

Europe, the first institution for tertiary education, the Medical School, was set up by the British Colonial government. Sociology was to be absent from Singapore's university education for another sixty years. The young resident sociologists — none of them are over 55 years old — have been busy with descriptive work and empirical testing of available conceptual frameworks. The young age of resident scholars and the brief history of local sociological research, are not insurmountable obstacles preventing theoretical contributions, but these are parts of the social setting that help us understand the accomplishments as well as the limitations of local sociological work.

The social setting is also very important in understanding the three positive trends outlined earlier on empirical testing, data analysis and comparative research. These improvements have been sustained by a parallel growth in research facilities and research funds in Singapore. The main institutional setting for family sociology research continues to be the Department of Sociology at the National University of Singapore (NUS). The research facilities at NUS have improved by leaps and bounds since 1980 when the university moved to the new Kent Ridge campus. Today, the research facilities at NUS may be the best in East Asia with the exception of Japan.[1] In addition to these facilities, there is also increasing financial support. While in the 1960s and 1970s resident scholars depended primarily on research funds provided by international foundations, today NUS offers research grants and actively encourages faculty members to submit research proposals. Furthermore, while the Department of Sociology at NUS is the only institutional setting for academic research and teaching in sociology, NUS is not the only institution interested in family research. Three government bodies, the Ministry of Community Development, the Ministry of Health, and the Housing and Development Board — Singapore's public housing authority — conduct periodic studies on various aspects of family life such as child care arrangements, care of the aged, family values, attitudes towards marriage, and fertility behaviour and attitudes. It is common for sociologists at NUS to be invited as consultants for the planning and implementation of these projects or, alternatively, to be asked to conduct a more detailed analysis of data collected by the research personnel at one of these government bodies.

Having identified the main research trends and some relevant features of the social setting after 1980, I want to turn now to specific sociological work accomplished during this current period. Two of the themes popular in the 1970s continued to capture the attention of some sociologists in the 1980s. These themes were fertility and the status of women. But, in contrast to the previous decade, these themes have not dominated research efforts in the 1980s and 1990s. Other important aspects of family sociology have also received consideration, for example, family policy, gender roles socialization, marriage, parenthood, divorce, family life and family values. While a comprehensive review of all material is not practical in this chapter, a discussion of the published work produced since 1980 will suffice to illustrate the trends I have identified (unpublished work will be excluded).

Fertility and population growth

As explained earlier, research on family planning, financed by international foundations and geared towards regional or global comparisons, was primarily a phenomenon of the 1970s in Singapore. One of these cross-national projects, the "Ethnicity and Fertility in Southeast Asia" project initiated in 1977, continued to occupy the efforts of some sociologists during the first half of the 1980s. This project involved five countries, Indonesia, Malaysia, Philippines, Singapore and Thailand, and it was conducted in two phases. The first phase on "Culture and Fertility" took place from 1977 to 1979 (Chang, Ong and Chen 1980). The second phase began in 1980 and was intended to investigate further the findings from Phase I that showed that ethnicity was a significant factor in fertility behaviour "among the various ethnic groups in Southeast Asia" (Kuo and Chiew 1984, xiii). An interesting aspect of this project was the cooperation between two Singaporean institutions: NUS and the Institute of Southeast Asian Studies (ISEAS). All the sociologists involved, except one, were from NUS but the research grant from the International Development Research Centre was administered by ISEAS, which also served as the publisher of the various reports including the Singapore report by Kuo and Chiew (1984), and the overall report on comparative analysis in Southeast Asia by Wong and Ng (1985).

From the perspective of this discussion on family sociology, the relevance of the Ethnicity and Fertility project lies in the second of its two objectives, namely the analysis of "fertility preferences", that is, people's perception of "the ideal family size and desired number of children." The other objective of the project was to investigate the "fertility outcome" or the number of children born (Wong and Ng 1985, 3). The conceptual contributions of the project were modest. Instead of a comprehensive review of the theoretical literature, the researchers described the network of interrelated hypotheses they tested to explain fertility preferences and fertility outcomes (Kuo and Chiew 1984, 2-6, Wong and Ng 1985, 1-11).

Their "theoretical model" was based on a few major conceptual propositions in the international sociological literature. These conceptual propositions were: (1) that ethnic differences disappear gradually "as ethnic groups become assimilated into the majority culture"; (2) that ethnic groups vary in their social class position in society; (3) that differences in cultural values and practices affect fertility; and (4) that individuals differ in their "attitudes and preferences with regard to childbearing" (Wong and Ng 1985, 2-3). Operating at the level of working hypotheses, it was not surprising that the conclusions were empirical generalizations rather than conceptual formulations geared towards the improvement of theories. It was found that ethnicity is not a major determinant of fertility, but that social class factors such as education, occupation and income are more important (Kuo and Chiew 1984, 174-177, Wong and Ng 1985, 367-369). The overall finding that people's preference for a large number of children diminish in inverse proportion to their socioeconomic status, is a finding that fits well the outcome of fertility studies in Western countries.

The Ethnicity and Fertility comparative project was based on representative samples of the population in each of the five countries involved. The research teams from each country used a standard codebook in preparing their respective raw data tapes. The tapes were then sent to Singapore where all the five countries' data were analyzed using the computing facilities at the National University of Singapore and some of the statistical techniques of the SPSS, including multiple classification analysis (Wong and Ng 1985, 31, Kuo and Chiew 1984, 30-31). Similar work on the theme of ethnicity and fertility was published by Hassan (1980) and Arnold and Kuo (1984). A related theme on the aspect of family planning efforts in Singapore, is found in the papers by Wong and Salaff (1983) and Wong and Cheung (1987) who continued the discussion of incentives and disincentives in population policies, popular in the 1970s.

The status of women and gender roles

The other research topic that originated in the 1970s and continues in the 1980s and 1990s is the status of women in Singapore, and it has been primarily the work of one female sociologist, Aline Wong. Wong's approach to this issue has not been conceptual. Her work is primarily a description of women's economic status and a discussion of practical perspectives to help working women in their capacity as wives and mothers (Wong 1981, Wong 1983, Wong and Ko 1984, Salaff and Wong 1984, Wong, Tan, Chew and Lai 1985, Salaff 1988, Wong and Leong 1993).

The analysis of women in Singapore has also been studied from a rather different sociological approach, that is, from the perspective of gender roles and sex-role socialization. By focusing on the analysis of gender roles and sex-role socialization, women's issues are approached not as a political and ideological theme but, rather, as an integral part of family sociology. The first study following this approach dealt with the impact of the school and school textbooks upon the children's learning of sex-role stereotypes (Quah 1980). That paper reviewed the relevant literature on the impact of the school on the learning of sex-role stereotypes. The main concepts discussed and explored in this study were: the concept of sex-roles as defined by Chetwynd and Hartnett (1978) and Guttentag and Bray (1976); the concepts of "two-role ideology" and "shared-role ideology" introduced by Bernard (1972); and key concepts from role theory including anticipatory socialization (Cottrell 1942, Burr 1973), role conflict, and role strain (Burr 1973, Goode 1960).

Two types of empirical data were collected in that study (Quah 1980). One type was first hand data obtained from the content analysis of school textbooks used in the five grades of elementary school in Singapore during the three years prior to the research. The other type of data consisted of official statistics on labour force participation in Singapore including rates of participation, wage differentials between male and female workers, and a comparison with industrialized countries. My findings (Quah 1980) supported two propositions. First, school textbooks legitimized the traditional sex-role stereotypes of men as economic providers and women as housewives and mothers — the "one role ideology" — thus carrying traditional sex-role stereotypes into adult life as part of anticipatory socialization. Second, the real-life economic pressures in Singapore required and opened opportunities for women to alternative roles in the labour force and, yet, society did not provide women with the necessary means for a congruent working life (Quah 1980, 227). Basically, the situation conveyed by the "two-role ideology" prevailed. The inclination towards traditional sex-roles was also documented in a descriptive study of adolescents' values on family and courtship (Saw and Wong 1981).

I addressed the analysis of gender roles in a later study on the link between family roles and health behaviour (Quah 1990a). I brought together in this analysis relevant conceptual formulations from sociology of the family and medical sociology in the form of three hypotheses found in the sociological literature: the "sex-role" hypothesis, the "role set" hypothesis, and the "stress" hypothesis (see for example Mechanic 1964, Suchman 1972, Nathason 1975, Marcus and Siegel 1982, Cleary, Mechanic and Greenly 1982, Gore and Mangione 1983, Westbrook and Viney 1983, Kessler and McLeod 1984, Verbrugge 1985). The "sex-role" hypothesis states that, in contrast to men, women are culturally expected to be dependent and fragile and it is thus more socially accepted for women to fall ill. The "role-set" hypothesis assumes that people with important role obligations are less likely to acknowledge illness and to use health services and that women — as housewives — are perceived as having less role obligations than men. The "stress" hypothesis proposes that women's roles in society are objectively more stressful than men's roles and that such stress is manifested in higher rates of actual ill-health among women (Quah 1990a, 51-55).

The Singapore data discussed in that paper substantiate the assumption that socially defined gender roles have a pervasive influence upon the preventive health behaviour of men and women. Such influence is manifested not only through diverse role responsibilities within the family and stress levels of those roles, but also through the attitudes instilled in the role players. Singapore women, as women in other countries, are socialized into nurturant roles, where health is a key aspect of the caring for their families (Quah 1990a, 66-67).

The latest study on gender roles (Chapter 5 in Quah 1998) is a follow-up analysis updating the examination of contradictory role demands women face in Singapore first discussed 12 years ago (Quah 1980). The study focuses on what may well be a uniquely "Singaporean" combination of three contradictory signals women face and on the way in which women try to make sense of them and organize their lives around them. These three contradictory signals are the traditional values regarding the role of women including Confucianism; the exigencies of Singapore's industrial economy that encourage and reward female participation in the labour force; and the modern values of gender equality to which an ever increasing number of young Singapore women are exposed through higher education. The first part of the study reviews pertinent work in the sociological literature on the concepts of sex-role ideologies and gender equality and compares the situation in Singapore to that in Europe, North America and Japan. The second part of the study illustrates with empirical evidence the two main approaches that Singapore women use to reconcile these contradictory signals. One approach is to compartmentalize roles in order to minimize role strain and role conflict when one's role obligations are incompatible. This is an application to Singapore of the concepts from role theory and symbolic interaction discussed by Wesley Burr and others (Burr 1973, Burr, Leigh, Day, and Constantine 1979, 82-84). The other approach used by Singapore women to reconcile contradictory social demands is the separation of attitudes from behaviour, that is, trying to think liberal but to act conservative (Quah 1998,167).

Themes on family structure and family values

Four aspects of family structure and family values have been discussed by resident sociologists since 1980, namely, ideology, divorce, marriage and parenthood. Wong (1983) and Kuo (1987) presented their own interpretation of possible changes in family ideology due to socio-economic development in Singapore. Wong (1983) suggested a tendency towards modernization in family values. Kuo (1987) believed that the values of "individualism, utilitarianism and achievement orientation" prevalent in modern Singapore "debunked" the Confucian tradition of preference for a large family and for sons, and the traditional perception of children as one's security in old age. The values and the process of spouse selection in the Singaporean Indian community were analysed by Siddique and PuruShotam (1993).

The first — and so far the only — detailed study of divorce in Singapore was completed by Wong and Kuo (1983). As in the case of other unpublished studies or restricted circulation reports[2] the divorce study was commissioned in 1979 by the Singapore Ministry of Social Affairs to the Applied Research Corporation which, in turn, approached Wong and Kuo as consultants. The original detailed report of the study submitted by the consultants was released first by the Applied Research Corporation. The published version (Wong and Kuo 1983) includes a brief review of sociological studies on divorce particularly Goode's (1976) views on the link between the process of industrialization, the conjugal family, and the changes in divorce rates. The authors stated that the objective of their study was "not so much to test the theories developed in other societies" but to "attempt to convey a sociological understanding of divorce in the local context of Singapore" (Wong and Kuo 1983, 5-6). The study excludes Muslim Singaporeans. The data were collected using two methods: "a documentary analysis of non-Muslim divorce files kept with the High Court"; and "a survey of divorcees, based on personal interviews". The sample of 389 individuals for the survey was drawn from "the total number of divorces granted in 1974/75 and 1978/79" as listed in the files at the High Court (Wong and Kuo 1983, 9).

The study covered the divorce patterns, including grounds for divorce; social factors such as age at marriage, number and age of children and occupational status; family background; marital problems; the divorce situation; problems brought about by divorce and post-divorce adjustment. The authors concluded that the rise in divorce rates among non-Muslims in Singapore was "consistent with the trend observed in most developed societies" (1983, 101-102). However, they asserted that "the major forces constraining the divorce rate here [in Singapore]...are the social and moral sanctions and the deeply-ingrained cultural values attached to a stable marriage and family life" (1983, 104).

The other aspects of family structure that have been the subject of three studies in Singapore during the past five years are marriage and parenthood. One of these, a study on the decision to postpone the birth of the first child (Quah 1988), discussed three theories offered in the international literature. These theories are the "biological drive theory", the "normative theory", and the "choice and exchange theory" (Newton 1973, Chodorow 1978, Nye 1979, Reading and Amatea 1986). The study probed the premises of the choice and exchange theory, arguing that there are four main motivating factors in the choice made by a wife to postpone the birth of the first child, namely, her subjective perception of the main purpose of marriage; her perception of her husband's agreement with her basic values and views; her perception of her own fertility; and her perception of the possible health risks of late pregnancies (Quah 1988, 7-15). The data used to probe these assumptions came from a survey — structured personal interviews — of a specific target population of Singapore married women who had postponed the birth of their first child for more than two years. Using factor analysis, the study found that the demographic variables age at marriage and number of years married are the best predictors of age at first birth, as found in most other countries. Nevertheless, the proposed set of four attitudinal factors derived from the choice and exchange theory were also significantly associated with the decision to delay motherhood (Quah 1988, 39-41).

The issue of marriage and parenthood as personal goals was studied in more detail two years later (Quah 1990c). Two of the objectives of that paper were: to present a comprehensive review of empirical evidence from Singapore on the assumption that marriage and parenthood are among the top personal goals of Singaporeans; and to link the findings to those from similar family studies in other countries. Data collected from various sources in different studies during the 1970s and 1980s clearly indicated that Singaporeans have a positive attitude towards marriage and parenthood. As it is reported in other countries, "modernity has not meant a rejection of marriage", and "parenthood is a highly valued goal in the private lives of Singaporeans" (Quah 1990c, 264, 271).

Another study on family structure (Chapter 2 in Quah 1998) deals with the process of family formation in Singapore. That study is primarily based on an analysis of census data from 1947 to 1990 but it also includes data from other sources. Three main aspects are discussed: marriage, parenthood, and some features of family life. On the aspect of marriage, the study deals with changes in marriage patterns, marriage postponement, marriage and work outside the home, and marriage dissolution, in terms of salient factors such as age, education, occupation, ethnicity and religion. Parenthood is analysed from two perspectives: its timing and its socioeconomic and cultural variations. The trends in family life include changes in household structure — household size and residential patterns — and the distribution of roles among family members concerning childcare, housekeeping and wage earning. As this study has the principal objective of documenting family formation trends over a period of five decades, and it is addressed not only to researchers but also to policy-makers and to the general public, it is basically descriptive and there is no discussion of sociological concepts or theories.

This analysis of census data from 1947 to 1990 (Chapter 2 in Quah 1998) identifies eight main trends in family formation. First, modernization "has not eroded the value of marriage". Second, the proportion of single people over the age of 35 is increasing. Third, there is an increasing rate of female participation in the labour force. Fourth, there is also an increasing proportion of married women who prefer to combine both home and job obligations, and "a corresponding decline in the proportion of women who prefer to be full-time homemakers". Fifth, the rate of divorce is still lower than in industrialized countries but it is, nevertheless, increasing. Sixth, parenthood is "as important today as it has been in the past", and the ideal number of children is two. Seventh, "the most preferred living arrangement is a two generation family in its own dwelling" but the larger family network involving older and younger generations remains important. Finally, there is a trend towards involvement and cooperation of grandparents, particularly in childcare (Quah 1998, 69-72).

Three other studies deal with family structure. The potential conflict created by the pressures of career, family and motherhood in Singapore is discussed by Straughan (1997) based on her findings from in-depth interviews with a purposive sample of eight working mothers. Lyons-Lee (1998) reviews the relevant literature on family formation and reports the situation of eleven educated single women in Singapore within the context of social pressures to marry and have children. Chan and Dorais (1998) examine the impact of forced migration on Vietnamese families through interviews with 21 Vietnamese refugees living in Quebec. As expected, their nuclear families lost their links to the larger kin network and the traditional system of power relations within the family.

Family policy

The other topic on family sociology that has received close attention in Singapore is family policy. Interestingly, it is not uncommon to find policy recommendations in the concluding sections of some studies on the family (see for example, Wong and Kuo 1983, Kuo and Chiew 1984, Wong and Cheung 1987), but these works did not discuss in depth the sociological perspectives on government intervention in family life. In contrast, my personal interest in exploring family policy from a sociological perspective began in the early 1980s. The first study (Quah 1981a) sought to probe the question "can the family be strengthened by legislation?" It discussed the issue from three angles. First, the paper reviewed and discussed the definitions and conceptual perspectives on family policy in the relevant literature including, among others, the work of Lasswell (1968), Kamerman and Kahn (1978), Tallman (1979), Moroney (1979), and Grotberg (1981). Second, after reviewing the experiences from other countries, the Singapore legislation was analyzed critically in terms of policies affecting the family directly and indirectly, and a five-step strategy of institutional or government intervention was identified (Quah 1981a, 36-48). The final angle of analysis discussed the problem of contradictory policy pressures on the family and pointed out the need "to plan and coordinate policies that will enable the family to strengthen its capabilities" and the fact that "family policy does not make better families but it certainly establishes the social mechanisms to ensure that the family will be able to satisfy its needs" (Quah 1981a, 50).

A decade later, a comparative study of family policy was published in Singapore (Quah 1990b) covering seven countries in four continents (North America, Europe, Asia and Australasia) including Singapore. The main sociological perspectives on family policy were critically discussed. This analysis led to the identification of (a) three main schools of thought namely, "the opponents", the "moderates" and the "advocates" of family policy; and (b) five basic issues on the "feasibility and desirability of family policy" (Quah 1990d, 16-18). The Singapore component of that comparative study (Quah 1990c) dealt with the policy aspects of marriage and parenthood. The comparative study concluded with an analysis of major trends and experiences shared by the seven countries covered in the analysis (Quah 1990e).

The problems involved in the provision of childcare services have also been analysed from the perspective of family policy (Chapter 4 in Quah 1998). The main conceptual arguments both in favour and against government intervention are reviewed and discussed, including the views of Lasch (1979), Steiner (1981), Henslin (1985), and Kamerman and Kahn (1988). Then, the case of childcare services in Singapore is presented as an illustration of moderate state intervention. This paper is a follow-up of an earlier study on welfare services for children in Singapore (Quah 1979).

Another work that requires some comments at this juncture is a book by Salaff (1988) on the "State and Family in Singapore". If one takes its title seriously, this book would be classified as a study on family policy. Salaff declared that she wanted to demonstrate "how the society of the Republic of Singapore was transformed by state-sponsored social policies" (1988, 3). Unfortunately, the book's title is misleading and the author's stated objective is not reached. Considering the material presented and discussed by Salaff, a more accurate title would be "The lives of some Chinese couples in Singapore in the late 1970s". The best parts of the book, comprising

51% of its total text, are those chapters dealing with an ethnographic account of the daily life of 100 Chinese couples she selected and interviewed in the mid-1970s — Chapters 3 and 5 — and Chapters 7 and 8 where she describes the lives of the 45 couples from the original group, whom she re-interviewed in 1981. The other six chapters must be read with caution as they contain inaccurate information on the situation of Singapore during the study's six-year period, and they ignore the significant changes that have taken place after 1981.

More specifically, despite the ethnographic value of some of its chapters, Salaff's (1988) book has two serious weaknesses: its time frame and the use of an inadequate research approach. Concerning the time frame, Salaff observed changes in the 45 couples she re-interviewed after a six-year period — from 1976 to 1981,— and then presented her findings as a current study of industrial "restructuring", oblivious to the significant changes in the socio-economic development of Singapore during the 1980s. Salaff's research approach was an in-depth analysis of selected case histories. But she was apparently unaware of the severe limitations of this approach to reach her study objective: she used a micro-level approach to do a macro-analysis of Singapore's development (for further comments on Salaff's book see Quah 1990f).

In a more recent publication focusing on the State's promotion of family formation, Straughan (1999) argues that emphasis is given to the "normal" family that is based on a heterosexual marriage with the husband as head of the family. But, agreeing with other studies, Straughan argues that Singaporeans face contradictions created by the contrast between the official effort to "glorify" marriage and parenthood and the realities of family and work obligations.

Conclusion

This chapter has provided an account of the work on family sociology in Singapore. The development of the study of the family has been traced over three periods. The first period covered the early years of Singapore from its foundation in 1819 until 1965. During most of the 19th century, the pioneer "researchers" were interested but untrained European observers. Later on, nearing the end of

British colonial rule, two British anthropologists began the scholarly type of research that characterized the later periods. The second main period of development, from 1965 to 1979, was a period of consolidation of research efforts. The beginning of this period was marked both by the independence of Singapore as well as by the establishment of the Department of Sociology at the University of Singapore. The third and current period of development may be said to have begun in 1980 when the National University of Singapore, was established from the amalgamation of two previous universities (the Chinese-medium Nanyang University, and the English-medium University of Singapore) and moved into the new Kent Ridge campus.

Some main trends have been identified in each of these three development periods. Concerning major research themes, the pioneer period was characterised by general descriptions of the family, its structure, its values and the modes of everyday family life. Researchers during the consolidation period took a rather different approach, looking into specific aspects of family behaviour in detail, primarily interethnic marriage and fertility behaviour. The current period has continued the detailed analysis of family phenomena, but the range of family aspects studied after 1980 is much wider than before.

Comparing the three development periods in terms of data sources and methods of data analysis, the trend has clearly been towards the collection of more sophisticated and accurate empirical information. The pioneers relied almost entirely on small groups of informants and on their personal observations of the local families with whom they lived during their fieldwork in Singapore. Researchers in the consolidation period were still inclined to base their studies on small and specially selected groups, but there were also some who, being part of cross-national projects, began using large-scale surveys involving personal interviews with representative samples of targeted populations. During the current period, surveys of large representative samples continue to be among the most frequently used methods to study family behaviour. Similarly, data analysis in the early 1950s consisted mainly of the attractive narration from the researcher's field notes and the tendency to make inferences on the total community from a few observed individuals. But the trend in data analysis after 1965, and particularly after 1980, has been towards the use of comprehensive statistical techniques such as factor analysis, regression analysis, path analysis and multiple classification analysis, for the purpose of identifying and understanding population trends in family behaviour, attitudes and values.

Another interesting dimension in this comparison refers to the use of theories, or conceptual assumptions to be tested empirically. The pioneer researchers were not interested in theoretical analysis preferring, instead, to dedicate their efforts to ethnographic descriptions. The preoccupation with concepts and conceptual frameworks began during the consolidation period, although it was a feature found only in some of the studies published at that time. In contrast, the inclination to probe concepts and theoretical propositions from the international body of sociological theory has been more evident during the current period of development.

The final dimension that emerges from the comparison of the three phases of development in the study of the family concerns the disciplines and the type of researchers involved. At the beginning, it was anthropology. Imported to Singapore under the British and through colonial-sponsorship, anthropology was the first social science to be applied systematically to the study of family in Singapore. This was a feature that Singapore shared with most other colonies, British or otherwise, on account of the European powers' perception of their colonies' native peoples as exotic cultures. Sociology entered the scene later, in the second period of development, and in a more scholarly manner, as a university department. In contrast to the pioneer period, the published studies on the family in Singapore conducted during the current period show the overwhelming predominance of sociology.

In the analysis of the history and development of the social sciences in Third World countries, it is very important to identify the contributions of foreign scholars versus the contributions of resident or native scholars. Very often one finds Third World countries still depending for their intellectual growth and for the study of their own cultures, on the input of foreign expertise. In Singapore, the dependency on foreign expertise was total during the colonial period. The two pioneer scholars were both British anthropologists brought into the island on contract by the British colonial government to undertake specific studies. This state of affairs changed after independence. Indeed, one of the main characteristics of the development of sociology of the family in Singapore and of the published research produced after 1965 has been the predominance of resident — as opposed to foreign — sociologists. This is true of all the family themes discussed in this chapter. Studies involving foreign researchers are the exception rather than the rule. One of these few studies is the paper on ethnicity and the value of children by Arnold and Kuo (1984). The other three are on the issue of the status of women, namely, Wong and Salaff (1983), Salaff and Wong (1984), and Salaff (1988). Incidentally, the latter is classified here as a study on the status of women because it deals with the lives of small group of married women and it is thus not a study on family policy as suggested by Salaff.

Adding to the numerous articles discussed in the preceding pages, by 1999, we have three books on the sociological analysis of the family in Singapore. In addition to Kuo and Wong's (1979) volume, my own book's first edition (Quah 1994) has been followed by the revised and expanded second edition (Quah 1998). In this second edition I pursue the analysis of sociological concepts from role theory, symbolic interaction, and conflict theory, among other perspectives, focusing on the micro-macro linkage as far as possible. Examples of these efforts are the discussion of contradictory expectations of social and perceived definitions of gender roles (1998, 144-175); grandparents as social capital (1998, 201-216), the resilience of the parent-child relationship (1998, 219-246); institutional arrangements for family conflict resolution (1998, 176-200); family and work roles (1998, 247-270); and the process of value transmission and value transformation (1998, 273-283). The most recent study on family behaviour and attitudes is a work in progress sponsored by the Ministry of Community Development with the first report of findings published in mid-1999 (Quah 1999). The study is based on personal interviews with representative samples of the main ethnic groups in Singapore. It addresses the marital relationship, parenthood, child upbringing practices, the situation of dual-career (or dual-earner) families, family stress and coping strategies, and the public's perception of family policies. It will serve as a benchmark study for a longitudinal analysis of family developments in Singapore.

What about the future? Today the prospects for Singapore look bright in terms of the political will to sustain the country's international competitiveness in the information and knowledge sectors by providing a strong financial support to research and development efforts in universities and research institutions. Once the current economic recession subsides one may expect further improvements at two levels. On the one hand, there will be an increase in the number of resident sociologists with Ph.D. degrees interested in systematic and scholarly research. On the other hand, the research facilities and research funds for sociological research will either be sustained at the current level or will continue to improve. These two likely trends may also be accompanied by increased cooperation between university research sociologists (as consultants) and government and non-government institutions (as funding agencies) in the study of family matters, including divorce, adolescent pregnancies, family violence and child socialization. Perhaps most significant is the fact that the distinguished work of resident family sociologists in the consolidation period (1969-1979) laid the foundation for serious sociological research which subsequent generations of sociologists have emulated.

While these working plans are practically written on the wall, what is more difficult to predict is whether or not resident sociologists in Singapore will contribute to theory building in future. In the history of human knowledge, outstanding theoretical contributions in any science have been few and far between. Some people suggest that it has to do, among other things, with the presence of a critical mass: in a country with a large population of scientists, the probability of having prominent producers of knowledge among them is much higher than in a country where the number of scientists is small. In Singapore, the odds are against us. The total population of the small island is just over three million, and the number of resident sociologists engaged in scholarly research in a university setting is small compared to other countries. Still, I believe that with continuous dedication to sociological investigation scholars everywhere may improve their ability to contribute to theory building. Scholarly dedication may defeat the critical mass argument. After all, there were only a handful of people engaged in sociological investigation when great scholars like Tonnies, Durkheim, or Weber emerged.

Endnotes

*   This chapter is an updated version of Chapter 1 in S. R. Quah (1998). *Family in Singapore Sociological Perspectives,* Singapore: Times Academic Press, pp. 3–33.

1.   According to the 1990 census of population, the large majority of Singaporeans (77.7%) are of Chinese descent, while 14.1% are Malays, 7.1% are Indians, and 1.1% are people from a variety of other ethnic groups (Department of Statistics 1991, 4).

2.   Indeed, 99.7% of Malays are Muslims; 68% of Chinese classify themselves as Buddhist or Taoist; and 53.2% of Indians follow Hinduism. The Indian community shows the greatest variation in religious affiliation. After Hinduism, the next largest religion is Islam: 26.3% of the Singapore Indians are Muslims; and 12.8% of the Indians are Christians (Department of Statistics 1991, 12).

3.   The total land area, including the main island and about 58 offshore islets, is only 626.4 square kilometres (Ministry of Communications and Information 1991, 1).

4.   The 1990 census indicates that 85.7% of Singapore resident households own and live in public housing high-rise apartments (Department of Statistics 1991, i).

5.   A few additional indicators of rapid economic development will complete the picture. The indigenous gross national product per capita in 1977 was $5,712; it increased steadily to $12,584 in 1983, and to $17,909 in 1989. Annual electricity consumption per person was 1,938 kwh in 1977; 3,054.7 kwh in 1983; and 4,724.6 kwh in 1989 (Ministry of Culture 1984, 46, Ministry of Communications and Information 1991, 32). According to an international study of quality of life indicators by the 1990 Population Crisis Committee comparing 100 countries, Singapore ranked 1st in housing standards (availability of utilities), 1st in noise level; 5th in food cost as percentage of income; 6th in public health (based on infant mortality); 7th in traffic flow; 20th in public safety (based on murder rate); 20th in communications (number of telephones); 40th in education (percentage of population with secondary education); and 42nd in living space (Economic Planning Committee 1991, 24).

6. Chapter 2 on "The urban kinship network in Singapore" was written especially for this book by Wong and Kuo. Their figures on urban kinship networks cast some doubt on the popular notion that most Singaporean families in the 1970s were isolated nuclear families. Chapter 3 on "Women's status and changing family values" is a reprint of a previous article by Wong published in 1976 in *Journal of Economic Development and Social Change in Asia and the Pacific*. Chapter 4 on "Daughters and Working Mothers" by Chee-Yin Boey is based on her original study of a small group of Chinese school girls. Following the work of Hoffman (1960, 1963, 1974), Douvan's (1963) and Banducci's (1967) — among others — on the effect of mother's employment, Boey tested a few hypotheses on the possible impact of mothers' working status on their daughters' self-esteem and on their daughters' perception of female roles. Boey concluded that her data supported "the contention that...maternal employment helps liberalise the daughter from the traditional female role definition" and that daughters of working mothers showed "higher achievement motivation and academic performance than do those of non-working mothers" (1979, 85). Chapter 8 on "Ethnic inter-marriage in a multiethnic society" is a revised version of Kuo and Hassan's (1974) *Sociology Working Paper* No 32 discussed earlier. Five other chapters were entirely dedicated to describe the local situation and did not attempt comparisons with sociological studies conducted elsewhere. These were: Chapter 5 on "Social change and the Malay family" by Tham Seong Chee; Chapter 6 on "Nuptiality patterns among women of childbearing age" by C.T. Chang; Chapter 9 on "Caste and marriage among the Singapore Indians" by A. Mani; Chapter 11 on "Marriage counselling as part of social welfare" by J. Ang; and Chapter 12 on "The family and the law in Singapore" by K. Wee. The latter two authors, Ang and Wee were the only non-sociologists contributing chapters to this book. Ang is a social worker and Wee is a lawyer. Kuo and Wong's (1979) book is largely exploratory, reporting data from small non-representative samples of some subpopulations in Singapore. More specifically, Chapter 2 on urban kinship networks deals with 88 "working-class" and 80 "middle-class" married couples, mostly

Chinese (1979, 19). Chapter 3 on women's status is based on data from 900 Chinese mothers (1979, 41). Chapter 4 on daughters of working mothers involved 152 female students in their third year of Secondary school (1979, 65). Chapter 5 on the Malay family was based on Tham's Ph.D. thesis and dealt with 60 Malay families and 45 Malay university undergraduate students interviewed by the author (1979, 88, 95, 102). And in Chapter 9 on Indian marriage, Mani reported that he obtained his data from "a purposive sample" of 200 "Indian Tamil Hindus" comprising 50 members from each of four castes, namely, Vellalars, Chettiars, Kammalans, and Adi-Dravidas (1979, 193). Findings based on non-representative samples must be used with caution. In contrast, three other chapters are more likely to provide an accurate picture of the situation in the 1970s: the chapters on nuptiality patterns, divorce and intermarriage had a wider empirical base as they covered official population records.

7. Every faculty member has a personal computer linked to the campus three mainframe computers which offer a rich variety of software for data analysis in addition to electronic access to local and international library databases. NUS has an IBM 3090 mainframe computer, a NEC SX-1A supercomputer, and a MD 19/600P library computer. The Optical Fibre based NUS campus network, NUSNET, links all three systems with over 3,000 staff workstations and student workstations and gives campus users access to the international networks BITNET and INTERNET. The larger of the two is INTERNET which allows researchers at the university to get access to overseas library catalogues such as the Research Libraries Information Network (RLIN), and Harvard Online Library Information System (HOLLIS), among others. INTERNET also links NUS researchers to other networks such as ACSnet (Australian Computer Science Network), EARN (European Academic Research Network), XEROX Internet, VNET (IBM's internet network), JANET (England's Joint Academic Network) and others.

8. An example of the latter type is the Report on National Survey on Married Women, Their Role in the Family and Society (Singapore Ministry of Social Affairs), released in 1984.

9. The best parts of Salaff's book, comprising 51% of its total text, are those chapters dealing with an ethnographic account of the daily life of 100 Chinese couples she selected and interviewed in the mid-1970s — Chapters 3 and 5 — and Chapters 7 and 8 where she describes the lives of the 45 couples from the original group, whom she re-interviewed in 1981. The other six chapters must be read with caution as they contain inaccurate information on the situation of Singapore during the study's six-year period, and they ignore the significant changes that have taken place after 1981. More specifically, despite the ethnographic value of some of its chapters, Salaff's (1988) book has two serious weaknesses: its time frame and the use of an inadequate research approach. Concerning the time frame, Salaff observed changes in the 45 couples she re-interviewed after a six-year period — from 1976 to 1981 — and then presented her findings as a current study of industrial "restructuring", oblivious to the significant changes in the socio-economic development of Singapore during the 1980s.

References

Ahmad bin Muhammad Ibrahim (1965) "The Status of Women in Family Law in Malaysia, Singapore and Brunei", *Malaya Law Review*, 7: 54-94.

Ang, J. (1979) "Marriage Counselling as Part of Social Welfare Service to Families", in E. Kuo and A. Wong (eds) *The Contemporary Family in Singapore*, Singapore: Singapore University Press.

Arnold, F., Bulatao, R. A., Buripakdi, C. et al. (1975) *The Value of Children. A Cross-national Study*, Honolulu: East-West Centre Population Institute.

Arnold, F. and Kuo, E. (1984) "The Value of Daughters and Sons: A Comparative Study of the Gender Preferences of Parents", *Journal of Comparative Family Studies*, 15 (2): 299-318.

Banducci, R. (1967) "The Effect of Mother's Employment on the Achievement, Aspirations, and Expectations of the Child", *Personnel and Guidance Journal*, 46: 263-67.

Bernard, J. (1972) "Changing Family Life Styles: One Role, Two Roles, Shared Roles", in L.K. Howe (ed) *The Future of the Family*, New York: Simon & Schuster.

Boey, C. Y. (1979) "Daughters and Working Mothers", in E. Kuo and A. Wong (eds) *The Contemporary Family in Singapore*, Singapore: Singapore University Press.

Braddell, R. (1921) "Chinese Marriages as Regarded by the Supreme Court of the Straits Settlements", *Journal of the Royal Asiatic Society, Malayan Branch*, No. 83.

Buckley, C. B. (1902) *An Anecdotal History of Old Times in Singapore, 1819-1867*, Singapore: Fraser & Neave.

Burr, W. R. (1973) *Theory Construction and the Sociology of the Family*, New York: John Wiley & Sons.

Burr, W. R., Leigh, G. K., Day, R.D. and Constantine, J. (1979) "Symbolic Interaction and the Family", in W.R. Burr, R. Hill, F.I. Nye, and I.L. Reiss (eds) *Contemporary Theories About the Family, Vol. 2, General Theories/Theoretical Orientations*, New York: The Free Press.

Chan, K. B. and Dorais, L.-J. (1998) "Family, Identity and the Vietnamese Diaspora: The Quebec Experience", *Sojourn*, 13(2): 285-308.

Chang, C. T. (1979) "Nuptiality Patterns among Women of Childbearing Age", in E. Kuo and A. K. Wong (eds) *The Contemporary Family in Singapore*, Singapore: Singapore University Press.

Chang, C. T., Ong, J. H., and Chen, P. S.J. (1980) *Culture and Fertility: The Case of Singapore*, Singapore: Institute of Southeast Asian Studies.

Chen, P. S. J. (1974) "Social and Psychological Aspects of Fertility: Findings from Family Planning Research in Singapore", *Sociology Working Paper 23*, Singapore, Dept. of Sociology, University of Singapore.

Chen, P. S. J. and Fawcett, J. T. (eds) (1979) *Public Policy and Population Change in Singapore*, New York: The Population Council.

Chen, P. S. J., Kuo, E. and Chung, B.J. (1979) *Dilemma of Parenthood: A Study of the Value of Children in Singapore,* Singapore: Institute of Southeast Asian Studies [Also published under the same title by Maruzen Asia in 1982].

Chetwynd, J. and Hartnett, O. (eds) (1978) *The Sex Role System,* London: Routledge & Kegan Paul.

Chew, S. B. (1982) *Fishermen in Flats,* Sydney: Monash Papers on Southeast Asia No. 9.

Chodorow, N. (1978) *The Reproduction of Mothering. Psychoanalysis and the Sociology of Gender,* Berkeley: The University of California Press.

Chung, B. J., Chen, P. S. J., Kuo, E. and PuruShotam, N. (1979) *The Dynamics of Childrearing Decisions: The Singapore Experience,* Singapore: Institute of Southeast Asian Studies [Also published under the same title by Maruzen Asia in 1981].

Cleary, P. D., Mechanic, D. and Greenly, J. R. (1982) "Sex Differences in Medical Care Utilization: An Empirical Investigation", *Journal of Health and Social Behaviour,* 23: 106-12.

Comber, L. (1954) *Chinese Ancestor Worship in Malaya,* Singapore: Donald Moore.

Cottrell, L. S. (1942) "The Adjustment of the Individual to His Age and Sex Roles", *American Sociological Review,* 7: 617-20.

Del Tufo, M. V. (1949) *A Report on the 1947 Census of Population. Malaya Comprising the Federation of Malaya and the Colony of Singapore,* London: The Crown Agents for the Colonies.

Department of Statistics (1991) *Census of Population 1990 Advanced Data Release,* Singapore: Department of Statistics.

Djamour, J. (1959) *Malay Kinship and Marriage in Singapore,* London: Athlone Press.

Djamour, J. (1966) *The Muslim Matrimonial Court in Singapore,* London: Athlone Press.

Doolittle, J. (1986) *The Social Life of the Chinese,* Vols. I and II, Singapore: Graham Brash [Reprinted from the original published in 1895 by Harper & Brothers, New York.

Douvan, E. (1963) "Employment and the Adolescent", in F.I. Nye and L.W. Hoffman (eds) *The Employed Mother in America*, Chicago: Rand McNally.

Economic Planning Committee (1991) *Towards a Developed Nation: The Strategic Economic Plan*, Singapore: Ministry of Trade & Industry.

Edgar, D. (1990) "The Social Reconstruction of Marriage and Parenthood in Australia", in S. R. Quah (ed) *The Family as an Asset. An International Perspective on Marriage, Parenthood and Social Policy*, Singapore: Times Academic Press.

Edmonds, J. (1968) "Religion, Intermarriage and Assimilation: The Chinese in Malaya", *Race*, 10 (1): 55-67.

Firth, R. (1966) *Housekeeping Among Malay Peasants*, London: Athlone Press.

Freedman, M. (1950) "Colonial Law and Chinese Society", *Journal of the Royal Anthropological Institute of Great Britain and Ireland*, 30, Parts I and II: 97-126.

Freedman, M. (1957) *The Chinese Family and Marriage in Singapore*, London: Her Majesty Stationery Office & Colonial Office, Colonial Research Studies No. 20.

Freedman, M. (1962) "Chinese Kinship and Marriage in Singapore", *Journal of Southeast Asian History*, 3 (2): 65-73.

Goode, W. J. (1960) "A Theory of Role Strain", *American Sociological Review*, 25: 488-96.

Goode, W. J. (1976) "Family Disorganization", in R.K. Merton and R. Nisbet (eds) *Contemporary Social Problems*, 4th ed., New York: Harcourt Brace Jovanovich.

Gore, S. and Mangione, T. W. (1983) "Social Roles, Sex Roles and Psycho-logical Distress: Additive and Interactive Models of Sex Differences", *Journal of Health and Social Behaviour*, 24: 300-308.

Grotberg, E. H. (1981) "The Federal Role in Family Policies", in H.C. Wallach (ed) *Approaches to Child and Family Policy*, Washington: AAAS, 9-24.

Guttentag, M. and Bray, H. (1976) *Undoing Sex Stereotypes*, New York: McGraw-Hill.

Hareven, T. K. (1987) "Historical Analysis of the Family", in M. B. Sussman and S. K. Steinmetz (eds) (1987) *Handbook of Marriage and the Family*, New York: Plenum Press.

Hassan, R. (1980) *Ethnicity, Culture and Fertility: An Exploratory Study of Fertility Behaviour and Sexual Beliefs*, Singapore: Chopmen Publisher.

Hassan, R. and Benjamin, G. (1972) "Ethnic Outmarriage Rates in Singapore: the Influence of Traditional Socio-cultural Organization", *Sociology Working Papers*, No. 1, Singapore: Dept. of Sociology, University of Singapore.

Henslin, J. M. (ed) (1985) *Marriage and Family in a Changing Society*, 2nd ed., New York: The Free Press.

Hoffman, L. W. (1960) "Effects of the Employment of Mothers on Parental Power Relations and the Division of Household Tasks", *Marriage and Family Living*, 22: 27-35.

Hoffman, L. W. (1963) "Mother's Enjoyment of Work and Effects on the Child", in F.I. Nye and L.W. Hoffman (eds) *The Employed Mother in America*, Chicago: Rand McNally.

Hoffman, L. W. (1974) "Effects on Child", in L.W. Hoffman and F.I. Nye (eds) *Working Mothers*, San Francisco: Jossey-Bass.

Husin A. S. (1981) *The Malays: Their Problems and Future*, Singapore: Heinemann Asia.

Kamerman, S. and Kahn, A. J. (1978) *Family Policy*, New York: Columbia University Press.

Kamerman, S. and Kahn, A. J. (1988) *Mothers Alone, Strategies for a Time of Change*, Dover, Mass.: Auburn House Publishing Co.

Kamerman, S. and Kahn, A. J. (1989) *Privatization and the Welfare State*, Princeton, N.J.: Princeton University Press.

Kessler, R. C. and McLeod, J. D. (1984) "Sex Differences in Vulnerability to Undesirable Life Events", *American Sociological Review*, 49(5): 620-25.

Koopman-Boyden, P. G. (1990) "The Study of Family Policy: Sociological Approaches and Perspectives", in S. R. Quah (ed) *The Family as an Asset. An International Perspective on Marriage, Parenthood and Social Policy*, Singapore: Times Academic Press.

Kuo, E. (1974a) "Industrialization and Family Type: An Overview", *Sociology Working Papers*, No. 21, Singapore: Dept. of Sociology, University of Singapore [Also published under the same title in *International Journal of Sociology of the Family* 1974, 4: 75-90].

Kuo, E. (1974b) "Field Theory as a Conceptual Framework for Divorce Study", *Sociology Working Papers*, No. 36, Singapore: Dept. of Sociology, University of Singapore [Also published under the same title in *International Journal of Sociology of the Family* 1976, 6: 239-51].

Kuo, E. (1975) *Families under Economic Stress: The Singapore Experience*, Singapore: Institute of Southeast Asian Studies Monograph.

Kuo, E. (1987) "Confucianism and the Chinese Family in Singapore: Continuities and Changes", *Sociology Working Papers*, No. 83, Singapore: Dept. of Sociology, National University of Singapore.

Kuo, E. and Chiew, S. K. (1984) *Ethnicity and Fertility in Singapore*, Singapore: Institute of Southeast Asian Studies.

Kuo, E. and Hassan, R. (1974) "Some Social Concomitants of Interethnic Marriage in Singapore", *Sociology Working Papers*, No. 32, Singapore: Dept. of Sociology, University of Singapore [Also published under the same title in *Journal of Marriage and the Family*, 1976, 38: 549-59].

Kuo, E. and Hassan, R. (1979) "Ethnic Intermarriage in a Multi-ethnic Society", in E. Kuo and A. K. Wong (eds) *The Contemporary Family in Singapore*, Singapore: Singapore University Press.

Kuo, E. and Wong, A. (eds) (1979) *The Contemporary Family in Singapore*, Singapore: Singapore University Press.

Lasch, C. (1979) *Heaven in a Heartless World: The Family Besieged*, New York: Basic Books.

Lasswell, H. (1968) "The Policy Orientation", in D. Lerner and H. Lasswell (eds) *Policy Sciences*, Stanford: Stanford University Press.

Lee, G. R. (1987) "Comparative Perspectives", in M. B. Sussman and S. K. Steinmetz (eds) (1987) *Handbook of Marriage and the Family*, New York: Plenum Press.

Lenero-Otero, L. (ed) (1977) *Beyond the Nuclear Family Model. Cross-Cultural Perspectives*, London: SAGE.

Levinger, G. (1965) "Marital Cohesiveness and Dissolution: An Integrative Review", *Journal of Marriage and the Family*, 27: 19-28.

Levy, M. J. (1949) *The Family Revolution in Modern China*, Cambridge, MA: Harvard University Press.

Levy, M. J. (1965) "Aspects of the Analysis of Family Structure", in A.J. Coale et al. (eds) *Analysis of Family Structure*, Princeton: Princeton University Press.

Lyons-Lee, L. (1998) "The 'Graduate Women' Phenomenon: Changing Constructions of the Family in Singapore", *Sojourn*, 13 (2): 309-27.

Majlis Pusat (1990) *Some Aspects of Malay Customs and Practices*, Singapore: Ministry of Community Development.

Mani, A. (1979) "Caste and Marriage among the Singapore Indians", in E. Kuo and A. Wong, (eds) *The Contemporary Family in Singapore*, Singapore: Singapore University Press.

Marcus, A. C. and Siegel, J. M. (1982) "Sex Differences in the Use of Physician Services: A Preliminary Test of the Fixed Role Hypothesis", *Journal of Health and Social Behaviour*, 23: 186-190.

Mechanic, D. (1964) "The Influence of Mothers on their Children's Health Attitudes and Behaviour", *Pediatrics*, 33: 444-50.

Ministry of Communication and Information (1991) *Singapore Facts and Pictures 1990*, Singapore: Ministry of Communication and Information; Ministry of Culture (1984) *Singapore Facts and Pictures 1983*, Singapore: Information Division, Ministry of Culture.

Moen, P. (1989) *Working Parents. Transformations in Gender Roles and Public Policies in Sweden*, Madison: University of Wisconsin Press.

Moroney, R. M. (1979) "The Issue of Family Policy: Do We Know Enough to Take Action?" *Journal of Marriage and the Family*, 41 (2): 461-64.

Nathanson, C. A. (1975) "Illness and the Feminine Role: A Theoretical Review", *Social Science and Medicine*, 9 (2): 57-62.

Newton, N. (1973) "Interrelationships Between Sexual Responsiveness, Birth and Breast Feeding", in J. Zubin and J. Money (eds) *Contemporary Sexual Behaviour: Critical Issues in the 1970s*, Baltimore: Johns Hopkins University Press, 94-105.

Nye, F. I. (1979) "Choice, Exchange and the Family", in W.R. Burr, R. Hill, F.I. Nye and I.L. Reiss (eds) *Contemporary Theories About the Family, Vol. 2, General Theories/Theoretical Orientations*, New York: The Free Press.

Purcell, V. (1952) *The Chinese in Southeast Asia*, London: Oxford University Press.

Quah, S. R. (1979) "Child Welfare and Socio-economic Development: The Singapore Experience", in T.N. Chatuverdi (ed) *Administration for Child Welfare*, New Delhi: Indian Institute for Public Administration.

Quah, S. R. (1980) "Sex-role Socialization in a Transitional Society", *International Journal of Sociology of the Family*, 10: 213-32.

Quah, S. R. (1981) "The Impact of Policy on the Family: Can the Family be Strengthened by Legislation?", *Southeast Asian Journal of Social Science*, 9(1): 33-53.

Quah, S. R. (1988) *Between Two Worlds: Modern Wives in a Traditional Setting*, Singapore: Institute of Southeast Asian Studies.

Quah, S. R. (1990a) "Gender Roles, Family Roles and Health Behaviour: Pursuing the Hidden Link", *Southeast Asian Journal of Social Science*, 18(2): 51-69.

Quah, S. R. (1990b) (ed) *The Family as an Asset. An International Perspective on Marriage, Parenthood and Social Policy*, Singapore: Times Academic Press.

Quah, S. R. (1990c) "The Social Significance of Marriage and Parenthood in Singapore: Policy and Trends", in S. R. Quah (ed)

The Family as an Asset. An International Perspective on Marriage, Parenthood and Social Policy, Singapore: Times Academic Press.

Quah, S. R. (1990d) "Family as Hindrance or Asset? An Overview of Current Controversies", in S.R. Quah (ed) *The Family as an Asset. An International Perspective on Marriage, Parenthood and Social Policy*, Singapore: Times Academic Press.

Quah, S. R. (1990e) "Family and Social Policy: The Shared Experiences", in S.R. Quah (ed) *The Family as an Asset. An International Perspective on Marriage, Parenthood and Social Policy*, Singapore: Times Academic Press.

Quah, S. R. (1990f) "Review of J. Salaff's "'State and Family in Singapore'", *Pacific Affairs*, 63(1): 124-26.

Quah, S. R. (1993a) [E] *Asian Sociologists at Work*, London: Current Sociology, 41(1).

Quah, S.R. (1993b) "Marriage and Family", in A. Wong and W.K. Leong (eds) *Singapore Women. Three Decades of Change*, Singapore: Times Academic Press [Also as Chapter 2 in Quah 1994a].

Quah, S. R. (1993c) "The Family Court", *Singapore Journal of Legal Studies*, July, 16-34 [Also as Chapter 6 in Quah 1994a].

Quah, S. R. (1994a) *Family in Singapore. Sociological Perspectives*, Singapore: Times Academic Press [See Chapter 5 "Gender Roles: Striving for Coherence", 177-217].

Quah, S. R. (1994b) "Social Policy in Family Life: The Case of Childcare in Singapore", *International Journal of Sociology and Social Policy*, 14(1): 126-48.

Quah, S. R. (1998) *Family in Singapore. Sociological Perspectives*, Second Edition Revised and Expanded, Singapore: Times Academic Press.

Quah, S. R. (1999) *Study of Singapore Families*, Singapore: Ministry of Community Development.

Rapoport, R. and Rapoport, R. (1982) "British Families in Transition" in R. N. Rapoport, M.P. Fogarty and R. Rapoport (eds) *Families in Britain*, London: Routledge & Kegan Paul.

Reading, J. and Amatea, E.S. (1986) "Role Deviance and Role Diversification: Reassessing the Psychological Factors Affecting the Parenthood Choice of Career-oriented Women", *Journal of Marriage and the Family*, 48: 255-60.

Reith, G. M. (1907) *1907 Handbook of Singapore*, Singapore: Fraser & Neave.

Salaff, J. W. (1988) *State and Family in Singapore. Restructuring an Industrial Society*, Ithaca: Cornell University Press.

Salaff, J. W. and Wong, A. (1984) "Women's Work: Factory, Family and Social Class in an Industrialising Order", in G. Jones (ed) *Women in the Urban and Industrial Workforce: Southeast and East Asia*, Canberra: Australia National University Development Studies Centre.

Saw, S. H. and Wong, A. K. (1981) *Adolescents in Singapore: Sexuality, Courtship and Family Values*, Singapore: Singapore University Press.

Siddique, S. and PuruShotam, N. (1993) "Spouse Selection Patterns in the Singapore Indian Community", in K.S. Sandhu and A. Mani (eds) *Indian Communities in Southeast Asia*, Singapore: ISEAS, 811-26.

Singapore Children's Society (1958) "Family Life Among the Malays in Singapore", *International Child Welfare Review*, XII (2): 51-82.

Siraj, M. (1965) "Status of Muslim Women in Family Law in Singapore", *Intisari*, 2 (2) 9-17.

Steiner, G. Y. (1981) *The Futility of Family Policy*, New York: Brookings Institution.

Straughan, P. (1997) "Career, Family, Motherhood: Conflict or Consensus?", in H.M. Dahlan, H. Jusoh, Hing Ai Jun, and Ong Jin Hui (eds) *ASEAN in the Global System*, Kuala Lumpur: Universiti Kebangsaan Malaysia.

Straughan, P. (1999) "The Sociological Contradictions of the Normal Family: Challenges to the Ideology", *Sociology Working Paper Series* No. 135, Singapore: Dept. of Sociology, National University of Singapore.

Suchman, E. A. (1972) "Social Patterns of Illness and Medical Care", in E.G. Jaco (ed) *Patients, Physicians, and Illness*, New York: The Free Press.

Sussman, M. B. (1959) "The Isolated Nuclear Family: Fact or Fiction?" *Social Problems*, 6: 333-40.

Sussman, M. B. and Burchinal, L. (1962) "Parental Aid to Married Children: Implications for Family Functioning", *Marriage and Family Living*, 24: 231-40.

Sussman, M. B. and Steinmetz, S. K. (eds) (1987) *Handbook of Marriage and the Family*, New York: Plenum Press.

Swift, M. G. (1958) "A Note on the Durability of Malay Marriages", *Man*, October (207-208): 155-59.

Tallman, I. (1979) "Implementation of a National Family Policy: The Role of the Social Scientist", *Journal of Marriage and the Family*, 41(3): 469-72.

Tan, T. T. W. (1986) *Your Chinese Roots: The Overseas Chinese Story*, Singapore: Times Books International.

Tan, T. T. W. (1990) (ed) *Chinese Dialect Groups: Traits and Trades*, Singapore: Opinion.

Tai, C. L. (1979) "Divorce in Singapore", in E. Kuo and A. Wong (eds) *The Contemporary Family in Singapore*, Singapore: Singapore University Press.

Tham, S. C. (1979) "Social Change and the Malay Family", in E. Kuo and A. Wong (eds) *The Contemporary Family in Singapore*, Singapore: Singapore University Press.

Topley, M. D. (1954) "Chinese Women's Vegetarian Houses in Singapore", *Journal of the Malayan Branch Royal Asiatic Society*, 27(1): 51-57.

Verbrugge, L. M. (1985) "Gender and Health: An Update on Hypotheses and Evidence", *Journal of Health and Social Behaviour*, 26(3): 156-63.

Wee, A. (1954) "Some Aspects of the Status of Women in Malaya" in A. Appadorai (ed) *Status of Women in Southeast Asia*, Bombay: Orient Longmans.

Wee, K. (1979) "The Family and the Law in Singapore", in E. Kuo and A. Wong (eds) *The Contemporary Family in Singapore*, Singapore: Singapore University Press.

Westbrook, M.T. and Viney, L. L. (1983) "Age and Sex Differences in Patients' Reactions to Illness", *Journal of Health and Social Behaviour*, 24: 313-17.

Winstedt, R. (1981) *The Malays. A Cultural History*, Singapore: Graham Brash [Revised edition by Tham Seong Chee of original published in 1947 by Routledge & Kegan Paul, London].

Wong, A. (1974a) "Women as a Minority Group in Singapore", *Sociology Working Papers* No. 29, Singapore: Dept. of Sociology, University of Singapore.

Wong, A. (1974b) "The Continuous Family Revolution in China – Ideology and Changing Family Patterns", *Sociology Working Papers*, No. 31, Singapore: Dept. of Sociology, University of Singapore.

Wong, A. (1975) (ed) *Women in Modern Singapore*, Singapore: University Education Press.

Wong, A. (1977a) "The Value of Children and the Household Economy — A Review of Current VOC Studies in the Developing World", *Sociology Working Papers*, No. 58, Singapore: Dept. of Sociology.

Wong, A. (1977b) "Socio-economic Development and Women's Basic Needs in Singapore", in Asian & Pacific Centre for Women and Development (APCWD), *Selected Country Papers Presented at the APCWD Expert Group Meeting*, Teheran: APCWD, 81-89.

Wong, A. (1979) "Women's Status and Changing Family Values", in A. Wong and E. Kuo (eds) *The Contemporary Family in Singapore*, Singapore: Singapore University Press.

Wong, A. (1979) "The National Family Planning Programme and Changing Family Life", in A. Wong and E. Kuo (eds) *The Contemporary Family in Singapore*, Singapore: Singapore University Press.

Wong, A. (1981) "Planned Development, Social Stratification and the Sexual Division of Labour in Singapore", *Signs*, 7(2).

Wong, A. and Cheung, P. (1987) "Demographic and Social Development: Taking Stock for the Morrow", in L.G. Martin (ed) *The ASEAN Success Story*, Honolulu:University of Hawaii Press.

Wong, A. and Ko, Y. C. (1984) "Women's Work and Family Life: The Case of Electronics Workers in Singapore", *Office of Women in International Development Working Paper* No. 64, USA: Michigan State University.

Wong, A. and Kuo, E. (1979) "The Urban Kinship Network in Singapore", in A. Wong and E. Kuo (eds) *The Contemporary Family in Singapore*, Singapore: Singapore University Press.

Wong, A. and Kuo, E. (1983) *Divorce in Singapore*, Singapore: Graham Brash.

Wong, A. and Leong, W. K. (eds) (1993) *Singapore Women Three Decades of Change*, Singapore: Times Academic Press.

Wong, A. and Ng, S. M. (1985) *Ethnicity and Fertility in Southeast Asia: Comparative Analysis*, Singapore: ISEAS.

Wong, A. and Salaff, J. (1983) "Incentives and Disincentives in Population Policies", *The Draper Fund Report*, (12): 13-16.

Wong, A., Tan, T., Chew, S. B. and Lai, A. E. (1985) "Family Life Styles of HDB Residents", in A. Wong and S.H.K. Yeh (eds) *Housing a Nation: Twenty-five Years of Public Housing in Singapore*, Singapore: Maruzen Asia.

Yeh, S. H. K. (1964) "Chinese Marriage Patterns in Singapore", *Malayan Economic Review*, 9(1): 102-12.

Yeh, S. H. K. (1970) *Report on the Census of Malay Settlement Areas, Singapore, 1967*, Singapore: Economic Research Centre.

Yeh, S. H. K. (1973) *Public Housing in Singapore: An Analysis of Programme Implementation*, Manila: EROPA.

4

Education

Johannes Han-Yin Chang

Over 40 years ago, Peter Drucker (1959, 114) made a sharp statement, shocking many a scholar in the world of educational research:

> The uneducated is fast becoming an economic liability and unproductive. Society must be an "educated society" today — to progress, to grow, even to survive. ...the highly educated man has become the central resource of today's society, the supply of such men the true measure of its economic, its military and even its political potential.

To these remarks we can add that education has also become an increasingly important means for the status attainment of the individual, and hence for the upward mobility of lower class people as well.

Largely because of the enormous importance of modern education, a considerable amount of research has been conducted on Singapore's education system in the past three decades. What, then, has been achieved in the research? What can we expect in future inquiries on education when Singapore moves into the new millennium? These are the questions this paper attempts to address — from the viewpoint of the sociology of education.

The Theoretical Backdrop

To a large extent, educational research in Singapore has been stimulated and informed by a repertoire of international sociological theories on education, especially functionalism, Marxism, the Weberian perspective, and symbolic interactionism. It is helpful, therefore, to begin with a brief review of these theories in order to ensure a grasp of the nature, content and rationale of research carried out in Singapore.

Emile Durkheim was the first functionalist to systematically identify and highlight the influence society has on education, arguing that the former determines the nature and content of the latter. In his perspective, education is not meant to develop the abilities and potentialities of any individual for their own sake; rather, it is to develop them to meet the needs of a society:

> The man whom education should realise in us is not the man such as nature has made him, but as society wishes him to be; and it wishes him such as its internal economy calls for (Durkheim 1956, 122).

The most fundamental needs of a society are its survival and development. However, when the life conditions of a society change over time, its specific needs would change accordingly. This change will necessarily result in the alteration of the content of education. Durkheim did not mean to ignore the interests of the individual. However, in his view, individuals are fashioned by society and their interests can best be satisfied when the needs of society are met.

Durkheim's functionalism was further developed by his followers, such as Parsons (1961), Davis and Moore (1945), and Clark (1962). Like Durkheim, Parsons argues that a crucial way by which education serves to meet society's needs is to offer a systematic regime of socialisation. He (1961, 434) defines the socialization functions of education as "the development in individuals of the commitments and capacities which are prerequisites of their future role-performance". In his view, values regulate social systems, which in turn condition the motivations, actions and interactions of the individual. As such, values operate at the top of the hierarchy of social control in any society. It is from this point of view that he argues for the necessity of value consensus and values education. In addition, Parsons identified another function of education, namely selection (for "role allocation" in society). Clark (1962) developed a technical-function theory of education. In his view, educational expansion and development in contemporary society may be explained in terms of technological and economic advances as well as society's new needs which they give rise to. The impressive contribution of Kingsley Davis and Wilbert Moore (1945) from a functionalist view is their classic argument on the presumed "naturalness" or inevitability of social stratification and the relationship between social stratification and education. These functionalist formulations basically remain at the societal level, using macro-social influences to account for education.

The Marxist approach takes social class as its basic unit of analysis. This analytical focus allows the researchers to examine the diverse conditions of different classes and their impact on education, on social reproduction, and on the preservation of the existing social-economic system. Concepts that are important for understanding agency such as "capital", "power", and "praxis" are also introduced into the research. It takes a critical view of class differences and class inequality in education as well as of society at large.

Bowles argues that the US schools system is pervaded by class inequalities; class-based differentiation occurs within each level of schooling across schools as well as within each school. "Both the amount and the content of ...[the students'] education greatly facilitates their movement into positions similar to their parents" (Bowles 1977, 141). The social relations of the school replicate the social relations of the workplace. To account for class inequality in education and its social consequences, Bowles identifies three factors: (1) differential class culture in regulating students' learning behaviour; (2) differential class power in affecting education-related policies; and (3) the capitalist system in which (1) and (2) are rooted.

Bourdieu is another scholar whose thinking has been heavily influenced by Marx's ideas. His major contribution is reflected in his analysis of "the structural dynamics of class relations" in explaining inequality of education and reproduction of social structure. According to him, different classes possess different resources. These resources may be classified into economic capital, social capital, cultural capital, and symbolic capital. He is more interested in cultural capital in order to understand the relationship between social classes and education. Cultural capital is defined as "linguistic and cultural competencies". He sees an unequal distribution of cultural capital in favour of the upper and middle classes. Cultural capital may be transmitted from generation to generation through family socialisation. When acquired by children, fundamentally it takes the form of "habitus", namely a system of predispositions. Habitus covers two dimensions — cognition and evaluation. The latter consists of interests, tastes, appreciation, and values. Habitus is developed through lasting experience under specific class conditions and varies accordingly. It is located between class structure and practice. To students from upper and middle class families, their habitus can generally function as a key to decode the system of knowledge transmitted in schools. Because the coding system used in schools is largely a reflection of the upper and middle class culture, the habitus acquired by lower class children tends to be ineffective or less effective in decoding it. This leads to differential effectiveness of learning and greater probability of lower class children being eliminated at lower levels of education in the selective process. Consequently, appropriation of cultural capital in schools also becomes stratified in favour of upper and middle class children. This process supplements the unequal appropriation of cultural capital that occurs in the home environment. The end result: class-based reproduction of distribution of cultural capital. In Bourdieu's judgement this sort of cultural reproduction is responsible for the reproduction of the structure of social classes (Bourdieu 1977).

Like Bourdieu, Bernstein substantially follows the Marxist tradition as well. His well-known research focused on two particular aspects of cultural capital: command of speech codes and development of cultural sensitivities associated with such codes. He divided speech into two categories — the elaborated code and the restricted code. The restricted code is context-specific; simple (very often broken); lacking in variation; weak in explicitness, sharpness and precision; and scanty in causal analysis and explanation. The elaborated code is the opposite. Upper and middle class children tend to be proficient in both codes, whereas lower class children are generally familiar with the restricted code only – due to the fact that their parents largely use the restricted code when communicating with them.

According to Bernstein (1961, 294), "The speech marks out a pattern of stimuli to which the child adapts." In other words, the use of different speech codes in interaction creates different kinds of environment to stimulate children's response and learning. Since learning is determined in part by the environment of stimulation, differences in what are learned thus emerge between children of different class backgrounds. Consequently, children not only acquire different codes of speech according to their class backgrounds, they also develop different levels of cognitive sensitivity accordingly, for example, sensitivity to classification and reasoning.

In addition, lower class parents' typical authoritarian and simplistic manner of communication with their children also tends to encourage obedience and conformity in the children and depress their tendencies for inquisitiveness and reasoning. These consequences differ from the more favourable development of open-mindedness, rationality and reasoning in upper and middle class children. Thus, it is only natural for upper and middle class children to perform better in schools.

The Weberian scholars are highly critical of the deterministic tendencies of both functionalism and Marxism. They follow and develop Max Weber's tradition, ie, to advocate a vision of education that celebrates power-based action as an alternative:

> Education has the characteristics it does because of the goals pursued by those who control it... change occurs because new goals are pursued by those who have the power to modify education's previous structural form, definition of instruction and relationship to society... education is fundamentally about what people have wanted of it and have been able to do to it (Archer 1984, 1).

In the Weberian approach action may take place at both the individual and group levels. In either case it is competitive in nature. Social life is an arena in which individuals and groups struggle with and try to dominate each other in an attempt to obtain privileges. The privileges include power, status and wealth. Education is used as one of the means of attaining these ends. Thus, it becomes a sort of "market place", "in which social actions simultaneously attempt to attain certain goals." However, power is not equally distributed among individuals and groups in the competition. Those who have greater power are likely to dominate those who have less, thereby placing themselves in a more influential position in controlling the educational system and defining its goals, contents, and consequences (Collins 1979, Lenski 1984). By analysing power-based action and interaction, the Weberian perspective gained a relative advantage compared to the Marxist approach: it succeeds in extending the Marxist concepts of class and class-specific power to cover groups other than classes. It also has the potential to analyze actions at the individual level.

Symbolic Interactionism shares with the Weberian approach in emphasising the role of action and interaction in constructing social reality (including education). It also shares with the latter in referring to action at both group and individual levels. However, what symbolic interactionism is interested in is "self"-conditioned and meaning-guided action rather than power-based action (for example, see Hargreaves 1975). As such it provides an effective tool for understanding education from the viewpoint of meaning and "self", especially at the micro-level.

So far I have presented some major arguments of the four most influential theoretical traditions in the international sociology of education. They constitute the theoretical background against which research on Singapore's education has been pursued and developed.

Research on Singapore's education concentrates on the following aspects: (1) economic returns to education; (2) education and social change; (3) education and social reproduction; (4) education and ethnicity; and (5) effectiveness of the current educational system. (1), (2) and (5) are largely studied within the framework of functionalism, supplemented with some other theories such as symbolic interactionism and the Weberian perspective. The investigations on (3) and (4) are basically informed by Marxist and Weberian perspectives respectively.

Economic Returns to Education

Tham (1989, 489) observed that "the central concern [of the Singapore government] that has evoked [its] thinking and prompted its policies in education has been the matter of human resource development... The underlying assumption is that failure to meet this fundamental development requirement would lead to an irreversible downward slide in the economy, with all its attendant consequences." This concern has been translated into educational reality. An economically-oriented, highly competitive mass education system with high standards has been firmly established and continuously expanded since 1959 to cater to the needs of industrialization and post-industrial development (also see Yip, Eng and Yap 1997; Gopinathan 1997).

Contrary to the anti-functionalist arguments about lack of connection between education and needs of economic development (Collins 1979; Archer 1984), it is found that in Singapore, education has performed a crucial role in promoting industrialization. Macro-level economic returns to education are substantial (Low, Toh and Soon 1991, Chang 1998, cf. Han 1998). Similarly, returns to education at the individual level are also highly salient (Clark and Pang 1970, Chiew 1977, Ko 1991, Chang 1995). According to Ko's research (1991), his respondents' education "stands out as the most important determinant of first job attainment," exceeding the direct impact of parents' education and parents' occupation on first-job attainment.

However, returns to the individuals are not evenly distributed. Ko (1991, 223) found that "the correlation of education and first-job status... is 0.6 for women but 0.4 for men." Some other scholars observed that the Chinese-educated earned significantly less than the English-educated (Clark and Pang 1970, Chiew 1977, Gopinathan 1998, Tan 1999). People educated in Malay and Tamil earned even less.

Education and Social Change in Singapore

In contrast to the dominant concern in the current sociology of education regarding the impact of education on social reproduction, scholars in Singapore observed that education can also play an important role in promoting social change, especially in social stratification. The effects of education in this regard are expressed in two basic ways: (1) by facilitating economic development, thereby helping to create a functional imperative to expand the proportion of professionals, technicians, executives and managers, ie, to expand the relative size of the upper division of the class hierarchy; and (2) by equipping members of underprivileged groups with necessary qualifications to respond to this imperative and move upward to join the upper division — thus leading to the change of the social composition of the upper division (Chang 1995, 455).

Thanks to the contribution of education and a number of other factors, Singapore's economy has gained tremendous advances in the past four decades (Low *et al.* 1991, Chia 1989, Chang 1998). This has given rise to continual change in the occupational structure. It was found that in 1966, 12% of the labour force were government officials, employers, executives, professionals and paraprofessionals. These people and their dependants may be classified as members of the upper and middle classes. By 1996, the percentage had jumped to 37% (Chang 1995, 1998). This change implies that the upper and middle classes had expanded by about 2.1 times in three decades up to 1996.

The expansion of the upper and middle classes has created a large number of opportunities for members of the lower classes, especially lower class children to move up. Lower class children have responded to the opportunities by competing for higher education, hoping to use it as a means for upward mobility.

Among all the traditional disadvantaged groups, women have gained the largest margin of upward mobility judging by their proportion in the student body at the tertiary level. In 1993 about 53% of university graduates were females, 6 percentage points more than males. Among the ethnic groups, the proportional educational gains over time of the Malay group were the greatest. In 1964 about 1.2% of the graduates of the local universities was Malay. By 1993 it had reached 3.8%, an increase by 2.2 times. The representation of the lowest class in tertiary education has also made a significant improvement. In 1980, for example, the chance of gaining access to university education for children living in 1-3 room HDB flats was one-sixth of the odds for children living in private houses/flats; the ratio increased to 1:3 by 1990 (Chang 1995).

Education and Social Reproduction

Despite the salience of social change in the past four decades, reproduction has remained the dominant feature in the social dimension. Social reproduction is a central issue because it relates to perpetuation of the capitalist system, reproduction of the general configuration of class stratification, preservation of the overall profile of ethnic differentiation, and inter-generation transmission of social status within each social class and ethnic group.

Education is found to have contributed to such reproduction in two fundamental ways. One is to shape a public ideology which justifies educational stratification and the subsequent occupation-based social differentiation by means of streaming and educational meritocracy (Chang 1998, cf. Bourdieu 1977, Bowles 1977). The other way is to allow the operation of differential cultural capital and economic capital within the framework of educational meritocracy (Chang and Mani 1995). Quah (1991, 63-64), Tan (1997, 287), and Quah et al. (1997, 326) found that parents' educational qualifications were closely correlated with children's education. Chen (1973) observed that according to a large survey conducted in 1971 and 1972, 94% of the upper class respondents spoke English while only 8.5% of the lower class ones could speak English. Parents' education and proficiency in English may be taken as indicators of parents' cultural capital which can be transmitted to children. Thus, the difference in parents' cultural capital will be translated into difference in children's cultural capital, which in turn will affect children's learning performance in schools. Ko (1991, 224) found that father's education and occupation and mother's education can explain 22% and 20% of variance respectively in women's and men's educational achievement. To a lesser degree, financial capital can also be transformed into uneven distribution of educational achievements among social classes and ethnic groups. In Singapore's context, varied educational achievements effectively generate social stratification and contribute to the inter-generation transmission of social status (Chang and Mani 1995).

Education and Ethnicity

Marked education improvement has been found in Singapore as a whole as well as in every individual ethnic group in the past forty years. The tertiary-primary student ratio increased from 4:100 in 1965 to 34:100 in 1995 (Chang 1995b, 1999a). However, the gains secured by each ethnic group are not equal in proportion (Hashim 1992, Chang 1995a). In 1990 among the resident non-student population aged 10 years and over, those who have received university education constituted 5.1%, 4.1%, and 0.6% of the Chinese, Indian and Malay groups respectively. The proportion of the Malays among all university graduates in 1993 was 3.8% compared to 1.2% in 1964. Despite the remarkable 216% increase, however, this 3.8% was far below the percentage of the Malays in the general population (14.2%).

Hamid et al. (1995) found that the learning performances of Malay students correlate with the following factors: (1) parents' educational qualifications (65% or more of the high- and over-achievers had parents whose educational qualifications were at the 'O' level or above whereas only 25% or less of the under- and low-achievers had such parents); (2) parental supervision, for example, in controlling TV watching hours; (3) private tuition; (4) home environment; (5) reading materials available at home; (6) students' language skills; and (7) students' resourcefulness in seeking assistance from others. By implication, these findings suggest that Malay students' weaker position in educational competition may partially have resulted from their relative weakness regarding these conditional factors.

The issue of differential educational competitiveness aside, Abdullah (1994) and Babar (1999) also found that a section of the Malay community has become increasingly concerned about the cultivation of Islamic values through formal education. There is an increased tendency for some Malay parents to send their children to the "Madrasah" or Islamic religious schools since Islamic values are not intentionally transmitted in the government schools. Currently, there are four "Madrasah" schools in operation. A demanding challenge to them is to balance Islamic values with the core values of the whole nation on the one hand and on the other, to ensure the competitive competence of their students in mathematics, science, English, etc at a level not inferior to that of a quality government school.

Effectiveness of the Current Educational System

Effectiveness may be measured against two sets of criteria: (1) how well it helps to increase Singapore's chances of survival and development; and (2) how well it helps to develop the productive potential of the individual. The first set may be indexed with the service rendered by education to Singapore's industrialization, social stability and nation building; it should also be indexed, in part, with the possible service Singapore's education may provide for the country's post-industrial development now and in the future. The second set may be approximated using proxies such as the proportion of the population who have received education and at what level; the relationship between education and upward mobility; and the market value of credentials. The research on most of these indicators previously reviewed suggests that Singapore's education system is generally successful so far. It may be noted that in addition to the areas examined, education has also played an effective role in Singapore's nation building according to some scholars (Kuo and Jernudd 1994, Gopinathan 1997, 1998, Hill and Lian 1995, Pakir 1997, Chang 1998).

Kuo and Jernudd (1994) argued that "given the multiethnic and multilingual nature of Singapore, two language-related issues are of fundamental significance and are closely related to the task of nation building." One is the question of "communicative integration"; and the other the issue of "develop[ing] a new national identity which is additional to, and above and beyond, the identity and loyalty at the ethnic and sub-ethnic levels, one which serves the government's vision of economic, social and cultural development." In dealing with these two issues, the Singapore government has adopted a policy of "pragmatic multilingualism." The policy prescribes four official languages (Malay, English, Mandarin Chinese, and Tamil) to be treated equally, but with English as the common working language emphasized in business, education, and government functions. The use of English, the only language that is regarded as "neutral" for inter-group relations in Singapore, serves to shape and express the emerging supra-ethnic national identity. Kuo and Jernudd observed that this language policy has been actively implemented in the education system. By 1987 all primary one students were already enrolled in the unified national education system using English as the first language. English is now the medium in all classes at all levels except when special considerations warrant use of one of the other official languages. This situation clearly facilitates the creation of the "supra-ethnic national identity" for nation building. Similarly, Hill and Lian (1995) systematically documented Singapore's language policy and note that as a result of the implementation of this policy, English has finally emerged as the common language in this city-state. As such it has successfully broken down "the ethnic barriers of vernacular education" and, at least in this sense, contributed to Singapore's nation building.

Nonetheless, Singapore's education system is not without problems. Chang (1998) observed that the existing education system is basically one of transmitting knowledge for application and shaping attitudes and personality traits that emphasise discipline, conformity, hard work, and a strong sense of national interest and national identity. The products generated by such a system were suitable for a Singapore in the early stage of industrialization when the "train model" of development was practiced (1998). The train model is characterized by the decisive leading role of the government (like the locomotive of a train) in promoting industrialization and nation building. A major part of the role is reflected in the government's successful effort in attracting MNCs to invest in Singapore and in borrowing advanced technology and other resources from abroad for the benefit of Singapore's industrialization. A high-standard application-oriented education was efficient in producing sufficient numbers of managerial personnel and professionals as well as skilled labourers to cater to the needs of the MNCs, which dominate Singapore's manufacturing sector. There was no urgent need for Singapore to develop original sophisticated technology so far as its own industrialization was concerned. Furthermore, the train model at the societal level, the management pattern of the MNCs and the operational style of the local enterprises and other institutions at the intermediate level, all require discipline and conformity on the part of the subordinates. Therefore, the discipline orientation of the education system also catered well to these needs.

However, the situation has changed as Singapore enters the stage of post-industrial development in an era of rapid globalization and intense competition in a knowledge economy. Singapore's further development requires a radical expansion of its economic scope and depth. As regards scope, it needs to substantiate and consolidate its goal of regionalization and then extend it to the sphere of globalization. With reference to depth, it needs to make a big step forward in developing the knowledge economy. Hence it needs to cultivate and mobilize human resources for entrepreneurship and creativity, especially creativity to generate original sophisticated technology. When taking into consideration this new need, the existing education system is found wanting (also see Sharpe and Gopinathan 1997, 369-83).

Some lesser problems have also been identified. Hill and Lian (1995, 82-83) noted that as early as 1965 Lee Kuan Yew had expressed his fear that the consequence of English education would be the de-culturalization of the population. It was mainly for this reason that a second language was made compulsory in secondary schools, for Lee believed that the learning of a second language, the mother tongue, was synonymous with learning a whole value system that would help maintain the fabric of society against the negative excesses of Westernisation. However, Hill and Lian (1995, 84) argue that "it was questionable whether a bilingual policy was effective in fortifying the resilience of Asian communities against 'undesirable changes' precipitated by rapid economic development."

Chang (1999) discovered in his recent study that among the 811 students (secondary or above) surveyed, nearly 22% of the Chinese respondents said, if given a chance, they would rather be born into a non-Chinese race – mostly to become a Caucasian or Japanese. By contrast, 94.9% of the Chinese parents surveyed indicated that they would prefer to be Chinese again. Similarly, 18% of the Indian students surveyed were not willing to take it as their first choice to be Indian again, compared to a mere 7% of their parents. The average score of feelings of attachment to Singapore was significantly lower for those who were less willing to identify with their native ethnic groups than for those who were more willing to do so. The average score of appreciation of the non-native local ethnic groups was also lower for those who were more willing to identify with Caucasians and Japanese. Further, Chang's research findings revealed that among both students and their parents, a significantly larger proportion of those who use English as the major medium of communication at home were less willing to identify with their native ethnic groups compared to those who mainly speak their mother tongue at home (with the exception of the Indian respondents).

Gopinathan (1994), following D. Tyack, sees language as "part of the contested terrain of power and values". According to his observation, Singapore's language policy has undergone repeated accommodative adjustments in response to changing power relationships since 1956. All the adjustments have been reflected in education. He feels that the adjustments, while solving some of the old problems, have created "new fault lines": "Within Singapore, the disfunctionality of an English-driven modernization process is becoming more apparent in both class and cultural terms, and the response of the government to problems arising from the process may cause new problems (for example, the "Speak Mandarin" campaign as a response to the anxiety of the Chinese-educated once "alarmed the minorities"). The balancing of fundamental and competing claims [regarding language and education] must often be re-negotiated anew."

A Comparative Evaluation

The research conducted on Singapore's education is a fruitful part of the worldwide effort in educational inquiry and it has also helped to promote Singaporeans' understanding of their own educational system.

Research on educational stratification and social reproduction is the most abundant and most prominent in the sociology of education, especially in the so-called "core countries" (eg, Lareau and Horvat 1999, Ballantine 1997, Levine and Levine 1996, Colclough and Beck 1986, Burnhill 1981, Bourdieu 1977, Bowles and Gintis 1976). Educational research in Singapore has effectively extended the research from the core countries to a different type of society – a newly industrialized Asian society. This attempt has generated a significant amount of new knowledge. Similarly, Singapore's research on the education of minority ethnic groups and on the economic impact of education at the macro level has also contributed to the expanded "database" of the international sociology of education. More importantly, the educational research on bilingualism has actually transcended the existing theoretical horizon known in the core countries (see Kuo and Jernudd 1994, Hill and Lian 1995, Gopinathan 1997, Chang 1999b). Sadly, Singapore's investigations pale in the remaining areas of empirical research where international research has much credit to claim. For illustration, let us closely examine two such areas, namely, research on ability tracking and school climate.

According to research conducted in Europe and America, the dominant motivation underlying ability tracking is to improve efficiency of teaching by finding the best "fit" between students and teachers, learning materials and teaching methods (Reid 1986, Ballantine 1997). In reality, however, ability tracking is found to have generated three kinds of major effects:

1. Socially it tends to increase social stratification (Darling-Hammond 1994). Students in lower-ability groupings tend to be from lower-class families. They receive less attention from teachers and are often stigmatized. Their scores keep falling in relation to other groups. This situation is likely to affect their subsequent job attainments and earnings. In contrast, higher ability groups tend to include a disproportionate number of upper- and middle-class children. They are more motivated. Teachers give more feedback and praise to them and plan more creative activities for them. They have higher achievement, class rank, and test scores. These give them a better start after graduation.

2. Academically, the research findings are controversial. Some studies showed that ability tracking tends to benefit gifted students and the others who are placed in high tracks, while low ability students tend to suffer in learning (Douglas 1964, Barker Lunn J.C. 1970, Hallinan 1990, Pallas et al. 1994). Other studies found little evidence of positive effects (Slavin 1990, Hill 1995).

3. Psychologically, students in lower-ability groupings tend to be psychologically depressed, their aspirations and self-esteem lowered (Ballantine 1997).

How relevant are these findings to Singapore? Actually, streaming is one of the most controversial topics in the country. Yet no systematic research, or anything similar to the study conducted in Europe and the United States, has ever been pursued to clarify the situation.

An influential study conducted by Coleman and his associates (1981) found that in America private schools provide superior education to public schools because the school atmosphere in private schools is generally more conducive to learning. Factors that influence school atmosphere include principals' perception and leadership; staff cooperation; classroom policy; teachers' values, perception, expectations, and morale; students' values, self-concept, and norms as well as the racial and economic background of the students. After Coleman and his associates published their report, a number of other studies have also been conducted to explore further the impact of school climate on students' learning and achievement.

Brookover and colleagues (1996) reported the following findings: Schools can make a difference in students' learning; the staff of improving schools place more emphasis on accomplishing basic reading and mathematics objectives; they believe all students can master basic objectives and they hold high expectations; they assume responsibility for learning and accept being held accountable; principals in such schools function as instructional leaders and disciplinarians. To put the concept of "school climate" into practice in an experimental program in the Chicago public school system, Brookover and his associates managed to help alter school climate and consequently, school achievement levels were raised significantly.

An important component of the school climate is teacher expectations and teacher-student interaction. Rosenthal and Jacobson (1968) were the first scholars to bring to public attention some surprising effects of teacher expectations on interactions, achievement levels, and intelligence of students. Their experimental findings led to the emergence of the phrase "self-fulfilling prophecy": The teacher expects certain behaviour from the child and the child responds to the expectations; depending on the type of expectations received, students with similar other conditions (age, sex, and IQ scores) will differ in their learning behaviour, leading to marked difference in their learning achievements — so much so that the difference can more or less match and "justify" the artificial difference in the initial teacher expectations. Similar results have also been observed by other scholars (Peters 1971, Good 1981, Bonetari 1994).

Cooper (1995) and Brookover et al. (1996) found that teacher expectations are affected by a variety of factors such as the student's test scores; his sex, race, dress, name, name, physical appearance, language, and accent; his parents' occupations; his motherhood status; the way he responds to the teacher; his status in ability grouping; and even his sitting position in the classroom (lower expectations are typically transmitted to students who sit on the sides and in the back of a classroom). These findings suggest that lower class children are more likely to suffer from teachers' lower expectations and more likely to develop a sense of "futility" (feelings of hopelessness and the impression that teachers do not care about their academic achievement). The feelings of futility are damaging to school climate as well as students' learning effort and achievement.

This important theme has barely been touched upon in Singapore's research. Consequently, little understanding has been gained of the processes, mechanisms, and consequences of the operation of the various kinds of school climate in Singapore. For example, should we attribute the better examination results of Singapore's independent schools to the higher pre-enrolment exam-related quality of their students and more financial resources they possess or to any one or more other factors relevant to their school climate?

Two other inadequacies of Singapore's research should also be noted. One is that its theoretical originality is generally lacking. The existing research is mostly reactive and applied. Besides, the existing research has failed to provide sufficient well-researched, feasible solutions to the problems of educational effectiveness cited in the previous section.

The Next Lap

Given its current state, educational research in Singapore obviously needs substantial improvement in the coming years. Theoretically, serious effort may be needed to produce breakthroughs. This may be realized by developing new theories or new insights within the frames of the existing theories. For example, the concept of "power" in the Weberian perspective does not have to be analyzed exclusively in terms of competition and conflict centring around individual or group interests; the analysis may be extended to understand how power may be used to promote education-related interests of the whole society, for example, to examine under what conditions the power of the state may be effectively used to promote education on behalf of the overall interests of society.

One of the major arguments of functionalism is that culture and values regulate social interaction, social institution as well as individual behaviour. Functionalist theorists, such as Durkheim and Parsons, have related the argument to moral education. But they have largely neglected how culture may regulate the education system in a country as a whole. Much may be discovered and theoretically capitalized on in this neglected area.

The application of symbolic interactionism in the sociology of education is the least satisfactory. Most of the theoretical resources contained in the framework of Mead, Blumer and Strauss have remained untouched. Creative application in this regard may be worked out at least in the following three aspects: (1) to study the connection between meaning and power in affecting education; (2) to investigate the connection between Mead's "I" and culture in understanding cultural production and reproduction in affecting education; and (3) to review the connection between perception and individual conduct in understanding the impact of meaning on the effectiveness of teaching and learning.

Further, much scientific understanding needs to be developed for applied sociology of education as well. In the Singapore context, this development may be achieved in studying, sociologically, how to deal with a number of practical issues related to the local education system. The following issues warrant special attention:

1. How to effectively cultivate students' capacity for creativity and entrepreneurship?
2. How to improve students' emotional quotient to match Singapore's need for post-industrial development?
3. How to prevent students in the lower stream from suffering the negative consequences of streaming?
4. How to further help students of the underprivileged groups to sharpen their competitiveness?
5. How to conduct moral education and values education more effectively?

Educational research needs substantial advances. There are good reasons to believe that such advances can be realised on the basis of creative imagination in combination with a broader pragmatic orientation.

References

Abdullah, Kamsiah (1994) "Maintaining Cultural Values and Identity: The Case of Malay Language Teaching in Singapore", in E. Thomas (ed) *International Perspectives on Culture and Schooling: A Symposium Proceedings*, London: University of London.

Archer, M. (1984) *Social Origins of Educational Systems*, London: Sage.

Ballantine, J. H. (1997) *The Sociology of Education*, Upper Saddle River, N.J.: Prentice-Hall.

Babar, Mukhlis Abu (1999) "Islamic Education in Singapore", Paper presented at the 4th ASEAN Inter-University Seminar on Social Development, Prince of Songkla University (Pattani), Thailand, 16-18 June, 1999.

Barker Lunn, J. C. (1970) *Streaming in the Primary School*, Slough: NFER.

Bernstein, B. (1961) "Social Class and Linguistic Development: A Theory of Social Learning", in A.H. Halsey, J. Floud, and C. Arnold Anderson (eds) *Education, Economy and Society*, New York: Free Press.

Bernstein, B. (1990) *The Structuring of Pedagogic discourse: Class, Codes and Control*, Vol. 4, London: Routledge.

Blumer, H. (1969) *Symbolic Interaction: Perspective and Method*, Englewood Cliffs, N.J.: Prentice-Hall.

Bonetari, D. (1994) "The Effects of Teachers' Expectations on Mexican-American Students," Paper presented at the annual meeting of the American Psychological Association, New Orleans.

Bourdieu, P. (1977) "Cultural Reproduction and Social Reproduction", in J. Karabel and A. Halsey (eds) *Power and Ideology in Education*, New York: Oxford University Press.

Bowles, S. (1977) "Unequal Education and the Reproduction of the Social Division of Labour", in J. Karabel and A.H. Halsey (eds) *Power and Ideology in Education*, New York: Oxford University Press.

Bowles, S. and Gintis, H. (1976) *Schooling in Capitalist America: Education and the Contradictions of Economic Life*, New York: Basic Books.

Brookover, W. B., Erickson, F. J. and McEvoy, A. W. (1996) *Creating Effective Schools: An In-Service Program for Enhancing School Learning Climate and Achievement*, Holmes Beach, Fla.: Learning Publications.

Burnhill, P. (1981) "The Relationship between Examination Performance and Social Class", *CES Collaborative Research Newsletter*, 8.

Chang, J. H. Y. (1995a) "Singapore: Education and Change of Class Stratification", *Southeast Asian Studies*, 32(4): 455-76.

Chang, J. H. Y. (1995b) "Singapore: Access to Tertiary Education and Prospect of Change", in *Proceedings of the Annual ASAIHL Seminar on Higher Education for All*, Bangkok: Bangkok University.

Chang, J. H. Y. (1998) "The Functions and Limitations of Education in Singapore", *Commentary*, 15: 22-28.

Chang, J. H. Y. (1998) "State Values, Education, and Reduction of Social Inequality", Paper presented at the Second Euroseas Conference at the University of Hamburg, Germany, 3-6 September 1998.

Chang, J. H. Y. (1999a) "Education: Government Values as an Effective Determinant", Paper presented at the 4th ASEAN Inter-University Seminar on Social Development, Prince of Songkla University (Pattani), Thailand, 16-18 June 1999.

Chang, J. H. Y. (1999b) "The Trend of Change in Ethnic Identification: A Selected Summary of Survey Findings", A research report to the Cabinet of Singapore.

Chang, J. H.Y. and Mani, A. (1995) "Higher Education in Singapore: Dual Constraints of Less Competitive Groups", *Southeast Asian Journal of Social Science*, 23(2): 42-61.

Chen, P. S.J. (1973) "Social Stratification in Singapore", Working Papers, No. 12, Dept. of Sociology, University of Singapore.

Chia, S. Y. (1989) "The Character and Progress of Industrialization", in K. S. Sandhu and P. Wheatley (eds) *Management of Success, The Moulding of Modern Singapore*, Singapore: Institute of Southeast Asian Studies.

Chiew, S.-K. (1977) "Educational and Occupational Attainment of Singapore's Chinese Women and Men", Sociology Working Paper, No. 59, Dept. of Sociology, University of Singapore.

Clark, B. R. (1962) *Educating the Expert Society*, San Francisco: Chandler.

Clark, D. and Pang, E.-F. (1970) "Returns to Schooling and Training in Singapore", *The Malayan Economic Review*, XV: 79-103.

Colclough, G. and Beck, E.M. (1986) "The American Educational Structure and the Reproduction of Social Class", *Sociological Inquiry*, 56(4): 456-73.

Coleman, J. et al. (1966) *Equality of Educational Opportunity*, Washington, D.C.: US Dept. of Education.

Coleman, J.S., Hoffer, T. and Kilgore, S. (1981) *Public and Private Schools, Report to the National Center for Education Statistics*, Chicago: National Opinion Research Centre.

Collins, R. (1979) *The Credential Society*, New York: Academic Press.

Cooper, H. and Conswella, J. M. (1995) "Teenage Motherhood, Mother-Only Households, and Teacher Expectations", *Journal of Experimental Education*, 63(3): 231-48.

Darling-Hammond, L. (1994) "Performance-based Assessment and Equation Equity", *Harvard Educational Review*, 64: 5-30.

Davis, K. and Moore,W. (1945) "Some Principles of Stratification", *American Sociological Review*, 10: 242-49.

Douglas, J. W. B. (1964) *The Home and the School*, London: MacGibbon and Kee.

Durkheim, E. (1956) *Education and Sociology*, New York: Free Press.

Fischer, C. S., Hout, M., Jankowski, M. S., Lucas, S. R., Swidler, A. and Voss, K. (1996) *Inequality by Design: Cracking the Bell Curve Myth*, Princeton, N. J.: Princeton University Press.

Gibson, M. A. & Oybu, J. U. (1991) *Minority Status and Schooling: A Comparative Study of Immigrant and Involuntary Minorities,* New York: Garland.

Good, T. L. (1981) "Teacher Expectations and Student Perceptions: A Decade of Research", *Educational Leadership*, 38: 415-22.

Gopinathan, S. (1994) "Language Policy Changes 1979-1992: Politics and Pedagogy", in S. Gopinathan et al. (eds) *Language, Society and Education in Singapore: Issues and Trends*, Singapore: Times Academic Press.

Gopinathan, S. (1997) "Education and Development in Singapore", in J. Tan, S. Gopinathan and W. K. Ho (eds) *Education in Singapore: A Book of Readings*, Singapore: Prentice-Hall.

Gopinathan, S. (1998) "Educational Development in Singapore: Connecting the National, Regional and the Global", *Commentary*, 15: 1-13.

Hallinan, M. T. (1990) "The Effects of Ability Grouping in Secondary Schools: A Response to Slavin's Best-Evidence Synthesis", *Review of Educational Research*, 60(3): 501-504.

Hamid, H. A., Mohd Azhar Khalid, Mohad Alami Musa and Yusof Sulaiman (1994). *Factors Affecting Malay/Muslim Pupils' Performance in Education*, Singapore: Association of Muslim Professionals.

Han, F. K., Fernandez, W. and Tan, S. (1998) *Lee Kuan Yew, The Man and His Ideas*, Singapore: Times Editions.

Hargreaves, D. (1975) *Interpersonal Relations and Education*, London: Routledge and Kegan Paul.

Hashim, Zarina Binte (1992) *The Malay Middle Class*, Unpublished Academic Exercise, Dept. of Malay Studies, National University of Singapore.

Hill, H. (1995) "Ideas and Programs to Assist in the Untracking of American Schools", in H. Pool and J. Page (eds) *Beyond Tracking*, Bloomington, IN: Phi Delta Kapa Educational Foundation.

Hill, M. and Fee, L. K. (1995) *The Politics of Nation Building and Citizenship in Singapore*, New York: Routledge.

King, R. (1980) "Weberian Perspectives and the Study of Education", *British Journal of Sociology of Education*, 3(1).

Jencks, C. et al. (1972) *Inequality: A Reassessment of the Effects of Family and Schooling in America*, New York: Basic Books.

Jones, J., Vanfossen, B. E. and Ensminger, M. E. (1995) "Individual and Organizational Predictors of High School Track Placement", *Sociology of Education*, 68(4): 287-300.

Ko, Y. C. (1991) "Status Attainment", in S. Quah, S. K. Chiew, Y.C. Ko and S. M. Lee, (eds) *Social Class in Singapore*, Singapore: Centre for Advanced Studies, National University of Singapore.

Kuo, E. C. K. and Jernudd, B. H. (1994) "Balancing Macro- and Micro-Sociolinguistic Perspectives in Language Management: The Case of Singapore", in S. Gopinathan, A. Pakir, W. K. Ho and V. Saravanan (eds), *Language, Society and Education in Singapore*, Singapore: Times Academic Press.

Lareau, A. and Horvat, E. M. (1999) "Moments of Social Inclusion and Exclusion: Race, Class, and Cultural Capital in Family-School Relationships", *Sociology of Education*, 72(1): 37-53.

Lee, W. O. (1991) *Social Change and Educational Problems in Japan, Singapore and Hong Kong*, Basingstoke: MacMillan.

Lenski, G. (1984) *Power and Privilege*, Chapel Hill: University of North Carolina Press.

Levine, D. U. and Levine, R. F. (1996) *Society and Education*, Boston: Allyn and Bacon.

Low, L., Toh, M. H. and Wong, S. T. (1991) *Economics of Education and Manpower Development: Issues and Policies in Singapore*, Singapore: McGraw-Hill.

Mark, D. L. H. (1993) "High Achieving African-American Children in Low-Income Single Parent Families", Paper presented at the annual meeting of the American Educational Research Association, Atlanta.

Mead, G. H. (1962) *Mind, Self and Society: From the Standpoint of a Social Behaviorist*, Chicago: University of Chicago Press.

Pakir, A. (1997) "Education and Invisible Language Planning: The Case of the English Language in Singapore", in J. Tan et al. (eds) *Education in Singapore: A Book of Readings*, Singapore: Prentice-Hall.

Pallas, A. M. et al. (1994) "Ability Grouping Effects: Instructional, Social, or Institutional?", *Sociology of Education*, 67: 27-46.

Parsons, T. (1961) "The School Class as a Social System: Some of Its Functions in American Society", in A.H. Halsey, J. Floud, and C. A. Anderson (eds) *Education, Economy, and Society*, New York: Free Press.

Peters, W. (1971) *A Class Divided*, New York: Doubleday.

Quah, M. L., Sharp, P., Lim, A. S. E. and Heng, M. A. (1997) "Home and Parental Influence on the Achievement of Lower Primary School Children in Singapore", in J. Tan et al. (eds) *Education in Singapore: A Book of Readings*, Singapore: Prentice-Hall.

Quah, S. R. (1991) "Education and Social Class", in S. R. Quah, S. K. Chiew, Y. C. Ko and S. M. Lee (eds) *Social Class in Singapore*, Singapore: Centre for Advanced Studies, National University of Singapore.

Reid, I. (1986) *The Sociology of School and Education*, London: Fontana Press.

Rosenthal, R. and Jacobson, L. (1968) *Pygmalion in the Classroom*, New York: Longman.

Sharpe, L. and S. Gopinathan (1997) "Effective Island, Effective Schools: Repair and Restructuring in the Singapore School System", in J. Tan, S. Gopinathan, and W. K. Ho (eds) *Education in Singapore*, Singapore: Prentice Hall.

Sharp, R. and Green, A. (1975) *Education and Social Control*, London: Routledge and Kegan Paul.

Slavin, R. E. (1990) "Achievement Effects of Ability Grouping in Secondary Schools: A Best-Evidence Synthesis", *Review of Educational Research*, 60(3): 471-99.

Stockton, C. (????) in M.A. Gibson and J.U. Ogbu (eds) *Minority Status and Schooling*, New York: Grand Publishing.

Tan, E. (1999) *Seeing and Crafting Chinese Selves: A Study on Being Chinese in Singapore*, Honours thesis, Dept. of Sociology, National University of Singapore.

Tan, J. (1997) "Independent Schools in Singapore: Implications for Social and Educational Inequalities", in J. Tan et al. (eds) *Education in Singapore: A Book of Readings*, Singapore: Prentice-Hall.

Tham, S. C. (1989) "The Perception and Practice of Education", in K. S. Sandhu and P. Wheatley (eds), *Management of Success, The Moulding of Modern Singapore*, Singapore: Institute of Southeast Asian Studies.

Treiman, D. J. (1970) "Industrialization and Social Stratification", *Sociological Inquiry*, 40: 207-34.

Yip, J. S. K., Soo, P. E. and Yap, J. Y. C. (1997) "25 Years of Educational Reform", in J. Tan et al. (eds) *Education in Singapore: A Book of Readings*, Singapore: Prentice-Hall.

5

The Sociology of Work in Singapore

Hing Ai Yun

The field of Labour Studies in general is particularly beset with contention at present because the field has been so receptive to interdisciplinary and cutting edge approaches. In fact, this area of study has undergone a radical shift in coverage and focus during the past decade, reflecting the rapid material changes taking place in the real world. In comparison, thinking and research on work and labour in Singapore have been characterized by a singular lack of intellectual vitality. However, good work is being done now, not only by sociologists, but by economists, management specialists and legal practitioners as well. It is interesting to note that a major site for innovative thinking lies in the area of "feminist" labour studies and in the refreshing turns taken by theses so painstakingly crafted by students.

The centrality of the relationship between work and society for Sociology as an academic discipline is unquestioned. Since "life involves before everything else eating and drinking, a habitation, clothing and many other things, the first historical act is thus production of the means to satisfy these needs, the production of material life itself" (Marx and Engels 1974, 48). Furthermore, as production takes place in cooperation with others, the social relations in labour provide for the emergence of classes and shared ideas. In sum, these processes — work, division of labour, class, class relations and the role of ideas — are central to the understanding of complex capitalist societies and set the questions that are at the forefront of the analysis of labour and work. Foremost amongst the major issues studied in the field of the Sociology of Work is the problematising of work itself, for by now it is recognized that there is a massive variety of ways in which work can be socially organized. Other interrelated questions focus on the determinants of work organizations and how work organizations shape patterns of inequality in society. And finally, the kind of relationships people get involved in while working.

Drawing on their approach and orientation, I would say that literature on work in Singapore and related aspects can be identified as falling into one of three major types: official publications of tripartite agencies, the work of institutional economists, and sociological inquiries on work.

Tripartite Agencies Characterize Labour

The most prolific and up-to-date body of literature on labour is comprised of documents, handbooks and reports issued by official bodies constituting Singapore's tripartite system of labour regulation. This great stream of information provides a veritable feast of descriptive figures, which are useful for secondary analysis.

The Ministry of Labour is a repository of much valuable information on trends in major aspects of work and labour. Its data sources are regularly up-dated by large-scale national surveys set up explicitly to measure various dimensions of labour and aspects of behaviour which are thought to affect it. Most notable amongst its many regular publications are the Report on the Labour Force of Singapore (LFS) and the Singapore Yearbook of Labour Statistics (YLS). Initiated in 1974, the LFS is a useful source of longitudinal information on the size and characteristics of Singapore's labour force. It is currently based on a two-stage sample survey of about 26,000 households carried out in May-June of each year using primarily personal interviews. The YLS provides additional information on industrial accidents and diseases; the industrial relations scene; training and pay; sectoral shifts, and the composition and conditions of the labour market. *The Annual Report of the Ministry of Labour* provides a useful update on labour legislation and lists the most recent amendments to labour related provisions. A recent addition to this fast expanding body of statistical information on the Singapore Labour market is the *Digest of Singapore Labour Market Statistics* which takes a broader view of labour by paying attention to details of Singapore's female workforce and the older category of workers. The inclusion of comparative statistics is useful in contextualising Singapore's workforce in the world labour market. Both the YLS and the Digest are cognizant of the linkages between the conditions of labour and the general economic climate for they have included in their compendium a copious array of statistics indicating the state of the Singapore economy, past and present. Whether these are used as references or read in a systematic manner, they have something to offer the sociologist interested in many of the main topics of employment research. Though the contents need to be treated with the usual caution that we have learned to apply to "official statistics", for anyone willing to put a little effort into thinking beyond their formal presentation, they provide valuable information on the national labour scene.

Apart from this wide range of labour statistics, bodies integral to Singapore's tripartite labour regulation system have contributed substantially in other ways in enlarging the knowledge base in the field of labour studies in Singapore. I refer to the many ad hoc studies carried out to look into specific issues relevant to these institutions and organizations, with the sole purpose of searching for solutions to the many practical concerns facing them. A typical example is the report by the Committee on Third Shift titled "Promoting the Third Shift" (1998). I would like to make some comments on exercising caution so that these reports can be used in a more judicious manner. To correct the peculiar slant of these reports, one should always be conscious of the rationale behind the commissioning of these studies. Normally, some of these reports would draw on unpublished studies made by various government departments. Where the methodology is not explicitly stated and where slices of findings are drawn to support or to reject particular positions, the reader would have difficulty in assessing and thus in verifying supporting evidence cited and the conclusions arrived at. Wherever possible, it would be wise to obtain supplementary information, preferably from non-partisan sources, to arrive at a more "balanced" view. The reader should also be acquainted with the composition of the members making up the Committee preparing the study. As an example of the need to mesh findings originating from state with non-state sponsored sources, it would be instructive to briefly examine comparative findings from these two disparate sources on shift work.

According to the Committee on Third Shift, "COTS, the committee on Third Shift was formed to study issues relating to the third shift (11 pm – 7 am). It was to recommend measures to promote the acceptance of the third shift in the Singapore workforce, in order to increase Singapore's economic competitiveness and to meet demands of greater capital investment and automation" (1988, i).

The core of supporting evidence for this Report on Promoting the Third Shift (1988) came from three major unpublished studies conducted by the Ministry of Labour. One was a study by the Department of Industrial Health on the Health of Nightworkers in the Electronics Industry carried out in September-November 1986, based on self-administered questionnaires form 594 female production workers. The second was a survey on shift work in Singapore carried out in 1985, basically to ascertain patterns of shift work in various sectors. The last study comprises a survey on workers' attitudes toward shiftwork based on a sample of 1,750 workers. Drawing on the findings of these two impact studies on health and attitudes, the Committee then concluded that "the results... indicate no serious health problems even amongst those with fairly long periods of night shiftwork" and "there is no conclusive evidence that shift work, including the third shift, affects workers' health" because 76% of the respondents had expressed satisfaction with the system. 19.3% said they were somewhat satisfied while only 4.7% were not satisfied. The answers varied according to the different types of shift pattern refereed to. The COTS committee was constituted by seven members from the government (including one from a Statutory Board), six private sector members and three labour representatives.

Findings from COTS, however, should be read in the context of the study by the National Productivity Board (NPB) of 419 firms (comprising 927 manufacturing firms sampled, thus a response rate of 45.2%) on the prevalence, systems, gender participation rate and the difficulties experienced by employers in implementing shift work (National Productivity Board, 1980). This study concluded that "Despite difficulties experienced by these companies, it was highly unlikely that shift work would be abandoned" (1988, 110). Among the litany of problems cited were: lower output, high labour turnover and worker's refusal to work under the shift system.

Though not strictly comparable, the Young Christian Worker Report on the 12-Hour shift, done under auspices of three Christian groups and submitted to the Acting Minister of Labour is concerned also about the impact of shift work. Curiously enough, this study based on a survey of 74 workers with shift work experience in 17 companies and 176 workers without such experience was not mentioned by the COTS report. Carried out in December 1983, the survey by YCW which used 30 interviewers obtained some interesting findings which showed that 63% of the respondents now spend less time with their family; 67.6% were spending less time with friends and for 70% of the workers, their participation in self-improvement programmes was disrupted. Whereas COTS had concluded that workers need to adapt to shiftwork and adjustments must be made by both management and labour to help achieve this goal, the YCW Report had urged that the shift system be tempered to allow workers live a more humane and leisurely life. The YCW Report went on to assert that "the 12-hour shift is not an important factor in Singapore's continued economic growth. In fact, it runs counter to our national productivity campaign ... the introduction of the 12-hour shift has put many workers in a dilemma. For the sake of a job and for an increase in take-home pay, workers place their health, leisure, family life, self-esteem and various roles in jeopardy" (1988, 45).

The view of COTS and YCW therefore comprise two distinct approaches to the handling of emerging work practices necessitated by intensified competitive manufacturing. While the state and employers would urge workers to adapt to the "inevitable" consequences of capitalist processes, the church championing the workers thought otherwise. The NPB study indicates that blind adoption of capitalist strategy to maintain competitiveness can rebound on the operating efficiency of organizations. In order to achieve efficiency goals, studies of workers' discomfort and implicit resistance should be taken seriously to come up with more sensible corporate remedies. The sociological approach would give due recognition to the interplay between centralized formulation of corporate priorities and site-level management of labour. Despite widespread deployment of the rhetoric of competition, the sociological understanding would advise against an interpretation of management conduct which automatically assumes strategic coherence and operational efficiency.

Labour Studies to Improve Productivity

The second type of scholarly work on labour in Singapore is mainly derived from the work of economists and management specialists often employing sophisticated statistical techniques which contrast vividly with rather straightforward and simple conclusions. These are usually focused studies with limited objectives of proving or disproving particular hypotheses, with most having the tendency to nourish theories of "one best way" development path (universalism). When competently executed, however, they provide solid evidence useful to the study of Singapore's political economy.

The best example of the simple, descriptive, straightforward and easily readable type of work is the series of studies on Singapore's labour market closely associated with Pang Eng Fong (Pang 1980, Pang and Lim 1989). Pang (1980) traces the development of Singapore's economy, its labour force and the types of consumer goods owned by the general population. The comparative dimension is introduced in Pang and Lim(1989) which can also be characterized as a purely descriptive piece of work delineating the industrial process in the NIEs (Newly Industrialized Economies), their growing requirement for hi-tech labour; steps taken by governments to boost their supply of skilled labour and the impact of hi-tech on labour, on which there is indeed very little published data. Another work typical of this genre is that of Chew and Chew (1992). This study locates Singapore's workforce within the context of an increasingly competitive environment. It's objective is to assess labour market behaviour of both the employer and employee in order to maximize the utilization of Singapore's labour force. The study concludes that "with correct emphasis on job loyalty, heavy commitment of retraining, promotion of the flexible wage system and the CPF cum-social security scheme, and some form of preferential treatment of citizens, the Singapore Labour Force can remain competitive and stay at the top of Beri's list of quality workforce" (Chew & Chew 1992, 183).

It is however heartening to note that a new generation of more critical studies has emerged to add depth to the more simple descriptive writings of an earlier era. In reply to Pang and Lim (1982) which comprises a simple listing of the advantages and disadvantages of using foreign labour, Stahl (1984) provides some empirical evidence to rebut their arguments, which he criticized were "general in nature and not substantiated empirically". Stahl went a step further to show by means of a graphic model the losses incurred by supplier countries like Malaysia. While both these works combined can give us a clearer understanding of the use of foreign labour in Singapore, these accounts could have been made more comprehensive if they had placed their discussions on Singapore within the global process of economic restructuring.

The work of economists and management experts have in large measure been a gloss on public documents, and often differentiated little in tone and approach from handbooks published by various tripartite agencies. These studies normally take work structures and their emergence and evolution as given and non-problematic, within their explanatory framework eg those within neo-classical economics. In recent times, however, by imaginative use of statistical sources, some of these works have come close to addressing the relationship between labour process and the wider social relations. In particular, I would like to mention the work of Anantaraman (1990) which discusses how the distinctive forms of corporatist and populist forms of state regulation of labour in Singapore have conditioned workplace social relations, arguing that the state must be integral to any analysis of the politics of production.

Anantaraman's slim volume provides a comprehensive, authoritative and most important, credible account of the evolution of Singapore's industrial relations institutions and practices. Singapore's economic success is said to owe a great deal to its system of industrial relations. Anantaraman's account of the radical transformation of Singapore's industrial relations system is rooted in the linkage between unions, the ruling party and the State. The central focus is therefore on how labour discipline is enforced in Singapore. It is easy to forget in today's amicable industrial relations climate that the new corporatist mode of labour discipline stems from a background of violent contestation, all little more than four decades ago. Anantaraman's approach is rare in that it is shaped by a political economy perspective. Four features make this book distinctive. First, it contextualizes the evolution of Singapore's industrial relations system within the historical development of society and polity. Second, it links current structures of labour discipline to its historical roots since 1948. Thirdly, it locates the discussions within current theoretical debates on perspectives in industrial relations. Fourthly, it provides practitioners — both management and trade unionists – with a well-documented analysis of major labour legislation, collective bargaining prerequisites/ procedures and insightful comments on new directions. The discussions are presented in a concise and lively style. That Anantaraman's study forms a baseline for other studies is illustrated by the paper of Tan and Chew's (1997) which attempts to project Singapore's industrial relations system as a possible optimum role model for trade unions of the 21st century. Unfortunately, this projection ignores the historical development of Singapore's political economy which has seen the emergence of a strong state.

Another work by economists worthy of mention is that of Islam and Kirkpatrick (1986). The value of this work is that it addresses the effects of macro-economic developments on the lives of individuals and households via their participation status in the labour market. They first describe the evolution of Singapore's macro-economic structures from 1960-1984, characterizing it as "highly open" with "extreme dependence on foreign capital", with developmental phases shifting in sync with state machinations. The authors then show shifts in sectorial emphasis and how these in turn are reflected in labour market developments. The latter constitutes the core of Islam's analysis for its bearing on individual employment behaviour and remuneration. In all this, the state is shown as playing the pivotal role, for major policy shifts are intimately connected to new phases in Singapore's industrial development: "the short-lived regime of import substituting industrialization of the 1960s, the highly successful export-oriented industrialization throughout the 1970s, and the current phase of industrial restructuring" (Islam and Kirkpatrick 1986, 4). In coupling macro-economic features with labour market performance, income distribution and active state intervention, Islam and Kirkpatrick thus confront the social consequences of macro-economic issues which are often lost sight of, given the regular media ritual of presenting official figures on economic growth and performance. Both the work of Islam and Anantaraman's have located institutions and processes of labour relations within a wider analysis of the interplay between state policies, employer initiatives, production, and market imperatives.

The Sociology of Work in Singapore

While no sociological account on labour and changes today can be credible or comprehensive without locating it in the interplay between economy and society, the Sociology of Work definitely requires grounding in political economy. Sociological fare on labour grounded in political economy did not emerge in Singapore until the landmark work of Deyo (1981, 1989). The central concern for Deyo is the attempt to analyze and to account for the success of export-oriented industrialization. His study of the four Asian NIEs, Taiwan, South Korea, Hong Kong and Singapore shows how rapid growth experienced by these four economies was predicated upon the exploitation and subordination of the working classes even as these workers have attained significant real wage gains over the past several decades. Like most of the macro-economic studies discussed previously, works of Deyo attempt to find an answer to the first question in the Sociology of Work ie what determines and influences the organization of work as it is constituted in various contexts and societies by examining paths of industrialization and present labour organization in the four NIEs.

I have dwelt at some length on the work of economists and management consultants because they are the ones who have done most to further the field of Labour Studies albeit within their own rather positivistic and confined perspective. On the other hand, I have also noted encouraging signs of convergence in approaches with and increasing number of economists using the historical, dynamic and inter-relational mode of analysis. At the same time sociologists like Deyo have encroached into the field of economics by basing their work primarily within political economy, which is still considered by some sociologists here as non-mainstream.

In contrast, the work of "main-stream" sociologists in Singapore can be described as historical and synchronic. Quah et al. (1991) typifies this approach in their study of social stratification in Singapore and in doing so only manage to partially answer the second mega-question posed initially by this review — explaining the relationship between the organization of work (particularly the division of labour) and patterns of inequality in a society. Quah et al. (1991) is a classic example of the dominant employment aggregate approach to the study of stratification. Such studies have the tendency to be concerned with the application of particular stratification schemes by using a very limited number of dependent variables of which self-assigned class and party preference are most commonly taken as measures of class consciousness and socio-political affiliation. While not denigrating the effort and ingenuity that have gone into the operations of such studies, nor underestimating the importance of associated studies of social mobility and educational opportunity which are indispensable to an understanding of the dynamics of class at the macro-social level, it can be said that this type of classificatory approach displays only a very rudimentary theory of class formation and class processes. This is partly and not entirely due to the quite specific aim of this kind of stratification study which is overly concerned with observing methodological rigour. The narrow and precise goals of such studies are also reflected in Quah (1991, 244) "the three principal goals of this descriptive study are: to replicate the internationally known occupational prestige scales in the context of Singapore; to provide empirical information on Singapore's current social stratification hierarchy, that is, its social pyramid..."

In the same vein, one can describe the work of Mak and Leong (1993) which looks at three dimensions of the middle class — their socioeconomic position, political attitude and behaviour, and values and lifestyle. Their work is concerned with defining class boundaries by operating within a refashioned schema originally provided by Goldthorpe. Mak and Leong however, try to move away from the production of neat and tidy set of middle class categories. A chapter containing in-depth interviews with 18 individuals provide useful insights into the state of apathy and impotence of the middle class.

As it is however, much more attention needs to be paid to the process of class formation in Singapore. Studies on class should now include observations on how class processes are gendered and ethnicized, and how their incumbents come to acquire distinctive identities and organizational representation of their interests. This means getting away from chronic "boundary problems" of occupational class schemes, abandoning the distinct separation between class structure and class formation that goes with them, and at the very least, supplementing the findings of large scale cross sectoral survey research with detailed case studies that examine the process of class formation over time.

Up until now, this review has broadly concentrated on macro-analyses of labour-related issues covering areas that constitute dominant themes underlining conventional approaches to the study of work, for instance, industrialization, capitalism and rationalization. The reason is that in Singapore, until very recently, not much attention has been directed to examining labour issues at the micro level. This is unfortunate on two counts. First, one can scarcely hope to understand the problems of labour and industry without knowing the details of the labour process. Furthermore, the heart of the new Sociology of Work which draws heavily on labour process theory, feminism and segmented labour market analysis, has become the dominant approach since 1970s. The result has been the most powerful and empirically rich, non-reductionist accounts of the political and cultural constitution of labour relations.

Amongst the token representations of micro-level studies in Singapore are conventional investigations of work attitudes/ values. The work of Wimalasiri (1984) is mainly descriptive, relating a number of value items (subjective assessment of job standing, earnings, pride in work, job involvement, desire for job activity, striving for higher job level) with demographic variables like income, education, age, gender, ethnicity, and sector. Putti et al. (1989) in a similar type of study looked at the relationship between work values and company involvement and identification. Such studies have tended to transplant scales developed elsewhere onto the Singapore worker without any regard for their suitability.

While Wimalasiri studied a non-random sample of 75 workers from 48 different organisations, Putti et al.'s paper was based on a random sample of 350 (only 175 questionnaires were returned) workers in an American multinational corporation. In common with the parsimony and aim of such studies, the primary focus is describing the attitudes of workers. Interest in independent variables are confined to running correlational tests of attitudes with basic demographic components. Both investigations have failed to consider the worksite as a major influence in shaping workers' attitudes.

Located at one of the hot spots of the global economy today, it is inevitable that radical labour studies spawned in the West would soon take hold in Singapore, albeit after a short time lag. In eloquent contrast to Wilmalasiri (1984) and Putti et al. (1989) who are management specialists, micro-level analyses of labour carried out within the tradition of Sociology do not study workers as unrelated objects operating in a vacuum. Instead, micro-level labour studies in Sociology have focused attention on shop-floor experiences as crucial in shaping the wage earner's politics and identity. There is also interest in the texture of the wage earners' daily lives.

Beginning with the work of some commanding figures like E.P. Thompson and E.Hobsbawn, who are Marxists of an innovative strain, the field of labour studies began sometime ago to move from simple economic determinism. Doubts and revisions have since been proliferating, moving hand-in-hand with worldwide crises in labour politics. The failure of workers to initiate a new sociopolitical order and especially with the fall of communism, the strength of ethnic over class identities, and frustrations with inadequacies in dealing with gender inequality have all combined to challenge the focus on workplace and community, to force reorientation toward the issue of identity and an expanded sense of the political. While the study of culture and discourse at the workplace has drawn from symbolic anthropology (represented most notably by C. Geertz) and the literary theory of French philosopher Jaques Derrida, and the English cultural movement represented most prominently by Stuart Hall, expansion of the category of the political dimension was much influenced by the feminist movement, the later work of Foucault and the Gramscian current in recent Marxism.

There are some pioneering studies in Singapore which look at the social construction of work definitions and structures based on the new rhetorical paradigm for labour relations. Using phenomenogical and ethnomethodological ideas as "organizing device" (Chung 1989, 8), Chung's work has yielded rich data about "the everyday lives of women in a factory". In her words, the ethnography "explores the meanings and relevance of such terms as 'patriarchy', 'sexual division of labour', 'women's subordination' in experiential and interactional terms. The focus is on thoughts, aspirations and perceptions of women as social actors" (Chung 1989, 27). The core of this thesis is made up of three parts. The first is about "the meaning of waged work to the women". This section shows vividly "how factory and family are juxtaposed in the lives of the women and the gendered dimensions of both domains". In the second section, she discusses the processes through which "gender, class and work consciousness interlock". Chung very ably uses the example of the "target" in work performance to demonstrate how the implementation of managerial control intertwines with everyday resistance to produce patterns of power and subjectivity mediated through gender identities. The final part on the "nature of ethnicity" was added on as the research unfurled, indicating the salience of ethnicity on the shop-floor while at the same time demonstrating the superiority of the ethnographic method in the discovery of serendipity. This section is particularly rich in its apt quotations and in the subtlety of the analyses. The thesis is a valuable contribution to the growing area of feminist studies as well as to the library of shop-floor studies.

In a curious way, this study points to the limitations of the shop-floor based ethnography, a limitation partially brought about by a recognition of the central importance of gender. Part of it has to do with the methodology used, in that, such authors have the tendency to point to the way to read and understand the quotations and accounts on daily life on the shop-floor. Chung (1989, 145) asserted that "an attempt to feminise the job by management was to be seen in its adoption of the language of the domestic sphere as vocabulary of the work place. The term 'housekeeping' was used to mean tidying and clearing up of her workstation by an operator". Perhaps Chung was not aware that "housekeeping" is commonly used in factory environments regardless of the gender of the work force. In fact, it is not a pejorative term as this function is deemed crucial in the smooth running of a modern factory. In male-dominated work environments, housekeeping is one basic task to be performed by every worker and there is no connotation that it is a woman's job. It is similar to the requirement that workers should be clean and neatly dressed when they report for work. In a similar vein, Chung (1989, 145) pointed out that the supervisors addressed the operators as "girls" ... male operators were not referred to as "boy". A comparative design would reveal that in other sectors, bosses sometimes refer to their workers as "boys" – denoting power and possession over them rather than using the term for gender construction.

Ethnographic studies such as that of Chung have their use, even to policy makers who are more concerned to support their arguments with facts and figures provided by large-scale quantitative studies. I would like now just to juxtapose the distinct approaches taken by the ethnographic, survey and comparative studies to show how well they complement each other and should therefore be considered together for crafting policies that are effective and relevant to the lives of workers.

The Report of the Sub-committee on Manpower (1986, 9) stated, "According to the Annual Labour Force survey, a large majority of the non-working women indicated that they are unable to accept job offers because of housework and child care". Chung's study could be considered as a rebuttal to this commonsensical and simple answer.

"Yes, the women I studied felt the pressures of the domestic domain, but struggled against these as and when these forces contested their work lives. In their struggle, I find that the women were in fact committed to the work. If they were not, they would surely have given up the struggle" (Chung 1989, 82). The additional dimension raised on the work commitment of our female workforce should give a new slant to the problem of getting our female workforce onto the shop-floor. Are we not over-burdening our women by insisting that those tasks associated with the reproduction of society be their sole responsibility? In seeking their contribution to the nation's economic growth, should we not also as a nation assist in shouldering the responsibility of reproduction?

The Sub-committee on Manpower (1986, 41-42) also raised the issue of factors inhibiting productivity. Quoting from the National Survey on Knowledge, Attitude and Practice of Productivity (1984), they mentioned a list of hindrances to productivity performance and they include "(c) Poor work attitude" and "(d) uncertainty over the benefits of higher productivity". I point to these two obstacles to productivity just to show how Chung's work could help enlighten us further on these two serious "hindrances". From Chung's observations on how much work gets done on the shop-floor, we learn the mechanisms of pacing.

"This account however, revealed the essential tension, sometimes obvious, sometimes oblique, that existed between the women operators ... supervisors and management over the target that could be achieved. The women shared the belief that management was never satisfied. Once an operator showed that her target could be raised a little, management would keep trying to raise that. It was therefore important for the women not to let that happen and to maintain what they considered were the realistic and achievable levels of target ... In their everyday work, the operators paced themselves according to some kind of internal timing system" (Chung 1989, 148).

Glossing over factors (c) and (d) as "inhibiting factors" is futile for raising productivity, without giving due consideration to the costs and benefits of productivity. If Chung had had the opportunity to read the ethnographic work of Kuttan (1992) on productivity inducing strategies of shipyard managers, she would be in a better position to tease out what was peculiarly gender specific about the target. The remarkable work of Kuttan (1992, 79) reveals that targets are a more appropriate form of productivity control in assembly line work compared to work in the relatively more uncontrollable open space exemplified by work on the docks. Both these forms of work organization are observable in the shipyard. Targets are therefore not gender but task specific. It is through a comparative perspective that the researcher can gain such insights.

To recapitulate, this review has so far examined literature addressing two of the three questions posed in the Sociology of Work. The first question deals with the multiple forces shaping work organisations and how these have impacted on patterns of social inequality. The other question looks at relationships at the workplace. I now come to the third broad question asked in the Sociology of Work and that has to do with the meaning of work itself. For a long time now, studies on work have focused on male manual labour as the standard employment relationship. Two recent developments have contributed to questioning this long held image of labour as epitomized by the male proletariat. Both developments however, have roots in the same source. The increasing integration of housewives into the formal employment system has made them "visible" and as consequence, capitalist organizations are increasingly reluctant to support a system which assumes that males should be the breadwinner in a marriage. Likewise, flexible specialization and the search for new accumulation regimes have raised questions regarding standard forms of employment and given rise to the need to deconstruct work categories. The debate on flexible specialization is partly about the different ways in which labour may be organized and rests on the assumption that the standard form of employment is subject to possible variation. On the other hand, the debate about women's work derives from a recognition that there is in fact little that is given about who must perform what sort of labour.

The Singapore study that serves to point to this broader concept of work is *Superior Servants* by K.Gaw (1988). Despite a disclaimer to the contrary, this is a serious study of Cantonese women from the province of Kwantung in South China, who emigrated to Hong Kong, Malaya and Singapore, mainly in the 1930s to work as domestic servants. Despite non-academic credentials, Gaw has cleverly located this spate of female migration as a part of the extension of a world market for labour which started in the fifteenth century. By describing details of the labour process "involved in three main areas of domestic activity: minding the children, cooking, and household work" (1988, 9l), Gaw has given prominence to the importance of housework in so far as his account has drawn attention to the fact that labour in the house entails both ideological and material processes (raw inputs have to be purchased, meals have to be made from materials supplied). And, in tracing the story of these female workers to the customs and history of their village of origin, Gaw showed how these women's struggle to become first generation female waged workers was related to their fight to break the "web of disadvantage" traditional women were caught in.

On the traditional concept of work, Quah's (1984) work comparing four classes of professionals (doctors, lawyers, architects and engineers) should be mentioned for its clarity and comprehensiveness. This is an interesting and detailed historical study of four professions starting from the colonial period and covers three aspects of the professions: structural features, collective consciousness (more or less equivalent to self-perception) and influence. This work provides a solid starting point for anyone interested in working on any dimension of professional work in Singapore.

Conclusion

This review of existing literature on work in Singapore is highly selective. In particular, the review has highlighted three orientations guiding studies in this field of specialization. First, official bodies of Singapore's tripartite system of labour regulation have generated a huge body of literature defining the nature of work and labour relations in Singapore. Their main objective is to improve the competitiveness of Singapore's human resources in the world market for labour. Despite their peculiar slant, they often provide useful facts and figures for the discerning reader who can understand them within a sociological perspective. The second type of investigations, primarily by institutional economists can be characterized generally as more detailed extensions of studies undertaken by the state, employers and the unions. More critical and holistic studies, however, have now appeared, with a more historical and dynamic orientation. In taking this tack, the work of economists has begun to converge with that of sociologists whose work have a base in political economy.

The new sociology of labour rooted in feminism and the Foucauldian sense of politics has scarcely taken hold in Singapore. On the rare occasion when the new rhetoric on labour which conflates culture and politics has been used in Singapore, more often than not we do not see mainstream "practising" sociologists using this frame. Instead, the new scripting on labour studies has only begun to be deployed by the more innovative students working at both the post-graduate and undergraduate level. Apart from Chung (1989), studies sporting the language of radical discourses have now gradually come on stream, including the academic exercise of Wu P. (1993)

References

Anantaraman V. (1990) *Singapore Industrial Relations System*, Singapore: Singapore Institute of Management/Mc Graw-Hill Book Co.

Blum, A. A and Pataranapich, S. (1987) "Productivity and the Path to House Unionism: Structural Change in the Singapore Labour Movement", *British Journal of Industrial Relations*, 25(3): 389-400.

Chew, S. B. and Chew, R. (1992) *The Singapore Worker*, Singapore: Oxford University Press.

Chung, Y. K. (1989) *Gender, Work and Ethnicity: An Ethnography of Female Factory Workers in Singapore*, Ph.D. thesis, Dept. of Sociology, National University of Singapore.

Deyo, C. F. (1981) *Dependent Development and Industrial Order*, New York: Praeger Publishers.

Deyo, C. F. (1989) *Beneath the Miracle: Labour Subordination in the New Asian Industrialism*, Berkeley: University of California Press.

Deyo, C. F. (1989) "Labour and Development Policy in East Asia", *Annals of the American Academy of Political and Social Science*, 505: 152-57.

Digest of Singapore Labour Market Statistics (1991), Singapore Institute of Labour Studies.

Gaw, K. (1988) *Superior Servants*, Singapore: Oxford University Press.

Islam, I. and Kirkpatrick, C. (1986) *Wages, Employment and Income Distribution in a Small, Open Economy: The Case of Singapore*, New Delhi: ILO-ARTEP.

Kuttan, S. G. (1992) *Industrial Workers in Modern Singapore*, M.Soc.Sc. Thesis, Dept. of Sociology, National University of Singapore.

Mak, L. F. and Leong, C. H. (1993) *East Asian Middle Class Research Project: The Singapore Middle Class* (Unpublished Report).

Marx, K. and Engels, F. (1974) *The German Ideology*, Part 1, London: Lawrence and Wishart.

Ministry of Labour Annual Report.

National Productivity Board, Annual Report.

National Productivity Board (1980) *Shift Work in Industry*, Singapore.

National Productivity Board (1984) *National Survey on Knowledge, Attitude and Practice of Productivity*, Singapore.

Pang, E. F. (1980) "Employment, Development and Basic Needs in Singapore", *International Labour Review* 19(4): 495-504.

Pang, E. F. and Lim, L. (1982) "Foreign Labour and Economic Development in Singapore", *International Migration Review*, 548-76.

Pang, E. F. and Lim, L. (1989) "Hightech and Labour in the Asian NICs", *Labour and Society*, 14: 43-57.

Putti, J. et al. (1989) "Work Values and Organizational Commitment", *Human Relations*, 42(3): 275-88.

Promoting the Third Shift (1988) Committee on Third Shift.

Quah, S. (1984) *Balancing Autonomy and Control*, Centre for International Studies, MIT.

Quah, S. R. et al. (1991) *Social Class in Singapore*, Singapore: Times Academic Press.

Report on the Census of Industrial Production, Research and Statistics Unit, Economic Development Board.

Report on the Labour Force of Singapore, Research and Statistics Department, Ministry of Labour.

Report of the Sub-committee on Manpower (1986).

Report on Wages in Singapore, Research and Statistics Department, Ministry of Labour.

Singapore Yearbook of Labour Statistics (various years), Ministry of Labour.

Stahl, C. W. (1984) "Singapore's Foreign Workforce: Some Reflections on Its Benefits and Costs", *International Migration Review,* XVIII (I): 37-49.

Tan, E. S. and Chew, I. (1997) "The New Role of Trade Unionism in the 21st Century: Lessons from Singapore", *The Economic and Labour Relations Review,* 8(1): 7-21.

Wimalasiri, J. (1984) "Correlates of Work Values of Singapore Employees", *Singapore Management Review,* 6(1): 51-75.

Wu, P. (1993) *Life and Work in a Small Factory,* Dept. of Sociology, Academic Exercise, National University of Singapore.

The YCW Report on 12-Hour Shift (1983) The Young Christian Workers Movement, The Justice and Peace Commission, and The Christian Family Social Management.

6

Medical Sociology

Paulin T. Straughan

This chapter will detail the development of medical sociology in Singapore. Although medical sociology was introduced as an undergraduate module in the Department of Sociology only in 1996, research on medical sociology has been conducted since the 1970s. As in the US where medical sociology enjoys a prominent position in the discipline, work on medical sociology in Singapore tends to be multidisciplinary in nature, and reflect a collaboration between sociologists and members of the medical faculty. Grants for medical sociology research have been obtained from both international sources (including World Health Organization) and the National University of Singapore.

An overview of the work published since 1976 shows that the progress of medical sociology in Singapore can be categorized into two main areas: work on the impact of the social environment on health, and research on the dynamics at play in the health care system.

The Social Environment and Health

Much of the research that falls in this category tends to be applied in nature and focused primarily on preventive health behaviour. The studies investigated the barriers to and facilitators of preventive health measures. These studies are critical in that they invoked social factors as key players in health promotion and disease prevention, and thus, steered away from traditional medical models which stipulated that disease prevention is merely confined to germ theory and biological warfare. In order for such findings to be effectively translated to policy, it is necessary that social scientists find partners in the medical profession. By and large, the studies conducted so far are the result of cooperation between social scientists and medical professionals. Recent studies include a multiphase project collaboration between Sociology, Community Medicine, and the Ministry of Health on breast screening in Singapore, a large-scale community-based survey on health care utilization and attitudes towards health care issues, and a multi-institutional collaboration between Sociology and psychiatrists on mental health.

Acceptability of Cancer Screening

In 1995, a National Breast Screening Exercise was initiated by the Ministry of Health to assess the efficacy of mammography in reducing mortality due to breast cancer among Asian women. While the primary concern of the Exercise was to assess efficacy of mammographic screening, it was recognized that public acceptability of the screen was a critical issue too. To assess acceptability, a four-phase multidisciplinary project was initiated, and collaborators from Sociology, Department of Community, Occupational, and Family Medicine, and National Breast Screening Project Committee worked together to achieve a better understanding of the barriers to and facilitators of breast screening.

The first phase of the project was a qualitative, focus groups study aimed at generating hypotheses that illuminated barriers faced by Singapore women with regard to cancer and cancer prevention. The researchers felt that screening acceptability is culturally sensitive and thus, models derived and validated in western cultures may not necessarily suit the local context. This proved to be a critical decision. In the focus groups interviews, several important and unpredicted concepts surfaced (for details, see Straughan and Seow 1995). In particular, the notion of fate was a dominant theme, particularly for the Chinese respondents. The women interviewed were cautious about screen tests because of a strong belief in fate, or predestination. Those who were more fatalistic tend to avoid discussions on cancer, and refused to participate in screen tests designed to detect cancer.

To test this and other hypotheses generated from the qualitative study, a community-based survey of a representative sample of women between 45-69 years was launched. Several barriers and facilitators were identified and tested against acceptability of several cancer screen tests, including mammography, clinical breast examination, breast self-examination, and the Pap smear test for early detection of cervical cancer. One major contribution of this phase of the study was the validation of some new scales that were designed specifically for the local cultural context. These scales had significant explanatory power in the analysis of variation in health screening behaviour. For example, a seven-point index measuring fatalism was designed and validated. The scale was significantly associated with acceptability of the four cancer screen tests (see Straughan and Seow 1998).

When the Breast Screening Exercise was launched, the team also surveyed the women who were invited to the free screening. A survey of the participants was conducted at the screening site, and non-participants were interviewed at home. The barriers and facilitators identified were documented in two articles (Seow et al. 1997, Seow et al. 1998). Overall, the findings reinforced findings of earlier studies (Seow 1994, Lim 1993, Straughan 1991). Women who were more educated, of higher income, and who were socially connected were more likely to participate in breast screening.

In addition to perceived attitudes, one key finding that surfaced in both the qualitative study and the surveys was the importance of social support. Since the surveys were all cross-sectional in design, cause and effect could not be established. To lend weight to the argument that social support has an influence on acceptability of mammograms, a prospective study was done at the last stage of the project.

With funding from the University Academic Research Grant and the Breast Cancer Screening Project, a randomised trial was conducted on a nationwide representative sample of 1,500 women. Two test instruments were designed to promote attendance. The first was a personalized pamphlet with information directed at fears and concerns that were highlighted in the community-based surveys. The second intervention involved invoking social support. Instead of addressing the benefits of breast screening to the women involved, the pro-screening information was directly conveyed to the women's spouse or adult children. It was hypothesized that if social support was effective, then the spouse/adult child would be able to motivate the woman to attend the free screening.

The women were randomly divided into three groups, and all three groups were invited to a free mammogram. One group was designated to be the control group, and the group members were sent a standard reminder letter to the free screening. The second group was test group 1, and women in this group were sent the standard reminder letter as well as the personalized health pamphlet. The third group was test group 2, and trained female field workers visited the homes of these women and delivered the standard reminder letter as well as the personalized health pamphlet to the addressee's spouse or adult child. The results showed that the attendance rate for test group 2 was significantly higher than the other two groups (Seow et al. 1998).

Other Preventive Health Measures

The second major study on medical sociology completed recently was a community-based survey on health care utilization and health perceptions. This study is an attempt to follow up on earlier studies done on preventive health in Singapore. Data analysis is on-going.

The same investigator had used the Health Belief Model to study preventive health behaviour in Singapore (Quah 1985a). In the earlier study, Quah used the factors stipulated in the Health Belief Model (which included perceived susceptibility, benefits, and severity of the disease) as well as some background factors (social class, age, religion, sex, exposure to mass media and future orientation) to explain variation in three forms of preventive health behaviour: cancer, heart disease and tuberculosis. The results showed that the Health Belief Model was not appropriate for analyzing preventive health behaviour in Singapore. The data failed to support the three key criteria laid down by the Health Belief Model. Instead, the findings showed that ethnicity was an important consideration in explaining variation in preventive health behaviour. In addition, the study also showed that in the analysis of alcohol consumption and smoking behaviour, gender should be controlled as cultural norms in Singapore tend to restrict women from such activities.

Quah published two other articles on another aspect of preventive health in Singapore — the concept of self-medication. In lieu of the rising formal health care costs, the promotion of self-medication is one possible strategy to decrease public demand on institutional health services.

The first study found that about 40% of Housing and Development Board (public housing) dwellers in Singapore practised self-medication (Quah 1977). Self-medication was mainly in the form of having over-the-counter medication; a smaller proportion reported that they stored traditional medication at home. The analysis revealed that formal education is the strongest predictor of whether an individual practices self-medication. This is expected since a rise in formal education correlates with greater exposure to the mass media. And through the mass media, information on drugs and their efficacy are channelled. This study confirmed the importance of education on health behaviour.

A later study on the same topic six years later found a rise in the number who practised self-medication (Quah 1985b). In addition to education, ethnicity and gender were significant factors correlated with the practise of self-medication. However, only bivariate analysis was carried out, so it is not certain if these correlations will be sustained when other factors are controlled for.

In light of the growing concern on AIDS and other sexually transmitted diseases, several studies have been published in these areas. The latest focused on public attitudes towards AIDS and AIDS prevention (Quah 1992b). The study found significant differences in perceptions among the various ethnic groups. The paper offered some tentative explanations to account for the differences.

Condom use as a means of prevention against sexually transmitted diseases (including AIDS) was investigated in two studies. The first was a survey of 806 sex workers in Singapore who attended a public STD clinic for mandatory regular STD and HIV screening. The survey showed that while 73.3% of the sex workers always negotiated for condom use, they succeeded only half the time in convincing their clients to use a condom (see Wong et al.

1992). Subsequently, a qualitative study was conducted on a sub-sample of 40 sex workers to explore the perceived barriers and approaches in the negotiation of condom use (see Wong et al. 1994). Questions on perceived susceptibility to acquiring AIDS, personal values on health, self-efficacy and strategies used in getting clients to use condoms were discussed in detail in the face-to-face interviews.

In the 1970s when birth control was a social issue, two papers were published in this area. Quah (1979) looked at the socio-economic variations in the perception of the side-effects of contraceptives in Singapore. Specifically, three methods of contraception (the pill, intrauterine device and sterilization) were examined. Overall, two main sets of results surfaced. First, there was significant variation in the perception of the side effects of contraceptive across the different ethnic groups as well as social classes. Second, there was a class-based as well as gender-based difference in the level of knowledge of contraception. In addition to the empirical contributions, the study also provided a clear, comprehensive description of family planning policy and sterilisation patterns in Singapore in the 1970s.

On a more general note, a preliminary study was completed by Phoon et al. (1976) on the health status of residents in three Housing and Development Board estates (Queenstown, Jurong and Toa Payoh). Three major findings surfaced. First, the preference for, and the selection of, the first source of medical treatment varied with social class. Second, ethnicity was statistically associated with self-medication. And third, education had a significant effect on when antenatal care was received. In addition, the study also probed into some aspects of mental health. Social class was found to be associated with the level of worry and anxiety experienced.

There is a growing awareness of the importance of sociology in mental health research. To date, two mental health projects have been successfully completed. Both were results of collaboration between social scientists and medical professionals. The first project on work stress gained much media attention. The multidisciplinary research team (comprising three sociologists, two medical researchers and one psychologist) explored the sources of work stress and coping mechanisms engaged by six professional groups (teachers, lawyers, nurses, engineers, doctors and life insurance personnel) (see Chan et al. 2000). The results suggested a high correlation between subjective assessment of work stress and internal control. The methods of coping with perceived stress were detailed in the report. Most of the methods relied on individual efforts at behaviour modification (eg, working harder, finding alternative means to solve problems, learning to live with the problem). Not surprisingly, seeking professional or psychological help was among the least frequently used means of coping with work stress. Of the six professional groups studied, the teachers interviewed reported the highest level of work stress.

The second project on mental health resulted in two well-publicised papers on post-stroke depression (Chan et al. 1995, Ng et al. 1995). The findings were based on a study of 52 stroke patients at the Tan Tock Seng Hospital. In addition to the profile description of the stroke patients, the authors also found that post-stroke depression was unlikely to be caused by neuronal injury due to the cerebrovascular accident (as suggested in the mental health literature). On the contrary, the findings implied that post-stroke depression might be a reaction to physical and social disabilities. Therefore, the efficacy of social intervention in post-stroke patients in preventing the onset of depression should be re-evaluated. One paper won the Singapore Psychiatric Association Scientific Research Prize (1993). The abstract of the other was cited in *Focus on Depression* (Netherlands) and *CME Review* (NUH, Singapore).

Evaluating the Health Care System

Unlike the studies highlighted in the previous section, work that falls in this category is more theoretical in nature. They are work done by sociologists, and focused generally on analysing the dynamics at play in the health care system. Compared to applied medical sociology, these papers are also more evaluative and critical.

The research reviewed in this category can be grouped into three sections: evaluating health policies, sociology of medical professionals, and analysis of the doctor-patient relationship.

In "Health Policy and Traditional Medicine in Singapore", Quah (1981) addressed the role of government management in Singapore's health policy. The article took a historical perspective in analysing the evolution of Singapore health policies from 1965 till 1970s. Quah argued that the Singapore health policy went through four major phases since 1965. The first involved the reorganization of public health and primary health care services. This was followed by the expansion of the primary health care services. The third stage saw the provision of highly specialised, hospital-based health care services. Finally, the fourth phase involved the emphasis on health education and other preventive health services. In relation to the latest stage of progress in health policy, Quah also highlighted the importance of a dual health care system, where traditional Chinese healers work hand-in-hand with the modern health care providers.

In relation to the dual-utilization of traditional and modern medical systems, Quah's book, *The Triumph of Practicality* (1989a), provided a thorough and comprehensive analysis of how the two seeming opposing medical systems coexist in society. Insights were drawn from five Asian countries undergoing rapid modernization (China, Japan, Hong Kong, Thailand and Singapore). Three key concerns were addressed in the book. The first focused on the prominent patterns of dual utilization, the second explored the impact of modernization on dual utilization, and the third highlighted the role of the government in the integration of the two medical systems. In Quah's essay ("The best bargain: medical options in Singapore"), a history of the medical options available in Singapore is detailed. In the chapter, she also developed the notion of "pragmatic acculturation", the process which explained how Singaporeans practise dual-utilization. Quah argued that Singaporeans would adopt health care practices that are perceived to be beneficial to them, even if the practices contradict their own cultural beliefs and practices. Thus, while the western biological model differs very much from the traditional medical systems, Singaporeans successfully extracted elements from these different systems that are perceived to be effective in promoting their health status. They resolve the contradictions in a pragmatic fashion ie, as long as the combination of health care practices worked, they internalized the "hybrid" system.

One major concern in health policies is how we deal with diseases that are highly stigmatized. In her essay on AIDS, Quah

(1992b) focused on the social obstacles to AIDS prevention. The prevention of AIDS, the author proposed, may operate through influencing individual behaviour (micro-level intervention) and through social policies (macro-level intervention). With respect to effecting changes in individual behaviour, three main obstacles to AIDS prevention were highlighted. The first obstacle was the issue of privacy. High-risk behaviours (like casual sex and drug abuse) which put the individual in the dangerous position of contracting the AIDS virus belonged to the realm of the individual's private choices. It is very difficult to effect change in the individual's private choices. The second obstacle to AIDS prevention was the tendency for individuals (even those who were in the high risk group) to believe that they would never contract AIDS. The final obstacle put forth by the author, and perhaps the most formidable obstacle to seeking medical help for AIDS, was the fear of social stigmatization. This fear also hindered the AIDS patient from informing his significant others of the disease and therefore, contributed to further spread of the virus. With respect to social policies that affect AIDS prevention, four aspects were addressed in the paper: the screening of blood for transfusion, mandatory testing for HIV, reaching sexual contacts of HIV infected persons, and educational campaigns.

There is also research that examines various aspects of the health care system. To fully understand the social status of the medical profession in any society, one has to trace the historical evolution of that profession. Quah (1989b) engaged a historical perspective to examine the structure of the medical profession in Singapore. The paper detailed the structure of the medical profession, the internal organization of the profession, and how these factors influence the social position of the profession in Singapore.

A more recent project funded by the University looked at professionalisation of nurses in Singapore. Like most developed countries, Singapore faces a severe shortage of nurses. To cope with the shortage, hospitals have to resort to hiring foreign nurses. To address this pressing problem, the project looked at factors that affected attrition among hospital nurses. Several new scales on job satisfaction, occupational values, and professionalism were designed and validated (Straughan and Tan 1998, Tan and Straughan 1996). The effects of shift work were also investigated in a preliminary paper (Straughan and Tan 1996).

Two papers looked at the relationship between the medical profession and the general public through the doctor-patient interaction. The first examined a crucial dimension of the doctor-patient relationship, the patient's right to know. Quah (1989c) discussed this issue from three perspectives. First, the patient's right to know about his medical condition was argued based on three key features of the doctor-patient relationship (namely the common goals shared by the doctor and patient, the potential for conflict in the relationship, and the "bumpkin" fallacy which assumes that the patient is ignorant and therefore, in no position to assess objectively any medical information given to him). Following this, the second perspective looked at the assumed benefits and consequences of the patient's ignorance, and finally, the patient's right to know in relation to the concept of informed consent is elaborated on.

A more general look at the doctor-patient relationship was the focus of an Academic Exercise by Kerk (1992). Kerk looked at how patient satisfaction and compliance were influenced by the subjective experiences within the doctor-patient encounter. The paper compared a patient-centred approach to a doctor-dominant approach in the doctor-patient relationship. The author concluded that, with the rise in education and consumerism, patients were more aware of their right to be treated as equal partners in the doctor-patient encounter.

Future Directions for Medical Sociology Research

So far, the range of research interests in medical sociology in Singapore has been a strong applied orientation. The course of research has helped us understand more about how the social environment affects mental and physical well-being. The findings demonstrated quite clearly the important contributions sociology can make in an area which has been dominated by the hard sciences. From a micro perspective, we learned more about the influence of social factors on preventive health behaviour and the perception of health. The macro research revealed the dynamics involved in the health care system and how the various components (like the formal health care agents vis-à-vis the traditional healers, patient-doctor interactions) negotiate the distribution of power. Where should medical sociology research proceed from here?

As in most of the industrialized developed nations, medical costs in Singapore are on the rise. Recently, in an attempt to combat rising costs, the Singapore Government revised the Civil Service medical benefits scheme. Under the old medical benefits scheme (Co-Payment on Ward Scheme), the Government assumed responsibility for the health status of the civil servants. All outpatient and pharmaceutical costs were paid for by the employer and the employer also reimbursed the bulk of the hospitalization charges. The two new schemes, Comprehensive Co-Payment Scheme (CSS) and the Medisave Cum Subsidized Outpatient Scheme (MSO), place more responsibility on the employee. Under the CSS, employees are responsible for 15% of all medical costs incurred (ie, costs which were formally subsidized by the employer). The MSO scheme focuses even more on rewarding the employer who maintains a good level of health. Under the MSO, the employer no longer subsidizes hospitalization costs. In lieu of hospitalization benefits, an additional 1% of the gross salary will be channelled into the employer's Medisave account (which can be used to pay for medical expenses incurred by the employee and his/her dependants).

Clearly, the State is now putting the onus of well-being on the individual. In a climate where health care costs are rising and where the individual is no longer protected by generous employee medical benefits, preventive health is a crucial issue. If preventive health is widely practised, the incidence of illnesses would decrease. More importantly, when serious diseases are detected in the early stages of development, the costs incurred (both in terms of fiscal cost of treatment as well as intangible costs of pain, emotional trauma etc) are also likely to be much lower.

Thus, in terms of suggestions for future research in the discipline of medical sociology, preventive health issues are important areas which deserve much focus. There are several areas of possible research. First, the utilization of accessible screen tests (like mammograms, pap smear, cholesterol blood tests). There are many serious diseases which can be arrested if detected early. For example, if breast cancer is detected in the early stages of development (ie stage 1), there is a very high likelihood that the cancer can be arrested with relatively low discomfort to the patient (ie there is no need for mastectomies, intensive radiotherapy or intravenous chemotherapy). Therefore, medical sociology research can contribute invaluable information on the social factors that predispose individuals to adopt regular screening for early detection of serious diseases.

The second research area on preventive health which warrants attention is in preventive health behaviour. There is a significant link between health status and lifestyle. In particular, consumption behaviour (especially diet) and regular exercise both lead to healthier dispositions. Empirical research on lifestyles of Singaporeans with special emphasis on health concerns will help build a valuable database for public health policy makers to tap on.

In relation to the above-mentioned research concerns, it is also important to explore the cultural meanings attached to preventive health. In many societies, public health officials are constantly baffled by the irrational decisions people make regarding preventive health. For example, many women do not practise breast self-examination or go for regular mammograms because they believe that such actions would "tempt fate". In a multiethnic society like Singapore, it is of interest both sociologically as well as from the medical perspective to explore the different meanings to preventive health attributed by the various cultures.

Medical sociology research in the US has explored quite extensively the influence of informal social networks on health issues. For example, it was found that individuals who were socially integrated in informal support networks (eg they were married, they had more social contact with friends and family) have been shown to enjoy greater psychological well-being (see O'Leary 1984), have greater life satisfaction (Thoits 1982), enjoy less stressful lives (Pearlin et al. 1981), have better self-perceived health (Hibbard 1985, Krause 1987, Straughan 1988) and live longer (Berkman and Syme 1979, Eisenberg 1979). In particular, the landmark study conducted by Berkman and Syme (1979) in Alameda County (California) found that respondents with few social contacts suffered higher rates of morbidity and mortality. Later studies by Howe (1981) and Gravell et al. (1985), found that women who were involved in quality support networks were more likely to engage in breast self-examination (BSE) each month. Both studies reported that women who received social support from their informal networks for performing BSE tend to perform BSE more regularly. In addition, a survey conducted in the US found that women who were integrated in their informal support networks were more likely to adopt regular screening for early detection of cervical cancer (see Straughan 1991).

All these studies lend support to the argument that the informal support network (of family members and close friends) is an invaluable resource, especially in the area of health research. In addition, the work by Straughan and Seow on breast screening in Singapore had also demonstrated the effectiveness of mobilising the informal support network in cancer screening. The role of the family support network as well as the support network of non-kin in the prevention of morbidity and mortality should be further investigated in Singapore. In an era where health care costs are on the rise, the link between informal social support and well-being could prove to be important. As a resource, informal support networks are inexpensive, easily accessible and, more importantly, it is a resource that is available to almost everyone.

Preventive measures can only be effective if we can understand the aetiology of diseases. While statistical correlations may highlight certain trends, we can only use these results to effect disease prevention if we can understand **why** these correlations exist. For example, the mortality statistics in Singapore show a consistent ethnic correlation with certain diseases. To understand why the Chinese, for example, are predisposed to colorectal cancer, we have to contextualise the link between ethnicity and cancer. There is a large multidisciplinary project in progress that addresses this concern. The project looks at the implications of ethnicity for heart disease and colorectal cancer (Quah et al. 1999).

Finally, in relation to the high costs of formal medical care, more attention should be focused on the alternative forms of healing in our society. For example, more research should be directed at the availability and utilization of chiropractors, natural and homoeopathist, as well as traditional Chinese healers. With formal health care costs on the rise, more people are likely to turn to alternative forms of healing. Therefore, from a sociological perspective, it is important for us to achieve a better understanding of these alternative healers and how they complement modern medicine.

In the next millennium, one area that will dominate headlines is medical technology. With the advent of developments that can prolong life as well as generate life, we need to take a critical look at the social implications of these technological advancements. For example, the availability of assisted reproductive technologies (ART) which includes invitro-fertilisation (IVF) and other subfertility treatments, the implications for involuntary childless couples is tremendous. Tan's (1999) preliminary data details some of the rich, intriguing dynamics at play when sub-fertile couples embark on fertility treatment. It documents some of the contradictions that surface in the advent of new technologies. Her qualitative data details the state of liminality that sub-fertile couples are locked in. Because reproductive technology represents hope for these couples, they define themselves as "not yet pregnant" and the women continue to subject their bodies to medical intervention, in hope that at some point, they will acquire biological parenthood.

The practice of medicine does not occur in isolation. Issues of health and illnesses are very much embedded in a social setting and the intricacies can only be fully understood with the contribution of sociology. Health care issues affect everyone. The health care system, with its many players, is a dynamic set-up governed by social processes. Unless we understand these processes, there will be many "unsolved mysteries" in an area that touches each of us personally.

References

Berkman, L. F. and Syme, S. L. (1979) "Social Networks, Hosts Resistance, and Mortality: A Nine-year Follow-up Study of Alameda County Residents", *American Journal of Epidemiology*, 109(2): 186-204.

Chan, K. L., Ng, K. and Straughan, P. T. (1995) "Post Stroke Depression: Outcome Following Rehabilitation", *Australian and New Zealand Journal of Psychiatry*, 29: 609-14.

Chan, K. B., Lai, G., Ko, Y. C., and Boey, K. W. (2000) "Work Stress among Six Professional Groups: The Singapore Experience", *Social Science & Medicine,* 50: 1415-432.

Eisenberg, L. (1979) "A Friend, Not a Doctor a Day, Will Keep the Doctor Away", *American Journal of Medicine,* 66: 551.

Gravell, J., Zapka, J. G. and Mamon, J. A. (1985) "Impact of Breast Self-examination Planned Educational Messages on Social Network Communications: an Exploratory Study", *Health Education Quarterly,* 12(1): 51-64.

Hibbard, J. H. (1985) "Social Ties and Health Status: an Examination of Moderating Factors", *Health Education Quarterly,* 12(1): 23-34.

Howe, H. L. (1981) "Social Factors Associated with Breast Self Examination among High Risk Women", *American Journal of Public Health,* 71 (3): 251-55.

Kerk, W. S. (1992) *A Sociological Analysis of Doctor-Patient Relations,* Academic Exercise presented to the Dept. of Sociology, National University of Singapore.

Krause, N. (1987) "Satisfaction with Social Support and Self-rated Health in Older Adults", *The Gerontologist,* 27: 301-8.

Lim, Weiling (1993) *Preventive Health Behaviour: A Study of Breast Self-Examination Among Women in Singapore,* Academic Exercise presented to the Dept. of Sociology, National University of Singapore.

Ng, K. C., Chan, K. L. and Straughan, P. T. (1995) "Study of Post-stroke Depression in a Rehabilitation Centre", *ACTA Psychiatrica Scandinavica,* 92(1): 75-9.

O'Leary, T. J. (1984) *Alone at the Wheel: a Study of Social Solidarity and Automobile Accidents,* Dissertation presented to the Graduate Faculty of the University of Virginia.

Pearlin, L. I., Lieberman, M. A., Menaghan, E. G. and Mullan, J. T. (1981) "The Stress Process", *Journal of Heath and Social Behaviour,* 22: 337-56.

Phoon, W. O., Quah, S., Tye, C. Y., and Leong, H. K. (1976) "A Preliminary Study of the Health of a Population Staying in High Rise Apartments in Singapore", *Annals of Tropical Medicine and Parasitology*, 70(2): 231-46.

Quah, S. R. (1977) "Self-medication: a Neglected Dimension of Health Behaviour", *Sociological Symposium*, 19: 20-36.

Quah, S. R. (1979) *Socio-economic Variations in the Perception of Side-effects of Contraceptives*, Singapore: SEAPRAP Research Report No. 34.

Quah, S. R. (1981) "Health Policy and Traditional Medicine in Singapore", *Social Science and Medicine*, 15A(2): 149-56.

Quah, S. R. (1985a) "The Health Belief Model and Preventive Health Behaviour in Singapore", *Social Science and Medicine*, 21(3): 351-63.

Quah, S. R. (1985b) "Self-medication in Singapore", *Singapore Medical Journal*, 26(2): 123-29.

Quah, S. R. (1986) "Social Science and Illness Prevention: an Overview of the Health Belief Model", *Journal of Social and Economic Studies*, 3(4): 345-47.

Quah, S. R. (1989a) *The Triumph of Practicality*, Singapore: Institute of Southeast Asian Studies.

Quah, S. R. (1989b) "The Social Position and Internal Organisation of the Medical Profession in the Third World: the Case of Singapore", *Journal of Health and Social Behaviour*, 30: 450-66.

Quah, S. R. (1989c) "The Patient's Right to Know: Some Sociological Considerations", *Singapore Medical Journal*, 30(2): 184-88.

Quah, S. R. (1992a) "The Market Situation of Sociological Research and Expertise: the Case of Medical Sociologists", *Sociology of Health Newsletter*, 25: 3-9.

Quah, S. R. (1992b) "AIDS and Us: Are We Failing to Prevent a Highly Preventable Disease?" *Singapore Medical Journal*, 33(5): 484-88.

Quah, S. R. (1999) "Ethnicity, HIV/AIDS Prevention and Public Health Education", *Health and Social Policy*, 18(7/8): 1-26.

Seow, A., Straughan, P. T., Ng, E. H., Emmanuel, S. C., Tan, C. H. and Lee, H. P. (1997) "Factors Determining Acceptability of Mammography in an Asian Population: a Study among Women in Singapore", *Cancer Causes & Control,* 8: 771-79.

Seow, A., Straughan, P. T., Ng, E. H., Emmanuel, S. C., Tan, C. H. and Lee, H. P. (1998) "Population-based Mammographic Screening in Singapore: What are Participants' Views?" *Annals (Academy of Medicine),* 27: 154-60.

Seow, A., Straughan, P. T., Ng, E. H., and Lee, H. P. (1998) "A Randomised Trial of Print Material and Face-to-face Contact to Improve Mammography Uptake among Initial Non-attenders in an Asian Population", *Annals (Academy of Medicine),* 27(6): 838-42.

Seow, A., Wong, M. L., Smith, W. C. S. and Lee, H. P. (1994) "Beliefs and Attitudes as Determinants of Cervical Cancer Screening: a Community-based Study in Singapore", Unpublished paper.

Straughan, P. T. (1988) *Informal Support Networks and the Perceived Health Status of the Elderly in the US,* M.A. Thesis presented to the Graduate Faculty of the University of Virginia.

Straughan, P. T. (1991) *Social Integration and Preventive Health Behaviour: an Exploratory Study on the Use of the Pap Smear Test for the Early Detection of Cervical Cancer,* Dissertation presented to the Graduate Faculty of the University of Virginia.

Straughan, P. T. and Seow, A. (1995) "Barriers to Mammography among Chinese Women in Singapore: a Focus Group Approach", *Health Education Research,* 10(4): 431-41.

Straughan, P. T. and Seow, A. (1998) "Fatalism Reconceptualised: a Concept to Predict Health Screening Behaviour", *Journal of Gender, Culture, and Health,* 3(2): 85-100.

Straughan, P. T. and Tan, E. S. (1996) *Shift Work, Job Satisfaction, and Turnover Propensity: Nurses in a Singapore Hospital,* Dept. of Sociology Working Paper Series, 128, Singapore: National University of Singapore.

Straughan, P. T. and Tan, E. S. (1998) "Hospital Nurses and Occupational Values in Singapore", in H. Lim and R. Singh (eds) *Values and Development: A Multidisciplinary Approach with Some Comparative Studies*, Singapore: Centre for Advanced Studies.

Tan, E. S. and Straughan, P. T. (1996) "Tracking the Caring Profession: Hospital Nurses in Singapore", *Southeast Asian Journal of Social Sciences,* 24(2): 99-109.

Tan, K. (1999) *Awaiting the Stork: the Impact of Reproductive Technologies on Involuntary Childlessness*, Unpublished thesis.

Thoits, P. A. (1982) "Conceptual, Methodological, and Theoretical Problems in Studying Social Support as a Buffer against Life Stress", *Journal of Health and Social Behaviour,* 28: 306-19.

Wong, M. L., Tan, T. C., Ho, M. L., Lim, J. Y., Wan, S. and Chan, R. (1992) "Factors Associated with Sexually Transmitted Diseases among Prostitutes in Singapore", *International Journal of STD and AIDS,* 3: 323-28.

Wong, M. L., Archibald, C., Chan, R., Goh, A., Tan, T. C. and Goh, C. L. (1994) "Condom Use Negotiation among Sex Workers in Singapore: Findings from Qualitative Research", *Health Education Research: Theory and Practice,* 9(1): 57-67.

7

Class and Social Stratification

Ko Yiu Chung

Stratification is a term borrowed from geology. When used in sociology, it conveys a concept of society as consisting of a set of layers. This concept of society was proposed around the 1930s in America as a general framework for studying social structure and social processes. The main proponent of this perspective is Sorokin (1959), who conceptualizes social structure as being composed of a set of vertical and horizontal positions in which individuals can move about. Sorokin proposes that society can be characterized in terms of the degree of openness (based on the rates of social mobility) within the society. This view represents only one among the many assumptions underlying the characterization of a society. It is, however, commonly shared by sociologists who embark upon research in social stratification.

Individuals and groups in a society can be evaluated on the basis of many criteria: income, occupation, religion, age, gender, physical attribute, personality and so on. Thus a society can be stratified in many possible ways depending on the number of and the specific criteria used in evaluating and ranking the people or groups. Social change may involve transformation of the number of and the specific criteria used in social stratification. Because of space limitation, this paper seeks to review studies on three main types of social stratification in Singapore society, namely, class, ethnic and gender stratification.

Social Class in Singapore: Characteristics and Issues

Social class is a basic sociological concept. As Weber defined it, the term refers to any group of people who have the same "typical chance for a supply of goods, external living conditions, and personal life experiences, in so far as this chance is determined by the amount and kind of power, or lack of such, to dispose of goods or skills for the sake of income in a given economic order" (1946, 181). Under this definition, many social studies can be classified as research in the area of social class. For example, the research focused on poverty (Goh 1956, Cheah 1978) and housing conditions (Kaye 1960, Hassan 1977) are studies relevant to social class. In the 1950s and 1960s, social research conducted in Singapore was oriented to social problems in the society and many empirical studies were concentrated on the lower social class.

In the early 1970s, social scientists in Singapore began to turn their attention to the income distribution of the whole society. The central issue raised was whether income inequality would be greater or lesser when a society underwent rapid economic development (Chen 1974, Pang 1975a, 1975b, Rao and Ramakrishnan 1980). This question was brought up partly because it was then debated by economists and sociologists around the world at a time when most developing countries were experiencing rapid economic growth (Chen 1974). Secondly, Singapore had embarked on a massive industrialization programme since its independence in 1965 and was enjoying impressive growth rates (Rodan 1989, 1996). It would provide an ideal testing ground for the debates of the above issue.

A second issue that was brought up in the 1970s concerns whether Singapore society had emerged as a middle-class society or still remained as a working-class society (see review by Chen 1986, 53-54). Buchanan (1972, 201-223) characterized Singapore as a low-income working-class society based on the income and the occupational status of the majority of the population. Chen (1973, 1974), however, argued that Singapore was already a "middle-class society" by the 1970s. He estimated that 56% of respondents in an Economic Commission on Asia and Far East survey were "middle class".

Subsequent research on social class provided further views to this second issue. Lee (1991, 35) in *Social Class in Singapore* argued that the labels of middle-class or working-class society are somewhat arbitrary and of limited utility. Quah (1991, 255-68) in the same book supported Lee's position. She defined social class as basically socio-economic status, which can be seen from indicators such as educational attainment, occupational status and income. Since a person's position on these dimensions is represented by a numerical score, the composite measure of socioeconomic status is essentially a continuum. As such, the demarcation of social class has to be arbitrary and indistinct because the cut-off point of a continuum cannot be determined discretely.

If, however, we move away from the specific focus of Singapore to look at the whole region of East and Southeast Asia, the rise of the middle class has generally been regarded as an established phenomenon. Hsiao (1993) referred to the "discovery of the middle classes in East Asia" in his book which consists of essays about the middle class in various countries. Hsiao and other researchers (Robison and Goodman 1996) are interested in the social attitudes and political behaviour of the emerging middle class in a number of Asian and Southeast Asian societies. Following this trend of research, Mak and Leong published a study of the middle class in Singapore (Mak 1993, Mak and Leong 1993). They began their report by arguing that the rise of the middle class is inevitable following the "embourgeoisement of labour", as a consequence of "the world system of industrialization and the supportive role of the state" (Mak and Leong 1993, 1-2). House ownership and occupational change were used as the main indicators of the rise of the middle class in Singapore. They measured social class by adopting a revised Goldthorpe classification scheme. The main feature of the Goldthorpe scheme is its focus on occupation as the basis of classification of social class. Specifically the scheme proposes the use of the respondents' credentials and authority at the work place as the key dimensions of occupation by which social classes are determined (Mak and Leong 1993, 18-19). On this basis, Mak and Leong classified respondents in their study into three categories: capitalist, middle class and working class. They further stated that they believed middle class is the biggest among the three classes.

Although *Social Class in Singapore* and Mak and Leong's study used quite different methods to come up with a different set of social classes in Singapore, they shared common modes of data collection and data analysis. Both studies used survey as the method of data collection and both collected data on various attitudes and behaviours so that statistical comparisons between classes could be made. It would be interesting, therefore, to compare the findings of these two studies.

First of all, there seems to be a great similarity between "classes" with respect to social participation and political value. In *Social Class in Singapore*, the authors have not found significant differences in participation in voluntary organizations between the various social classes, nor are there any differences in their beliefs about the power of class (Quah et al. 1991, 97-105). Mak and Leong similarly have not found distinctive differences in patterns of lifestyle, political values and activities between the middle- and working- class respondents. The finding differs from the western literature, where a number of studies have established that "lower-class persons participate less in their society than those in the middle and upper classes" (Reissman 1967, 260).

To delineate the class distinction in western societies, Veblen used the term "conspicuous consumption" to describe the efforts members of a class make to develop significant status symbols so that they can be distinguished from other classes. But this was less obvious in Singapore than in western societies. Both the authors of *Social Class in Singapore* and the middle class study converged in that while members of each social class in Singapore could be identified by dress or language, these insignia were not reliable indicators of class position.

With respect to subjective class identification, the Singapore studies were similar to western literature. That is, the majority of respondents in Singapore would identify themselves as middle class even though they were presented with the choice between middle class and working class instead of between middle class and the derogatory label "lower class". It appears that social classes as found in the empirical studies were not sharply marked off from each other in terms of social participation, political value, conspicuous consumption and subjective class identification.

Theories of Class Inequality

Theories of class inequality developed in sociology have been dominated by the influences of Marx and Weber. While Marx and Weber have emphasized the increasing importance of class over time, they have developed a different concept of social class. For Marx, class is the exploitative relationship that is linked to the pattern of ownership and control of production. Weber, being a methodological individualist, is concerned with the problem of organized collective social action and sees the critical role of interest and power in the organization of collective action. For Weber, the unequal distribution of power is manifested in three spheres of activities. They are class, status and party. Class is the social formation found in the economic sphere of life. It consists of people who have similar access to, or command over, some economic resources. For instance, people who are property holders will have greater accessibility to resources in the market than non-property holders. For Weber, classes really consist of people who share the same positions in the market situation. There can be as many classes as there are economic positions, interest and power in the market situation.

Judging from the research interests pursued in Singapore's class studies, Weber's concept of class seems to be more applicable than the Marxian concept. The research focus on distribution of income, occupational status and educational attainment in Singapore studies shows a preference for using multiple dimensions in the definition of social class. As discussed earlier, one of the common topics studied in Singapore is the rise of the middle class. Since "Marxist-inspired approaches view class as a social relationship linked to the pattern of ownership and control of production", the "middle class" is an ambiguous term as "it lies outside the fundamental relationships involved in surplus extraction" (Rodan 1996, 29). Thus Rodan argues that "Many contemporary writers from the Marxist tradition have therefore drawn on Weber and incorporated some notion of domination between 'classes' in the technical division of labour to clarify the specificity of the middle class" (1996, 29).

One cannot, however, conclude that the Weberian approach has provided the main orientation in stratification research in

Singapore. It is more likely that different paradigms such as functionalism, status attainment model, and Goldthorpe's classification scheme are preferred, depending on the researchers' interest and training. The literature review shows that class and inequality in Singapore is of interest not only to sociologists but economists as well. Economists seldom refer to stratification as sociologists do. But some of their research is relevant for the study of social class such as their study of labour market and human capital. Economists also have their perspectives in studying social class. Given the diversity of perspectives used in class studies, we propose to highlight four theories that have guided research in the field of social class analysis in Singapore. They are development theory, status attainment theory, human capital theory and segmented labour market theory.

Development Theory

Development theory is built on empirical research that looks into economic growth as the source of change in the stratification system. The basic questions raised concern the effect of economic growth on income inequality and the role of the state in income distribution during the period of economic growth. A series of studies using various measures of income distribution consistently find that the degree of income inequality increases at the initial phase of rapid economic development and its rate of increase declines afterwards (Kuznets 1963, Lenski 1966). Stack and Zimmerman's study (1982) based on 43 nations also support these general findings.

Development theory attracted a great deal of interest in Singapore in the 1970s as the country had undergone unprecedented economic growth. Local social scientists were enthusiastic in using Singapore as a case study for testing the thesis suggested by the theory. The debate whether Singapore had reached the status of a middle class society was one of the issues generated by the application of the theory.

The findings that emerged from this research are quite unexpected. Consistent results show that the early phase of its economic growth in Singapore in the 1960s and 1970s have led to greater equity instead of increasing inequity as hypothesized by Kuznet and Lenski (Pang 1975a, 1975b, Rao and Ramakrisnan 1980). Pang explains this observation by the changing pattern of labour participation in the economy. He argues that in the rapid industrialiszation of Singapore, the manufacturing sector has expanded faster than the service and commercial sectors: "As the latter sectors are characterized by a higher proportion of self-employed and own-account workers, the result was an increase in the proportion of employees in the work-force. The income distribution of self-employed workers being more inequitable than that of employees, the net effect was a reduction in income inequity" (Pang 1975a, 24)

Chen examined the real income distribution rather than money income distribution and found that even the real income distribution has tended to be more equitable at the earlier phase of economic development in Singapore. He attributed this to the social policy of the state: "The money income disparities may be narrowed by social policies and redistributive instruments. In order to have a proper perspective of the picture of real income distribution, attention should therefore be given to certain policies and instruments which affect the redistribution of income" (1974, 126). According to Chen, these redistributive instruments include public housing, education, public health, transportation, and social welfare (Chen 1986, 52-53).

The development thesis has been commonly endorsed and utilized in subsequent studies. Tai's study of public housing in Singapore (1988, 83-94), for example, has emphasized the strong income redistribution effects of the Lands Acquisition Act and the Government's provision of subsidized low-cost housing to the population. Chiew (1994, 251-54) has also used the development thesis to explain the social class disparity between Chinese and Malays in Singapore and Malaysia before 1990. He argued that as the economy developed the Chinese in both countries were better able to exploit the economic opportunities than the Malays because the former could pool their capital and manpower resources and utilize their business networks. But since the government in Malaysia provided a wider range of affirmative action programmes to help the Malays as compared to the Singapore government, the social class disparities between Chinese and Malays in the two countries were affected correspondingly.

The weakness of the development thesis is its preoccupation with income distribution. There is no discussion of other aspects of the class structure. Also the thesis does not address how the process of economic development shapes the class structure of society. Although various independent variables such as labour force participation and the state policy have been introduced, they provide no discussion of the normative structure of and the linkage between the state, the labour market and the education system in Singapore. The explanation provided thus constitutes only an empirical case study and has limited capacity for formulating generalizations about economic development and social class.

Status Attainment Theory

The stratification research focused on status attainment and mobility began since the publication of Blau and Duncan's *The American Occupational Structure* in 1967. In the social mobility and social attainment research, Blau and Duncan shifted from the question of what causes structural inequality to how individuals are allocated different positions in society. They assumed a system of positions already exists in the society, the question is how people are allocated into these positions. Thus the focus of their study is who gets what and why, not on the social formation of class structure nor on the determinants of income distribution.

This theory draws attention to the family as a source of stratification (Bielby 1981). It distinguishes achievement and ascription as the two bases of producing inequality. According to this theory, inequality based on intelligence and education is justified while that based on social origin is not. A model is then constructed for assessing the relative influence of social origin, measured in terms of parents' socioeconomic characteristics, on a person's educational attainment. This educational attainment, together with social origins, is further assessed with respect to its influence on the individual's occupational status attainment. As a next step, the occupational status attainment, together with the educational attainment and social origin variables, is assessed with respect to their influence on income attainment. Because of the sequential nature of the model, it is called the path model.

Chiew was the first scholar to apply the model to study the educational and occupational attainment of males and females in Singapore (1977). He did not find that social origin had any substantive effect on both types of attainment and for both sub-samples. Ko later used the model to analyze data collected in a social class survey (1991). The findings show that social origin can explain no more than 20% of the variance in educational attainment, and the percentage of variance explained in occupational attainment by social origin is less than 10%. These results have confirmed research conducted in other countries that social origin, measured in terms of parents' socioeconomic status, have limited capacity to explain an individual's status attainment.

The weakness of this theory is its inability to explain inequality in the wider social structure as Marx and Weber have attempted. The variables included in the model are all attributes of an individual. There is no discussion of the role of labour market and the education system in status attainment. Without taking into account the structural factors, the pattern of inequality cannot be fully explained.

Human Capital Theory

Unlike sociologists, economists do not talk about stratification and class structure. But some of their research has led to theories that are relevant to the understanding of class inequality. One such theory is human capital theory first elaborated by Becker (1975). The human capital theory takes people as rational actors and assumes that they will invest in human capital to increase their qualification or productivity in line with where they think job opportunities lie. Human capital investments consist of formal education, on-the-job training and work experience. According to the theory, people invest their human capital mainly on the basis of income return. In other words, every individual attempts to maximise his lifetime income by investing in his or her human capital. As a result of differences in human capital, income returns to individuals are different.

In Singapore, Pang has presented several papers studying income returns to education level. The first paper is based on data collected in 1966 (Clark and Pang 1970). The second paper, published a decade later, compares the earlier findings with data collected in 1978. He notes that "the earnings differential between primary-educated and secondary-educated workers has narrowed greatly since 1966" (Pang 1980, 170). By comparison, the earnings gap between secondary-educated and tertiary-educated workers has widened. However, Pang argues that since then, "forgone earnings and direct costs of higher education have risen. On balance, it seems likely that both private and social rates of returns to higher education have not changed much since 1966" (Pang 1980, 170).

Regarding returns to language stream of education, Pang (1980, 169) notes that English education only benefits workers with higher education. English education bestows no income advantage on workers with little schooling. He explains that this is because unskilled jobs taken up by poorly educated workers do not require proficiency in the language.

Human capital theory is criticized for its unrealistic assumption about the labour market. As part of neoclassical economic theory, it assumes that employers and workers behave to maximise utility and have perfect information about opportunities and constraints when they make choices. Employers and workers are also assumed to operate in a perfectly competitive market, where there is perfect information and no barriers to mobility (Fligstein and Fernandez 1988).

Segmented Labour Market Theory

Another economic theory relevant to understanding inequality is the segmented labour market theory, which represents an effort to relax the neoclassical assumption of perfect competition. The theory argues that non-economic factors may divide the labour market into non-competing segments. Wages are paid differently in different segments. Income inequality is mainly a result of this fragmented structure of the labour market.

The idea of a segmented labour market first came from several members of the institutionists in economics during the post-war period of 1945-60. Its proponents include the well-known economists Clark Kerr and John T. Dunlop. The institutionists point out that American workers in the 1950s could not move freely within the labour market as most people would expect (Kerr 1977, 25). First of all, there was the tendency of employers and employees to work with people they liked. Secondly, the unions, professional associations, craft unions and the government tended to set up rules to restrict entry into jobs. These rules, whether they were written or merely understood, set up many barriers that divided the "totality of employment relationships into more or less distinct compartments" (Kerr 1977, 25). In general, Kerr argues, these rules in the labour market "establish more boundaries between labour markets and make them more specific and harder to cross. They define the points of competition, the groups which may compete, and the grounds on which they compete" (ibid, 37).

The idea of a segmented labour has been revived after the late 1960s by both economists (eg, Doeringer and Piore) and sociologists (eg Bonacich). Bonacich (1975), for example, has argued that the labour market in the US is split into white and black labour. The latter tend to be unskilled and are paid much lower than white labour. It is the racism of white unions and employers that creates barriers between the two labour forces.

After Kerr and Dunlop, a few perspectives have been proposed with regard to how the labour market is compartmentalized. The dual labour market perspective, for example, postulates the market as comprising the primary and secondary sectors (Doeringer and Piore 1971). The dual economy perspective, on the other hand, delineates the segmented labour market in terms of the characteristics of the firm as in Averitt's distinction of the core and periphery economies (1968). Other perspectives include O'Connor's distinction of the state, monopoly, and competitive sectors (1973).

Empirical research using the segmented labour market theory to study income inequality in Singapore is scant. The only one I have reviewed is Lee's application of the dual economy perspective to examine income difference between males and females in the manufacturing industries (Lee 1994, 281-300). Lee finds that core manufacturing industries in Singapore have high capital intensity, high productivity, high profit, are export-oriented, and comprise large firms, whereas periphery manufacturing industries have low capital intensity, low productivity, low profits, serve local markets, and are small in size. The data, however, does not confirm the prediction of the dual economy theory that core firms will pay higher wages than those offered by periphery firms.

Thus empirical data does not seem to support the segmented labour market theory. The theory may do well to explain wage differentials between the local and new immigrant workers. But it has limited powers of generalizability to other labour market conditions. This limitation is partly caused by the lack of a coherent and consistent approach explicating the causes and consequences of the dual structure of the economy in the research using the dual economy perspective (Oster 1979, 33). Precisely because researchers have not agreed on the sectoral differences along which the labour market is segmented, empirical studies based on this theory "produce inconsistent patterns of results and show a mixed pattern of support for dual economy predictions" (Zucker and Rosenstein 1981, 869).

The research in social inequality reviewed here has been guided by several specific research paradigms. The four research paradigms discussed in this paper are development theory, status attainment theory, human capital theory and segmented labour market theory. They emphasize different sources of inequality. Labour force participation and state policy are emphasized in development theory; social origin and education in status attainment theory; skill, education, training and work experience for human capital theory; barriers to mobility in segmented labour market theory. As far as data is available, social origin and segmented labour market do not seem to have great effects on creating class differences in Singapore before the nineties. The variables that seem to be important include state policy, education, and labour market participation.

Ethnic Inequality

Ethnicity refers to group differences based on cultural criteria. It is not, as in the case of caste and class, a ranked entity by definition. Hence the term "plural society" refers to the existence of multiple ethnic groups without the implication of a hierarchy. In the case when ethnic groups are ranked in terms of superiority and inferiority, sociologists usually use the term "ethnic inequality". When the inequality can be passed on from generation to generation, the system becomes a form of social stratification (Mayer and Buckley 1970).

Singapore is a multiethnic society, consisting of three main ethnic groups: Chinese, Malays and Indians. In terms of their economic status, Malays as a group are said to occupy the lowest position in the economy (Pang 1975a, Li 1989, Chiew 1991, 1994). Based on survey data given by Goh Keng Swee, Li (1989, 100) points out that, "Prior to 1959, the majority of Malays were not generally worse off economically than the majority of the Chinese". She argues that the position of the Malays as a group declined only since 1959.

Pang (1982) compares the economic status of the three ethnic groups over time. He observes that while there was a continuing decline in income inequality in the population during the period of economic growth in Singapore in the 1960s and 1970s, the income disparity between Malays and non-Malays appeared to have increased. He wrote: "Though all races in Singapore have benefited from rapid economic growth since 1965, the rates of advancement vary greatly ... In consequence, Malay incomes fell further behind that of non-Malays during the fastest period of Singapore's economic growth" (Pang 1982, 72).

Why did the Malays' economic status fall behind the non-Malays during the initial phase of economic development in Singapore? Pang (1975a) proposes three main factors, namely, the low rate of female labour force participation, the low educational attainment, and the employment problems of Malay youths. With regard to the first factor, he makes the following observation:

> In 1966, working-age Malay women had a labour force participation of only 8.5%, 20 percentage points below that of Chinese women. The large gap in participation rate suggests that cultural factors influenced Malay attitude towards female education and training and inhibited female Malay participation in the labour market in the 1960s. In 1980, Malay women had a participation rate of 46.2%, less than 2 percentage points below the Chinese rate (Pang 1982, 73).

The relatively low educational attainment of the Malays compared with the Chinese can be easily supported by Government statistics. According to Pang (1982) and Chiew (1991), the low educational attainment accounts for the fact that the Malays have concentrated in the production and service sectors while a much higher proportion of the Chinese and Indians have taken up occupations in the professions and administration.

The third factor mentioned by Pang is the employment problems experienced by Malay youth. This was the case because Malay youth were slow to be called to serve in the national service "as the government was planning to restore racial balance in the armed and police forces ... Their military status being unclear, employers were reluctant to hire them, thus contributing to their employment problem" (Pang 1982, 79).

Li, author of *Malays in Singapore* (1989), agrees with Pang that lower female labour force participation and lower educational attainment resulted in lower income for the Malays. But she presents a different reason for the low female labour force participation of the Malays. She believes that it is the absence of work opportunities rather than Malay attitudes that accounts for the low participation rate. She wrote, "While Chinese females could be employed in various capacities in the Chinese-speaking trade and manufacture sector, it was the growth in manufacturing in the multinational sector in the late 1970s that first provided mass employment opportunities for Malay women" (1989, 104-105). As a minority in the society, Malay women did not enjoy equal work opportunities as their Chinese counterparts.

In a more recent paper discussing the economic position of the Malays, Chiew (1994) highlights other factors in explaining income disparity between the Chinese and the Malays. Chiew compares Chinese and Malays in Singapore and Malaysia. He points out that both Singapore and Malaysia have experienced rapid economic growth in the past few decades, and in both countries the Chinese did much better economically than the Malays. There must be common factors that lie behind both situations. He proposes that the Chinese possess a higher level of "need for achievement" or what Ayal described as "behavioural propensities" than the Malays. Because of this motivational difference, the Chinese "are likely to be able to seize the opportunities created during economic development than the Malays. Then they use their new-found wealth to give their children more education than the Malays in order to prepare them for better paid jobs ..., and the economic advantage of the Chinese over Malays is thus maintained" (Chiew 1994, 255).

But statistics show that the income gap between the Chinese and Malays has been on the wane recently. Chiew thinks that this is the result of the intervention of the state. He hypothesizes that "as the economic disparity increases in size and reaches a point which is considered to be politically unacceptable to the leaders of the disadvantaged group, the government has to act in order to redress the real or 'perceived injustice' of the social system which distributes the benefits unequally" (Chiew 1994, 256).

Chiew makes use of the concepts of "need for achievement" and "behavioural propensities" in his explanation. But such notions are difficult to validate and substantiate. For Chiew, the low level of participation of Malays in entrepreneurship is an indication of their lack of "need for achievement" or "behavioural propensities". The lack of such motivation is then used by Chiew to explain why Malays are not doing well economically compared with the Chinese. His explanation is obviously tautological.

Li has provided an alternative view on the cause of the low participation of Malays in entrepreneurship in Singapore. She has not, however, excluded the motivational factor as the cause. She said that "unlike the merchants described by Weber, ... Singapore Malays do not consider wealth to be essential to salvation nor is it proof of holiness or social or moral worth" (Li 1989, 83). But for Li, the absence of a strong motivation for the accumulation of wealth does not fully explain why most Malay businessmen lack incentives to expand their business. To explain the phenomenon, Li points to the significance of the Malay system of property ownership. She wrote about the system as follows:

> In Malay and Javanese society, partners in marriage retain ownership of their own goods and earnings. Parents have complete ownership of their property and during their lifetime may give it to whom they please, not necessarily to their own children. Children, in return, do not have a clearly defined

> obligation to support their parents. They have no obligation to contribute to the support or material provisioning of their siblings with whom there is no joint estate (Li 1989, 8).

With this individualistic system of property ownership, the Malays tend to encounter "a practical constraint on starting a business due to the lack of pooling of capital and labour resources within the nuclear family unit" (Li 1989, 123). Compared with the Malays, the Chinese are more ready to obtain resources from the family and thus are more likely to enjoy a favourable condition for their involvement in entrepreneurship.

To summarize I make the following three observations. First, research in ethnic stratification has concentrated on only two ethnic groups: the Chinese and the Malays. The situation of the Indians seems to have largely been neglected. Secondly, the variables used by researchers to explain the income disparity between the Chinese and Malays have been drawn from the four theories of class inequality discussed rather than taken from one theory. The use of multiple theories in the analysis indicates that these theories are complementary to one another. Thirdly, in explaining ethnic stratification, researchers have highlighted the importance of culture and family structure. Nevertheless, there is so far no in-depth examination of how the education system and the labour market have influenced the unequal position of the ethnic groups in Singapore.

Gender Inequality

The income disparity between males and females in Singapore has been noted in several studies. A survey conducted in 1979 found that "an earnings gap between men and women exists at all educational levels. Male workers, on the average, earn one-third more than female counterparts" (Pang and Seow 1983, 166). Another study based on the 1980 census data similarly points out that "within each of the seven occupational groups, the women without exception earned less than the men" (Saw 1984, 58). A third study discloses that females earn only 63% as much as males in the manufacturing sector. The income difference remains large even after allowing for human capital factors such as education, skills and work experience (Lee 1994).

Several variables have been examined in an attempt to explain the income gap. With respect to educational attainment, one view expressed was that by the early 1980s it was no longer true that parents in Singapore prefer to educate their sons rather than their daughters (Pang 1982, 147-48). In fact, the average education of working females has not been lower than that of working males. Thus the gap cannot be due to the level of education. Another study compares the effects of family origins (measured in terms of father's education, mother's education and employment ratio of the household) on the educational and occupational attainment of a sample of working males and females in Singapore (Chiew 1977). It shows that the social origins of the family have negligible effect on status attainment, and this is true for both the male and female samples.

A third study attempts to explain the income gap using the dual economy theory (Lee 1994). According to this theory, the labour market is segmented into the core and periphery sectors. Females are disproportionately channelled into the periphery sector where wages are lower, and "it is their concentration in the periphery that explains their lower incomes" (Lee 1994, 282)

The author tested this hypothesis with a sample of workers who worked in the manufacturing sector. His results show that contrary to the prediction of the dual economy theory, females are not disproportionately clustered in the periphery. Furthermore, it is not true to say that the earnings in the core are higher than the periphery, for in both core and periphery industries, females earn less and are concentrated in lower paying jobs.

The last variable that has been put forth to explain the income gap is the increasing rate of female labour force participation. Would that affect women's wages? After one decade of rapid industrialization, the wage levels for women have not changed. A sociologist observes that the education and employment opportunities for women have expanded during this period. But women's economic participation has been bound to the pattern of foreign investment, with the majority engaged in low-status, dead-end and low-wage jobs (Wong 1981, 437). Similarly, an economist argues that the labour force participation has two opposing effects on female income returns to education. "On the one hand, it has raised female lifetime earnings. On the other, it has slowed down the rate of increase in the average earnings of women, particularly those of young females entering the job market for the first time" (Pang 1982, 112).

In conclusion, none of the factors reviewed (human capital, family origins, dual economy and economic participation) — factors that have been used to study income disparity between the Malays and Chinese — have been found to show any effects on reducing the income differentials between working males and females. Are the lower wages of working women compared with men simply a reflection of men's interest to preserve patriarchy?

Other than the issue of wage differentials, another popular topic of interest in the study of gender stratification is occupational segregation by gender. Even obvious to layman, many occupations in society are either dominated by males such as engineers or by females such as nurses. In view of the increasing rate of female labour force participation, social scientists have raised a number of questions. How would the increasing female participation in the labour market affect the distribution of males and females in occupation? Would male-dominated occupations continue? Would working females choose to take traditional occupations as their number increases?

The empirical evidence in occupational segregation by gender has been used to address the issue of choice for women. All along, social scientists have been concerned with the availability of choice for women in their careers, particularly in the decision to work or not to work (Gerson 1985). With reference to occupational segregation, feminists and structuralists argue that sex segregation in occupation is a result of men's interest to preserve patriarchy. As such, it is likely to remain stable and women will continue to be limited in occupational choices. In contrast, the human capital perspective in economics predicts increasing integration as more and more women enter the job market. There are two reasons stated for that. First, discrimination will end because of the competitive operation of the marketplace. Secondly, "increasing wages lead more women into the labour force for longer spells, which in turn leads them to invest more heavily in labour-market skills, which in turn should reduce the sexual differentiation of occupational choices" (Jacobs 1989, 161). Thus, the human capital perspective believes that women's choices in occupations are possible and they would affect occupational segregation.

A study in the occupational segregation by gender in Singapore finds that the index has decreased from 1957 to 1970 but has increased from 1970 to 1980. Overall it has been quite stable over the years (Ko 1996, 637). The author, however, warns that the issue of women's choice remains unsettled because among the greatest increase in female workers are two categories; those with a low proportion of females (professional and managerial work) and those with a high proportion of females (production-line work). While the decline of segregation in the first case is likely to be the result of women's choice as predicted by human capital theory, the increase in segregation in the second case may be an indication of lack of choice for women at the lower end of the job market (Ko 1996, 649-650).

Future Prospects of Stratification Research in Singapore

The literature reviewed in this paper has pointed to the importance of the education system and labour market as the main structural contexts in which social stratification and mobility occur in Singapore. However, the theoretical approaches used to study stratification (such as status attainment model of stratification and human capital theory) are more concerned with individual attributes. "They were assigned values as global covariates at the individual level (ie individuals were assigned values representing structural contexts such as industry codes, labour market segments, neighbourhoods) and included as predictors in structural models" (O'Rand 1996, 9). In this way the researchers bypassed the normative structures in which the stratification processes were embedded. "Consequently, the explanatory framework had an individualistic bias that could not account for subgroup variations (such as those associated with race, gender and industrial location) in attainment" (ibid).

There is thus a need to overcome the individualistic bias in local stratification research by directing attention to the normative structures in both the education system and labour market as suggested by the "new structuralism" approach to stratification and social mobility research (Kerckhoff 1995, 323). Under this focus, one can look at the streaming system, peer social networks, degree of central control, degree of stratification within a school, the number and specialised nature of credentials as well as other features in school that affect the distribution of academic aspirations and achievement. Similarly in studying the labour market one may examine firm structures, social networks, occupational and firm-specific job classifications, internal labour markets, vacancy chains, industrial sectors, and career lines, which influence job attainment and mobility.

Indeed, a promising direction has been initiated in a study of the *guanxi* networks and job mobility in China and Singapore (Bian and Ang 1997). In this study, data reveal that "a large number of job changers in both Tianjin (50%) and Singapore (75%) use *guanxi* to change jobs. In Singapore, *guanxi* is used to obtain both information and influence from social contacts for one's job mobility, and this flexibility may be responsible for the higher percentage of jobs changed through *guanxi* networks in Singapore than in Tianjin" (1997, 1000). Furthermore, it was also found that while job changers tend to be linked to their helpers through weak ties in western countries, in the case of Tianjin and Singapore, job changers are more closely linked to their helpers. This finding thus throws open the theoretical question of "how social resources are accessed through social ties of varying strengths" (ibid, 1001). Future research in network chains should shed light on this question.

Recent trends in international stratification research have also emphasised the processes and mechanisms through which social stratification and mobility are generated. Underlying these research efforts is the aim to go beyond the "new structuralism" which has been criticized as being "too narrowly concerned with the structural contexts within which social mobility occurs and has ignored the social psychological processes that help explain the effects of those contexts" (Kerckhoff 1996, xiii). Thus, in recent stratification and mobility research, the focus has shifted to include linkages between educational and labour force institutions – through studying the structural mechanisms that operate to organize the **careers** or life course of individuals. It is hoped that through such attempts, the process of structuration and individualization can be incorporated in the stratification process.

Finally, recent international stratification research has been moving beyond a single societal study to a cross-national comparative analysis because the cross-level effects and the multilevel process between the educational system and the labour market placements can best be examined by using the comparative databases (O'Rand 1996, 13). Singapore researchers should be prepared for the advanced methodologies that allow for such cross-national and multilevel analyses.

References

Averitt, R. (1968) *The Dual Economy: The Dynamic of American Industry*, New York: Norton.

Becker, G. S. (1975) *Human Capital*, Chicago: University of Chicago Press.

Bian, Y. and Ang, S. (1997) "*Guanxi* Networks and Job Mobility in China and Singapore", *Social Forces*, 75(2): 981-1005.

Bielby, W. T. (1981) "Model of Status Attainment", *Research in Social Stratification and Mobility*, 1:3-26.

Blau, P. M. and Duncan, O. T. (1967) *The American Occupational Structure*, New York: The Free Press.

Bonaciah, A. (1975) "Abolition, the Extension of Slavery and the Position of Free Blacks: A Study of Split Labor Markets in the United States", *American Journal of Sociology*, 81(3): 601-28.

Buchanan, I. (1972) *Singapore in Southeast Asia: An Economic and Political Appraisal*, London: G. Bell & Sons.

Cheah, H. B. (1978) "A Study of Poverty in Singapore", University of Singapore, M.Soc.Sc. thesis (unpublished).

Chen, P. S. J. (1973) *Social Stratification in Singapore*, Singapore, University of Singapore, Dept. of Sociology, Working Paper No. 12.

Chen, P. S. J. (1974) "Growth and Income Distribution in Singapore", *Southeast Asian Journal of Social Sciences*, 2: 119-30.

Chen, P. S. J. (1986) "Sociological Studies on Singapore Society", in B. Kapur (ed) *Singapore Studies: Critical Surveys of the Humanities and Social Sciences*, Singapore: Singapore University Press.

Chiew, S. K. (1977) *Educational and Occupational Attainment of Singapore's Chinese Women and Men*, Singapore, University of Singapore, Dept. of Sociology, Working Paper No. 59.

Chiew, S. K. (1991) "Ethnic Stratification", in S.R. Quah, S.K. Chiew, Y.C. Ko and S.M. Lee (eds) *Social Class in Singapore*, Singapore: Times Academic Press.

Chiew, S. K. (1994) "Social Class Disparity between Chinese and Malays in Singapore and Malaysia, 1957-1990", in S.K. Lau, M.K. Lee, P.S. Wan and S.L. Wong (eds) *Inequalities and Development: Social Stratification in Chinese Societies*, Hong Kong: The Chinese University of Hong Kong, Hong Kong Institute of Asia-Pacific Studies.

Clark, D. H. and Pang, E. F. (1970) "Return to Schooling and Training in Singapore", *Malayan Economic Review*, 15(2): 42-8.

Doeringer, P. B. and Piore, M. (1971) *Internal Labor Markets and Manpower Analysis*, Lexington, MA: Heath.

Fligstein, N. and Fernandez, R. M. (1988) "Worker Power, Firm Power, and Structure of Labor Markets", *The Sociological Quarterly*, 29(1): 5-28.

Gerson, K. (1985) *Hard Choices: How Women Decide about Work, Career, and Motherhood*, Berkeley: University of California Press.

Goh, K. S. (1956) *Urban Income and Housing*, Singapore: Government Printing Office.

Hassan, R. (1977) *Families in Flats: A Study of Low Income Families in Public Housing*, Singapore: Singapore University Press.

Hsiao, M. H. H. (1993) *Discovery of the Middle Classes in East Asia*, Taipei: Academic Sinica, Institute of Ethnology.

Jacobs, J. A. (1989) "Long-Term Trends in Occupational Segregation by Sex", *American Journal of Sociology*, 95(1): 160-73.

Kaye, B. (1960) *Upper Nankin Street, Singapore: A Sociological Study of Chinese Households Living in a Densely Populated Area*, Singapore: University of Malaya Press.

Kerckhoff, A. L. (1995) "Institutional Arrangements and Stratification Processes in Industrial Societies", *Annual Review of Sociology*, 21: 323-47.

Kerckhoff, A. L. (ed) (1996) *Generating Social Stratification: Toward a New Research Agenda*, Boulder: Westview Press.

Kerr, C. (1954) "The Balkanization of Labor Markets", in his *Labor Mobility and Economic Opportunity*, Massachusetts: M.I.T. Press, and Wiley. Reprinted in (1977) Labor Markets and Wage Determination: The Balkanization of Labor Markets and *Other Essays*, Berkeley: University of California Press.

Ko, Y. C. (1991) "Status Attainment", in S.R. Quah, S.K. Chiew, Y.C. Ko and S.M. Lee (eds) *Social Class in Singapore*, Singapore: Times Academic Press.

Ko, Y. C. (1996) "Trends in Occupational Segregation by Sex in Singapore", in S.K. Lau, P.S. Wan, M.K Lee and S.L. Wong (eds) *New Frontiers of Social Indicators Research in Chinese Societies*, Hong Kong: The Chinese University of Hong Kong, Hong Kong Institute of Asia-Pacific Studies.

Kuznets, S. (1963) "Quantitative Aspects of the Economic Growth of Nations, VIII: The Distribution of Income by Size", *Economic Development and Cultural Change*, 11(2): 1-37.

Lee, S. M. (1991) "Social Class in Singapore: An Overview", in S.R. Quah, S.K. Chiew, Y.C. Ko and S.M. Lee (eds) *Social Class in Singapore*, Singapore: Times Academic Press.

Lee, W. K. M. (1994) "Labour Market Segmentation and Gender Inequality in Singapore", in S.K. Lau, M.K. Lee, P.S. Wan and S.L. Wong (eds) *Inequalities and Development: Social Stratification in Chinese Societies*, Hong Kong: The Chinese University of Hong Kong, Hong Kong Institute of Asia-Pacific Studies.

Lenski, G. E. (1966) *Power and Privilege*, New York: McGraw-Hill.

Li, T. (1989) *Malays in Singapore*, Singapore: Oxford University Press.

Mak, L. F. (1993) "The Rise of the Singapore Middle Class: An Analytical Framework", in M. H. H. Hsiao (ed) *Discovery of the Middle Classes in East Asia*, Taipei: Academia Sinica, Institute of Ethnology.

Mak, L. F. and Leong, C. H. (1993) *East Asian Middle Class Research Project: The Singapore Middle Class*, Singapore: National University of Singapore, Dept. of Sociology.

Mayer, K. B. and Buckley, W. (1970) *Class and Society*, New York: Random House.

O'Connor, J. (1973) *The Fiscal Crisis of the State*, New York: St. Martin.

O'Rand, A. M. (1996) "Structuration and Individualization: The Life Course as a Continuous, Multilevel Process", in A.L. Kerckhoff (ed) *Generating Social Stratification: Toward a New Research Agenda*, Boulder: Westview Press.

Oster, G. (1979) "A Factor Analytic Test of the Theory of Dual Economy", *Review of Economics and Statistics,* 61: 33-39.

Pang, E. F. (1975a) "Growth, Inequality and Race in Singapore", *International Labour Review*, 3: 15-28.

Pang, E. F. (1975b) "Development and Social Equity in Singapore", in C.M. Seah (ed) *Trends in Singapore*, Singapore: Singapore University Press.

Pang, E. F. (1980) "Return to Schooling and Training: Postscript", in E.A. Afendras and E.C.Y. Kuo (eds) *Language and Society in Singapore*, Singapore: Singapore University Press.

Pang, E. F. (1982) *Education, Manpower and Development in Singapore*, Singapore: Singapore University Press.

Pang, E. F. and Seow, G. (1983) "Labour, Employment and Wage Structure", in P.S.C. Chen (ed) *Singapore Development Policies and Trends*, Singapore: Singapore University Press.

Quah, S. R. (1991) "Conclusion: The Realities of Social Class", in S.R. Quah, S. K. Chiew, Y. C. Ko and S. M. Lee (eds) *Social Class in Singapore*, Singapore: Times Academic Press.

Quah, S. R., Chiew, S. K., Ko, Y. C. and Lee, S. M. (eds) (1991) *Social Class in Singapore*, Singapore: Times Academic Press.

Rao, V. V. B. and Ramakrishnan, M. K. (1980) *Income Inequality in Singapore*, Singapore: Singapore University Press.

Reissman, L. (1967) "Social Stratification", in N.J. Smelser (ed) *Sociology: An Introduction*, New York: John Wiley & Sons.

Robison, R. and Goodman, D. S. G. (eds) (1996) *The New Rich in Asia: Mobile Phones, McDonalds and Middle-Class Revolution*, London and New York: Routledge.

Rodan, G. (1989) *The Political Economy of Singapore's Industrialization: National State and International Capital*, Basingstoke: Macmillan.

Rodan, G. (1996) "Class Transformations and Political Tensions in Singapore's Development", in R. Robison and D.S.G. Goodman (eds) *The New Rich in Asia: Mobile Phones, McDonalds and Middle-Class Revolution*, London and New York: Routledge.

Saw, S. H. (1984) *The Labour Force of Singapore*, Singapore, Dept. of Statistics, Census Monograph No. 3.

Sorokin, P.A. (1959) *Social and Cultural Mobility*, New York: Free Press.

Stack, S. and Zimmerman, D. (1982) "The Effects of World Economy on Income Inequality: A Reassessment", *The Sociological Quarterly*, 23(3): 345-58.

Tai, C. L. (1988) *Housing Policy and High-Rise Living: A Study of Singapore's Public Housing*, Singapore: Chopmen Publishers.

Weber, M. (1946) *From Max Weber: Essays in Sociology*, translated and edited by H.H. Gerth and C. W. Mills, New York: Oxford University Press.

Wong, A. K. (1981) "Planned Development, Social Stratification, and Sexual Division of Labour in Singapore", *Signs*, 7(2): 434-52.

Zucker, L. G. and Rosenstein, C. (1981) "Taxonomies of Institutional Structure: Dual Economy Reconsidered", *American Sociological Review*, 46(6): 869-84.

PART II

MODERNITY

8

"Race" and Ethnic Relations in Singapore

Lian Kwen Fee and Ananda Rajah

A critical sociological and anthropological examination of "race" and ethnic relations in Singapore must address what we consider to be two major concerns. First, it demands an evaluation of studies of "race" and ethnic relations in a Singaporean context in relation to the evolution of sociological and anthropological thinking on "race", its replacement by the notion of "ethnicity" and ethnic relations as a contextually situated phenomenon. Second, it requires a clear historical perspective on the emergence and consolidation of Singapore as a nation-state and society in its own right because the processes associated with these developments are inseparable from the phenomenology of, and the various discourses on, "race", ethnicity, and ethnic relations. In this chapter, we take studies of "race" and ethnic relations in Singapore broadly to include works not only in sociology and anthropology, but also those in political science and history and evaluate them on the basis of the two concerns mentioned. In so doing, we also seek to draw out what is sociologically relevant in these other studies.

Between Essentialism and Relativism

The study of "race" and ethnic relations has a long history and it will not be possible to trace its development here. We may, however, identify a number of pertinent themes. Early anthropological thinking was largely concerned with understanding the nature of human diversity and difference encountered in the colonial enterprise in the 18th and 19th centuries (Asad 1973). The anthropologically constituted "object", to put it another way, was an invented "primitive society" (Kuper 1988). This constitution was an undertaking not only by European scholars but colonial administrators and missionaries with a scholarly bent, the reflections of the one feeding on the observations of the other and vice versa. In such thinking, social and cultural diversity were intimately linked to and determined by biological difference. Furthermore, different societies could be placed at one or another stage of advancement in a linear evolutionary path, ie from primitive to civilized. Such notions were, of course, central to the employment of the term "race". Aside from markers of identity such as language and "customs" (or more precisely religion, family and kinship, and indigenous legal systems), it is important to note that, in general, different groups or communities were thought of as possessing inherently different behavioural characteristics or features and that such groups or communities were, accordingly, separated by fixed boundaries. The dominant aspect of such thinking was its essentialising character and studies based on this kind of thinking were often primarily concerned with the internal constitution, features or characteristics of ethnolinguistic groups rather than the relations between groups.

It is significant that in the period of decolonization and the proliferation of new nation-states after the Second World War, essentialist notions of this kind gave way to relativist conceptions of group identification and inter-group relations, the abandonment of the term "race" in favour of the more open-ended term "ethnic group", and a greater understanding of the permeability of group boundaries in social science thinking (see Lian and Rajah 1993). The relativist approach, in essence, represented a rejection of biological determinism of what have since been more clearly understood to be in principle mutable cultural features and a concern with, among other things, group identity and relations as a situational phenomenon either at the inter-ethnic or intra-ethnic level or both. The remarkable proliferation of theoretical work in sociology and anthropology (as well as other related social sciences such as political science) on ethnicity and ethnic relations in this period, especially in the 1960s and early 1970s, contributed to the establishment of the study of "race", ethnicity and ethnic relations as a major field of enquiry in these disciplines. It also saw, to some extent, a convergence of sociological and anthropological approaches in this field. A crucial aspect of this disciplinary development was (and continues to be) the theoretical attention given to the post-colonial nation-state. This was not simply a fortuitous progression on the discovery of "plural" societies in colonies or former colonies first set out by Furnivall (1948). It was a response to two sets of crucial societal conditions and dynamics: first, ethnic conflict in relation to political development in post colonial nation-states; second, the increasing ethnic diversity of those European states which had been colonial powers. Such societies were now faced with the "problem" of ethnic relations which manifested itself in terms of racism, socioeconomic differences and differential access to resources and opportunities — all of which controverted the assumption of the inviolability of equal rights of citizens in western liberal democracies. This has resulted in an extraordinarily large corpus of work on racial or ethnic conflict, national identification as against "primordial" ethnic affiliations, the relationship between "race" and class, "race" or ethnic relations, the dynamics of minority and majority group relations, split labour markets, and sociolinguistic studies of language competence in conditions of diglossia. Work in this area was given further impetus and elaboration in the wake of forced and unforced migration as a result of the Vietnam war and its aftermath in Southeast Asia; which further "pluralized" countries such as America, Australia and Canada, thus providing additional perspectives from the point of view of refugee and migration studies. A re-conceptualization of these states as being not simply plural but "multicultural", coupled with intellectual trends away from neo-Marxist theoretical pre-occupations in the 1960s have in turn generated new approaches which call for evaluation.

These more recent trends have now impacted on the sociological and anthropological study of ethnicity and ethnic relations although the ultimate, long-term significance of this is by no means clear. These developments, associated with "post-modernism", "deconstructionism" or sometimes "cultural studies", defy easy, summary description. Their concerns include the relationship between knowledge and relations of power and the bearing that it has on identities, group and individual, a high degree of reflexivity and an even greater degree of relativism, the employment of methods derived from literary and textual criticism, a focus on "narratives" as the object of deconstruction, the avoidance of privileging any particular intellectual position, among others. What follows is an attempt at a critical examination of studies of ethnicity and ethnic relations in Singapore, in the light of the issues we have identified as central to the sociology and anthropology of race and ethnic relations.

Plural Society and Ascriptive Ethnicity

One of the glaring omissions in the study of ethnic relations in Singapore is the absence of an awareness of the historical trajectory of the city-state from its colonial origins to the present. As far as the sociology of ethnic relations is concerned, two phases of the Republic's history may be identified. The first refers to the period up to the Second World War when colonial society and administration was established and consolidated in Malaya and Singapore. The second covers the years after the Second World War when Britain committed itself to decolonisation in the Far East and a post-independent Singapore.

At the height of its influence, British colonial administrative policies and practice were based on ascriptive ethnicity, a term used by Taylor (1982). The British imposed their perceptions of race and ethnicity upon Southeast Asian societies and ruled accordingly. Such policies and practice, in other words, rested on essentialist notions of ethnic difference. Ethnic groups were thought of as having particular propensities and were thus assigned economic and social roles (Stockwell 1982, Abraham 1983, Trocki 1992). The Malays were essentially peasant and rice-cultivators whilst a few with aristocratic ties were recruited into the lower ranks of the civil service. The Chinese were either mining coolies or middlemen engaged in trade and commerce; and the Indians laboured on rubber estates or public works. The colonial ascription of ethnicity has generally been analyzed by scholars as one based on social Darwinist assumptions of the development of the human population. In fact, as Kuper (1988, 2) has pointed out, such assumptions — which also characterized early anthropological thinking—are better described as crudely Lamarckian rather than Darwinian. The Lamarckian view essentially posits the emergence of greater organic complexity with evolutionary advancement whereas the Darwinian view explains diversity among species as a consequence of adaptation. Kuper is, therefore, quite right in making this distinction which has been missed. It is in the light of this distinction that we may also further argue that, in colonial conditions, the roles ascribed to the various ethnic groups were justified on ideological and essentialist grounds. In the colonial mind for example, Indians were regarded as docile and well-behaved, and were suited to the poorly paid and regimented life of plantations and government projects. The Chinese, on the other hand, had more self-reliance and the enterprise to rise above manual labour (Abraham 1983, 24). The Malays were regarded as rural, poor and backward, and in the colonial division of labour were most appropriate to the role of food producers and agriculturalists. There were underlying cultural reasons for the roles assigned to each ethnic community. Such cultural explanations were perpetuated not only in popular discourse by colonial officials, Chinese immigrants, and even Malay reformists (Li 1989, 168-72), but also in academic dissertations on Malay society in Singapore even in the 1970s (Bedlington 1974, Betts 1975). The inability of the Malays to match the economic and educational achievements of the Chinese and Indians was simply attributed to the traditional values that came with isolated, rural and agricultural-based communities. In this way, essentialist notions of ethnicity came to be infused in the work of scholars. Li's work on Malays in Singapore Society (1989), on the other hand, represents in part an attempt at situating Malay ethnicity in Singapore which is sensitive to its socio-political context, and thus displays the sociological and anthropological concern with the relativist position which distinguishes more contemporary approaches. We must add here that the first attempt at this kind of work is found in Alatas' seminal The Myth of the Lazy Native (1977).

Ascriptive ethnicity has its concomitant in the concept of plural society. Expounded by the British scholar-administrator, Furnivall in 1948, it conveyed the notion that Southeast Asian societies were characterized by the presence of ethnic communities who lived adjacent to each other within the same political unit but separately, and only came into contact at the marketplace out of economic necessity. The concept is significant because it has not only informed colonial policy and practice but also influenced the understanding of ethnic relations by scholars even to this day. In addition to the assignment of social roles to different ethnic groups, colonial administrative agencies and laws took cognizance of ethnic divisions, as in the setting up of the Chinese Protectorate and in the enactment of separate legislation to regulate Indian labour migration in Malaya (Trocki 1992, 113). Of greater consequence is that the British in Asia, from the mid-19th century, were community conscious, and viewed themselves and those they ruled as members of distinct communities first, and only as individuals second (Stockwell 1982, 56). In so doing colonial government became the administration of ethnic communities, and the local population responded as members of such communities. The contemporary significance of official classification of the population may be seen in the Peoples Action Party (PAP) government's use of the categories "Chinese", "Malays", "Indians", and "Others" as the basis of its policy of multiracialism, which will be discussed later. Here, we note that this classification shares the essentialist attributes of earlier colonial ascriptions of ethnicity but there is a major difference as well. Whereas the PAP government's use recognizes only four categories, colonial censuses recognized a far greater number of categories based on place of origin, language and dialectal variations (Hirschman 1987).

The utilization of the paradigm of "plural society" in scholarly studies of ethnic relations in Southeast Asia, and in Malaya (later Malaysia) and Singapore has been widespread. While most have used it as a descriptive concept, its explanatory power has been limited, if not disappointing. One major criticism of the paradigm is that it has encouraged a static conception of ethnic relations in Southeast Asia. As Taylor (1982, 7) explains, because ethnicity is viewed as being ascriptive in Western political thought since the rise of nationalism, antagonism between ethnic groups is assumed to be primordial rather than as a relational attribute reflecting ecological and subcultural characteristics. If the analytical utility of the paradigm has been limited, we should not however disregard the importance of its application by political actors in post-colonial society itself. Indeed the ascriptive definition of ethnicity, as opposed to a relational conception, is susceptible to reification.

One early study of Hodder (1953), titled "Racial Groupings in Singapore", used data collected from a government-sponsored land-use survey to map out ethnic concentrations of population in the city. Reflecting the plan first articulated by Raffles in 1822 to mark the separate quarters of the "native" population in the proposed town, he identified the Chinese as having settled in the congested core of the city, the Malays on the western fringes, and the Indians south of the central city where they worked on the railway and docks (ibid, 29). Raffles's plan, of course, can only be understood in terms of essentialist notions of "race" and their fixed boundaries which, accordingly, had to be spatially represented through segregation. What is of interest here is that Hodder's analysis reflects essentialist thinking at a much later period in history in a scholarly work. One of his conclusions (ibid, 31), apropos the Chinese, is that "with their low average standard of living and indefatigability in the pursuit of wealth, the Chinese generally prefer the congested core". The connection between the spatial segregation of ethnic communities, as illustrative of plural society, and their socio-cultural organization is unquestioningly accepted. Against this, however, we may place the work of, for example, Djamour on *Malay Kinship and Marriage in Singapore* (1959) and Freedman's studies, "Colonial Law and Chinese Society" (1950) and *Chinese Family and Marriage in Singapore (1957)*. These anthropological studies have helped to elucidate, without essentialising, aspects of the culture of ethnic groups in pre-independence Singapore.

Despite its limitations, the model of plural society has been used by Chiew (1983, 1985) to explain ethnic relations and the PAP government's ethnic policy in post-independent Singapore. Arguing that Singapore was a plural society prior to self-government in 1959 (Chiew 1985, 51-4), the PAP has gradually put in place a series of policies which have broken down the barriers which once separated the ethnic communities. Utilising the concepts of broker and parallel institution — the former referring to an institution which mediates and bridges two or more ethnic groups and the latter to one which is not shared but duplicated — he pointed out that the significance of broker institutions has increased while that of parallel ones has decreased through a state managed process of de-pluralization since 1959. Amongst the bridging institutions are integrated schools, bilingual education, public housing estates and the promotion of a national identity (a cultural institution) (ibid, 55-7). As a consequence, Singapore society enjoys high levels of structural integration and national identity (ibid, 61). Chiew's work is a useful attempt to draw on the model of plural society in explanatory terms, in contrast to the descriptive nature of much of the work using a similar paradigm. However, it should be pointed out that the de-pluralization thesis is unable to account for developments in government policy over the last decade, which has promoted the revitalisation of ethnic identity and its so-called "cultural roots", for example, in a more rigorous bilingual education policy, and ethnic-based initiatives in self-help.

Politics of Language and Identity

Political developments after the Second World War, critical to understanding how ethnic relations in Singapore have been structured, began in 1946 when the British established the Malayan Union for the purpose of creating a unitary state comprising the Straits Settlements, Federated and Unfederated Malay States. The proposed Union was a major departure from pre-war colonial policy because it extinguished the sovereignty of the Malay Rulers and the privileged position of the Malay community (Stockwell 1979, 17). It also extended citizenship to all regardless of race or creed (Andaya and Andaya 1982, 255), in recognition of the contribution of immigrants to the War effort and the Malayan economy. The Union however excluded Singapore for two reasons (ibid, 254). A liberal citizenship policy would have included large numbers of non-Malays including Singapore's predominantly Chinese population and would have been perceived by the Malays as a threat to their own position. Moreover, the British government considered Singapore a strategic naval base in the Far East and wished to retain it for that purpose.

However, committed to a policy of decolonization and the gradual devolution of independence in British territories in Southeast Asia, it left open the door for a possible unification of Singapore with the mainland at a later date.

This brief but important interlude of the Union in the history of Malaya and its relevance for Singapore has escaped the attention of scholars of the sociology of ethnic relations in the island. Until the formation of Malaysia in 1963 much of the politics of the island were dominated by the view that Singapore, for practical and sentimental reasons, could only survive as part of Malaya. Ethnic relations in the pre-independence period were conditioned by this singular event, and the sociological ramifications of this for post-independent Singapore have yet to be fully documented. During this phase of Singapore's history, two issues, the language and citizenship controversy, were prominent. In this brief essay we can only draw attention to the need for students of ethnic relations to consider this important phase of the island's history, particularly with regard to language, and suggest some directions for future research.

As Gopinathan (1980, 175) commented, it is hardly possible to speak of education in Malaya and Singapore without meaning language because most of the major decisions taken in education are language-related. The political significance of the Chinese language (specifically Mandarin) for the Chinese population in both territories may be traced to the birth and growth of modern Chinese education in the years 1894 to 1941 (Lee 1987, 49). Its philosophy was derived from the humiliating defeats inflicted on China first by the British in 1830 and subsequently by the Japanese, and the rise of Chinese nationalism under Sun Yat Sen, who frequently travelled to Southeast Asia to muster Nanyang Chinese support for the overthrow of the Manchu rulers. The only education available to the majority of the Chinese population in Malaya and Singapore during these years was privately-funded Chinese schools. Considering that the curriculum in such schools was based on Chinese nationalism inspired by the 1911 Revolution, a whole generation of Chinese children were brought up to identify themselves with the political destiny of an emerging nation-state in China.

It was against this backdrop that the first generation of English-educated PAP leaders, committed to the ideal of "multiracialism", were compelled to forge a political strategy that would not alienate the majority of Chinese-educated voters in Singapore yet provide sufficient signal to the mainland that they were committed to Malaya, later Malaysia. Following Communist-backed agitation by Chinese students on the island in 1954, an All-Party Committee, which included Lee Kuan Yew, was set up to look into the problem of Chinese education. Its most important recommendation was the principle of equal treatment for the four streams of education — Malay, Chinese, English and Tamil — which laid the foundation of Singapore's "multiracial" policy and subsequent bilingual education system.

It is relevant to bear in mind that the PAP's policies on language and multiracialism were intimately linked to the notion of equality of the "races" in a "Malaysian Malaysia" as against a "Malay" Malaysia in which Malays would be privileged above other ethnic groups. This particular concept of multiracialism has its origins in the political development of the island following the War and the abandonment of the British proposal to establish the Malayan Union, as a prelude to self-government and nationhood for Malaya. The one common characteristic of all the local political parties formed on the island in the 1950s was their non-communal origins — all of whom professed the principle of equality between races. Multiracialism continues to remain a cornerstone in the way in which Singapore has been constituted as a nation-state and society, particularly in the two decades following separation from Malaysia in 1965.

This brief overview is intended to drive home the point that the politics of language in Singapore has as much to do with ethnic relations as it has with nation-state formation. Research in the sociology of language in the post-independence years has been carried out with language and language policies being firmly embedded within a nation-building agenda. These included linguistic surveys (Kuo 1976, 1980); language policy and planning (Murray 1971, Gopinathan 1980, Pendley 1983, Pakir 1992, 1993); and the promotion of Mandarin by the government (Newman 1986, 1988). What these studies reflect is the increasing role of the state in structuring ethnicity and "managing" ethnic relations. A bilingual education policy is clear illustration of the state's management of ethnic relations. It also throws up the interesting question of how

Singaporeans' perceptions of ethnicity have been filtered by twelve years of bilingual education. Siddique's work on "The Phenomenology of Ethnicity" (1990) is a start in this direction. The consequences of bilingualism for language maintenance and ethnic identity have been well documented by Edwards (1984, 1985) with reference to Canadian society. Students of ethnic relations interested in the ramifications of language policy in Singapore society will do well to seek comparative lessons from Canadian literature (Wardhaugh 1983, Wotherspoon 1987).

The other important implication of the language issue for the study of ethnic relations, and here we must not forget intra-ethnic relations, is that as a consequence of the promotion of the four languages, we find in the 1990s (as argued by Pakir 1993, 84-5) signs of polarization between the Chinese-educated and the English-educated within the Chinese community. Drawing on two unpublished graduate student dissertations, Pakir reports that for the Chinese-educated the Chinese language is seen as central to maintaining Chinese identity; other markers of Chinese identity are more important for the English-educated. This will be elaborated later. Electoral politics in recent general elections have often focused on this perceived polarisation.

Intra-Chinese differences are not a new development. By the beginning of the twentieth century, Murray (1971, 60-1) noted, there appeared within the Chinese population in Singapore a polarization based on language and education, between a minority of Anglophile Chinese and the majority of Chinese-educated. The PAP government's preoccupation with economic development, the establishment of integrated schools with a common curriculum, and the emphasis on English language were responsible for minimizing the language schism. Nevertheless, the division remained nascent throughout these years, kept in check only by the policies of the PAP government. It is arguable whether the signs of polarization in the Chinese community are not also a manifestation of growing income disparities. If so the sociology of ethnic relations in Singapore has increasingly to take into account the relevance of class influence.

In discussing the relevance of political developments in the past to the study of ethnic relations, contributions from the sociology of migration should not be overlooked. Migration has for a long time

232 • *The Making of Singapore Sociology*

been a field of study in its own right but its theoretical incorporation into the sociology of ethnic relations and the nation-state is a more recent development (Zolberg 1982). Widespread interests in the breathtaking economic developments of East Asian societies and their regional impact on parts of the world like Southeast Asia have been accompanied by a "cultural revitalization" of the overseas Chinese. Such a revitalization has also been evidenced by academic interests in the so-called Chinese Diaspora and conceptions of Chinese identity. In an issue of Daedalus in 1991 entirely devoted to looking at the changing meaning of being Chinese today, Wang Gungwu (1991a, 136) remarks, "Sooner or later, it is impossible to avoid asking what being among foreigners does to one's perception of being Chinese ... For most Chinese abroad, it is the non-Chinese environment that impinges on their lives most directly. How that helps to define their Chineseness is an important starting-point". The "rediscovery" of "Chineseness", particularly amongst the overseas Chinese, has been given expression in numerous popular novels and academic papers by Chinese writers in the English language. As Ang (1993, 9) comments, "The experience of migration brings with it a shift in perspective ... for the migrant is no longer 'where you're from', but 'where you're at'" — and this will be the point of anchorage for migrant and ethnic identity.

For this reason the distinction between sojourners and settlers, so well known in sociological literature, may be given a new lease of life. One such development by Wang Gungwu (1991a, 135) describes the overseas Chinese as *huaqiao* (sojourners) and *huayi* who see themselves as descendants of Chinese but prefer to regard themselves as having settled abroad as foreign nationals. The political consequence of the distinction for the Chinese in Southeast Asia is discussed elsewhere by Wang Gungwu (1991b, 176-70) and it is worth recounting. The term *huaqiao* came into use at the end of the last century and the first decade of this century. It was quickly adopted by the Chinese government and various political parties as they vied for the support of the overseas Chinese for their political activities in China. The description is politically significant as it came to be applied to every overseas Chinese, the implication of which challenged the view that they could be loyal to any other country except China. *Huaqiao* came to be closely associated with Chinese nationalism as embodied in the Revolution of 1911. As a consequence, by the beginning of the Second World War, the local loyalties of the Chinese in overseas societies came under suspicion; and their settlement in Southeast Asia was perceived as a form of Chinese colonization.

It was this perception and their loyalty in question that the *huayi* (settlers who could trace their ancestry to several generations outside China), or better known as the Straits-born in Malaya, had to contend with; as they fought to establish their political rights in Malaya and Singapore in preparation for independence and nationhood after the War. With the expulsion of Singapore from Malaysia in 1965, the Chinese on the island found themselves in an unprecedented position in Southeast Asia. They now had the option to be settlers (Wang Gungwu, 1991b, 178) with a state they could call their own, but in a region in which they are perceived as an ethnic minority with a disproportionate economic influence. Studies in the construction of the ethnic identity of the Chinese in Singapore are still in an embryonic stage, with attempts made by Wee (1988) and Rudolph (1993). More undoubtedly will follow. These will need to take on board the insightful contributions of Wang Gungwu's work. Furthermore, resurgence in studies related to the cultural revitalization of the Chinese in Singapore may have a flow-on effect on other ethnic groups.

The reconceptualization of "Malayness" and Malay identity in Singapore more than 25 years after independence is one possibility. Scholarly investigations of this will need to take into consideration the fact that the composition of the officially designated category "Malay" is internally more complex and diverse than the term implies. At the same time, such investigations would also need to consider to what extent has "Malayness" come to be constituted as a Singaporean experience, and to what extent has this experience itself been conditioned by geographical proximity to Malaysia and cultural affinities with other related communities in Malaysia, the Riau archipelago, and Indonesia. One notable attempt is a study, by Mariam Ali (1985), of intra-ethnic perceptions of Malay identity on the north coast of Singapore. One way in which the indigenous inhabitants of the area identified themselves as "real" or "pure" Malays was by tracing their descent to place or location (ibid, 173-76). Another was to distinguish them according to *adat*, customary or refinement of behaviour appropriate to conceptions of "Malayness". Accordingly the ideal model of *adat* was associated with the Riau-Lingga court, which wielded power over the Riau archipelago and Johore in the 17th century. Indeed some of the inhabitants who were originally from Johore still see Singapore as part of the Johore kingdom and consider the political separation in 1965 as an artificial division. Such perceptions have undoubtedly created ambivalence amongst "Malays" about the Singapore government's tacit acceptance of those who profess Islam, practise *adat*, and speak the Malay language as general criteria for the definition of "Malay" on the island. This is a clear illustration of the use of ascriptive ethnicity for the purpose of government. In intra-ethnic terms "Malayness" should be perceived as a continuum, and explained by reference to ethno-history.

The issues raised here are equally pertinent to the "Indian" community in Singapore. Although they are a small minority in Singapore, the community is, ethno-linguistically, highly diverse, notwithstanding the fact that the Tamils make up a dominant proportion. Religious affiliations are also equally diverse. Most studies of Indians in Singapore have focused on the constitution of social organisation and culture in *sub-ethnic* groups, and have not paid much heed to sub-ethnic interactions or relations and the structural relationships between these sub-ethnic Indian groups and nation-building processes after independence and the separation from Malaysia. While existing studies are valuable in revealing aspects of the social history of such South Asian sub-ethnic groups and showing how their identities are maintained, they are insufficient as recent work by Gomez (1997), Sinha (1997), and PuruShotam (1998) show. While there appears to be a concerted drive, at the official level, by various communities such as the Eurasians and Tamils to respond to the state-sponsored revitalization of multiculturalism and Asian values in the last two decades, Gomez argues that the fragmented nature of the Malayalee community has made it difficult for the latter to seize the opportunities to consolidate their identity. Young Malayalees are pressured to identify with the hyphenated Singaporean-Indian-Malayalee, which are sometimes contradictory. As much as there are variations in the interpretation of *Indian-ness* by sub-ethnic groups, the same applies in the label

Hindu as Sinha's work shows. The work of Gomez and Sinha are attempts to deconstruct common-sense notions of being Indian in Singapore, largely created by the practice of ascriptive ethnicity. PuruShotam's study points to the considerable importance of the *negotiation* of ethnicity, especially with regard to language use, in domestic contexts among South Asians in Singapore in sub-ethnic intermarriage conditions.

In recent years the Eurasians have become increasingly conscious of their identity and position in Singapore society, as a minority who perceive themselves as having contributed significantly to the island state relative to its numbers. In part, this is a reaction to the policy of ethnic revitalization and the search for "Asian values" begun by the PAP government in the early 1980s. In contrast to the Eurasians, *Peranakan* (Straits-born Chinese) ethnicity and ethnic identity appears to have undergone a process of attrition or, alternatively, a transformation. Following decolonization and independence, the *Peranakans* have lost one of the major markers of their ethnicity, ie their language (*Baba* Malay) which is a creole of Malay and Chinese dialect, Hokkien or Teochew. The reason for this is that *Peranakans* are officially recognised as Chinese and consequently when *Peranakan* children are enrolled in schools they are required to learn Mandarin as their "mother tongue" (Rudolph 1994, 260-91). The case of the *Peranakans* reveals yet another aspect of the effects of government policies on ethnicity and ethnic relations. While some ethnic groups experience a revitalization of ethnic identity or identify themselves in terms of a particular "race" more than they otherwise would because of the cultural logic of Singapore's "multiracialism" (as argued by Benjamin and discussed below), it is possible for others to undergo a transformation of identity which takes them away from their "roots".

The expansion of interest in the study of ethnic identity, in both majority and minority communities, is only to be expected in a society which has had a dominant migrant background, and which is only now coming to terms with its own identity more than 30 years after reluctantly accepting independence and in the face of economic affluence. Such studies of identity, however, will need to be sensitive to the power differential between ethnic groups. How a minority group comes to terms with its identity is different from that of the majority group, the former is usually expected to adapt in favour of the latter (Lian 1982). In the process the state may be required to play the role of neutral arbiter.

Furthermore, apart from studying such groups as "groups in themselves", there is also a need to study the way in which group boundaries are crossed or transcended. An important work which concerns the crossing of ethnic boundaries is that by Hassan and Benjamin on "Ethnic Outmarriage and Socio-cultural Organisation" (1976). The work is concerned with explaining differences in rates of inter-ethnic marriage among Chinese, Malays and Indians in cultural terms. It is significant for revealing one mechanism by which ethnic boundaries are crossed, ie through intermarriage, and raises a fundamentally important question, viz. how and in what way is ethnic affiliation assigned to the children of such marriages. In Singapore, this is in fact administratively assigned on a patrilineal basis, for example at registration for identity cards. The work is also important because it raises the question of whether or not there exists a Singaporean culture. If individuals from different ethnic groups are indeed able to establish such intimate relations as that between spouses, given the dominance of the CMIO paradigm, what is it that makes it possible for them to do so? While the conditions of Singapore make this question a pertinent one, it also reveals that studies of inter-ethnic marriage elsewhere have failed to consider the dynamics of shared experience in ostensibly plural or multicultural situations in which such marriages occur. The Singapore instance offers possibilities for the development of sociological insights that go far beyond the study of intimate and familial relations. In Singapore, inter-ethnic marriages occur in inter-dialectal and inter-language contexts. For such marriages to occur, some competence in different dialects or in a common language constitute the preconditions before intimate relations can be established. But intimate relations are not simply about the translation of cultures as noted above. For intimate relations to occur, there must exist shared modes of thought. Regardless of the diglossic contexts, shared modes of thought are only possible if there is sufficient substance in the shared experience of everyday life. In Singapore, this shared everyday life experience is situated within a capitalist developmental trajectory, language competencies, religious affiliations, or even purely secular orientations and common concerns.

At first sight, these sociological and social anthropological themes may appear unrelated to larger themes such as symbolic representations of the nation-state in the National Day Parade of Singapore. However, Rajah (in press) has argued that the symbolic representations of the CMIO "races" in Singapore in National Day Parades are nothing but significations which seek to make and manage "traditions" in order to get Singaporeans to think in the same way about their relationship with the state, that they are Singaporeans who belong to a common community. As such, they are ideological constructs and are therefore mystificatory. The National Day Parades, however, contain a profound paradox in the expression of nation-ness in Singapore. Rajah argues that if there is to be any analysis of what is truly Singaporean, it would require a serious consideration of the ethic and norms of rational administration, bureaucratic efficiency, a high degree of planning and coordination and the use of English. These are impossible to represent in the *symbolic, performative* terms of these parades. It is such so called non-ideological elements of everyday life which constitute a Singaporean culture, admittedly experienced differently by various ethnic communities and social classes. It is, in other words, possible to take inter-ethnic marriage as a point of departure for investigations into whether or not there is a Singaporean culture and how such a culture may manifest itself in ways that are unrecognized because of the dominance of the CMIO model. These explorations, we argue, call for further studies and we believe that these studies will make a contribution to the sociological and anthropological understanding of inter-ethnic relations in general.

The State and the Management of Ethnic Relations

It may be gathered in this discussion so far that the state has played an increasingly influential role in ethnic relations. For this reason the policy on ethnic groups pursued by the state and its underlying assumptions require examination. A major contribution in this respect is Benjamin's (1976) discussion in "The Cultural Logic of Singapore's 'Multiracialism'". As he rightly points out, multiracialism is one of the founding charters (in the Malinowskian sense of the term) of the Republic (ibid, 116). A fuller appreciation of this requires a consideration of Singapore's past but intimate ties with Malaya and Malaysia. As an ideology multiracialism is significant in three ways (ibid, 115-16). First, it is a powerful force against ethnic discrimination. Second, it is woven almost invisibly into the everyday life of Singaporeans. Third, the multiracial idea-complex is the clearest expression and cognition of Singaporean culture.

Multiracialism, as PAP ideology, accords equal status to the cultures and ethnic identities of the various "races" in Singapore (Benjamin 1976, 115). It embodies the ideal of equal treatment of such races and in doing so, it also serves to define the population on the basis of races (the official CMIO classification refers to the three major "races", Chinese, Malays, Indians; and the rest are described as "Others"). However the CMIO categories is more than just an administrative construct. The assumption behind the classification, Benjamin states, is the government's view that the relationship between society, culture, race, ethnicity, and the individual is solidary (ibid, 118), and we may add language and community. In contrast to Chiew's depluralization thesis that ethnic distinctions in Singapore are gradually being whittled away by broker institutions, Benjamin argues that such ethnic consciousness has been deliberately nurtured by policies that support a revitalization of ethnic identity and cultural roots. This may be seen in recent developments such as self-help organizations, and a more strident promotion of Mandarin. The apparent contradiction between the two views is not necessarily irreconcilable; the view that the Singapore government strikes a balance between developing broker and parallel institutions is sustainable. What is also noteworthy is that the ideology of multiracialism, as espoused by the state, encourages a primordialist conception of ethnicity. Benjamin's analysis of multiracialism as ideology is an important contribution, a point not always acknowledged by subsequent work (see Clammer 1982, 1985, Siddique 1990). Any further development in this area should consider multiracialism as policy and practice, and their political implications. One such implication is that as a consequence of state policies, intra-ethnic differences are gradually being eroded leading to increasing homogenization within the categories "Chinese", "Malay" and "Indians".

As far as more recent international social science trends, such as cultural studies and postmodernism, there is a small but growing body of literature in Singapore concerned with ethnicity and, in particular, ethnic identity. The article by Ang referred to above is one example. More recently, Chua and Rajah (1997) have attempted to examine ethnic food in Singapore in terms of hybridization and creolization which reveal that food that is commonly and officially associated with the different ethnic groups in Singapore in fact exhibits a great deal of culinary borrowing. What is interesting is that despite this process, such food is "misrecognized" and is believed to be representative of these different "racial" groups. PuruShotam's (1998) most recent work is a serious attempt of the so-called 'deconstructionist' approach. It is a reflexive synthesis which encompasses a Schutzian phenomenological approach and an espousal of a Foucauldian perspective of the relations of power. As such, the work defies easy description. One of the more noteworthy features of the work is that it focuses on 'Language' as an ideological, politico-administrative tool in nation-building and the unintended consequences of nation-building. Yet another notable feature of the study is its convincing treatment of the structural relationships between micro- and macro-sociological issues in Singapore pertaining to "race" and ethnic relations. In view of the fact that intellectual developments in the social sciences elsewhere are very often eventually brought to bear on comparable issues in a Singapore context, we may expect to see more of such work published in the future. However, it is too early to assess what contributions these will make to our understanding of ethnicity and ethnic relations in Singapore.

Most of the work reviewed here acknowledges the importance of the state in the sociology of ethnic relations in Singapore. None, however, has made an attempt to conceptually and theoretical articulate the state within ethnic relations. The exception is Brown (1993) who uses the model of the corporatist state in his analysis of ethnic politics in the Republic in the 1980s. His discussion of the corporatist state, of which Singapore is one, and its relevance for understanding ethnic relations is premised on three interrelated concepts. First, political authority in the corporatist state is viewed in terms of absolute loyalty of citizens to the nation-state; in return the state acts as moral guardian and competent manager of the community. Second, the cultural identity of such a national community is constituted by the presence of various ethnic groups, but the values of each group are mutually compatible and constitute an overarching framework of reference. Third, interest associations such as ethnic groups are institutionalized through state-sponsored participation in activities approved by the government (ibid, 17). Hence self-help and ethnic-based organizations such as MENDAKI, AMP, CDAC and SINDA are deliberately nurtured. They reflect the corporatist ethnic politics which is rationalized within the complex of political authority-cultural identity-interest association discussed. Brown's study is of particular sociological interest, especially in relation to Chiew's, because of the common focus on mediating institutions, even though neither specifically employs the term. Whereas Chiew sees government-sponsored or broker institutions mediating between ethnic groups, Brown's study points to ethnically-based institutions set up by the government to mediate between the state and society. Whether the mediating function will succeed is a matter of debate between those who believe that such structures should be "natural" and spontaneous (Berger and Neuhaus 1977, 40) and those who argue that mediating contexts may be created, for example as a product of government policy (Nisbet 1986, 140). Brown's study, thus, reveals a distinctively characteristic feature of Singapore as a nation-state and society, ie the creation of mediating structures based on "race" by the state itself. While Brown's work constitutes a theoretical advance in understanding the role of the state in ethnic relations, which has hitherto only been assumed, the limitations of this model lies in its statist bias and its tendency to be reductionist. The PAP government works hard at mobilizing its citizens and ethnic groups, whose response has not always been one of equanimity.

From Colonization to Transnationalization

This brief but critical essay on "race" and ethnic relations in Singapore highlighted several issues. With few exceptions, writers who work in this area have used the terms "race" or ethnic group without critical reflection or awareness of their ideological and contextual implications. Essentialist notions of "race" translated into the colonial practice of ascriptive ethnicity have been such a dominant feature of colonial Malaya that they have not only been infused in everyday life but have come to be accepted as conventional wisdom by social scientists. Such notions continue to inform the rationale of government policies in a post-independent Singapore, the clearest expression of this is the ideology of "multiracialism". In a society where the state has been interventionist to effect not only economic development but also nation-building, it is difficult to ignore state influence in ethnic relations — however conceptual development here is embryonic.

Lian (1997, 3) argued that in the early years of independence, governments tend to essentialise ethnic identity for the purpose of constructing national identity and forging political legitimacy. With growing regionalization and globalization in Southeast Asia since the early 1980s, societies in the region, to a greater or lesser degree, are subject to the process of transnationalization. The exception is Singapore where transnationalization is deeply embedded in its history and development. The essential element of transnationalization is the multiplicity of involvements that transmigrants sustain in both home and host societies; as a consequence their identities may be expressed in transnational terms (Basch et al. 1994, 7-8), and even multiethnic terms in the case of Singapore. It is too early to argue that transnationalization will inevitably lead to the relativization of ethnic identities. It would be safer to argue that such identities oscillate between essentialist and relativist polarities. Studies of ethnic identity will dominate the sociology and anthropology of "race" and ethnicity in the next decade, as a once rootless society comes to terms with its being. However for such studies to be meaningful, sociologist and anthropologists will be required to inject a sense of the historical process, whether this be "objective" history or ethno-history, in their work. In the process, the richness of intra-ethnic and inter-ethnic relations may be uncovered. In the longer term as the class structure of Singapore society matures, we may see the greater convergence of the sociology of stratification and the sociology of ethnic relations.

References

Abraham, C. E. R. (1983) "Racial and Ethnic Manipulation in Colonial Malaya", *Ethnic and Racial Studies*, 6(1): 18-32.

Alatas, S. H. (1977) *The Myth of the Lazy Native*, London: F. Cass.

Andaya, B. W. and Andaya, L. Y. (1982) *A History of Malaysia*, London: Macmillan.

Ang, I. (1993) "To Be or Not To Be Chinese: Diaspora, Culture and Postmodern Ethnicity", *Southeast Asian Journal of Social Science*, 21(1): 1-17.

Asad, T. (1973) "Introduction", in T. Asad(ed) *Anthropology and the Colonial Encounter*, London: Ithaca Press.

Basch, L., Schiller, N. and Blanc, C. (1994) *Nations Unbound*, USA: Gordon and Breach.

Bedlington, S. (1974) *The Singapore Malay Community: The Politics of State Integration*, Unpublished Ph.D. Thesis, Cornell University.

Benjamin, G. (1976) "The Cultural Logic of Singapore's 'Multiracialism'", in R. Hassan (ed) *Singapore: Society in Transition*, Kuala Lumpur: Oxford University Press.

Berger, P. and Neuhaus, R. J. (1977) *To Empower People: The Role of Mediating Structures in Public Policy*, Washington D.C.: American Enterprise Institute for Public Policy Research.

Betts, R. H. (1975) *Multiracialism, Meritocracy and the Malays of Singapore*, Unpublished Ph.D. Thesis, Massachusetts Institute of Technology.

Brown, D. (1993) "The Corporatist Management of Ethnicity in Contemporary Singapore", in G. Rodan (ed) *Singapore Changes Guard*, Melbourne: Longman Cheshire.

Chiew, S. K. (1983) "Ethnicity and National Integration: The Evolution of a Multiethnic Society", in P.S.J. Chen (ed) *Singapore Development Policies and Trends*, Singapore: Oxford University Press.

Chiew, S. K. (1985) "The Socio-cultural Framework of Politics", in J. S. T. Quah et al. (eds) *Government and Politics of Singapore*, Singapore: Oxford University Press.

Chua, B. H. and Rajah, A. (1997) *Hybridity, Ethnicity and Food in Singapore*, Working Paper No. 133, Dept. of Sociology, National University of Singapore.

Clammer, J. (1982) "The Institutionalisation of Ethnicity: The Culture of Ethnicity in Singapore", *Ethnic and Racial Studies*, 5(2): 127-39.

Clammer, J. (1985) *Singapore: Ideology, Society, Culture*, Singapore: Chopmen Publishers.

Djamour, J. (1959) *Malay Kinship and Marriage in Singapore*, London: The Athlone Press.

Djamour, J. (1966) *The Muslim Matrimonial Court in Singapore*, London: The Athlone Press.

Edwards, J. (1984) "The Social and Political Context of Bilingual Education", in R.J. Samuda et al. (eds) *Multiculturalism in Canada*, Toronto: Allyn & Bacon.

Edwards, J. (1985) *Language, Society and Identity*, Oxford: Basil Blackwell and Andre Deutsch.

Freedman, M. (1950) "Colonial Law and Chinese Society", *Journal of the Royal Anthropological Institute of Great Britain and Ireland*, 30: 97-125.

Freedman, M. (1957) *Chinese Family and Marriage in Singapore*, London: Her Majesty's Stationery Office.

Furnivall, J. S. (1948) *Colonial Policy and Practice: A Comparative Study of Burma and Netherlands India*, Cambridge: Cambridge University Press.

Gomez, J. (1997) "Consolidating Indian Identities in Post-Independence Singapore: A Case Study of the Malayalee Community", *Southeast Asian Journal of Social Science*, 25(2): 39-58.

Gopinathan, S. (1980) "Language Policy in Education", in E.A. Afendras and E.C.Y. Kuo (eds) *Language and Society in Singapore*, Singapore: Singapore University Press.

Hassan, R. and Benjamin, G. (1976) "Ethnic Outmarriage and Socio-cultural Organisation", in R. Hassan (ed) *Singapore: Society in Transition*, Kuala Lumpur: Oxford University Press.

Hirschman, C. (1987) "The Meaning and Measurement of Ethnicity in Malaysia: An Analysis of Census Classification", *The Journal of Asian Studies*, 46(3): 555-82.

Hodder, B. W. (1953) "Racial Groupings in Singapore", *Singapore Journal of Tropical Geography*, 1: 25-36.

Kuo, E. C. Y. (1976) "A Sociolinguistic Profile", in R. Hassan (ed) *Singapore: Society in Transition*, Kuala Lumpur: Oxford University Press.

Kuo, E. C. Y. (1980) "The Sociolinguistic Situation in Singapore: Unity in Diversity", in E.A. Afendras and E.C.Y. Kuo (eds) *Language and Society in Singapore*, Singapore: Singapore University Press.

Kuper, A. (1988) *The Invention of Primitive Society: Transformations of an Illusion*, London: Routledge.

Lee, T. H. (1987) "Chinese Education in Malaya 1894-1911: Nationalism in the First Chinese Schools", in L. T. Lee (ed) *The 1911 Revolution — the Chinese in British and Dutch Southeast Asia*, Singapore: Heinemann Asia.

Li, T. (1989) *Malays in Singapore: Culture, Economy, and Ideology*, Singapore: Oxford University Press.

Lian, K. F. and Rajah, A. (1993) "The Ethnic Mosaic", in G. Evans (eds) *Asia's Cultural Mosaic*, Singapore: Prentice Hall.

Lian, K. F. (1982) "Identity in Minority Group Relations", *Ethnic and Racial Studies*, 5 (1): 42-52.

Lian, K. F. (1997) "Introduction: Ethnic Identity in Malaysia and Singapore", *Southeast Asian Journal of Social Science*, 25(2): 1-6.

Mariam, A. (1985) *"Orang Baru" and "Orang Lama": Ways of Being Malay on Singapore's North-Coast*, Unpublished M.A. thesis, National University of Singapore.

Murray, D. P. (1971) *Multilanguage Education and Bilingualism: The Formation of Social Brokers in Singapore*, Unpublished Ph.D. thesis, Stanford University.

Newman, J. (1986) "Singapore's Speak Mandarin Campaign: The Educational Argument", *Southeast Asian Journal of Social Science*, 14(2): 52-67.

Newman, J. (1988) "Singapore's Speak Mandarin Campaign", *Journal of Multilingual and Multicultural Development*, 9(5): 437-48.

Nisbet, R. (1986) *The Making of Modern Society*, Brighton: Wheatsheaf Books.

Pakir, A. (1992) "English-Knowing Bilingualism in Singapore", in K.C. Ban, A. Pakir, and C.K. Tong (eds) *Imagining Singapore*, Singapore: Times Academic Press.

Pakir, A. (1993) "Two Tongue Tied: Bilingualism in Singapore", *Journal of Multilingual and Multicultural Development*, 14(1 & 2): 73-90.

Pendley, C. (1983) "Language Policy and Social Transformation in Contemporary Singapore", *Southeast Asian Journal of Social Science*, 11 (2): 46-58.

PuruShotam, N. S. (1998) *Negotiating Language, Constructing Race: Disciplining Difference in Singapore*, Berlin and New York: Mouton de Gruyter.

Rajah, A. (In press) "Making and Managing Tradition in Singapore: The National Day Parade", in W.C. Chew (ed) *Our Place in Time*, Singapore: The Singapore Heritage Society.

Rudolph, J. (1993) *Notions of Baba Ethnicity 100 Years Ago and Today*, Unpublished paper presented at ASEAN Inter-University Seminars on Social Development, Kota Kinabalu, Sabah, Malaysia.

Rudolph, J. (1994) *Reconstructing Identities: A Social History of the Babas in Singapore*, Inaugural Dissertation, Friedrich-Alexander University.

Siddique, S. (1990) "The Phenomenology of Ethnicity: A Singapore Case-Study", *Sojourn*, 5 (1): 35-62.

Sinha V. (1997) "Unpacking the Labels 'Hindu' and 'Hinduism' in Singapore", *Southeast Asian Journal of Social, Science*, 25(2): 139-60.

Stockwell, A. J. (1979) "British Policy and Malay Politics during the Malayan Union Experiment, 1942-1948", *The Malaysian Branch of the Royal Asiatic Society*, Monograph No. 8.

Stockwell, A. J. (1982) "The White Man's Burden and Brown Humanity: Colonialism and Ethnicity in British Malaya", *Southeast Asian Journal Social Science*, 10(1): 44-68.

Taylor, R. (1982) "Perceptions of Ethnicity in the Politics of Burma", *Southeast Asian Journal of Social Science*, 10 (1): 7-22.

Trocki, C. A. (1992) "Political Structures in the Nineteenth and Early Twentieth Centuries", in N. Tarling (ed) *The Cambridge History of Southeast Asia*, 2: 79-130.

Wardhaugh, R. (1983) *Language and Nationhood: The Canadian Experience,* Vancouver: New Star Books.

Wang, G. W. (1991a) "Among Non-Chinese", *Daedalus*, 120(2): 135-57.

Wang, G. W. (1991b) *China and the Chinese Overseas*, Singapore: Times Academic Press.

Wee, V. (1988) *What Does "Chinese" Mean? An Exploratory Essay*, Working Paper, No. 90, Dept .of Sociology, National University of Singapore.

Wotherspoon, T. (1987) *The Political Economy of Canadian Schooling*, Toronto: Methuen.

Zolberg, A. R. (1982) "The Next Waves: Migration Theory for a Changing World", in N. Yeatman (ed) *Majority and Minority*, Boston: Allyn & Bacon.

9

Sociology of the Chinese

Kwok Kian Woon

In this chapter I offer a review of social research on "the Chinese in Singapore". In the first place, sociologists and anthropologists are led to ask a fundamental question: "What does 'Chinese' mean?" (Wee 1988). For them, the answer to this question cannot be an ahistorical one. The rubric "the Chinese in Singapore" provides a demarcation of the research field in a manner that is both more flexible and less misleading than that suggested by the terms "the Chinese community in Singapore" or "the Singapore Chinese community". For one thing, the latter terms tend to connote the idea of a single and more or less well-defined social group whose members share common cultural characteristics. This connotation is indeed stronger in the various common Chinese (Mandarin) terms used to describe Chinese (*huaren* ic "Hua people" or "Chinese") as a community or a group (*huaren shequn* or *huaren zuqun*, often abbreviated as *huashe* or *huazu*). In particular, the Chinese term for "ethnic group" (*zuqun*) overlaps with the term *minzu*, which carries various overlapping notions of collectivity such as "race", "people", and "nation".

There are two ways in which such connotations are problematic in the Singapore case. First, the idea of the Chinese as a single "community" or even as a "race" tends to reinforce — and be reinforced by — the post-independence Singapore state's official model of "multiracialism", albeit a colonial legacy, which discursively and administratively divides the population under the categories of "Chinese", "Malay", "Indian" and "Others" with each of the racial categories having its own "culture" and "mother tongue" (cf. Benjamin 1976, Lai 1995, PuruShotam 1998). To anticipate an argument that I shall develop in this review: one important research area concerns the *varieties* of "Chineseness" in Singapore, the diversity within the so-called "Chinese community", and the differences among various identifiable — and self-identifying — groups obtaining from their specific historical locations in the changing social structure of Singapore.

Second, the numerical predominance of Chinese in the population and the perception, among some, of the economic and political dominance of the Chinese as a majority "race" also tends to figure into the idea of Singapore as a "Chinese society". There is a basis for such a perception since "nowhere else outside of the People's Republic of China and Taiwan, do Chinese form the majority of the citizenry of a nation-state and hold the majority of positions at the highest levels of government" (Kwok 1998a, 200). It is sociologically relevant to consider if members of the "Chinese majority" or of "minority" groupings in Singapore – or even casual foreign observers or serious scholars – view the larger society as a *Chinese* society, meaning either a "*predominantly Chinese* society" or a "*Chinese-dominant* society" (cf. Mani 1997). Strictly speaking, however, Singapore cannot be unproblematically placed under the rubric of "Chinese societies", which conventionally includes China, Hong Kong, Macao, and Taiwan. For one thing, scholars may inquire into the "Chineseness" of each "Chinese society" in comparison to another. In the case of Singapore, however, it is more appropriate for scholars to refer to "Chinese society *in* Singapore" – as suggested by the title of a section in Maurice Freedman's *The Study of Chinese Society* (1979). In an overview of the Chinese in Singapore (Kwok 1998a, 200), I provide an argument for not placing Singapore under the rubric of "Chinese society":

> The inappropriateness of that description ... is apparent the moment one compares the proportion of Singapore's non-Chinese population with those of the other "Chinese societies": while Singapore's is more than 22%, China's non-Han population of "national minorities" is 7% of its billion-plus population; Taiwan's aborigines are less than 2%, of its 21 million people, while Hong Kong's expatriates are no more

than 2% of its 6.4 million inhabitants. Thus Singapore is multiethnic and "plural" to a degree not shared by these other societies. Furthermore, Singapore is located at the heart of the Malay Archipelago and not in that domain, generally referred as East Asia and understood to cover Japan, Korea and Vietnam, whose civilization is traceable to ancient China. In addition, it is a completely independent state whose national identity has to be sufficiently broad to include ethnic groups other than the Chinese.

It is not just for reasons of demographic composition or political correctness that Singapore should not be sociologically considered as a Chinese society. Here I advance a general thesis that I shall develop in my concluding section: "Singapore" as a historical entity can be conceived as one that was "born into" modernity, as contrasted with most other societies — including the so-called "Chinese societies" — whose modernity emerged in relation to a pre-existing indigenous traditional social order (cf. Kwok 1993, 7-10). By this, of course, I do not mean that we cannot speak of a "premodern" Singapore, but that "Singapore society" can be considered "modern" from the very beginnings of its historical evolution as a colony — a colonial society — under British rule. Put simply, this represented the spread of Western modernity on the global stage and the induction of a growing local and migrant population into the political and economic structures of modernity. In terms of a history of British colonial rule, Hong Kong presents a comparable case but, as indicated, its more homogeneous population, its physical and cultural proximity to the mainland, and its recent return to Chinese sovereignty (as a Special Administrative Region in 1997) also make it less comparable. Following colonial rule over a relatively short time span of one and half centuries, Singapore's transformation as a nation-state, since breaking away from Malaysia — and the Malayan past — in 1965, was led by a developmentalist and interventionist state which not only built upon the legacy of the colonial past but also initiated and managed rapid modernization (cf. Lian 1999, Kwok 1999, 55-58).

I shall conclude this review with a set of reflections on the problematic of "modernity" (or, more appropriately, "modernities") and on the ways in which the Chinese in Singapore can be located within the problematic. For the main part of the review, however, I outline existing areas and trajectories of research on the Chinese in Singapore, and then move on to highlight some research benchmarks and lacunae. This review is not meant to be comprehensive, let alone exhaustive, in scope. The selection and treatment of issues reflect my reading of the literature and the sociological concerns and theoretical perspectives that I have been preoccupied with. Moreover, some of the literature is more appropriately covered in other chapters in the present volume, especially those relating to, for example, ethnicity and ethnic relations, the sociology of religion, the sociology language, and the sociology of education.

Overlapping Research Areas

Research on the Chinese in Singapore is relevant to the sociological understanding of Singapore society or, more generally, Singapore Studies. What has been the place of the "Chinese" in the making of Singapore as a society? What have been the roles played by different groups of Chinese? What varieties of Chineseness have developed in an evolving multiethnic society? Research on the Chinese in Singapore, however, does not only contribute to an understanding of Singapore society. For example, as both a social anthropologist and a sinologist, Freedman (1979) saw the particular case of the Chinese in Singapore and Malaya (and in Southeast Asia) as offering insights for Chinese Studies, especially the study of patterns of Chinese familial, associational, and religious life. Indeed, Philip Kuhn (1997) has even made a case for the study of the Chinese overseas as an intrinsic part of the study of "late-imperial and modern China: not because Chinese culture and institutions are simply a reflection of China, nor that Chinese civilization in any way determines how Chinese overseas think and behave, but because the process of emigration, and the kinds of people who went through it, turn out to be important parts of Chinese history of the past several centuries".

The study of Chinese society in Singapore as a species of Chinese Studies can flow in two directions of interest, both of which were found in Freedman's work. On the one hand, his research also included investigations on social life in Hong Kong and China as part of understanding the sociology (or social anthropology) of "Chinese society" in its various manifestations in and out of China. On the other hand, Freedman's studies on the Chinese in Singapore and Malaya, followed by William Skinner's studies on the Chinese in Thailand (Skinner 1957), have been significant in the development of a larger terrain of study — that of the Chinese in Southeast Asia. This terrain also overlaps with the study of "Nanyang Chinese", a term referring to the Chinese who settled in the Southeast Asian coastal lands via the Nanyang or, literally, Southern Ocean, conventionally known as the South China Sea (Wang Gungwu 1992, 11-57). The history of the Nanyang Chinese points to the intimate historical and economic links between China and Southeast Asia over the course of a millennium (Reid 1996). In this sense the study of Chinese in Southeast Asia is not only part of Chinese Studies but also an important part of Southeast Asian Studies. In particular, the comparative study of different Chinese communities in the region not only illuminates patterns of Chinese social life and conditions in China but also the specific local context of each Southeast Asian society (Skinner 1996).

The study of the Chinese in Southeast Asia, however, is in turn a major part of what has been called "overseas Chinese studies" — of which the most succinct overview has been provided by Wang Gungwu (1998). Although it has been estimated that the Chinese in Southeast Asia make up more than 85% of 25 million outside of China (now including Hong Kong) and Taiwan (see Wang 1998), the study of Chinese in other parts of the world also offer scope for comparative work on the Chinese in Southeast Asia; this, however, has not developed in any significant way. The term "overseas Chinese" has been loosely synonymous with the Chinese term *huaqiao* — which literally means "Chinese sojourners" — a term coined in the 1880s and officially used in subsequent decades to refer to all Chinese abroad, including those who have settled in new lands, implying that they were still subjects of and protected by China (Wang Gungwu 1992, 1-10). With mass migration and settlement, and, finally, the attainment of citizenship, many ethnic Chinese no longer fall under the rubric of *huaqiao* but are more often called *huayi* (descendents of Chinese).

In contemporary scholarship, the term *huaqiao* has given way to *haiwai huaren*, which is translated into English as "Chinese overseas" (causing some confusion to the lay person who may see it as little different from the term "overseas Chinese"). For example, consider the later writings of Wang Gungwu such as those collected in *China and the Chinese Overseas* (Wang Gungwu 1991). It should be noted here that some scholars who study the place of the Chinese in contemporary Southeast Asian societies have sought to move away from either of these terms. In the collection *Ethnic Chinese as Southeast Asians*, Suryadinata (1997, vii), as editor, took pains to suggest that the existing terms perpetuate a "mainland China-centric view" and that this has confused the position and identity of the Chinese in Southeast Asia, with serious political implications as Southeast Asian Chinese are still considered to be "Chinese overseas" or "Overseas Chinese", not "Southeast Asians". In particular, he is keen to separate the Chinese in contemporary Southeast Asia from those in Hong Kong, Macao and Taiwan (*Gang-Ao-Tai* in the abbreviated Chinese term). The term of identification *Zhongguo ren* (either Chinese in the classical sense of being from the Middle Kingdom or in modern sense of being citizens of the Chinese nation-state) does not readily apply to the *huayi* in Southeast Asia, as much as some older-generation Chinese may continue to use it when they interact with their counterparts in the diaspora.

Moreover, the term "Greater China" has appeared in the 1990s, loosely subsuming not just *Gang-Ao-Tai* but, in some versions, also Singapore and, more generally, Chinese in and out of China who are economically linked across national and regional boundaries (Suryadinata 1997, 3, Pan 1998, 17). It should be noted that a number of writers tend to consider Singapore alongside China, Hong Kong, and Taiwan as part of "Greater China" (eg Kotkin 1992, Naisbitt 1994, Seagrave 1996, cf. Carino 1996). This was prefigured by the idea of a larger "East Asian" region put forward in the context of the economic rise of newly industrializing economies by the early 1980s — and hence Singapore, more economically advanced than her Southeast Asian neighbours, also tended to be considered as part of the East Asian nexus (eg Hofheinz Jr. and Calder 1982, Berger 1986, Berger and

Hsiao 1988). And given the predominance of the Chinese population, Singapore was included alongside the industrial-capitalist East Asian societies such as Japan, South Korea, Taiwan, Hong Kong as posing a "post-Confucian challenge" (MacFarquhar 1980, cf. Kahn 1979). In a comparable perspective, (Huntington 1993, 1996) offers his thesis of the potential "clash of civilizations", a world divided into civilizational blocs including a Confucianist bloc, of which Singapore is a member.

Stressing a shared universe of cultural discourse rather than a similarity or networking along economic lines among Chinese in different parts of the world, Tu Wei Ming (1991, 1994) has proposed the idea of a "Cultural China" (*wenhua Zhongguo*). This idea provides an alternative to the term *haiwai Zhonghua* or "overseas China", which Tu says "carries the political connotation of a Chinese-style commonwealth encompassing the mainland, Hong Kong, Taiwan, and Singapore" and has been debated in both China and Taiwan (Tu 1994, 264). Tu's conception of a "Cultural China" is composed of three "symbolic universes": first, "societies populated predominantly by cultural and ethnic Chinese"; second, Chinese communities in other societies; and third, non-Chinese individuals in scholarly, business and professional fields whose intellectual understandings of China are disseminated in their own languages. Singapore is included in the first category, alongside China, Taiwan and Hong Kong.

Suryadinata (1995a, 1995b) had earlier edited two volumes on "Southeast Asian Chinese". In my view, he is concerned with the integration of Chinese not as *Southeast Asians* — as if there has already developed a common regional consciousness — but rather as *citizens* in Southeast Asian *nation-states*. In contrast, the proponents of the notions of "Greater China" and "Cultural China" are concerned with *transnational* relations among people whose basic common denominator is that they can be considered to be of Chinese descent. For example, the inclusion of Singapore under such a term brings it into the East Asian ambit and gives short shrift to its geographical and cultural location in Southeast Asia. Suryadinata has a point in emphasizing the ties of Chinese to their Southeast Asian settings, but he does so at the risk of downplaying their ancestral origins or any continuing form of self-identification as

"Chinese" on their part, including, for example, as a minority group in the host society or as part of the wider diaspora.

In any case, beyond the Chinese in Southeast Asia, the term "Chinese overseas" is already a slight, if clumsy, improvement over the historically specific term "overseas Chinese". Although it can still be criticized as a China-centric term, it has acquired some currency with the publication of the *Encyclopedia of the Chinese Overseas* edited by Lynn Pan (1998). Here the coverage on the Chinese in countries and regions across the world (outside of China and *Gang-Ao-Tai*) is accompanied by interpretive essays on origins, migration, institutions, and relations (with China and with non-Chinese).

Finally, the worldwide scope of the research enterprise represented by the *Encyclopedia* suggests that overseas Chinese studies or the study of Chinese overseas are now also conceived of as part of the study of the "Chinese diaspora" in particular (see, for example, Pan 1994) and "diaspora studies" in general. The very notion of a Chinese *Diaspora* — a term which has been used to refer to Jews living dispersed among the Gentiles after the Babylonian exile and, in contemporary times, outside of the state of Israel — underlines China as the original centre of dispersal. In my view, the notion of a "homeland" which the Chinese overseas must, if not return to, continue to have some kind of bond with, should not be automatically assumed in any particular case, including, for example, the various groups of "Chinese" in Singapore. Tu Wei Ming has even suggested that "because the Chinese diaspora has never lost its homeland, there is no functional equivalent to the cathartic yearning for Jerusalem." Rather, "the ubiquitous presence of the Chinese state — its awe-inspiring physical size, its long history, and the numerical weight of its population — continues to loom large in the pyschocultural constructs of diaspora Chinese." (Tu 1994, 18-19) Yet this view appears rather sweeping. It begs further questions: In what sense have the Chinese overseas, living among non-Chinese, never lost their homeland? To what extent does an orientation to China — including "Cultural China" — continue to shape and define the Chineseness of the Chinese overseas? These are questions that the case of the Singapore may throw up theoretically interesting answers.

Benchmarks and Lacunae

To sum up, the study of the Chinese in Singapore can be located as part of the following areas and corresponding trajectories of research:

- Singapore Society / Singapore Studies: Chinese in the making of Singapore society; in particular, the historical development of Chinese identity in a colonial and then post-colonial multiethnic society.
- Sinology / Chinese Studies: Chinese society in Singapore in relation to the study of "Chinese societies"; comparative study of Chinese institutions and practices, and the study of Late Imperial and Modern China.
- Southeast Asian Studies: Chinese in Singapore as part of Southeast Asian or Nanyang Chinese; comparison with Chinese in other Southeast Asian societies, throwing light on the specific characteristics of such societies.
- Overseas Chinese Studies / Study of Chinese Overseas: Chinese in Singapore as *huaqiao* and *haiwai huaren.*
- East Asian Studies: Singapore as a predominantly Chinese society as part of "Confucian" and "industrial" East Asia or as part of "Greater China" or "Cultural China".
- Study of Chinese diaspora / Diaspora Studies: Chinese in Singapore as part of the global Chinese diaspora and in comparison with other diasporas.

In this review, the first of these areas serve as the core area around which the others overlap. But it is unproductive to draw clear lines to distinguish where one area ends and another begins. This is especially so when social scientists aim to move beyond the particularity of any case in order to consider larger substantive and theoretical implications. In particular, the study of the Chinese in Singapore is rich in possibilities; it can begin from different points of departure and can be of relevance to a number of fields. Moreover, research on the Chinese in Singapore may also yield insights for general sociology or sociological theory. It is tempting to consider this ambition as a conventional disciplinary distinction between history and sociology. Hence also the idea of a division of labour between the historian and the sociologist, the one ploughing away at the archives and unearthing the relevant oral, written, and material records, the other offering explanatory schemas and theoretical insights. Both the disciplinary distinction and the division of labour are artificial and unhelpful. It is true that earlier generations of scholars have been trained under the influence of strict disciplinary boundaries. To be sure, the bulk of the research output on the Chinese in Singapore has been contributed by scholars trained as historians. But useful works — whether by historians or sociologists — are distinguished by some combination of both empirical depth and interpretive power (cf. Lian 1992). In this sense the historian and the sociologist, history and sociology, cannot do without each other. With these points in mind, I now highlight benchmarks and lacunae in the existing literature along broad chronological lines which I have found useful elsewhere in providing an account of the Chinese in Singapore (Kwok 1998a).

Historical Formation and the Growth of a Diversified Community

If 1819 marks the beginning of "modern Singapore", it behoves scholars to have some understanding of pre-modern and pre-colonial Singapore. The little available textual materials need to be highly qualified as historiographical sources, while the archaeological work has been relatively recent, with much already lost to the ravages of time (Kwa 1985, Miksic 1985). In any case, there is evidence to suggest that the island was known to the Chinese empire, perhaps as early as the 12th century — the surrounding region known much earlier — and that early trading links were established. Indeed, the history of Singapore should be understood as intimately connected with the surrounding region, especially in the context of the Johore maritime polity, which also stretched to the Riau islands (Trocki 1979, 1990). A more general point can be made: the researcher's mental map of Singapore is not confined to its territorial borders as a sovereign nation-state since 1965; instead, he or she should be aware of the shifting and porous boundaries – political, economic, and cultural — that constitute "Singapore society" over time. In this light, the study of the Chinese in Singapore, too, both benefits from and contributes to a historical-sociological understanding of Singapore's place in the Southeast Asian and wider Asian region, and in the global context, at the crossroads of Indian Ocean civilizations and as a key node in the modern capitalist world system from the time of British colonialism.

Although there is no firm evidence of a settled Chinese community before the British founding, Chinese cultivators, traders, and labourers from neighbouring lands moved swiftly into the island after 1819 (Trocki 1990, Wang Gungwu 1991a, Wong 1980, cf. Lee 1978). Thus, from the earliest beginnings of Chinese migration into the island, there were groups of Chinese who were already familiar with local customs and practices, and with British and Dutch administrations, even as new arrivals (*sinkeh*), many of them relatives, came from Southern China. Against the backdrop of migration patterns over time (Pan 1988, Saw 1970), there developed different groups of Chinese in Singapore, making for a diversified community or a "community of communities". From early colonial times, therefore, the basic distinction is that between the Straits Chinese (Straits-born) or Babas and the China-born *sinkeh*, many of whom came to the colony as coolies (Pitt 1984). But within these two categories, distinctions were made between people according to place of origin, speech group, occupation or trade, and kinship. Seah U Chin, himself a China-born who made his way into the Straits Chinese community, left two translated and published scholarly studies (Seah 1847, 1848) on the social and economic life of the early Chinese immigrants: the first, a study of annual remittances of China-born coolies to their homeland and the second, a study of the occupational patterns of the Chinese. The latter showed that the Straits Chinese — called "Malacca men" — were largely from the non-labouring classes.

There have been a number of studies on the Babas, a culturally distinctive group of Chinese, who had deep roots in the region over generations and who thrived economically and socially under the aegis of British rule by virtue of their early settlement and their possession of skills, including knowledge of English, useful to the British. The most comprehensive study to date is Jurgen Rudolf's *Reconstructing Identities: A Social History of the Babas* (1998), covering the vicissitudes of the community from the earliest times to the mid-1990s, from their status as the

"King's Chinese" to what has been seen as their near-extinction in contemporary Singapore. This is a rich and informative study that is superior to the more superficial treatment provided by Clammer (1980) and to popular accounts, for example, by Tan (1993) and Chia (1994). It is also a study that is theoretically and methodologically sophisticated, solidly located within the tradition of interpretive sociology.

But the Babas constituted one group, albeit a socially significant group in spite of their smaller numbers, within a diversified community whose internal structure and functioning in relation to colonial society in Singapore was multilayered and complex. The social organisation of the China-born numerical majority is extensively covered in the writings of Yen Ching Hwang (1986 and 1995b), especially with regard to patterns of migration, the functioning of dialect and clan organizations, secret societies and overall social structure. Cheng (1985 and 1990, cf. Mak 1995) has highlighted the enduring nature of *bang* structure and the proliferation of traditional associations, many of which continue to exist in present-day Singapore (Pang and Low 2000).

Given the continued existence of Chinese secret societies in contemporary Singapore, it is necessary to develop an understanding of the role and functioning of this type of organisation in colonial society. In this respect, Mak's study (1995) stands out as an explicitly sociological treatment which looks back to the history of secret societies in the early Straits Settlements. Carl Trocki (1990) has advanced a bold thesis about the role of secret societies in the colonial order, whose existence and functioning depended heavily on the opium trade. In particular, he links the secret society as a type of organisation to the *kongsi* (cf. Wang Tai Peng 1995) and to the operation of the system of opium revenue farms on the island. In analyzing the frequent clashes between rival *kongsi* (eg the Hokkien-Teochew riots of 1846-47), he points to a larger class struggle between Chinese labourers and the colonial socio-political order supporting the opium trade. This thesis, which can be criticized for its use of an orthodox Marxist approach, offers a related line of analysis from Lee Poh Ping's explanation of the instability in the society as resulting from the conflict between the "gambier and pepper society" and the emerging "free trade society".

Edwin Lee (1991), in turn, offered the view that such instability was a continuation of the political and social disorder in China brought into Singapore by those who had experienced such disorder. Lian (1992, 101) has called such an argument "equally unconvincing" and suggested, following the work of Lyman (1974), that autonomous traditional associations and secret societies developed to fill the vacuum created by the lack of central government authority, in effect playing the role of a "parallel government". There is merit in this line of analysis, which is not totally at variance with Trocki's argument concerning the attenuation of such forms of solidarity with the further extension of colonial rule towards the end of the nineteenth century (cf. Kwok 1998, 204-205). The debate along all these lines can hardly be considered to be settled, and there is still a need for sociological interpretation of the consolidation of the colonial socio-political order vis-à-vis the diversified Chinese community in the 19th century.

Into the Rwentieth Century

The study of Chinese social structure in the colonial order during the decades before the Second World War has been extensively covered by historians such as Yong (1991), Chui (1991), and Ng (1992), focusing on the structure of Chinese political and community leadership and the study of specific organizations and movements, including the Chinese Chamber of Commerce, the Malayan Kuomintang Movement and the Malayan Communist Movement (cf. Yong 1997). Yen Ching Hwang (1995) also offers essays on the Overseas Chinese nationalist movements, the Confucian Revival Movement, and the Revolutionary Propaganda Organizations during the early decades of the century. This period saw the intersection of a number of sources of cultural and political influence on different groups among the Chinese in Singapore. Many among the China-born evinced a strong orientation towards developments in the mainland: hence the support given to the Kuomintang, Communist and, in the 1930s, the anti-Japanese movements. The Straits Chinese, too, had their own organizations which were, on the one hand, part of the elite colonial structure and, on the other, part of efforts to relate meaningfully to developments on the mainland, the Confucian movement being a prime example (Lee Ting Hui 1988).

Five areas may be highlighted as lacunae in the research on the Chinese in Singapore in the pre-World War II decades. The first of these is both methodological and substantive in nature; it relates to the sociological theme of the relationship between biography and history. Indeed, there have been some examples of work in this direction, for example, Li Yuan Jin's detailed study of Lim Boon Keng (1990), Qiu Xinmin's brief study of Khoo Seok Wan (Qiu Shuyuan), and on a lesser scale, Ching Seow Ying's thesis on Song Ong Siang (1972). C.F. Yong (1987) has provided an authoritative study of Tan Kah Kee, the archetypal *huaqiao* patriot, whose memoirs has also been more recently translated (Ward et al. 1994). In particular, Yong also covered Tan's important economic role as an industrialist over the pre-war decades. But there have been no comparable biographical or sociological studies of other important Chinese business leaders, especially in relation to the rubber, banking and other industries in particular, and processes and vicissitudes of Chinese capital accumulation in general.

Ke Mulin has provided a useful compendium of short biographies of "Chinese historical figures" based on a variety of sources (including Song 1984). Yet there is a paucity of specific works on key protagonists, and often the links between biography and history — between personalities and social conditions are not adequately teased out. Li Yuanjin's consideration of men such as Song Ong Siang, Lim Boon Keng and Khoo Seok Wan — contemporaries from contrasting backgrounds — as "Chinese intellectuals" opens up a new area of inquiry, especially as a backdrop to an understanding of the changing roles of intellectuals in Singapore (Li 1999, cf. Hong 1975 and Kwok 1995). Both intellectual history and the sociology of intellectuals can be considered to be underdeveloped fields in Singapore, and a study of Chinese — both Chinese-speaking and English-speaking — local intellectuals, who emerged from various educational backgrounds since colonial days should be included in any understanding of the construction of intellectual traditions and cultures in Singapore.

Second, the study of individual "community leaders" also need to be accompanied by the study of the social and intellectual movements that they led or participated in, including the ways such movements manifest the historical moment as experienced by not only the "elites" but also the "masses". Most of the works on the movements already cited — the Communist, anti-Japanese, and Confucian movements — are not guided by any explicit sociological perspective on social movements and, indeed, there is room for a comparative sociology of social movements. In the same vein, the concepts of "public sphere" and "civil society" have hardly been used in the study of the early 20th-century movements, although an exception is T.N. Harper's stimulating study (1997) of "the making of a diasporic public sphere" in Singapore, breaking away from the focus on any one personality or social movement but instead looking at both the "creation of the intellectual culture that embodies both the demands of globalism and the desire for authenticity" and "the multiple layers of sociality within colonial society". Most of the existing studies can still be reworked and interpreted within and beyond the scope of the kind of conceptual vocabulary that Harper brings to the sociology of colonial Singapore.

Third, more work needs to be done on the patterns of social differentiation among the Chinese beyond that represented by the Babas and *sinkeh*, as well as the *bang* divisions. In particular, attention has been paid to the development of education in the colony, which created a division between those who were schooled in different language streams (Chelliah 1947, Lee Ting Hui 1987, Gopinathan 1991, Borthwick 1988 and 1990). This development is of significance in view of the subsequent bifurcation between the "Chinese-educated" and the "English-educated", one which in a number of aspects continue to persist in present-day Singapore. In particular, the differentiation could be analyzed along the dimensions of language use, sources of cultural influence, political affiliation, socioeconomic class. To be sure, there is no one-to-one fit between educational background and a set of specific attributes, but the point is to identify the patterns more clearly and to look into their sociological consequences for the shaping of Singapore society.

Fourth, the process of "Malayanization" in the pre-war decades has hardly been explored beyond studies on the literatures of the Chinese in Singapore and Malaya. These studies can be divided into those that deal with literary writings in Chinese (Fang 1977, Yeo 1993, Yeo and Leung 1985, Tang 1988, Loh 1989) collectively called *mahuawenxue* (Malayan Chinese Literature) and those concerning writings in English (Koh 1993 and 1995). The literature in English and in Chinese — including those written in Chinese by the China-born who have transplanted themselves in Singapore and Malaya — indicate strong ties to their adopted homeland. There have also been writings on the so-called "Nanyang school" of painting, the artists in this school seeking to express their immersion in the Southeast Asian landscape and their encounter with international art, while retaining some characteristics of Chinese painting traditions (see eg Shi 1989). Beyond their relevance for the sociology of literature or the sociology of art in Singapore, these writings detail a brief period of "Malayanization", elements of which were also seen in some of the pre-war intellectual and social movements and given new life in the post-war era of decolonization but finally attenuated with Singapore's independence. This area deserves attention because of its theoretical implications for the study of Chinese and other identities during the pre-war and pre-Independence era.

Fifth, it may appear that the thrust of the foregoing discussion leans heavily towards historical-sociological research that is based on leaders and the educated, those who have left behind a trail of achievements and written materials. Indeed, the study of the "nameless" or the "masses" from the perspectives of social history — or "history from below" — and the sociology of everyday life is generally underdeveloped in the literature on the Chinese in Singapore. Warren's work (1986), focusing on the lives and times of rickshaw coolies, has the ambition of offering a "people's history of Singapore" (covering the period 1880-1940), but it has not been followed up by major studies. A people's history makes a place for historical actors who are easily taken for granted or forgotten, and whose social roles have not been recognized. There is, for example, a paucity of work on women and gender relations. With such an approach in mind, however, existing materials (including more recently collected oral-historical materials) can be of use in looking at many unexplored areas in the study of the Chinese in Singapore. Materials that have not been used in extant research also need to be uncovered. I have in mind, for example, letters that immigrants — including illiterate immigrants employing the services of professional letter-writers — write home to relatives in China as a source of information about everyday life of the Chinese in Singapore.

The Japanese Occupation and Decolonization

The Japanese Occupation was a traumatic experience for the Chinese in Singapore because their widespread support for the anti-Japanese movement in Singapore and in China during the late 1930s singled them out for brutal treatment. The Malayan Chinese resistance to Japan has been relatively well documented by Chinese scholars (eg Shu and Chua 1984, Foong 1997). In addition, the War has received strong attention from official bodies in contemporary Singapore (eg National Heritage Board 1995) and figures prominent in the writing and teaching of national history for reasons related to nation-building and the promotion of the idea of national self-reliance (cf. D. Wong 1996). In this context, the figure of Lim Bo Seng has been focused upon as a war hero, although it is also generally recognized by now that Lim was fighting for the Kuomintang cause (Thio 1991, Kwok 1998). In contrast the war efforts of those who were identified with the Malayan Communist Party, especially the Malayan People's Anti-Japanese Army, have received little attention in Singapore (cf. Cheah 1983; Hara 1995). This can be explained by the official anti-communist ideology. It is also a case of history being written and represented from the perspective of Singapore as a nation-state, such that the War as a wider Malayan experience has figured less prominently. In any case, as Diana Wong (1996, 2000) shows, the Japanese Occupation in Malaya and Singapore can be studied from the perspective of sociology of memory. Here, it might also be suggested that the impact of the Occupation on the Chinese-educated is remembered in stronger terms as reflected, for example, in post-war literary writings in Chinese (Yeo and Ng, 2000).

But there are also substantive issues concerning the extent to which lines can be drawn between the nascent Malayan nationalism and the *huaqiao* patriotism that had developed over the preceding four decades. This, in turn, is complicated by the polarization within the *huaqiao* community in Singapore, between the supporters of the Kuomintang and those of the Communists. This leads us to some of the thorny issues in the immediate post-war context of decolonization, which also saw the rise of English-educated Chinese and non-Chinese who saw themselves developing Malayan nationalism along with anti-colonialism, independent of the political developments in China. The People's Action Party (PAP), led by a core group of English-educated professionals, emerged as the leading political power out of, as Willmott (1989, cf. Bloodworth 1986) puts it, "a struggle between different communions, two groups with different and conflicting collective sentiments. Politically it was a struggle between the leaders of the more numerous Chinese-educated community, who were trying to retain their power in Singapore, and the emerging English-educated professional class, who were trying to capture it". The struggle between the two groups, however, was not clear-cut, as there were Chinese-educated who early on rallied to, and promoted, the PAP cause. Thus there were key leaders such as Ong Pang Boon, Lee Khoon Choy and Jek Yeun Thong, who comprised the "Chinese-educated political vanguard" of the PAP (Sai and Huang 1999). Yet another example is that of Chan Choy Siong, who also led the cause of women at a time when socialist ideas concerning women's rights were integral to the party's developing ideology (cf. Lin 1993).

In the postwar years, the ranks of the Chinese-educated had swelled through the expansion of Chinese education; likewise, the graduates of Chinese schools had less access to employment opportunities in an environment, especially in the civil service, that favoured those who functioned in English (Borthwick 1988 and 1990). Coupled with the legacy of the China-orientation of their predecessors as well as their own exposure to the modern movements on the mainland, their anti-colonial and Malayan-oriented sentiments were often held suspect. Moreover, there were no opportunities for higher education for the Chinese-educated in the colony. It was against this background that the idea of a Chinese-language university, Nanyang University was mooted by Chinese leaders, in particular Tan Lark Sye, whose role and contribution has not attracted in-depth study although he has been remembered by the Nanyang University Alumni in a commemorative volume (1997). But Nanyang University also represented a larger social movement among the Chinese-speaking masses, dovetailing the anti-colonial and nationalist movements with the Chinese-educated and lower-income sector of the population. Indeed, there is a need for more study of the origin, development, and demise of Nanyang University in particular and as part of the larger problematic of the development of Chinese-medium education and the deeply felt marginalization of the Chinese-educated in post-war Singapore society. Dispassionate analysis, although guided by a concern to reflect different voices and points of views, is called for not least because memories among older generations of the Chinese-educated and Nanyang graduates still make their presence felt in contemporary Singapore, more often than not privately rather than publicly (see Li Hui Ling 1999).

In any case, an understanding of the post-war period of decolonization is relevant to any analysis of the Chinese in post-Independence Singapore, when the project of nation-state formation came into full force. In particular, many at the China-born population who had settled in the island had shifted the focus of their political affiliation away from China and had sought to become citizens, following the successful campaign of the Singapore Chinese Chamber of Commerce for gaining citizenship for those with an eight-year residential requirement but without knowledge of the English language (Drysdale 1984, 67, Yong 1992, 279). The idea of citizenship also gained legitimacy with David Marshall's effort in having the leadership in the People's Republic of China confirm that Chinese with Singapore citizenship owed their political loyalty to Singapore and not to China; an understanding of his role is now aided by the posthumous publication (Marshall 1996) of his letters written during his visit to China in 1956.

The decolonization period saw not simply the rise of the PAP but also the formulation of a "pragmatic strategy" (Wu 1999) which guided official policies concerning the Chinese language and education within the broad framework of multiracialism. Indeed, the role of the PAP — and the role of Lee Kuan Yew and other party leaders — cannot be overemphasized because of its centrality in determining the course of the nation-state project. In addition to earlier accounts of the PAP's triumph over the Communists (eg Bloodworth 1986, Drysdale 1984), there has been more recent efforts to tell "the Singapore story" either as part of the "National Education" programme of the state or as part of individual recollections of the past, as in the autobiographical accounts of Lee Kuan Yew (1998, cf. Han et al. 1998) and in published interviews with other important leaders (Chew 1996). Here again, with the exception of Lee Kuan Yew's writings, such published individual accounts are rare and, if available, need to be located within interpretive analyses of the period of decolonization. In particular, the accounts of those Chinese-educated leftist leaders who were the proverbial "losers" or "victims" in history are conspicuous by their absence. For example, other than Lim Chin Siong's brief interview in Chew's *Leaders of Singapore* (1996), historical-sociological understanding of the actions and motivations of leaders such as him, and the events that they were part of, is severely hampered by the lack of publicly available accounts, in effect making for a tendency for this period to be understood in terms of the more-or-less "official" or "authoritative" narrative of "*the* Singapore story" rather than in terms of multiple narratives and different versions of the events during the tumultuous pre-Independence years (cf. Wee 1999).

The Making of a New Nation

In his essay on the Chinese "as immigrants and settlers" focusing on the case of Singapore, Wang Gungwu (1991a, 166-78) concluded by suggesting that when Singapore separated from Malaysia, "a completely new kind of future was put before the Chinese there. For the first time in the history of the Chinese in Southeast Asia, there was every reason for one group of Chinese to settle" (Wang Gungwu 1991a, 178):

> …These Chinese…are determined to change the image of the Chinese as opportunistic transients. It is still too soon to determine whether they will succeed. It will not be easy to convince their suspicious neighbours that they have fully escaped from their history and that, whatever economic and geopolitical problems the region may have to face in the future, they are in Singapore to stay. For them, as the majority people of Singapore, ancestral values will remain useful for social intercourse and business purpose. For them, whatever links remain between Singapore and China would have to be on the same basis as those between Singapore and any other country.

Wang Gungwu provides one key to what might be considered the "exceptionalism" of Singapore. Three qualifications, however, may be added to Wang's insightful way of summing up the situation of the Chinese in post-Independence Singapore. First, historically, there have been Chinese and Chinese descendants who have settled in Southeast Asian societies and adopted them as homelands. The case of the Babas in Singapore stands out in this regard. Wang's reference, therefore, concerns the majority of the China-born who stayed on as Singapore citizens upon independence, thus "escaping" from the history of the Chinese in Southeast Asia as *huaqiao* or sojourners and from the ties to China as the original homeland. Second, by 1965, the Chinese "as the majority people of Singapore" could not be considered unproblematically as one people or community, one of the major divisions being, as we have seen, educational background, which in turn is aligned with patterns of language use, occupational status, and political affiliation. Third, with Independence, "it is now the sovereign state that becomes the pivotal actor in redefining the collective memory — and shaping the identity — of the Chinese in Singapore" (Kwok 1995, 225).

Thus, much of the scholarly literature on the Chinese in post-Independence Singapore has focused on what might be termed "the politics of identity". Moreover, the literature on this more recent period tends to be contributed by sociologists rather than historians — reflecting another aspect of the conventional but artificial distinction between sociology and history, the former dealing with contemporary society and the latter with the past. But sociology can be properly considered as the study of "the history of the present", and thus a number of sociological analyses of the Chinese in post-Independence Singapore do adopt an implicit or explicit historical perspective, although one that ranges over a long-term span of Singapore history. For example, Chiew (1995 and 1997) has offered two essays which survey the transformation of the Chinese in Singapore "from colonial times to the present" and chart their transition "from overseas Chinese to Chinese Singaporeans". In both these essays Chiew's historical discussion is thin but he provides a slew of statistical data documenting, in his first essay, demographic change along the dimensions of religious affiliation, age distribution, literacy, educational attainment, occupational distribution, gender differentiation. In the second essay he discusses "national integration" in terms of school integration, disaggregated public housing, and what Chiew terms "social integration" as shown by interethnic interaction. As for demographic data, much more can be learned and analysed from the 1990 Census, especially those concerning changes in patterns of language use among the Chinese since the 1980s (Lau 1992, Tham 1996).

In both essays, however, Chiew also highlights "the China factor", that is, the potential impact of China's economic rise, especially on those Chinese Singaporeans who invest or work in China. This opens up a new area of research, and conversely there should also be research on the influx of professionals from China into the Singapore job market, especially in view of Singapore's policy of attracting foreign talent, and in particular from Asian countries. Statistical data on these recent migrants and on their length of stay and the numbers granted permanent residence or citizenship, however, are not made publicly available (Kwok 1998, 201). This is a matter of great significance in the study of the Chinese overseas or Overseas Chinese Studies because it is part of the phenomenon of what Wang Gungwu has called "a new era of the *huaqiao*" with the migration of Chinese from Taiwan, Hong Kong and mainland China, raising the question of whether they return to their roots (*guigen*) or "grow roots" (*shenggen*) in their new homes (Wang Gungwu in Wang L. C. and Wang Gungwu 1998, viii). In the Singapore case, it raises questions about the processes of "Singaporeanization" on the part of the new Chinese migrants and "sinicization" on the part of the local Chinese.

From the mid-1960s, however, the state has played a proactive role in constructing an ideological framework and gaining ideological consensus in the new nation-state (Chua 1995). This has involved a complex of policies in the areas of language planning, education, and cultural planning. The key works relating to the overall policy on multiracialism have been mentioned at the beginning of the review, the *locus classicus* being Benjamin's 1976 essay on the "cultural logic" and ramifications of official thinking and practice on issues concerning race, ethnicity and language. During the time of its publication, ideas about "essentialism" and the "essentialization" of identity were hardly in the conceptual vocabulary of social scientists but Benjamin's essay already made an opening towards analysis along such lines, which have now become part of newer analyses (eg Lian 1999). This area, however, is in need of not just theoretical discussion but also empirical investigation. Two recent works partially fill this lacuna. On the one hand, Lai's anthropological study (1995) of interethnic relations in a housing estate fleshes out some aspects of Benjamin's argument but also shows in empirical detail how Singaporeans of various ethnic backgrounds negotiate the boundaries that have been officially delineated. On the other hand, PuruShotam's analysis (1998), based on empirical material, especially data from narrative interviews, employs a more sophisticated conceptual framework in detailing the construction of race in the formulation and implementation of language policies, effectively "disciplining differences" in Singapore.

Although these works are not specifically focused on the Chinese population, they provide the larger backdrop against which the impact of state interventions on the development of "Chinese identity" can be understood. In addition to the surveys on bilingual policies that have already been cited, more work are required on the watershed changes introduced by the Report on the Ministry of Education (Goh et al 1979) and the issues that they raise concerning not only the shifts in language patterns among the Chinese but also patterns of educational and social mobility with respect to those who come from dialect-speaking backgrounds (cf. Kwok 1999). There have been more general studies on language policies (Pendley 1983, Kuo 1985), but this area has developed so quickly as in, for example, recent changes in policies related to the teaching of Chinese — which are received by different sectors of the Chinese population in different ways, some of whom have shared in the concerns that Lee Kuan Yew have raised concerning "westernization" and "decentralization" (Loy et al. 1991) and for the very same reason are less prepared to see a lowering in standards of teaching. There has also been no major study of the Speak Mandarin Campaign. In contrast, a number of studies have looked at the promotion of Confucianism in the late 1980s, including as part of the Religious Knowledge programme (Tu 1994), leading into the construction of "Shared Values" as newer efforts in ideological legitimation on the part of the state in the light of rapid modernization and capitalist development in the region (Davis 1993, Kwok 1995, Chua 1995, Kuo 1996, Clammer 1993, cf. Clammer 1983, J. Wong 1996). None of these studies on state ideology and identity formation, however, have taken a comparative approach, a model of which is provided by Chun (1996), comparing ideological discourses in Taiwan, Hong Kong and Singapore and by Ang and Stratton (1995) in which the discussion of the Singapore model of multiculturalism is also related to the Australian case.

Yet another focus of research returns to the issue of the Chinese-educated that has already been highlighted in this review. In particular, the changes in education, especially the demise of Chinese education and the expansion of bilingual education has brought about a generation of bilingual Chinese Singaporeans who do not carry the same burden of memory that their parents and teachers did in relation to their marginalized status in Singapore society (Kwok 1996, Sai 1997). Yet the social memory of marginalization — for example, the memory of the demise of Nanyang University — have yet to be substantially erased among the older generations of the Chinese-educated (Li 1994, Liu 1994, Lim 1997). There is scope, therefore, for more work on this area, especially from the standpoint of sociology of memory and in connection with the study of "the differential politics of Chineseness" (Ang 1993). As a corollary, research can also be directed at the phenomenon of "Chinese intellectuals" (*huawen zhishifenzi*). It may be suggested (see Ke 1999) that the younger, bilingual, generation of Chinese-speaking intellectuals are more prepared to break out of the concern with language, education, and culture that earlier generations have been engaged with as they faced the decline of Chinese education. In particular, this signals a distancing from the politics of identity of the past and an interest among some of the younger Chinese-speaking to speak to wider national issues, and to see themselves beyond the role of preserving tradition — in effect in engaging in issues of social transformation and modernity.

The Chinese in Singapore: Identities and Modernities

In his essay on "The Study of Chinese Identities in Southeast Asia", Wang Gungwu (1991a, 199-217), argued that "modern Southeast Asian Chinese, like most peoples today, do not have a single identity but tend to assume multiple identities"; indeed, he highlighted the phenomenon of "the simultaneous presence of many kinds of identity, eg, ethnic, national (local), cultural and class identities".

Following this perspective, it has been also suggested that in looking at the case of Lim Boon Keng, a man who inhabited multiple identities, the "world of the turn-of-the-century Straits Chinese was, in a sense, a nascent 'postmodern' world in which identity was unstable, fluid, fragmentary, and shifting" (Kwok 1995, 237, cf. Ang 1993). The conceptual concern with "identity" among scholars and the apparent practical concern with "identity" among social (and political) actors as seen in this review leads me to my final point: that the concept of identity is intimately linked to the concept of modernity (Kwok 1996, cf. Lian 1999). Indeed, Wang Gungwu (1991a, 216) has pointed out that "the Chinese have found no word for it before the last decade or so. The technical term is now translated as *rentong* meaning "to identify that which is the same", but this yet to be used in ordinary speech". Today, however, the concept is fairly routinely used in everyday public discourse, but the point is this: "identity" becomes a problem or a quest only in the context of modernity (Kwok 1996).

If anything, "the Singapore story" and the story of the Chinese in Singapore can be conceived as not simply a story of modernization but a series of "multiple modernities" or "interlocking modernities" among various groups and sectors in society, and overlapping with modernities developing on a regional and global scale (cf. Ang and Stratton 1995, Nonini and Ong 1997). In my view, Wang Gungwu offers a provocative insight in his idea about the Chinese in Singapore having to "escape from their history". Singapore's development from the colonial era to the present can perhaps be also seen as a series of ways in which it "escapes from history". This is not the place for a fuller treatment of such a perspective, but its outlines can be sketched here. It may be said that modernity understood both as the experience of historical discontinuity and as a set of social phenomena bringing into force the structures of the modern world is the leitmotif of the history of Singapore, beginning with colonial modernity and the modernity experienced by peoples who migrated out of a "traditional" social order and into the new environment that Singapore offered. Under the colonial order, Singapore was inducted into the political economy of the modern capitalist world system. And with independence, its modernization has been spearheaded by a developmentalist state in the contemporary global economic and inter-state system.

Such a perspective, I think, provides a multi-faceted way of analysing the Chinese in Singapore and teasing out the interconnections between the various areas and trajectories of research that I have earlier outlined. The overseas Chinese (for example, those who migrated to Singapore) were the harbingers of a form of modernity that could not be developed in mainland China as the society faced its own path of modernity in a series of revolutions, marked by the end of Imperial China in 1911, the May Fourth Movement of 1919, the founding of the People's Republic in 1949, and the Cultural Revolution of 1966-76. These revolutions on the mainland were assaults on the traditional order which the migrants by and large bypassed but in so doing pursued "a smaller revolution" or "cumulatively a series of little modernizations" (Wang Gungwu 1991b, 245-60, cf. Kwok 1998b, 121). In this view, therefore, Goh Keng Swee was closer to the mark when he earlier argued (Goh 1972, 63) that traditional institutions such as the extended family may be obstacles to economic development than when he claimed in his foreword to a book on Chinese entrepreneurs in Singapore (Chan and Chiang 1994) that they were the purveyors of the "Confucian ethic" which was compatible with the promotion of capitalist entrepreneurship (Goh 1994, cf. Kwok 1999, 65). Moreover, such a perspective also allows us to look at the different kinds of modernity, the "multiple modernities", represented by different groups of Chinese throughout Singapore history, for example, the Babas and *sinkeh* or *huaqiao* and, in more recent times, the Chinese-educated and the English-educated. The English-educated provided the kind of modernity that lay at the centre of the developmentalist vision and programme of the PAP-led government (cf. Wee 1993). And the wheel was to come full circle when an economically successful Singapore positioned itself and was positioned by others as part of an emerging "East Asian modernity" (Wee 1996, cf. Ong 1997).

In conclusion, a sociological point may be made concerning the role of the individual in confronting the condition of modernity. Again, Wang Gungwu provides us with a useful perspective. In "Ethnic Chinese: The Past in Their Future" (1999), he writes: "My study of the Chinese overseas has led me to believe that confronting one's past is a necessary part of the community's growth and survival". He suggests four ways of relating past and future among the Chinese overseas: 1. The communal identification with selected aspects of Chinese history; 2. The search for a new national history with fellow citizens in the adopted country; 3. The identification with a common human past, which transcends national borders; and 4. The inclusive and flexible weaving of a personal past. The last option encompasses the earlier three, and becomes more possible with the extension of modern education and communications technology:

> Among ethnic Chinese in Southeast Asia, this could include bits of their cultural past as Chinese, including select parts of Chinese history, but also those parts of local national history that they can accept. It could extend to the history of other countries and other continents, and the criteria as to why each is chosen can be highly varied ... The point is that a personalised and inclusive past could be enlightening and liberating without threatening one's prior loyalties to community and nation-state.

In my view, Wang Gungwu's perspective avoids any kind of historical or sociological determinism in the study of the Chinese overseas, especially in the analysis of how they face the problematic of modernity and identity. In the case of the Chinese in Singapore, historically, different individuals and groups have had different degrees of personal autonomy in defining the past in their future. As much as they were influenced by the larger forces of the historical moment, whether enabling or constraining, ultimately the choices that they exercised were personal choices, with consequences for the shaping of the "Chinese community" and "Singapore society". With the apparent expansion of personal choice under contemporary conditions, the study of "the Chinese in Singapore" may lead to moving beyond the very rubric itself. In time, the term "Chinese" may hardly encapsulate — and do justice — to the many inclusive and flexible ways in which people identify themselves.

References

Ang, B. C. (1998) "The Teaching of Chinese Language in Singapore", in S. Gopinathan, A. Pakir, W.K. Ho and V. Saravanan (eds), *Language, Society and Education in Singapore: Issues and Trends,* (2ⁿᵈ ed) Singapore: Times Academic Press.

Ang, I. (1993) "To Be or Not to Be Chinese: Diaspora, Culture and Postmodern Ethnicity", *Southeast Asian Journal of Social Science,* 21(1): 1-17.

Ang, I. (1994) "The Differential Politics of Chineseness", *Southeast Asian Journal of Social Science,* 22: 72-79,

Ang, I. and Stratton, J. (1995) "The Singapore Way of Multiculturalism: Western Concepts / Asian Cultures", *Sojourn,* 10(1): 65-89.

Benjamin, G. (1976) "The Cultural Logic of 'Multiracialism'", in Riaz Hassan (ed), *Singapore: Society in Transition,* Kuala Lumpur: Oxford University Press.

Berger, P. L. (1986) *The Capitalist Revolution: Fifty Propositions About Prosperity, Equality, & Liberty,* New York: Basic Books.

Berger, P. L. and Hsiao, H. H. M. (eds) (1988) *In Search of an East Asian Development Model,* New Brunswick, NJ: Transaction Books.

Bloodworth, D. (1986) *The Tiger and the Trojan Horse,* Singapore: Times Books International.

Borthwick, S. (1988) "Chinese Education and Identity in Singapore", in J. Cushman and G.W. Wang (eds), *Changing Identities of the Southeast Asian Chinese since World War II,* Hong Kong: Hong Kong University Press.

Borthwick, S. (1990) "Chinese Education and Employment in Singapore" in L. Guo (ed), *Zhanhou Haiwai Huaren Bianhua: Guoji Xueshu Yantaohui Lunwenji* (The Postwar Transformation of Overseas Chinese), Beijing: Zhonggua *Huaqiao* Chubashe.

Carino, T. C. (1996) "Recent Writings on Role of Southeast Asia's Chinese", *Trends, Business Times,* 25 May.

Chan, K. B. and Chiang, C. (1994) *Stepping Out: The Making of Chinese Entrepreneurs*, Singapore: Centre for Advanced Studies/Prentice Hall.

Cheah, B. K. (1983) *Red Star Over Malaya*, Singapore: Singapore University Press.

Cheng, L. K. (1985) *Social Change and the Chinese in Singapore: A Socio Economic Geography, with Special Reference to Bang Structure*, Singapore: Singapore University Press.

Cheng, L. K. (1990) "Reflections on the Changing Roles of Chinese Clan Associations in Singapore", *Asian Culture*, 14: 57-71.

Chelliah, D.D. (1947) *A History of the Straits Settlements with Recommendations for a New System Based on Vernaculars*, Kuala Lumpur: The Government Press.

Chew, E. C. T. and Lee, E. (eds) (1991) *A History of Singapore*, Singapore: Oxford University Press.

Chew, M. (1996) *Leaders of Singapore*, Singapore: Resource Press.

Chia, F. (1994) *The Babas Revisited*, Singapore: Heinemann Asia.

Chiew, S. K. (1995) "The Chinese in Singapore: From Colonial Times to the Present" in L. Suryadinata (ed) *Southeast Asian Chinese: The Socio-Cultural Dimension*, Singapore: Times Academic Press.

Chiew, S. K. (1997) "From Overseas Chinese to Chinese Singaporeans", in L. Suryadinata (ed) *Ethnic Chinese as Southeast Asians*, Singapore: Institute of Southeast Asian Studies.

Ching, S. Y. (1972) "A King's Chinese: A Study of Song Ong Siang", Unpublished BA Honours Academic Exercise, Dept. of History, University of Singapore.

Chua, B. H. (1995) *Communitarian Ideology and Democracy in Singapore*, London: Routledge.

Chui, K. C. [Cui Guiqiang] (1991) "Political Attitudes and Organizations, c. 1900 –1941" in E.C.T. Chew and E. Lee (eds), *A History of Singapore*, Singapore: Oxford University Press.

Chun, A. (1996) "Discourses of Identity in the Changing Spaces of Public Culture in Taiwan, Hong Kong and Singapore", *Theory, Culture, and Society*, 13(1): 51-75.

Clammer, J. (1980) *Straits Chinese Society: Studies in the Sociology of the Baba Communities of Malaysia and Singapore*, Singapore: Singapore University Press.

Clammer, J. (1983) "Chinese Ethnicity and Political Culture in Singapore", in L.A.P. Gosling and L.Y.C. Lim (eds), *The Chinese in Southeast Asia, Vol 2: Identity, Culture and Politics*, Singapore: Maruzen Asia.

Clammer, J. (1993) "Deconstructing Values: The Establishment of a National Ideology and its Implications for Singapore's Political Future", in G. Rodan (ed), *Singapore Changes Guard: Social, Political and Economic Directions in the 1990s*, Melbourne: Longman Cheshire.

Cui, G. Q.[Chui Kwei-Chiang] (1994) *Xinjiapo Huaren: Cong Kaibu Dao Jianguo* [The Chinese in Singapore: Past and Present], Singapore: EPB Publishers.

Cohen, J. (1994) "Being Chinese: The Peripheralization of Traditional Identity", in W.M. Tu (ed) *The Living Tree: The Changing Meaning of Being Chinese Today*, Stanford: Stanford University Press.

Davis, G. (1993) "Star Wars and the Confucian Ethic", in M. Lee and A.D. Syrokomla-Stefanowka (eds) *Modernization of the Chinese Past*, Sydney: The University of Sydney, School of Asian Studies Series No. 1.

Drysdale, J. (1984) *Singapore: Struggle for Success*, Singapore: Times Books International.

Fang, X. (1977) *Notes on the History of Malayan Chinese New Literature 1920-1942*, translated by Angus W. McDonald, Jr., Tokyo: The Centre for East Asian Cultural Studies.

Foong, C.H. (ed) (1997) *The Price of Peace: True Accounts of the Japanese Occupation*, Singapore: Asiapac (trans. Clara Show; original Chinese edition 1995).

Freedman, M. (1979) *The Study of Chinese Society*, G.W. Skinner (ed), Stanford: Stanford University Press.

Goh, K. S. (1972) *The Economics of Modernization*, Singapore: Asia Pacific Press.

Goh, K. S. (1994) "Foreword", *Stepping Out: The Making of Chinese Entrepreneurs*, by Chan Kwok Bun and Claire Chiang, Singapore: Centre for Advanced Studies, NUS and London: Prentice Hall (New York).

Goh, K. S. et al. (1979) *The Report on the Ministry of Education 1978*, Singapore: Ministry of Education.

Gopinathan, S. (1991) "Education", in E. C. T. Chew and E. Lee (eds), *A History of Singapore*, Singapore: Oxford University Press.

Gopinathan, S. (1998) "Language Policy Changes 1979-1997: Politics and Pedagogy", in S. Gopinathan, A. Pakir, W.K Ho. and V. Saravanan (eds), *Language, Society and Education in Singapore: Issues and Trends*, (2nd ed.) Singapore: Times Academic Press.

Han, F. K., Fernandez, W. and Tan, S. (1998) *Lee Kuan Yew: The Man and His Ideas*, Singapore: Singapore Press Holdings, Times Editions.

Hara, F. (1995) "The Japanese Occupation of Malaya and the Chinese Community", in P.H. Kratoska (ed), *Malaya and Singapore During the Japanese Occupation*, Journal of Southeast Asian Studies Special Publication Series No. 3.

Harper, T. N. (1997) "Globalism and the Pursuit of Authenticity: The Making of a Diasporic Public Sphere in Singapore", *Sojourn*, 12(2).

Hofheinz Jr., R. and Calder, K. E. (1982) *The Eastasia Edge*, New York: Basic Books.

Hong, L. (1975) "The Intellectual and Social Reforms of the Chinese in Singapore (1894-1910)", Unpublished BA Honours Academic Exercise, Dept. of History, University of Singapore.

Huntington, S. P. (1993) "The Clash of Civilizations?", *Foreign Affairs*, 72(3): 22-49.

Huntington, S. P. (1996) *The Clash of Civilizations and the Remaking of World Order*, New York: Simon & Schuster.

Josey, A. (1980) *Lee Kuan Yew: The Struggle for Singapore* (3rd ed) Singapore: Angus & Robertson Publishers.

Kahn, H. (1979) *World Economic Development: 1979 and Beyond*, London: Croom Helm.

Ke, M. L. (ed) (1995) *Xinhua Lishi Renwu Liezhuan* [*Biographies of Singapore Chinese Historical Figures*], Singapore: Singapore Federation of Chinese Clan Associations, EPB Publishers.

Ke, S. R. [Quah Syren] (1999) "Shehue de Bianchui yu Xiandaixin de Zhongxing: Xinjiapo Huawen Zhishifenzi de Jingyu" [The Periphery of the Society and the Centre of Modernity: Singapore Chinese Intellectuals in Context], Paper presented at conference on The Role and Responsibility of Singapore's Chinese Intellectuals in the 21st Century, organised by the Hwa Chong Alumni, 28 February 1999.

Koh, T. A. (1993) "Literature in English by Chinese in Malaya/Malaysia and Singapore: Its Origins and Development", in L. Suryadinata (ed) *Chinese Adaptation and Diversity: Essays on Society and Literature in Indonesia, Malaysia, and Singapore*, Singapore: Centre for Advanced Studies, NUS and Singapore University Press.

Koh, T. A. (1995) "History as Her Story: Chinese Women's Biographical Writing from Indonesia, Malaysia and Singapore", in L. Suryadinata (ed) *Southeast Asian Chinese: The Socio-Cultural Dimension*, Singapore: Times Academic Press.

Kotkin, J. (1992) *Tribes: How Race, Religion, and Identity Determine Success in the New Global Economy*, New York: Random House.

Kuo, E. C. Y. (1985) "Language an Identity: The Case of Chinese in Singapore", in W.S. Tseng and D.Y.H. Wu (eds) *Chinese Culture and Mental Health*, Orlando: Academic Press.

Kuo, E. C. Y. (1996) "Confucianism as Political Discourse in Singapore: The Case of an Incomplete Revitalization Movement", in W.M. Tu (ed) *Confucian Traditions in East Asian Modernity: Moral Education and Economic Culture in Japan and the Four Mini-Dragons*, Cambridge, Mass: Harvard University Press.

Kuhn, P. A. (1997) "Why Should Sinologists Study the Chinese Overseas?", Paper delivered in Singapore in April 1997. Mimeo.

Kwa, C. G. (1985) "Appendix: Records and Notices of Early Singapore", in J.N. Miksic (1984) *Archaelogical Research on the 'Forbidden Hill' of Singapore: Excavations at Fort Canning*, Singapore: National Museum Singapore.

Kwok, K. W. (1993) "The Problem of 'Tradition' in Contemporary Singapore", in A. Mahizhnan (ed), *Heritage and Contemporary Values*, Singapore: Institute of Policy Studies / Times Academic Press.

Kwok, K. W. (1995) "Social Transformation and the Problem of Social Coherence: Chinese Singaporeans at Century's End", in *Asiatische Studien / Etudes Asiatiques*, XLLX (1): 217-41.

Kwok, K. W. (1996) "Myth, Memory, and Modernity: Reflections on the Situation of the Chinese-Educated in Post-Independence Singapore", Paper presented at conference 'Identity: Crises and Opportunity' organised by the Hwa Chong Alumni, 28 July 1996.

Kwok, K. W. (1998a) "Singapore", in L. Pan (ed) *The Encyclopedia of the Chinese Overseas*, Singapore: Archipelago Press and Landmark Books.

Kwok, K. W. (1998b) "Being Chinese in the Modern World", in L. Pan (ed) *The Encyclopedia of the Chinese Overseas*, Singapore: Archipelago Press and Landmark Books.

Kwok, K. W. (1999) "The Social Architect: Goh Keng Swee", in P.E. Lam and K. Y. L. Tan (eds), *Lee's Lieutenants: Singapore's Old Guard*, Sydney: Allen & Unwin.

Lai, A. E. (1995) *Meanings of Multiethnicity: A Case-study of Ethnicity and Ethnic Relations in Singapore*, Kuala Lumpur: Oxford University Press.

Lau, K. E. (1992) *Singapore Census of Population 1990: Demographic Characteristics (Statistical Release 1)*, Singapore: Dept. of Statistics.

Lee, E. (1991) *The British As Rulers: Governing Mulitiracial Singapore 1867-1914*, Singapore: Singapore University Press.

Lee, K. Y. (1998) *The Singapore Story: Memoirs of Lee Kuan Yew*, Singapore: Times Editions.

Lee, P. P. (1978) *Chinese Society in Nineteenth Century Singapore*, Kuala Lumpur: Oxford University Press.

Lee, T. H. (1987) "Chinese Education in Malaya 1894-1911: Nationalism in the First Chinese Schools", in L.T. Lee (ed), *The 1911 Revolution: The Chinese in British and Dutch Southeast Asia*, Singapore: Heinemann Asia.

Lee, T. H. (1988) "The Historical Development of Confucianism in Singapore, 1819-1948", *Asian Culture*, 11:14-26.

Lee, T. H. (1993) "Ideologies and Literature: The Development of Chinese Language Poetry in Post-War Singapore", in L. Suryadinata (ed) *Chinese Adaptation and Diversity: Essays on Society and Literature in Indonesia, Malaysia, and Singapore*, Singapore: Centre for Advanced Studies, NUS and Singapore University Press.

Lee, T. H. (1977) *The Open United Front: The Communist Struggle in Singapore, 1954-1966*, Singapore: The South Seas Society.

Li, H. L. (1999) *"Pan Shou de Nanda Leihen"* [Pan Shou's Sorrow Concerning Nanyang University] *Lianhe Zaobao*, 6 March.

Li, Y. J. [Lee Guan Kin] (1990) *Lin Wenqing de sixiang - Shongxi wenhua de huiliu yu maodun* [The Thought of Lim Boon Keng: Convergence and Contradiction between Chinese and Western culture], Singapore: Singapore Society of Asian Studies.

Li, Y. J. (1994) *"Xinjiapo Huawenjiao yu Bianqian (1959-1987) xia, Zhishifenzi de Baogen Xintai"* [Changes in Chinese Education in Singapore and the Attitude of Intellectuals towards the Preservation of Roots] in *Traditional Culture and Social Change*, Singapore: Tung Ann District Guild.

Li, Y. J. (1999) *"Zuo Chu Lishi, Kua Yue Shiji: Xinjiapo Huawen Zhishifenzi Jueshe de Yanbian"* [Transcending History, Crossing the Century: The Changing Roles of Chinese Intellectuals in Singapore], Paper presented at conference on The Role and Responsibility of Singapore's Chinese

Intellectuals in the 21st Century, organised by the Hwa Chong Alumni, 28 February.

Lian, K. F. (1992) "In Search of a History of Singapore", *Southeast Asian Journal of Social Science*, 20 (1): 93-106.

Lian, K. F. (1999) "The Nation-state and the Sociology of Singapore", in P.G.L. Chew and A. Kramer-Dahl (eds), *Reading Culture: Textual Practices in Singapore*, Singapore: Times Academic Press.

Liu, P. F. (1994) *"Lishi Changhezhong de yiduan Jiyi"* [A Section of Memory in the Long River of History] *Lianhe Zaobao*, 25 September.

Lim, J. K. (1997) "Forget the Sedan Chair, Let's Get on a Jetliner – Together: A Chinese-educated's View on the Tang Liang Hong Affair", Speech delivered at the 3rd National Education Seminar on 23 January 1997, Ngee Ann Polytechnic.

Lin, J. L. (ed) (1993) *Voices & Choices: The Women's Movement in Singapore*, Singapore: Singapore Council of Women's Organisations and Singapore Baha'I Women's Committee, Times Editions.

Loh, S. C. (1989) "The Singapore Chinese Community: From Sojourners to Citizens 1900-1957", Unpublished BA Honours Academic Exercise, Dept. of History, National University of Singapore.

Loy, T. J., Tong, S. H. and Pang, C. L. (eds) (1991) *Lee Kuan Yew on The Chinese Community in Singapore*, Singapore: Singapore Federation of Chinese Clan Associations and Singapore Chinese Chamber of Commerce & Industry.

Lyman, S. (1974) *Chinese Americans*, New York: Random House.

MacFarquhar, R. (1980) "The Post-Confucian Challenge", *The Economist*, 9 February.

Mak, L. F. (1981) *The Sociology of Secret Societies: A Study of Chinese Secret Societies in Singapore and Peninsular Malaysia*, Kuala Lumpur: Oxford University Press.

Mak, L. F. (1995) *The Dynamics of Chinese Dialect Groups in Early Malaya,* Singapore: Singapore Society of Asian Studies.

Mani, A. (1997) "Comments on 'From Overseas Chinese to Chinese Singaporeans", in L. Suryadinata (ed) *Ethnic Chinese as Southeast Asians*, Singapore: Institute of Southeast Asian Studies.

Marshall, D. (1996) *Letters from Mao's China* (M. Leifer (ed)) Singapore: Singapore Heritage Society.

Miksic, J. N. (1985) *Archaelogical Research on the 'Forbidden Hill' of Singapore: Excavations at Fort Canning*, 1984. Singapore: National Museum Singapore.

Naisbitt, J. (1994) *Global Paradox*, New York: Avon Books.

Nanda Shiye Youxian Gongsi / Xiang Gang Nanyang Daxue Xiaoyouhui (1997) *Chen Liushi: Bainiandan Jinian Wenji* [Tan Lark Sye: A Commemorative Collection on the Hundredth Anniversary of his Birth], Singapore: Bafang Wenhua Qiye Gongsi.

National Archives of Singapore, Singapore Heritage Board (1995) *The Japanese Occupation: 1942-1945: A Pictorial Record of Singapore During the War*, (Text by Tan Beng Luan and Irene Quah), Singapore: Times Editions.

Ng, W. C. (1992) "Urban Chinese Social Organization: Some Unexplored Aspects in *Huiguan* Development in Singapore, 1900-1941", *Modern Asian Studies*, 26(3): 469-94.

Nonini, D. M. and Ong, A. H. (1997) "Chinese Transnationalism as an Aletrnative Modernity", in A.H. Ong and D. Nonini (eds), *The Cultural Politics of Modern Chinese Transnationalism*, New York: Routledge.

Ong, A. H. (1997) "Chinese Modernities: Narratives of Nation and Capitalism", in A.H. Ong and D. Nonini (eds), *The Cultural Politics of Modern Chinese Transnationalism*, New York: Routledge.

Pan, L. (1994) *Sons of the Yellow Emperor*, New York: Kodansha International.

Pan, L. (ed) (1998) *Encyclopedia of the Chinese Overseas*, Singapore: Archipelago Press / Landmark Books [Cambridge, Massachusetts: Harvard University Press].

Pang, C. L. and Low, F. (2000) "Chinese Civic Traditions in Singapore", in G. Koh and G. L. Ooi (eds), *State-Society Relations in Singapore*, Singapore: Institute of Policy Studies and Oxford University Press.

Pendley, C. (1983) "Language Policy and Social Transformation in Contemporary Singapore", *Southeast Asian Journal of Social Science*, 11 (2): 46-58.

Pitt, K. W. (1984) "Chinese Coolie Immigrants in Nineteenth Century", in *Review of Southeast Asian Studies (Nanyang Quarterly)*, XIV (June): 31-59.

PuruShotam, N. S. (1998) *Negotiating Language, Constructing Race: Disciplining Difference in Singapore*, Berlin and New York: Mouton de Gruyter.

Qiu, X. M. (1993) *Qiu Shu Yuan Sheng Ping* [The Life of Qiu Shuyuan], Singapore: Seng Yew Book Store.

Redding, S. G. (1990) *The Spirit of Chinese Capitalism*, Berlin: Walter de Gruyter.

Reid, A. (ed) (1996) *Sojourners and Settlers: Histories of Southeast Asia and the Chinese*, Sydney: Allen & Unwin.

Reid, A. (1996) "Flows and Seepages in the Long-term Chinese Interaction with Southeast Asia", in A. Reid (ed) *Sojourners and Settlers,* Sydney: Allen & Unwin.

Rudolf, J. (1998) *Reconstructing Identities: A Social History of the Babas in Singapore*, Aldershot, England: Ashgate [Based on Ph.D. dissertation, Philosophischen Fakultät I (Philosophie, Geschichte und Sozialwissenschaften) der Friedrich-Alexander-Alexander-Universität, Erlangen-Nürnberg, 1994].

Sai, S. M. and Huang, J. L. (1999) "The 'Chinese-educated' Political Vanguards: Ong Pang Boon, Lee Khoon Choy and Jek Yeun Thong", in P.E. Lam and K.Y.L. Tan (eds) *Lee's Lieutenants: Singapore's Old Guard*, Sydney: Allen & Unwin.

Sai, S. Y. (1997) "Post-Independence Educational Change, Identity and Huaxiao-sheng Intellectuals in Singapore: A Case Study of

Chinese Language", *Southeast Asian Journal of Social Science,* 25(2): 79-101.

Saw, S. H. (1970) *Singapore Population in Transition,* Pennsylvania: University of Pennsylvania Press.

Seagrave, S.(1996) *Lords of the Rim,* London: Corgi Books.

Siah, U. C. (Seah Eu Chin) (1847) "Annual Remittances to China", *Journal of the Indian Archipelago and Eastern Asia,* (1): 35-37.

Siah, U. C. (Seah Eu Chin) (1848) "The Chinese of Singapore", *Journal of the Indian Archipelago and Eastern Asia,* (2): 283-90.

Shi, X. T. (1989) *Xiang Tuo Cong Gao* [Manuscripts of Xiang Tuo], Singapore: Wan Li Shu Ju.

Shu, Y. T. and Chua, S. K. (eds) (1984) *Malayan Chinese Resistance to Japan 1937-1945: Selected Source Materials* (Based on Colonel Chuang Hui-Tsuan's Collection), Singapore: Cultural & Historical Publishing House.

Skinner, G. W. (1957) *Chinese Society in Thailand: An Analytical History,* Ithaca, New York: Cornell University Press.

Skinner, G. W. (1996) "Creolized Chinese Societies in Southeast Asia", in A. Reid (ed) *Sojourners and Settlers,* Sydney: Allen and Unwin.

Song, O. S. (1984) *One Hundred Years' History of the Chinese in Singapore,* Singapore: Oxford University Press.

Suryadinata, L. (ed) (1993) *Chinese Adaptation and Diversity: Essays on Society and Literature in Indonesia, Malaysia, and Singapore,* Singapore: Centre for Advanced Studies / Singapore University Press.

Suryadinata, L. (ed) (1995a) *Southeast Asian Chinese: The Socio-Cultural Dimension,* Singapore: Times Academic Press.

Suryadinata, L. (ed) (1995b) *Southeast Asian Chinese and China: The Politico-Economic Dimension,* Singapore: Times Academic Press.

Suryadinata, L. (ed) (1997) *Ethnic Chinese as Southeast Asians,* Singapore: Institute of Southeast Asian Studies.

Tan, C.B. (1993) *Chinese Peranakan Heritage in Malaysia and Singapore,* Kuala Lumpur: Penerbit Faja Bakti Sdn Bhd.

Tang, E. T. (1988) "Uniqueness of Malayan Chinese Literature: Literary Polemic in the Forties", *Asian Culture*, 12 : 102-15.

Tham, S. C. (1996) *Multi-Lingualism in Singapore: Two Decades of Development (Census of Population, 1990, Monogragh No 6)*, Singapore: Dept. of Malay Studies, National University of Singapore.

Thio, E. (1991) "The Syonan Years, 1942-1945", in E.C.T. Chew and E. Lee (eds), *A History of Singapore*, Singapore: Oxford University Press.

Tu, W. M. (1984) *Confucian Ethics Today: The Singapore Challenge*, Singapore: Curriculum Development Institute of Singapore, Federal Publications.

Tu, W. M. (1991) "Cultural China: The Periphery as the Centre", *Daedalus*, 120(2): 1-32.

Tu, W. M. (ed) (1994) *The Living Tree: The Changing Meaning of Being Chinese Today*, Stanford: Stanford University Press.

Tu, W. M. (ed) (1996) *Confucian Traditions in East Asian Modernity: Moral Education and Economic Culture in Japan and the Four Mini-Dragons*, Cambridge, Massachusetts: Harvard University Press.

Trocki, C. A. (1979) *Prince of Pirates: The Temenggongs and the Development of Johore and Singapore, 1784 – 1885*, Singapore: Singapore University Press.

Trocki, C. A. (1990) *Opium and Empire: Chinese Society in Colonial Singapore, 1800-1910*, Ithaca: Cornell University Press.

Wang, G. W. (1964) "A Short Introduction to Chinese Writing in Malaya", in T. Wignesan (ed), *Bunga Emas: An Anthology of Contemporary Malaysian Literature (1930-1963)*, Kuala Lumpur: Rayirath (Raybooks) Publications.

Wang, G. W. (1991a) *China and the Chinese Overseas*, Singapore: Times Academic Press.

Wang, G. W. (1991b) *The Chineseness of China: Selected Essays*, Hong Kong: Oxford University Press.

Wang, G. W. (1992) *Community and Nation: China, Southeast Asia and Australia*, Sydney: Asian Studies Association of Australia and Allen & Unwin.

Wang, G. W. (1994) "Among Non-Chinese", in W.M. Tu (ed) *The Living Tree: The Changing Meaning of Being Chinese Today*, Stanford: Stanford University Press.

Wang, G. W. (1996) "Sojourning: The Chinese Experience in Southeast Asia", in A. Reid (ed) *Sojourners and Settlers*, Sydney: Allen and Unwin.

Wang, G. W. (1997) "Malaysia-Singapore: Two Kinds of Ethnic Transformations", *Southeast Asian Journal of Social Science*, (25): 183-87.

Wang, G. W. (1998) "The Status of Overseas Chinese Studies", in L.C. Wang and G.W. Wang (eds) *The Chinese Diaspora: Selected Essays, Vol. 1*, Singapore: Times Academic Press.

Wang, G. W. (1999) "Ethnic Chinese: The Past in their Future", *Asian Culture*, 23 (June): 1-9.

Wang, L. C. and Wang, G. W. (eds) (1998) *The Chinese Diaspora: Selected Essays, Volume I*, Singapore: Times Academic Press.

Wang, T. P. (1995) *The Origins of Chinese Kongsi*, Kuala Lumpur: Pelanduk Publications.

Ward, A. H. C., Chu, R. W. and Salaff, J. (eds) and trans. (1994) *The Memoirs of Tan Kah Kee*, Singapore: Singapore University of Singapore.

Warren, J. F. (1986) *Rickshaw Coolie: A People's History of Singapore (1880-1940)*, Singapore: Oxford University Press.

Wee, C. J. W-L. (1993) "Contending with Primordialism: The 'Modern' Construction of Postcolonial Singapore", *Positions*, 1(3): 715-44.

Wee, C. J. W-L. (1996) "The 'Clash' of Civilizations? Or an Emerging 'East Asian Modernity'?", *Sojourn*, 11(2): 211-30.

Wee, C. J. W-L. (1999) "The Vanquished: Lim Chin Siong and a Progressivist National Narrative", in P.E. Lam and K.Y.L. Tan (eds) *Lee's Lieutenants: Singapore's Old Guard,*, Sydney: Allen & Unwin.

Wee-Davies, G. [Gloria Davies] (1994) "East Asia's Link with Confucianism", *Trends, Business Times*, 31 December.

Wee, V. (1988) "What Does 'Chinese' Mean?: An Exploratory Essay", Working Papers, Dept. of Sociology, National University of Singapore.

Willmott, W. E. (1989) "The Emergence of Nationalism" in K.S. Sandhu and P. Wheatley (eds) *Management of Success: The Moulding of Modern Singapore*, Singapore: Institute of Southeast Asian Studies.

Wong, L. K. (1980) "The Chinese in Nineteenth Century Singapore: Review Article on Chinese Society in Nineteenth Century Singapore, by Lee Poh Ping", *Journal of Southeast Asian Studies*, 11 (1): 151-86.

Wong, D. (1996) "Memory Suppression and Memory Production: The Japanese Occupation of Singapore", Revised version of paper presented to conference on 'The Politics of Remembering the Asian/Pacific War', Hawaii, 7-9 September 1995.

Wong, D. (2000) "War and Memory in Malaysia and Singapore: An Introduction", in P.P.H. Lim and D. Wong (eds), *War and Memory in Malaysia and Singapore*, Singapore: Institute of Southeast Asian Studies.

Wong, J. (1996) "Promoting Confucianism for Socio-economic Development", in W.M. Tu (ed), *Confucian Traditions in East Asian Modernity: Moral Education and Economic Culture in Japan and the Four Mini-Dragons*, Cambridge, Massachusetts: Harvard University Press.

Wu, Y. H. [Goh Nguen Wah] (1999) *Wushi de Jueche: Renmin Xingdong Dang yu Zhengfu de Huawen Zhengche*, 1954-1965 [A Pragmatic Strategy: The People's Action Party and Government Policy on Chinese Language, 1954-1965], Singapore: Federal Publications.

Yen, C. H. (1986) *A Social History of the Chinese in Singapore and Malaya 1800-1911*, Singapore: Oxford University Press.

Yen, C. H. (1995a) *Community and Politics: The Chinese in Colonial Singapore and Malaysia*, Singapore: Times Academic Press.

Yen, C. H. (1995b) *Studies in Modern Overseas Chinese History*, Singapore: Times Academic Press.

Yeo, S. N. (1993) "Chinese Language Literature in Malaya and Singapore (1919-1942)", in L. Suryadinata (ed) *Chinese Adaptation and Diversity: Essays on Society and Literature in Indonesia, Malaysia, and Singapore*, Singapore: Centre for Advanced Studies/ Singapore University Press.

Yeo, S. N. and Leung, Y. S. (1985) "In Search of Identity: Chinese Literature in Malaysia and Singapore, 1991-1983", *Asian Culture*, 5: 18-23.

Yeo, S. N. and Ng, S. A. (2000) "The Japanese Occupation as Reflected in Singapore-Malayan Chinese Literary Works after the Japanese Occupation (1945-49)", in P.P.H. Lim and D. Wong (eds) *War and Memory in Malaysia and Singapore*, Singapore: Institute of Southeast Asian Studies.

Yong, C. F. (1987) *Tan Kah Kee: The Making of an Overseas Chinese Legend*, Singapore: Oxford University Press.

Yong, C. F. (1991) *Chinese Leadership and Power in Colonial Singapore*, Singapore: Times Academic Press.

Yong, C. F. (1997) *The Origins of Malayan Communism*, Singapore: The South Seas Society.

Acknowledgements

I would like to thank Lim Bee Ling and Chua Ai Lin for their help in locating some of the sources cited in this essay. I am also grateful to Lian Kwen Fee for his helpful comments on an earlier draft.

10

Sociology of the Malays

Syed Farid Alatas

An Approach to the Study of the Sociology of the Malays

The study of the sociology of the Malays, like the study of any sociology, is
a reflexive exercise. The focus is less the subject matter of the social world
and more that of sociology itself, to the extent that there is a sociology to
be found in Malay studies. The purpose of this bibliographic essay is to
explore the theoretical contribution of Malay studies to the discipline of
sociology in Singapore. The concern is with whether theories and
concepts from a wide variety of perspectives are applied to the study of
Malay society self-consciously or otherwise. In other words, does
sociological discourse on Malay society tend to be more descriptive or
theoretical and are new theoretical insights being developed?[1]

An essay of this nature cannot be exhaustive. Many important
studies that are relevant to the study of Malay society, particularly those
in allied disciplines of sociology, such as anthropology, history and
political science, cannot always be included. For example, one of the
earliest ethnographies of Singapore Malays, by Djamour (1959), was
written about 40 years ago.[2] This study of the sociology of the Malays,
however, will be restricted to the following aspects:

1.   For an earlier "state of the art" study see Clammer (1981).
2.   Ethnographies appearing later are few and include Mariam Mohamed Ali's
      "Orang Baru" and "Orang Lama" (1984/85) and her *Uniformity and Diversity
      Among Muslims in Singapore* (1989), Suriani Suratman's *The Malays of
      Clementi* (1986), and Tania Li's, *Malays in Singapore* (1989).

(a)   the question of Malay identity
(b)   ethnicity and class structure
(c)   patterns of ethnic relations
(d)   the rise of entrepreneurship amongst the Malays, underdevelopment, and the question of Malay capitalism
(e)   Islamic revivalism and ideology in Malay society.

These areas have been selected as most works of a sociological nature on Singapore Malay society fall into one of these areas.[3]

Malay Identity

There are two reasons why Malay identity in Singapore deserves sociological attention.

First, the nature of ethnic identity and boundaries, including the criteria used to define ethnicity as well as historical changes in ethnic identity, is obviously an important issue in a polyethnic society such as Singapore. This is particularly true for the Malays, in view of the fluidity of the Malay ethnic boundary and the historical processes of acculturation and assimilation of the various peoples of the Malay-Indonesian Archipelago as well as of Arabs and Indian Muslims to Malay society. This being the case, it is rather surprising that relatively little work on these issues has been done.

Secondly, some public debate on the position of the Singapore Arab community in Malay society has occurred in recent years. Many sociologically relevant issues were raised by the public. The debate started with a letter to *The Straits Times* criticizing a Singapore Broadcasting Corporation (SBC) Malay programme, "Potret Keluarga", for depicting "local Arabs as part of the Malay community" (bin Hafiz 1992). Very soon after that, a spokesman for SBC gave assurances to the effect that there was no intention on the part of SBC to depict Arabs as part of the Malay community (Cheng 1992).

---

3.   For broader surveys of a more bibliographic nature see Lim (1986), Hussin Mutalib, Hashimah Johari, Rokiah Mentol, Zaleha Othman and Zaleha Tamby (1996), and Hussin Mutalib (1996).

There were also reactions to references to "Malays of Arab descent".[4] Whatever the intention of the show, the question of Arab and, therefore, Malay identity, had been brought to the fore. In both Singapore and Malaysia, stories were carried in dailies suggesting that there was an identity crisis among the Arabs of Singapore, but that it was a minority who wished to hold on to their Arab identity.[5] It was also said that the process of integration of Arabs into Singapore Malay society that had been well under way for decades would not be jeopardised by the attitude of a tiny minority who wishes to set itself apart from the larger Malay society (A. Samad Ismail 1992). Furthermore, in asking the question of whether Arabs in Singapore are Malays, it was recognized that this could be situational (Mardiana Abu Bakar 1992b). The question of whether or not an Arab is a Malay raises the larger issue of what a Malay is. The historical processes of acculturation and assimilation of Arabs, Indian Muslims and the various ethnic groups from the Indonesian islands into Singapore Malay society is testimony to the accommodative nature of Malay identity. The fact that the issue has been alive in public discourse makes it all the more surprising that there has been hardly any sociological work on Malay identity in Singapore.

Exceptions include the work of Tham Seong Chee who looked at political, academic as well as non-Malay perspectives with regard to the definition of "Malay" (Tham 1992/93). Political definitions stressed race and territoriality or place of origin within the Malay world, while academic ones recognize the growing variation in what constitutes "Malay". Furthermore, the cultural lines separating Malays from Arabs, Indians and Chinese who are also Muslims are both subjective as well as objective. Tham's work raises many important issues in the study of Malay identity in Singapore but it is an essay rather than a theoretically informed or empirically based work on the subject.

4. This reference was made by Mardiana Abu Bakar (1992a) and was criticised by Syed Ali bin Hafiz (1992, 3).
5. "Krisis Identiti Melayu Arab", *Berita Harian* (Malaysia), 13 July 1992; "A Question of Identity", *Asiaweek* 31 July 1992; "Some Arabs Here 'Losing Their Sense of Identity'", *Straits Times*, 18 September 1992.

Relevant to the question of Malayness and Malay identity is the notion of "cultural involution" suggested by Benjamin, but not taken up by others. In cultural involution, culture "turns in on itself in a cannibalistic manner, struggling to bring forth further manifestations of its distinctiveness" (Benjamin 1976, 122). How cultural involution is related to the development of Malay identity and the self-image of the Malays would constitute a rich field of research primarily because it offers a different perspective from which to study the transformation of identity.

Mariam Mohamed Ali examines the different ways of being Malay. She questions treatment of the category "Malay" as referring to a socially and culturally monolithic entity. Malayness should not be understood as indicating adherence to fixed and unchanging cultural traits (Mariam 1984/85). In her study of the Malays of the North Coast of Singapore, Mariam demonstrates how the examination of the dynamics of the social and cultural organization of the Malays, falsifies the popular notions that "Malay" denotes a socially and culturally homogeneous community. Of particular interest is how the Malays themselves forge complex distinctions in the interests of maintaining social boundaries among themselves.

Another work of relevance, though not exclusively on Malays, is that of Sharon Siddique (Siddique 1990). This is addressed to how ethnic actors define their ethnic identities. Using the phenomenological approach, Siddique looks at how the content of CMIO (Chinese, Malay, Indian and Others) categories are conceptualized as an important component of commonly held knowledge. This entailed understanding how a group of individuals make sense of ethnicity in certain situations.

Finally, mention should be made of John Clammer's work which, although not confined to the Malays, develops a model to explore ethnic identity in Singapore (Clammer 1985a). This model looks at the six dimensions of family structure, majority/minority statuses, political economy, modernization, alternative modes of social stratification and national ideology. These "structuring elements" suggests that more work needs to be done on the relationship between structural and subjective factors with regard to inter-group and interpersonal relationships in plural Singapore (Clammer 1985, 149).

In general, work on Singapore Malay ethnic identity and boundaries, which attempt to develop theories of ethnicity in the context of plural societies, and which attempt to establish the criteria employed to define ethnicity, has not emerged in Singapore sociology. In this regard it should be mentioned that studies or reflections on Malayness and the question of Malay identity based on the Malaysian setting (Nagata 1974) or the larger Malay world of Southeast Asia (Benjamin 1993) are sometimes relevant to Singapore and should be taken seriously.

Ethnicity and Class Structure in Malay Society

Until today, Malays tend to be over-represented in the occupational categories of service and clerical workers, and are generally employed as clerks, office-boys, unskilled and semi-skilled workers, drivers and carpenters. They tend to be under-represented in the categories of professional, administrative, and managerial workers. When this is understood against the background of rapid economic growth in Singapore in the last three decades, it becomes evident that there is a need to examine the occupational and class structures of the Singapore Malays with a view to gauging the relative progress of this community.

It is common to distinguish between two approaches in the characterisation of the class structure of contemporary capitalist societies. These are based on relational and distributional theories, first identified by Ossowski (1963). The latter classify people into groups based on similarity of characteristics. Relational theories, on the other hand, understand classes in terms of their constituting a system of structured relationships with each other.[6]

It is conventional in the distributional approach to employ occupation and education as indices of class. Occupation, in particular is seen as a fairly accurate indication of income and wealth as well as status differences. The classic expression of the distributional approach is seen in the scheme that labels classes along a continuum from upper to lower that includes the upper

---

6.   For a concise discussion on these two approaches see Lucal (1994).

upper, lower upper, upper middle, lower middle, upper lower, and lower lower classes (Warner 1949).

Most works on the class structure of Singapore society are based on the distributional approach, whether the treatment is of Singapore society in general or of particular ethnic groups, and employ occupation or education as an index of class.[7] While such an approach does take into account important aspects of class such as wealth, power, esteem, prestige, and consumption habits, it is open to serious objections by proponents of the relational approach.

The argument is that concepts such as occupation and education, on the one hand, are qualitatively different from that of social class, on the other. In the relational approach, classes are not categorized along a continuum from upper to lower but according to the relations of power and domination (Wright 1979; Wright, Hachen, Costello and Sprague 1982). An example of the relational approach is the Marxist conceptualization of class, which is based on the position of individuals in the production process. Classes in society are differentiated in terms of relations to the means of production and the criteria of class include ownership of and control over the means of production, control over the labour power of others, and the mode of remuneration. In view of the fact that there tends to be an identification of race with economic function as far as Singapore Malays are concerned, it would be useful to work out the class structure of Singapore by ethnicity in terms of the relational approach. Then it would be possible to gauge how relative shares of income, wealth, power and status accrue not to arbitrarily defined income strata, but rather to strata that relate to each other in a hierarchy of political economic relations.[8] The importance of moving beyond occupational structure in class analysis for Singapore has been noted (Hassan 1970, 503) but there have not been any attempts to utilize the relational approach for the understanding of social class amongst the Malays of Singapore.

7. On Singapore in general, see Hassan (1970), Chen (1973), Lee (1991), Chiew (1991). On Singapore Malay society, see Hassan (1971).
8. For examples of such an approach in the context of other societies see Portes (1985) and Alatas (1991).

Ethnic Relations

A perennial debate in sociology concerns the race/class issue. More often than not, it involves a conflict between Marxist and non-Marxist viewpoints on the relative importance of race and class. Marxist scholars have generally argued for seeing race as a manifestation of class, while non-Marxists tend to assign an independent causal role to race (Mason 1986, 9). As a result of this debate as well as theoretical developments in sociology, there is a rich body of theoretical work on ethnic relations, which include the following perspectives:

(i)   orthodox Marxist interpretations of race and class (Cox 1948, Reich 1977, Szymanski 1976)
(ii) split labour market theory (Bonacich 1972)
(iii) relative autonomy model (Solomos 1986, 89-95)
(iv) autonomy model (Gabriel & Ben-Tovim 1978, 1979, Solomos 1986, 95-101)
(v)   migrant labour model (Miles 1980, 1982, Phizaklea & Miles 1980)
(vi) plural society theory (Furnivall 1939, Smith 1965, 1969)
(vii) Weberian perspectives (Rex 1986)
(viii) symbolic interactionist theories of race relations (Lal, 1986)[9]

Despite the availability of such theoretical tools and an appropriate empirical setting, there have been no attempts to develop the study of ethnic relations in the context of Malay society in Singapore. There are similar reasons for the need for studies on ethnic relations with regard to Malay society as there are for the study of the ethnic identity of this community. Nevertheless, there has been little work that goes beyond descriptive statements of ethnic relations as far as Malay society is concerned.

Most works on the question of ethnic relations in Singapore tend to fall into a number of categories in terms of their empirical focus:

(i)   national policy
(ii) interethnic marriage
(iii) political integration

9.   For a review of this perspective see Lal (1986).

Discussions of Singapore's national policy with regards to the Malays as well as other minority groups tend to focus on cultural and language policies, stressing the legal equality of all ethnic groups, freedom of worship, and the official status of four languages (English, Chinese, Tamil and Malay) (Chan 1984, Clammer 1988, Gopinathan 1979).

With respect to interethnic marriage, it was noted that assimilation between different ethnic groups becomes possible and viable only to the extent that there is compatibility between the cultures and worldviews of the ethnic groups concerned. In this sense, the possibility of Arabs and Indian Muslims being assimilated into Malay society appears to be much greater than assimilation into the Chinese and Indian communities (Clammer 1985a, 150). This point was made by Clammer in the context of noting the inapplicability of Gordon's theory of assimilation to the Singapore case. What Gordon saw as the integration of minorities (immigrants in America) into the social structure of the majority group (Gordon 1964) generally does not take place in Singapore due to the relatively great cultural divide between the Chinese majority and the other minority groups. To the extent that worldview is coterminous with religion, it is understandable that a great deal of ethnic intermarriage is intrareligious (Hassan & Benjamin 1973). An early study by Riaz Hassan concludes that interethnic marriage in Singapore occurs far more frequently here than in other parts of the world, but that these marriages were generally confined within Islam and Christianity (Hassan 1969/1970). In other words, persons marrying across ethnic lines had a common religion.

In asking the question of the extent to which Malay society is politically integrated into the national life of Singapore, the discussion had noted a number of factors which have bearing upon the process of political integration (Bedlington 1971):

(i)   the ethnic diversity among the Malays
(ii) the kinship and cultural ties that Singapore Malays have with Malaysia and Indonesia
(iii) the relative economic backwardness of the Malays
(iv) Malay ethnic identity

To the extent that political integration depends on loyalty, Bedlington's early study concluded that if the Malay community does not see itself as sharing equally in national development or sees its ethnic identity under threat, its loyalties may shift to extend beyond the territorial boundaries of the nation-state (Bedlington 1971, 53). Betts' dissertation on the integration of the Malays into the economic, social and political life of Singapore focuses on government intention and practice on the one hand, and Malay elite perceptions and reactions on the other (Betts 1975). Betts' conclusion that government efforts to mute Malay communalism may unintentionally contribute to the persistence of communalism complements that of Bedlington. Finally, Ismail Kassim's study looks at the problem of the political integration of the Singapore Malays from the point of view of elite cohesion, arguing that elite cohesion can promote stability and political integration (Ismail 1974).[10]

Underdevelopment and Malay Capitalism

The need to address the issue of Malay underdevelopment has long been recognized among Singapore academics. More than twenty years ago, it was suggested that "what is more important is perhaps not to focus on the obvious things such as per capita income, productivity, or capital investment. Instead, the study must include exclusively an inquiry into the causes of economic backwardness in this particular society and its development prospects" (Azhari 1970, 198). In fact, whatever few works there are on the economic conditions of the Singapore Malays tend to focus on the non-economic causes of Malay economic underdevelopment.

In terms of general overviews, the one worth mentioning is by Sharifah Zahra Aljunied (1978-80). She provides a descriptive analysis of the occupational and industrial structure of employment in the Malay labour force, examines the causes and implications of such a structure on Malay society, and makes some

---

10.   For more recent discussions, albeit of a non-sociological nature, see Association of Muslim Professionals (1996).

suggestions as to how to improve the economic conditions of the Malays in Singapore.[11]

The question of the relative economic backwardness of Malay society as a whole and the slow emergence of a Malay capitalist class in particular has received the attention of both scholars and the Malay elite. In general, the focus has been on the issues of (1) Malay entrepreneurship and (2) the relationship between Islam and development.

On Malay entrepreneurship a number of theories have been suggested to explain the relative underdevelopment of Malay capacities in this field:[12]

(i)   deficiencies in Malay education
(ii) the impact of colonial ideology
(iii) the structural argument
(iv) the cultural argument
(v)   the problem of the elite

The view that the problem of Malay entrepreneurial development is at heart a problem of education has been held for more than 30 years.[13] Malay underdevelopment has been attributed to the wrong kind of education, "a cultural education, which made the Malays contented and obedient. The result was that the Malay mind was not an inquiring one" (Sha'ari 1971, 3). It was noted that during the colonial period Malay education was "purely for the preservation and stability of the Malay traditional way of life" (Sharom 1971, 6) and was designed to prevent the emergence of an "educated class of malcontents" (Roff 1974, 25). Stevenson, in his work on the educational history of the Malays, shows how colonial educational policy maintained the division of Malay society between ruler and

11. For an overview of Muslim, including Malay businesses see Tyabji (1991).
12. A comprehensive discussion of these various theories is found in Sarbene (1994/95, chap 1).
13. For a descriptive overview of the socioeconomic status of Malays as seen from the level of educational attainment, occupational status and home ownership, see Wan Hussin Zoohri (1987).

ruled by providing vernacular education for the masses and English education for the sons of Malay *rajas* and chiefs (Stevenson 1975). Also of interest is Hough (1933) on the educational policy of Raffles. This work examines two minutes expressing Raffles' views on education with respect to the founding of the Singapore Institution and the Malay College at Singapore and, therefore, gives an insight into colonial views and policy with respect to education.

The continuity in educational policy between the colonial and early period of postcolonial Singapore was also suggested. As the Malays generally went to Malay schools, this left them relatively unaffected by modernization. The low economic value of Malay education from the standpoint of employment in government service and commercial firms was examined (Mokhtar 1969, Liaw 1969). References were made to various problems plaguing education in the Malay language, such as low scholastic achievement, high dropout rates, low English proficiency, low job aspirations, poorly qualified teachers, underdeveloped curriculum, lack of interest in science and mathematics, a paucity of textbooks in Malay, parental attitudes, and home environment (Tham 1971, 34, Haffidz et al. 1995).

This state of affairs has, of course, changed with the entry of more and more Malays into English-medium schools and the rise of organizations such as MENDAKI (Council on Education for Muslim Children), which addresses itself to the problem of education (Wan Hussin Zoohri 1989). Nevertheless, there have been no studies that attempt to gauge the impact of a modern, secular education on the development of Malay entrepreneurship.[14] Education was also linked to the problem of the elite in that to the extent that progress is a problem of leadership, the Malay-Muslim elite must be drawn from the "slowly expanding pool of the more highly educated" (Siddique & Yang Razali 1987, 167).

A more current issue surrounding education has been the role of the *madrasah* system in the education of the Malays. Since the 1980s, the *madrasah*s had been experiencing an increase in demand

---

14. There has, however, been some attention to the topic of the education of the Malays. See, for example, Kamsiah (1985).

(Zainah Alias 1997/98, 7). As a result, there has been concern in the government that 5-6% of the Malay cohort each year did not graduate from conventional schools (Straits Times 28 December 1997, cited in Zainah Alias 1997/98, 8). This is an issue mainly because of the fact that *madrasah* education is seen to be below the standards of conventional schools.[15]

Colonial ideology has been cited as another cause of the underdevelopment of the Malays. While the establishment of colonial monopolies and, eventually, the colonial state in Southeast Asia led to the disappearance of the indigenous trading class, the myth of lazy, incapable, treacherous and scheming natives was created by the British, functioning to justify colonial rule (Alatas 1977). What is of relevance here is the continuing effect of such colonial ideology in contemporary Singapore and the association of race with a "culture of laziness".

A more structural argument concerning the underdevelopment of Malay society focuses on the "structuring of constraints and opportunities which hinder the possibilities for the upward mobility of the Malays" (Sarbene 1994/95, 13). Stress is laid upon the role of rules, regulations and policies. Colonial policies with regard to immigration, land ownership and education have often been invoked as causes of Malay underdevelopment, because they excluded the Malays from full participation in the market economy.

The cultural explanation, on the other hand, postulates that the problem lies in the value system of the Malays. Islam and *adat* (customary behaviour and law) are seen to function as obstacles to development as they are conservative and intolerant to change.[16] Furthermore, it was noted by Tania Li that religious doctrines and perceptions of the afterlife do not "provide Singapore Malays with strong motivations for the accumulation of boundless wealth through business enterprise" (Li 1989, 84). Nevertheless, Li is generally critical of the cultural explanation, which are surveyed in her work and

15. See also Mukhlis Abu Bakar (1999/2000).
16. For such views in the context of Malaysia which are possibly applicable to the Singapore Malays, see Parkinson (1975a, 1975b). For a Singaporean view on the Malaysian Malay context see Tham (1983).

explained as ideological justifications for structural inequalities (Li 1989, 178-82).

Finally, Tham has appraised the literary efforts of Malay writers from the point of view of their value perceptions amidst modernization and change. He attempts to "structure the perceptual framework of the Malay writers in regards to values, beliefs and attitudes, as they relate to modernization" (Tham 1976).

Whatever little work that exists on the Malay elite in Singapore is mainly historical in nature and has tended to be critical of the role of the elite in the feudal past. The Malay elite of the pre-colonial period were regarded as a group "in whom is absent the qualities necessary for development...such as ethical integrity and standards, intellectual capacity and stamina for productive and creative endeavours" (Shaharuddin 1989, 96). The significance of this for contemporary Malay society in Southeast Asia lies in the notion that negative values inherited from the past obstruct development amongst the Malays today (Shaharuddin 1989, vi).

One way of demonstrating how such values promoted by the dominant elite in Malay society hinder development is to examine the ideal of excellence as reflected in the Malay concept of the hero. It is to this end that Shaharuddin Maaruf analyses the perception of Hang Tuah as a hero in Malay society, drawing attention to how the uncritical attachment to feudal heroism is still present in contemporary Malay society (Shaharuddin 1984). This line of inquiry into the value system of the Malay elite is continued in later work (Shaharuddin 1989). Here Shaharuddin draws his attention to the values of the Malay court in feudal times, and also to the cooperation between the Malay elite and colonial capitalism during the colonial period, with a view to exposing the dominant ideas of development that have shaped Malay thinking historically.

Along similar lines of analysis is the work of Sharifah Maznah who examines the nature and functions of Malay myths. The Malay elite, as creators and disseminators of myths, exert a great deal of influence over the development of the Malays. Sharifah Maznah attributes many contemporary problems in Malay society, such as the lack of scientific orientation, the romanticisation of feudal heroes, and blind loyalty to leaders as traits originating from the feudal past, and which owe their continuing presence to the persistence of myths (Sharifah Maznah 1993).

Although there has been some theoretical attention to the study of elite values and ideas in terms of the sociology of knowledge and theories of myth, in the works of Shaharuddin and Sharifah Maznah, there has been no sociological work focusing on the more objective aspects of Malay elites and their role in development.

Scholars based in Singapore have discussed the relationship between Islam and development in the context of Weber's work on the Protestant ethic and the development of capitalism in Western Europe as well as Weber's overall sociology of religion.

Capitalism as an economic system requires an attitude that Weber called the spirit of capitalism. This attitude was derived from Protestantism. Whereas the attitude in pre-capitalist times was one of traditionalism — man does not wish to earn more and more money but wants to live as he is accustomed to living and to earn as much as is necessary for that purpose – in the spirit of capitalism both labourer and entrepreneur regard work as an end in itself, as if it were a religious calling (Weber 1958, 60, 63). There was something about Protestantism which instilled an attitude in people that ultimately nurtured the capitalist drive.

Puritanism was a Protestant movement in the 16th and 17th centuries derived from the doctrines of Calvinism in England, and was based on asceticism. But it was not based on an other-worldly asceticism like Catholicism or other forms of monasticism which stress retreat from worldly affairs, but rather on a worldly asceticism which was neither against activity in this world nor wealth acquisition. The moral objection to wealth is the "relaxation in the security of possession, the enjoyment of wealth with the consequence of idleness and the temptations of the flesh, and above all distraction from the pursuit of a righteous life" (Weber 1958, 157).

The Protestant ethic freed the acquisition of wealth from the inhibitions of traditionalistic ethics (Weber 1958, 171). It also drove its adherents to hard work, discipline, and frugality since the attainment of wealth as a fruit of labour in a calling was a sign of God's blessing. The practical result of all this was an ascetic compulsion to work hard and to save, to avoid spontaneous enjoyment. For Weber, there was an elective affinity or congeniality between Calvinism and modern capitalist attitudes. Calvinists did not consciously seek to create a capitalist system; instead capitalism was an unintended consequence of the Protestant ethic.

Syed Hussein Alatas (1963) argues that, in the case of the Malays of Southeast Asia, the "calling" as well as various other aspects of the Protestant Ethic are to be found in Islam and that the spirit of capitalism was present amongst the early Muslim traders of the region. He attributes the loss of this spirit to factors other than religion.

Peacock, in taking his cues from Weber, attempts to demonstrate the extent to which cultural change amongst the Muslim of Singapore, Malaysia and Indonesia implies psychological rationalization (Peacock 1978). Peacock examines the psychological and cultural aspects of the lives of Muslim non-traditionalists in the three countries, looking at a broad range of items such as toilet training, language, social hierarchy, circumcision, theology, pilgrimage, schooling, and work.

Clammer makes a cautionary note with regard to the use of Weber for the study of Islam and development in Southeast Asia. First of all, he warns that "the hunt for varieties of the Protestant Ethic in Asia" is both fruitless and pointless from a Weberian viewpoint (Clammer 1985, 234). Weber did not claim that non-Protestant religions were not conducive to the development of capitalism (Clammer 1978, 17). What he did say, however, was that these religions were not based on an ascetic compulsion to accumulate capital in the way that Puritanism was. It is, therefore, pointless to search for the functional analogue to the Protestant ethic in other religions. Clammer also points out that it is necessary to move beyond Weber's Protestant ethic thesis to a consideration of his other areas of sociology such as the study of authority, legitimation, patrimonialism and law, which may be fruitfully applied to the study of development in Southeast Asia (Clammer 1985b, 234).

Ideology

The study of ideology, including Islamic revivalism, has received some degree of attention by scholars of Malay society in Singapore. Ideology, or the set of ideas and conceptions of a group, class or epoch, and which more or less reflect economic and political arrangements of a society, is variously expressed in Malay society and the literature has taken note of a number of such ideologies:

(i)   colonial ideology
(ii)   Malay nationalism
(iii) feudalism
(iv)   Islamic revivalism
(v)   secularism

Historical sociological research on colonial ideology had been carried out by Syed Hussein Alatas with a focus on (i) the political philosophy of Raffles and (ii) the myth of Malay laziness (Alatas 1971, 1977).

The account on Raffles detailed his political philosophy and its relation to the massacre of Palembang, his ethnic prejudice with regard to the different communities in the area, Raffles' alleged corrupt conduct in the Banjarmasin affair, and his ideology of imperialism, including where the latter concerns the Malays of Singapore and the rest of the Malay world. Alatas criticises colonial historiography for taking a "naive and docile" view towards Raffles in stressing his humanitarian characteristics when, in fact, he did not have the welfare of the Malays at heart and considered them to be a degraded community (Alatas 1971, 28, 39). Alatas' view is that the exaggeration of Raffles as a humanitarian reformer served the need for colonial myth making.[17]

The theme of colonial myths is taken up in more depth by Alatas in a later work which addresses it self to the myth of laziness of the Malays, Javanese and Filipinos in Southeast Asia (Alatas 1977). As far as the Malays are concerned, the purpose of this work is to show how the myth of the lazy native was created to instil a negative image of the native which could in turn justify colonial capitalist exploitation. An application of this idea to the case of Singapore Malays can be found

---

17.   A controversy over Alatas' work on Raffles developed in 1972. See "A Controversy on Raffles", *Suara Universiti* 3(1): 49-61, 1972.

in Chin (1996/97). Also worthy of mention is an academic exercise which discusses the survival of colonial stereotypes of the Malay in native Malay literature (Teo 1992/93).

Turning to Malay nationalism, its origins have been well documented (Roff 1974; Radin Soenarno 1960). The nationalist impulse in the Malay Peninsular was preceded by the rise of a religious revivalist movement at the turn of the present century in Singapore. In 1906 a Malay periodical by the name of *Al-Imam* (*The Leader*) began publishing in Singapore. Started by Syed Sheikh Ahmad al-Hadi, it was the first Malay newspaper that discussed issues of social change and politics (Radin Soenarno 1960, 6). Inspired by the Muslim modernist movement led by Muhammad Abduh in Egypt during the latter part of the last century and who was Syed Sheikh Al-Hadi's teacher, the movement behind *Al-Imam* was first and foremost a religious one.

Syed Sheikh Al-Hadi and his group came to be known collectively as *Kaum Muda* (Young Faction) as opposed to *Kaum Tua* (Old Faction). The latter consisted of the state religious hierarchy and the conservative Malay elite who derived their status from cooperation with the colonial state. The *Kaum Tua* sought to maintain their position under colonial rule. On the other hand, the *Kaum Muda* advocated the rejuvenation of Malay Muslim society along the lines of Western notions of progress. The *Kaum Muda* became politicised during the mid-1920s (Roff 1974, 87). Through the organ of two journals, *Seruan Azhar* (Voice of Azhar) and *Pilehan Timoer* (Choice of the East) published by Malay and Indonesian students at Al-Azhar University in Cairo, nationalist issues were raised.

The year 1926 saw the establishment of the first Malay political party, the *Kesatuan Melayu Singapura* (Singapore Malay Union). Its goal was to advance the social and economic interests of the Malays, to encourage the Malays to participate in politics and administration and to take an interest in higher education.

While there has been serious work on the origins of Malay nationalism in Singapore when it was a part of Malaya, this had not been followed up by explorations into Malay nationalist sentiments after Malayan political independence and the formation of Singapore as an independent nation.

Feudalism as a psychology and worldview and which is seen to be surviving in Malay society in Singapore and in Southeast Asia as a whole has also become the subject of historical sociological investigation in Singapore. While the topic of feudalism as an economic system or mode of production may seem more relevant to the study of Malaysia, the concern with feudalism among scholars based in Singapore was more with what came to be known as the feudal psychology.[18]

The role of myths in ideological justification is the focus of analysis by Sharifah Maznah, who explores myths perpetuated by the Malay ruling class of the feudal past in terms of their impact on contemporary social and political problems of Malay society. She looks at the emphasis on magic in Malay myths as they are found in Malay historical narratives, the Malay myth of golden age as an attempt to compensate for lost glory and pride, the myth of divine kingship, and how myths function in the abuse of religion and history (Sharifah Maznah 1993).

The study of feudalism in Malay society is also the interest of Shaharuddin Maaruf, who focuses on the survival and presence of feudal values in Malay culture (Shaharuddin 1984, 1989, 1992). According to Shaharuddin, feudalism is an element of tradition that inhibits modernization amongst the Malays. Although feudalism as an economic and political system no longer exists some feudal values still survive in Malay tradition (Shaharuddin 1992, 260). These include:

(i)   servility before authority and the acceptance of arbitrary notions of power
(ii)   lack of respect for the rule of law
(iii) non-distinction between the public and private domains of life
(iv) emphasis on grandeur and opulence
(v)   lack of concern for social justice
(vi) acceptance of unfair privileges for those in position and power

---

18.   The notion originated with Syed Hussein Alatas (1968).

These values, when internalized, make people less critical of corruption, inequality, and injustice.

Shaharuddin (1992, 261) points out that the feudal aspect in Malay tradition is in conflict with the Islamic aspect in Malay tradition. Islam challenges the negative feudal values with its emphasis on:

(i)   democratic conception of authority through consultation
(ii)   control of arbitrary power, abuses and excesses through the Shari'ah
(iii)   condemnation of corruption
(iv)   emphasis on frugal living
(v)   emphasis on social justice
(vi)   condemnation of unfair privileges
(vii)   condemnation of superstition and irrational beliefs

Shaharuddin concludes by saying that the success of modernization depends on the outcome of the conflict between Islamic and feudal values in Malay society.

On Islamic revivalism, there have been no works that attempt to approach the issue by way of analyses of ideology, other than a recent paper by Shaharuddin Maaruf that attempts a creative application of Karl Mannheim's concepts of ideology and utopia to Muslim thought in Southeast Asia. For the most part, however, rather than consider Islamic revivalism as constituted by ideological manifestations of Islamic sentiments in the context of political economic changes, writings on Islam in Singapore have remained at a descriptive and exhortative level (Kamsiah 1988, Wu 1988, Bambang 1988). This is unfortunate as theoretical work on Islam and ideology has been done for other countries and regions and there is, therefore, a pool of conceptual resources to draw upon.[19] Many of these works are undoubtedly of relevance to the Singapore Malay case as Islamic resurgence in various parts of the Muslim world has had some impact on the Malay-Muslim scene in Singapore (Omar 1988, Weyland 1990).

19.   See, for example, Binder (1964), Esposito (1984), Haddad (1982), Rahman (1970), Shepard (1987), Nagata (1984). On Islam and feminism, see Durrat bte Salleh (1996/97).

Conclusion

The terrain on which sociology and Malay studies meet has not been traversed intellectually. This bibliographic essay on Malay studies in Singapore has attempted to map out its sociological provinces. Ideally, such a project would focus on theory, pure sociology, narrative sociology, applied sociology, and sociology's value postulates. In doing so, the following issues could be dealt with:

(i) What is the value content of Malay sociology? What is the place of values in the choice of areas of inquiry and topics of research?
(ii) Social reality, in its objective, subjective, macro and micro dimensions can be apprehended by means of various theoretical perspectives such as structural-functionalism, ethnomethodology, structural Marxism and so on. Are theories from a wide variety of perspectives applied to the study of Malay society? Is sociological discourse on Malay society more narrative or theoretical?
(iii) In the study of Malay society in Singapore are new theoretical insights being developed? For example, in the study of Malay identity are there any valuable theoretical insights for the study of cultural or ethnic identity in general?
(iv) To what extent does research on Malay society in Singapore feed into policy formulation and implementation as far as both government agencies and non-governmental organizations are concerned. For example, do organizations such as Mendaki and the AMP (Association of Muslim Professionals) draw upon sociological works on the Malays and find such works useful in drawing up policies and programmes to deal with various problems facing Singapore Malays?

It is difficult to give equal weight to all of these questions. Satisfactory responses to them presuppose a rich body of sociological research to begin with. Nevertheless, some comments on the state of Malay sociology in Singapore can be made and can be summarized as follows:

(i) There is nothing by way of a clash of values in the literature on Malay society. While the various works that have addressed Malay problems are certainly guided by value postulates more or less in conformity with technical norms of efficiency and calculability and the capitalist ethos, these value postulates themselves have not been called into question. This is partly a reflection of the dominant interests of the Malay political elite and intelligentsia as well of the fact that the question of value-laden social science generally does not enter into sociological discourse in Singapore studies as a whole.

(ii) We do not find much theoretical application in the study of Malay society. With the exception of the study of Malay underdevelopment and Malay ideology, there has not been any critical thought, reflection and application of the wide range of sociological perspectives that have been available for decades.

(iii) A significant proportion of the works on Malay society cited above are not academic in nature although they often do make sociological statement and contain sociological insights. The semi-academic nature of such works and the general theoretical poverty of Malay sociology in general suggest that Malay sociology will not be able to play any appreciable role in the process of policy formulation and implementation.[20] Although we would agree with Liaw Yock Fang (1970, 185), writing in 1970, that Malay studies has the potential to contribute to national development, we find that it is not yet able to play this role.

Assuming a conducive political climate, a serious research tradition and well developed body of sociological knowledge needs to be created if Malay sociology is to contribute to the discipline of sociology and if it is to feed into policy formulation and implementation both at the governmental and non-governmental levels.

20. What is needed are efforts such as the setting up of the Research Institute of Malay-Muslim Affairs (Rimma) by the Association of Muslim Professionals. See Tuminah Sapawi (1995).

References

A. Samad Ismail (1992), "Melayu versus Arab", *Dewan Budaya*, September.

Alatas, Syed Farid (1991) "Notes on Race and Class in Malaysia", *Journal Institute of Muslim Minority Affairs*, 12(1): 115-27.

Alatas, Syed Hussein (1963) "The Weber Thesis and Southeast Asia", *Archives de Sociologie des Religions*, No. 15, Reproduced in Alatas, Syed Hussein (1972) *Modernization and Social Change: Studies in Social Change in Southeast Asia*, Sydney: Angus & Robertson.

Alatas, Syed Hussein (1968) "Feudalism in Malaysian Society", *Civilisation*, 18(4).

Alatas, Syed Hussein (1971) *Thomas Stamford Raffles 1781-1826: Schemer or Reformer*, Sydney: Angus & Robertson.

Alatas, Syed Hussein (1977) *The Myth of the Lazy Native*, London: Frank Cass.

Aljunied, Sharifah Zahra (1978-80) "A General Outlook of Malay Participation in the Singapore Economy", *Sedar*, 49-65.

Association of Muslim Professionals (1996) "Self Help and National Integration", AMP Occasional Paper Series No. 3-96, 1996.

Azhari Zahri (1970) "Brief Notes on Research into the Economic Life of the Malays", in *Research Programs in Singapore (Proceedings and Papers of a Seminar held under the Auspices of Nanyang University from 6 to 7 August, 1969)*, Singapore: Nanyang University.

Bambang Sugeng Kajairi (1988) "Into the 1990s: The Organizational Challenge for Singapore Muslims", *Fajar Islam*, 1(1): 79-85.

Bedlington, S.S. (1971) "Political Integration and the Singapore Malay Community", *Journal of the Historical Society*, 47-53.

Benjamin, G. (1976) "The Cultural Logic of Singapore's 'Multiracialism'", in Riaz Hassan (ed), *Singapore: Society in Transition*, Kuala Lumpur: Oxford University Press.

Benjamin, G. (1993) "Grammar and Polity: The Cultural and Political Background to Standard Malay", in W.A. Foley (ed) *The Role of Theory in Language Description*, Berlin: Mouton de Gruyter.

Betts, R. H. (1975) *Multiracialism, Meritocracy and the Malays of Singapore*, Ph.D. Dissertation, Dept. of Political Science, Massachusetts Institute of Technology.

Binder, L. (1964) *Ideological Revolution in the Middle East*, New York: John Wiley.

Bonacich, E. (1972) "A Theory of Ethnic Antagonism: The Split Labor Market", *American Sociological Review,* 37: 547-59.

Chan, H. C. (1984) "Language and Culture in a Multi-Ethnic Society: A Singapore Strategy", *Ilmu Masyarakat,* 5: 62-70.

Chen, P. S. J. (1973) "Social Stratification in Singapore", Dept. of Sociology Working Papers No. 12, University of Singapore.

Cheng, J. (1992) "No Intention to Depict Arabs as Malays", *The Straits Times,* 25 May.

Chiew, S. K. (1991), "Ethnic Stratification", in S.R. Quah, S.K. Chiew, K.Y. Chong & S.M. Lee, *Social Class in Singapore*, Singapore: Centre for Advanced Studies, National University of Singapore & Times Academic Press.

Chin, L. K. G. (1996/97) *The Myth of the Lazy Native Unbounded: A Sociological Examination of Achievement Values among Chinese and Malays in Singapore*, Honours Thesis, Dept. of Sociology, National University of Singapore.

Clammer, J. (1978) "Islam and Capitalism in Southeast Asia", *Sociology Working Paper No. 63*, Dept. of Sociology, National University of Singapore.

Clammer, J. (1981) "Malay Society in Singapore: A Preliminary Analysis", *Southeast Asian Journal of Social Science,* 9(1-2): 19-32.

Clammer, J. (1985a) "Ethnicity and the Classification of Social Differences in Plural Societies: A Perspective from Singapore", *Journal of Asian and African Studies,* 20(3-4): 141-55.

Clammer, J. (1985b) "Weber and Islam in Southeast Asia", *Journal of Developing Societies*, 1(2): 224-36.

Clammer, J. (1988) "Minorities and Minority Policy in Singapore", *Southeast Asian Journal of Social Science*, 16(2): 96-110.

Cox, O. C. (1948) *Caste, Class, and Race*, New York: Monthly Review Press.

Djamour, J. (1959) *Malay Kinship and Marriage in Singapore*, London: The Athlone Press.

Durrat bte Salleh (1996/97) *Feminism and Islam*, Honours Thesis, Dept. of Sociology, National University of Singapore.

Esposito, J. (1984) *Islam and Politics*, Syracuse: Syracuse University Press.

Furnivall, J. S. (1939) *Netherlands India – A Study of Plural Economy*, Cambridge: Cambridge University Press.

Gabriel, J. and Ben-Tovim, G. (1978) "Marxism and the Concept of Racism", *Economy and Society*, 7(2): 118-54.

Gabriel, J. and Ben-Tovim, G. (1979) "The Conceptualisation of Race Relations in Sociological Theory", *Ethnic and Racial Studies*, 2(2): 190-212.

Gopinathan, S. (1979) "Singapore's Language Policies", *Southeast Asian Affairs*, 280-95.

Gordon, M. (1964) *Assimilation in American Life*, New York: Oxford University Press.

Haddad, Y. (1982) *Contemporary Islam and the Challenge of History*, Albany: SUNY Press.

bin Hafiz, Syed Hassan Ali (1992) "Programme Suggested Arabs Belonged to Malay Community", *Straits Times*, 16 May.

bin Hafiz, Syed Hassan Ali (1992) "Always an Arab", *Al Shorouq*, 1(4).

Haffidz A. Hamid, Mohd Azhar Khalid, Mohd Alami Musa and Yusof Sulaiman (1995) "Factors Affecting Malay/Muslim Pupils' Performance in Education", AMP Occasional Paper Series No. 1-95.

Hassan, Riaz (1969/1970) "The Religious Factor in Interethnic Marriage in Singapore", *Sedar,* 2: 47-52.

Hassan, Riaz (1970) "Class, Ethnicity and Occupational Structure in Singapore", *Civilisations,* 20: 496-515.

Hassan, Riaz (1971) "Occupational and Class Structures of Singapore Malays", *Suara Universiti,* 2 (1): 29-32.

Hassan, Riaz and Benjamin, G. (1973) "Ethnic Outmarriage Rates in Singapore: The Influence of Traditional Sociocultural Organization", *Journal of Marriage and the Family,* 35 (4): 731-38.

Hirschman, C. (1984) "The Making of Race in Colonial Malaya: Political Economy and Racial Ideology", *Sociological Forum,* 1 (2): 330-61.

Hough, G. G. (1933) "Notes on the Educational Policy of Sir Stamford Raffles", *Journal of the Malayan Branch of the Royal Asiatic Society* 11, pt. 2: 166-71.

Hussin Mutalib (1996) "Singapore Malays, 1819-1994: A Bibliographic Survey", *Southeast Asian Journal of Social Science,* 24 (2): 22-48.

Hussin Mutalib, Hashimah Johari, Rokiah Mentol, Zaleha Othman and Zaleha Tamby (eds) (1996) *Singapore Malay/Muslim Community, 1819-1994: A Bibliography,* Singapore: Centre for Advanced Studies, National University of Singapore.

Ismail Kassim (1974) *Problems of Elite Cohesion: A Perspective from a Minority Community,* Singapore: Singapore University Press.

Kamsiah Abdullah (1985) "Attitudes and Motivation of Malay Students in Secondary Schools in Singapore towards the Learning of English and Malay", *Singapore Journal of Education,* 7 (1): 45-55.

Kamsiah Abdullah (1988) "Inculcating Islamic Values in Muslim Pre-School Education in Singapore", *Fajar Islam,* 1 (1): 59-67.

Lal, B. B. (1986), "The 'Chicago School', Symbolic Interactionism, and Race Relations Theory", in J. Rex and D. Mason (eds), *Theories of Race and Ethnic Relations,* Cambridge: Cambridge University Press.

Lee, S. M. (1991) "Social Class in Singapore: An Overview", in S. R. Quah, S. K. Chiew, K. Y. Chong and S. M. C. Lee, *Social Class in Singapore,*

Singapore: Centre for Advanced Studies, National University of Singapore & Times Academic Press.

Li, T. (1989) *Malays in Singapore: Culture, Economy, and Ideology*, Singapore: Oxford University Press.

Liaw, Y. F. (1969) "The Economic Value of Malay Education", *Intisari*, 3(3): 29-31.

Liaw, Y. F. (1970) "Malay Studies and National Development", in *Research Programmes in Singapore (Proceedings and Papers of a Seminar held under the auspices of Nanyang University from 6 to 7 August 1969)*, Singapore: Nanyang University.

Lim, P. H. P. (1986) *The Malay World of Southeast Asia: A Select Cultural Bibliography*, Singapore: Institute of Southeast Asian Studies [various sections on Singapore Malays].

Lucal, B. (1994) "Class Stratification in Introductory Textbooks: Relational or Distributional Models?" *Teaching Sociology*, 22: 139-50.

Mahathir Mohamad (1970) *The Malay Dilemma*, Singapore: Times Books.

Mardiana Abu Bakar (1992a) "The Arab Dilemma", *The Straits Times*, 11 June.

Mardiana Abu Bakar (1992b) "The Arab Dilemma", *The Straits Times*, 11 June.

Mariam Mohamed Ali (1984/85) *'Orang Baru' and 'Orang Lama': Ways of Being Malay on Singapore's North Coast*, Academic Exercise, Dept. of Sociology, National University of Singapore.

Mariam Mohamed Ali (1989) *Uniformity and Diversity among Muslims in Singapore*, Thesis (M.Soc.Sc.), Dept. of Sociology, National University of Singapore.

Mason, D. (1986) "Introduction. Controversies and Continuities in Race and Ethnic Relations Theory", in J. Rex and D. Mason (eds) *Theories of Race and Ethnic Relations*, Cambridge: Cambridge University Press.

Miles, R. (1980) "Class, Race and Ethnicity: A Critique of Cox's Theory", *Ethnic and Racial Studies,* 3(2): 169-87.

Miles, R. (1982) *Racism and Migrant Labour,* London: Routledge & Kegan Paul.

Mokhtar Abdullah (1969) "The Value of Malay Education in Singapore", *Intisari,* 3(3): 13-19.

Mukhlis Abu Bakar (1999/2000) "Islamic Religious Schools in Singapore: Recent Trends and Issues", Seminar Paper No. 26, Dept. of Malay Studies, National University of Singapore.

Nagata, J. A. (1974) "What is Malay? Situational Selection of Ethnic Identity in a Plural Society", *American Ethnologist,* 1 (2): 331-50.

Nagata, J. A. (1984) *The Reflowering of Malaysian Islam: Modern Religious Radicals and Their Roots,* Vancouver: University of British Columbia Press.

Omar Farouk (1988) "Malaysia's Islamic Awakening: Impact on Singapore and Thai Muslims", *Conflict,* 8: 157-68.

Ossowski, S. (1963) *Class Structure in the Social Consciousness,* New York: Free Press.

Parkinson, B. K. (1975a) "Non-Economic Factors in the Retardation of the Rural Malays", in D. Lim (ed), *Readings on Malaysian Economic Development,* Kuala Lumpur: Oxford University Press.

Parkinson, B. K. (1975b) "The Economic Retardation of the Malays – A Rejoinder", in D. Lim (ed) *Readings on Malaysian Economic Development,* Kuala Lumpur: Oxford University Press.

Peacock, J. L. (1978) *Muslim Puritans: Reformist Psychology in Southeast Asian Islam,* Berkeley: University of California Press.

Phizacklea, A. and Miles, R. (1980), *Labour and Racism,* London: Routledge & Kegan Paul.

Portes, A. (1985) "Latin American Class Structures: Their Composition and Change During the Last Decades", *Latin American Research Review,* 20(3): 7-39.

Radin Soenarno (1960) "Malay Nationalism, 1896-1941", *Journal of Southeast Asian History,* 1(1): 1-28.

Rahman, Fazlur (1970) "Revival and Reform in Islam", in *The Cambridge History of Islam*, Vol. 2, Cambridge: Cambridge University Press, pt. iv, Ch 7, pp. 632-56.

Reich, M. (1977) "The Economics of Racism", in D.M. Gordon (ed), *Problems in Political Economy*, Lexington, MA: Heath.

Rex, J. (1986) "The Role of Class Analysis in the Study of Race Relations – A Weberian Perspective", in J. Rex and D. Mason (eds) *Theories of Race and Ethnic Relations*, Cambridge: Cambridge University Press.

Roff, W. (1974) *The Origins of Malay Nationalism*, Kuala Lumpur: University of Malaya Press.

Sarbene Jantan, *Obstacles to the Rise of the Malay Entrepreneurial Class: The Case of Singapore*, Honours Thesis, Southeast Asian Studies Programme, National University of Singapore, 1994/95.

Sha'ari Tadin (1971) Opening Address by Inche Sha'ari Tadin, "Parliamentary Secretary to the Minister of Culture", in Sharom Ahmat and J. Wong (eds) *Malay Participation in the National Development of Singapore*, Singapore: Central Council of Malay Cultural Organisations,

Shaharuddin Maaruf (1984) *The Concept of the Hero in Malay Society*, Singapore: Eastern Universities Press.

Shaharuddin Maaruf (1989) *Malay Ideas on Development: From Feudal Lord to Capitalist*, Singapore: Times Books International.

Shaharuddin Maaruf (1992) "Some Theoretical Problems Concerning Tradition and Modernization Among the Malays of Southeast Asia", in Y.M. Cheong (ed), *Asian Tradition and Modernization: Perspectives from Singapore*, Singapore: Times Academic Press.

Shaharuddin Maaruf (1999) "Religion and Utopian Thinking Among the Muslims of Southeast Asia", Paper presented at the Asean Inter-University Seminars on Social Development, Prince of Songkla University, Pattani, Thailand, 16-18 June.

Sharifah Maznah Syed Omar (1993) *Myths and the Malay Ruling Class*, Singapore: Times Academic Press.

Sharom Ahmat (1971) "Singapore Malays, Education and National Development", in Sharom Ahmat and J. Wong (eds) *Malay Participation in the National Development of Singapore*, Singapore: Central Council of Malay Cultural Organisations.

Shepard, W. E. (1987) "Islam and Ideology: Towards a Typology", *International Journal of Middle East Studies*, 19: 307-36.

Siddique, S. (1986) "The Administration of Islam in Singapore", in Taufik Abdullah and S. Siddique (eds) *Islam and Society in Southeast Asia*, Singapore: Institute of Southeast Asian Studies.

Siddique, S. (1990) "The Phenomenology of Ethnicity: A Singapore Case-Study", *Sojourn*, 5(1): 35-62.

Siddique, S. and Yang Razali Kassim (1987) "Muslim Society, Higher Education and Development: The Case of Singapore", in S. Ahmat and S. Siddique (eds) *Muslim Society, Higher Education and Development in Southeast Asia*, Singapore: Institute of Southeast Asian Studies.

Smith, M. G. (1965) *The Plural Society in the British West Indies*, Berkeley: University of California Press.

Smith, M. G. (1969) "Some Developments in the Analytic Framework of Pluralism", in L. Kuper and M.G. Smith (eds) *Pluralism in Africa*, Berkeley: University of California Press.

Solomos, J. (1986) "Varieties of Marxist Conceptions of 'Race', Class and the State: A Critical Analysis", in J. Rex and D. Mason (eds) *Theories of Race and Ethnic Relations*, Cambridge: Cambridge University Press.

Stevenson, R. (1975) *Cultivators and Administrators: British Educational Policy towards the Malays 1875-1906*, Kuala Lumpur: Oxford University Press.

Suriani Suratman (1986) *The Malays of Clementi: An Ethnography of Flat Dwellers*, Master Thesis, Dept. of Anthropology and Sociology, Monash University.

Szymanski, A. (1976) "Racial Discrimination and White Gain", *American Sociological Review,* 41: 403-13.

Teo, P. L. G. (1992/93) *Portrait of the Malay: A Comparison of Colonial and Native Perceptions of the Malay,* Academic Exercise, Dept. of English Language and Literature, National University of Singapore.

Tham, S. C. (1971) "Education, Society and Economic Mobility Among the Malays in Singapore", *Suara Universiti,* 2(1): 32-40.

Tham, S. C. (1976) "Modernization and Value Perception Among Malay Writers", *Commentary,* 11(1): 36-47.

Tham, S. C. (1983) *Malay and Modernization: A Sociological Interpretation,* Singapore: Singapore University Press.

Tham, S. C. (1992/93) "Defining 'Malay'", Seminar Paper No. 6, Dept. of Malay Studies, National University of Singapore.

Tham, S. C. (1993/94) "Islam and Secularism: Dynamics of Accommodation", Seminar and Occasional Papers Series No. 14, Dept. of Malay Studies, National University of Singapore.

Tuminah Sapawi (1995) "New Centre Marks First Stage of Muslim Research Institute", *The Straits Times,* 8 September.

Tyabji, Aminah (1991) "Minority Muslim Businesses in Singapore", in Mohamed Ariff (ed) *The Muslim Private Sector in Southeast Asia,* Singapore: Institute of Southeast Asian Studies.

Vasil, Raj K. (1984) *Governing Singapore,* Kuala Lumpur: Eastern Universities Press.

Wan Hussin Zoohri (1987) "Socio-Economic Problems of the Malays in Singapore", *Sojourn,* 2(2): 178-208. This reappeared as *The Singapore Malays: The Dilemma of Development,* Singapore: Singapore Malay Teachers' Union, 1990.

Wan Hussin Zoohri (1989) "Education and the Malay Community", *Commentary,* 8(1/2): 86-93.

Warner, W. Lloyd, Meeker, M. and Eells, K. (1949) *Social Class in America,* New York: Harper & Row.

Weber, M. (1958) *The Protestant Ethic and the Spirit of Capitalism*, New York: Scribner.

Weyland, P. (1990) "International Muslim Networks and Islam in Singapore", *Sojourn,* 5 (2): 219-54.

Wright, E. O. (1979) *Class Structure and Income Determination*, New York: Academic Press.

Wright, E. O., Hachen, D., Costello, C. and Sprague, J. (1982) "The American Class Structure", *American Sociological Review,* 47: 709-26.

Wu, Ridzuan Abdullah (1988) "Erosion of Islamic Identity: The Singapore Challenge", *Fajar Islam,* 1 (1): 69-77.

Zainah Alias, *The Goals of the Madrasah Educational System in Singapore: Obstacles and Recommendations*, Honours Thesis, Dept. of Sociology, National University of Singapore, 1997/98.

11

Sociology of the Indians

Indira Arumugam

This survey of Indian sociology in Singapore is an exercise in the writing of a self-conscious history. The object of this historicizing is the scholarship by and about Indians in Singapore. While Indians as racially and ethnically constructed beings are implicated, the overwhelming emphasis is not on the Indians *per se* but on the archives created in defining Indians and Singapore Indians in particular, as objects of study. It is the knowledge itself that comes under scrutiny. However, this survey of the knowledge on Indians is a manifestation of the process of "signification" (Malik 1996, 5). Certain scholarly works have been chosen to convey meaning, to dissect and define the "Indian" experience in Singapore. The fact that there is this process of selection involved, intimates the historically and culturally specific as well as the constructed nature of the object of study. Thus, "Indian" is used as a social category to refer to peoples and cultural practices from the Indian sub-continent. It is not treated essentially but reflectively, to refer both to selected experiences as well as its social construction.

However, while much of the scholarly exercises about Singapore Indians are descriptively rich and ethnographically fascinating, there is a paucity of theoretically innovative or even up-to-date works. This is a rather sobering fact, significantly reducing the scope of this essay's content as well as its proposals for further research in this field. This has thus, necessitated references to works on Indians in countries other than Singapore, such as the Caribbean, Britain and the United States. Although the historical, contextual and cultural specificities may differ, the experiences that these works detail, and the theoretical and methodological possibilities they offer, are eminently relevant. Furthermore, they introduce a comparative element that acknowledges the heterogeneous nature of Indian experiences and the scholarship these experiences engender.

Some of the earliest work on racial composition and relations in Singapore stem from colonial, administrative sources (see Furnivall 1948 and Swettenham quoted in Allen 1964). This discourse emphasized the boundedness, homogeneity, coherence, stability and structure of race and culture (Brumann 1999). Such essentialist thinking was even translated into urban planning and settlement when Sir Stamford Raffles, colonial administrator par excellence, "allocated living areas to each of the major migrant groups who could then develop independently of the larger whole" (Siddique and PuruShotam 1982,12). Since the sociological scholarship of Singapore Indians is not that extensive or intensive, this bibliographic essay is composed of a palimpsest of history, anthropology, ethnography, political science and literature. The focus is on how works in these related disciplines contribute to sociological thinking on Singapore Indians. Theoretical and conceptual insights generated from the study of Indian experiences and communities in other countries in Southeast Asia as well as the United States and England are also incorporated. Though this greatly magnifies the scope of study, it also poses its own problems. Consequently, this bibliographic survey cannot be exhaustive. And like in any history, there is inclusion and exclusion, reclamation and refutation, clarification and obfuscation.

This essay will focus on four areas with which sociological analysis so far has been most concerned. These are:

(a) Indians and Identity: Ascribed Identity and Lived "Realities"
(b) Indians: Religion and Rituals
(c) Indians: Economy and Society
(d) Indians and Mobility: Sojourners, Migrants and diaspora

While such a bibliographic survey can only be selective, it is nevertheless of great value. Creative and critical work cannot occur in a vacuum. It must draw from what it knows. The past is always implicated in the present, as is history in sociology. Past work can never resolve issues but a knowledge of the relevant scholarly genealogy can clear the underbrush so that future work can be all the more precise and all the more relevant. This essay surveys research done on Indians in Singapore with a view toward future sociological and anthropological analyses of a critical and reflective nature.

Ascribed Identity and Lived "Realities"

There is an Indian parable that describes the experience of three blind men on their first encounter with an elephant. One touches the tail and proclaims that an elephant is long, thin and hairy at the end. Another fondles a tusk and declares that an elephant is smooth, curved and sharp. The last blind man feels the leg and decrees that an elephant is cylindrical, thick and wrinkly. An elephant is simultaneously all of that and none of that. This parable was used to illustrate the magnitude and inscrutability that was Hinduism to its followers (Dass 1984). But this allegory is just as appropriate to the problematic of Indian identity politics and the social scientific research that it has given birth to.

Singapore inherited its ethnic categories from British colonial practice. As PuruShotam (1998) has shown, the British were aware that their categorisations were merely umbrella categories that encapsulated many complexities (see Sandhu 1969 and PuruShotam 1998 for more on the intricacies and difficulties of colonial race ascription in Malaya)[1]. There was awareness that this list of races as constructed by the colonisers was not yet firm. The racial categories were fluid, with much overlapping among them. They were also not all inclusive, there was awareness of gaps in the knowledge. While the categories got more and more brief, the awareness of underlying intricacies remained. However, in the

---

1. For example, the "Indian" category was actually called the "Tamils and other natives of India" and included "Tamils", "Telugus", "Malayalis", "Punjabis", "Sikhs", "Pathans", "Mahrattas", "Gurkhas", "Dogras", "Gujeratis", "Marwaris", "Parsis", "Rajputs" and "Sindhis" (PuruShotam 1998, 32-33). Later this was compressed into just "Indians" but the latter mode was seen clearly to be used as shorthand for the earlier model.

process of translation and incorporation into a post-colonial, administration, these inherited racial shorthands were remade into main discursive categories and became "commonly used aspects of Everyday Life knowledge" (PuruShotam 1998, 33). When the racial taxonomies were remodelled after independence from colonial rule, their specific meanings underwent modifications as well. For example, the distinct, almost causal relationship between race, country of origin and language was emphasized. The CMIO[2] system, embedded in ideologies of multiracialism, mother tongues and meritocracy became the dominant discourse.

These state-ascribed ethnicities, with their attendant cultural manifestations and performances, became an integral part of Singaporeans' stock of knowledge. Where once conceptions of ethnicity had been different or fluid, they now came to be seen as fixed and reified. Indians had not perceived of themselves as "Indians" before colonialism and independence. A geographically bounded and strictly culturally and racially defined entity such as modern day India did not exist. Christophe Jaffrelot (1995) and John Brockington (1995) explain that while the "Other" did exist in pre-colonial Indian perceptions, the taxonomies were not really based on race as we understand it, but on culture and caste. Due to colonial authorisation as well as the ideology of multiracialism promoted by the elite in Singapore, peoples of South Asian origins were rendered as "Indians".

The question of identity and who exactly is an Indian and even what that ephemeral concept signifies is relevant to sociology, especially sociology practiced in such a diverse ethnic environment as that of Singapore. What is "Indian"? Where are the boundaries? Who determines them? While all the categories in the CMIO classification hide multiple realities and submerge countless positionalities, the "Indian" category seems to be the most problematic. The "Malay" category may theoretically have a unifying factor in Islam. The "Chinese" category may theoretically

2. This is the abbreviation for "Chinese", "Malay", "Indian" and "Others" which are the racial categories that are supposed to constitute the Singaporean population.

have a unifying factor in the Mandarin language. No such unifying factor or even the possibility of a unifying factor exists with regard to the Indian category. The Tamils may make up the numerical majority but this is far from a culturally or even linguistically hegemonic position. There are significant contradictions and cleavages in the "Indian" category. Caste, language, religion and even superficial skin colour, can all vary significantly within this category. So it is indeed very difficult to attribute homogeneity to the "Indian" category as the CMIO categorization assumes. Yet most works, especially the earlier ones have treated the concept of an Indian identity as unproblematic. The ascribed identity is taken as reality. It may be that many "Indian" actors conceive of their Indianness as unproblematic but a critical sociological and anthropological stance must explore how such essentialist thinking is mediated by circumstances in polyethnic Singapore.

The focus of much historic sociological and anthropological scholarship has been on the sub-ethnic diversities within the "Indian" category. Such work sheds much light on the multiplicities that comprise the "Indian" category. Valuable ethnographic data on some little known aspects of Indian communities are garnered from these studies. They document the social history of sub-ethnic groups and how the identities of these groups are maintained. They also offer precious insight into the changes that crucial components of community identity have undergone in multiethnic, rapidly modernizing Singapore. Mani's (1977) influential work on the caste system as it has been transplanted and translated into the Singapore milieu is a case in point. While caste is still an important component for most South Indian Singaporeans, they have adapted it to fit the interests of a capitalist economy. Many of the ritual and social restrictions have declined or been given up but the "essence" of the system — exclusion, hierarchy and endogamy — is preserved.

Other efforts that document sub-ethnic differences include Baguir's (1974) and Bibijan's (1977a) works, both of which explore the Muslim communities within a category that is defined as overwhelmingly Hindu. Lu (1976) and Mathew (1975) have as their focus the Christian communities within the Indian category, again posing questions about the assumed standardization of that category. Datt (1966) and Bibijan (1981) have produced ethnographies on the Sikh community, highlighting religion, language, cultural and sartorial markers that distinguish them from the majority of Indians. Yet they too are conveniently subsumed under the Indian category. Even the notion of origins as propounded by the dominant discourse as a firm determinant of ethnicity has been open to question. Indians do not automatically have India as their homeland. Rajah's (1958) study of the Ceylonese Tamils shows that while this community does share a language with the majority of the constituents of the Indian category, the circumstances that have shaped them are not entirely analogous.

Even as these community portraits enrich the ethnographic landscape of the poly-ethnic environment of Singapore, they are still largely descriptive. Although they do, by their very existence, question the neat racial categorisation prevalent in the dominant discourse, they do not contribute much theoretical input to the debate. Notions of race, ethnicity and culture, even in academic works still tend to utilize official or elite-defined notions of race, ethnicity and culture. Even with the tremendous theoretical and methodological challenges posed by post-colonialism, post-modernism and cultural relativism, few works have emerged to challenge essentialized and reified constructions of the complex and dynamic processes of race and ethnicity.

However, Benjamin's (1976) germinal piece, on the internal logic and contradictions embedded in Singapore's multiracial ideology (though not restricted to Indians) has changed the way in which race and ethnicity have been and are being conceived in Singapore. No other work so far has managed quite so successfully to juxtapose the roles of the nation-state, ideology and citizens in providing a coherent picture of the production and maintenance of racial and ethnic difference in Singapore. Benjamin argues that even as Singapore seeks to create a Singaporean identity, the emphasis on multiracialism results in the foregrounding of race and therefore the emphasis on difference and divisions. The survey of pieces on Indian sociology so far would seem to prove this, and his notion of "cultural involution" where a "culture turns on itself in a cannibalistic manner bring forth further manifestations of its distinctiveness" (Benjamin 1976, 122) is very relevant. The production of distinctiveness pits the "Chinese", "Malay" and "Others" categories against the "Indian" category and is produced not only within the state and everyday discourse but in academic work as well. Furthermore this production of distinctiveness in social as well as academic discourse does not stop at pitting the "Indian" category against the "other" three categories but is created within the "Indian" category as well. Difference rather than similarity is seen as worthy of scholarship. Therefore, the culture attendant to the "Indian category" in the CMIO system is made to feed on itself to produce further manifestations of distinctiveness. Not only is the "Indian" different from the "Chinese", "Malay" and "Others" but the *Malayalee*[3] differs from the *Gujerati*[4] as does the *Brahmin*[5] from the "Untouchable"[6] and the Tamil Muslim from the Sikh. Studies on Tamil Muslims, Sikhs, Bihari dairymen and countless other linguistic, geographic, caste and religious groups subsumed under the "Indian category" attest to the cultural cannibalism at work. Further analyses of this *process* of "cultural involution" and its impact on "Indian" identity are in order.

Some of the most interesting theoretical assumptions in ethnic and racial studies posit ethnicity as historical, socially constructed, situational, negotiable, dialectical and political (see Ang 1993, Robb 1995, Malik 1996, Stoler 1990, Tambiah 1996). There are very few works reflecting such new developments in the sociology of Indians in Singapore. This necessitates the utilization of examples from research on Indian migrants in other countries, to posit innovative avenues in this field for critical research. Works on Indians in the United States provide some of the most insightful

3. The *Malayalees* are an ethnic group from the state of Kerala in Southern India. They are usually Hindus, although there are significant numbers of Muslims and Christians as well. They speak Malayalam.
4. The *Gujeratis* are an ethnic group from North India.
5. *Brahmins* occupy the topmost position in the caste hierarchy. They are usually scholars and priests and are considered the most ritually pure according to the Hindu religious and caste systems.
6. The "Untouchables" occupy the lowest rank in the caste system are seen as the most ritually polluting. They were usually menials and slaves.

accounts of the intricate negotiations of ethnicity and identity in everyday life. For example, Kamala Visweswaran's (1997) paper on Indian immigrants over the years in the United States, acknowledges the discriminatory structures of American society and immigration policies. However, it also highlights the agency available to actors even in such an unaccommodating situation. Through active negotiations of categories of inclusion and exclusion and of "white", "Indian" and "Asian", the Indian immigrants evade the costs of minority entrepreneurship as well as maximize the benefits accruing from pro-minority legislation[7]. Rosemary Marangoly George's (1997, 32) research highlights the subtle yet complex tactics that South Asian immigrants use to survive in southern California, in the aftermath of Propositions 187 and 209[8]. She posits that South Asian immigrants in southern California try to fashion a conscious refusal of racial identity but the everyday experience of being mistaken for "Mexicans" disrupts this "purely ethno-cultural" self-identification, for it forces an acknowledgement of being "raced". The multifaceted interplay between structural constraints and resistance to those constraints is evocatively argued. Such theoretically and conceptually inventive studies on individual agency and negotiation as well as their disruption in the area of ethnic identity are rare in Singapore and warrant further attention.

7. In 1970, the first Congress decided that to become a naturalized citizen, a person must be "White". There was considerable debate as to what South Asians were. The infamous Ozawa case of 1922 upheld that Indians were Caucasians and were eligible for citizenship. In 1923, the Supreme Court rescinded the Ozawa ruling. Before this rescinding, South Asians had actively lobbied for citizenship; not by challenging the racial basis of the exclusion laws but by arguing that they were wrongly classified as 'Asian' (strategically deploying the Aryan invasion theory) and therefore wrongly excluded. After 1965, the strategy of the South Asian community has been to identify, and align itself, with other Asian groups for affirmative action benefits (Visweswaran 1997).

8. Propositions 187 and 209 repeal the affirmative action laws that based recruitment for jobs, education or politics on the basis of race. These propositions are aimed at manifesting "colour-blind" policies.

Having said that, Siddique's (1990) work (though not strictly about Indians) examines ethnicity from the point of view of the actors, upon whom identity is inscribed and how they incorporate elite-generated notions of ethnicity into their own conceptions. The creation and maintenance of ethnicity is not a unilinear process from the inscriber to the inscribed but a dialectical one. Some recent works by Sinha (1997) and PuruShotam (1998) acknowledge that. They illustrate the inadequacies of previous works on Indian ethnicity in Singapore and examine the various ways of being and performing "Indian". Sinha's paper deconstructs the labels of "Hindu" and "Hinduism" using ethnographic evidence to show the internal variation within the labels. She demonstrates that Indological and Orientalist constructions of Hinduism are homogenous, monolithic and essentialist, denying the socio-cultural and political specificities of their context of practice. PuruShotam's book is not strictly on Indians but uses them as a starting point to theorise about the nature of ethnic and racial relations in Singapore. This work offers some complex and compelling arguments that show how the discourse of race and multiracialism is used to discipline social actors. She also examines how the discourse of race is accepted by the actors such that it results in self-surveillance and discipline. However, such a discourse also allows for some choices to be made and some scope for manoeuvrability. These intricate negotiations are examined from a phenomenological standpoint through the prism of language, in an environment that stresses the intimate relationship between race and language. Sinha and PuruShotam are able to capture the complexity that is identity politics and signify a breakthrough amidst the tendency in Singapore sociology to use social categories superficially.

In general, while there has been tremendous scholarly activity in the area of Indian ethnicity from many disciplines, their contribution to critical social theories of race and ethnicity especially in a post-colonial, heterogeneous society is rather limited. As Cohen (1985) in his fascinating study of the composition of community contends, community is as much about who is excluded as it is about who is included. Identity incorporates the negative as much as it does the positive: it is as much about who you are not, as it is about who you are. In this mould, studies of what "other" ethnic groups in

Singapore such as the Malays and the Chinese conceive of as "Indian" may prove useful. What do these "other" ethnic groups think of Indians? Recent works that reflect on being Indian in Singapore could be augmented with works that address issues of Indian identity in other pluralistic societies in Southeast Asia. While the Sandhu and Mani (1993) edited volume on Indian communities in Southeast Asia does deal with this question, more in-depth studies of this nature should be considered.

Indians: Religion and Rituals

While the members of the Indian community practice many different religions, much of the scholarship has tended to focus on Hinduism. This in itself is quite limiting. Why do discourses on "Indian", even today, inevitably bring to mind "Hindu", "caste" and "rituals"? Having said that, over the years, some fascinating insights into the practice of Hinduism in Singapore have been offered. Babb's (1974, 1976a) papers on two of the most important religious occasions in the Singapore Hindu calendar are now classic. They are ethnographic pieces that elaborate the stages in the ritual occasion but they also offer a macro perspective to analyze these ethnographic data. His intriguing analysis of the whole sequence of rituals held at the Sri Mariamman temple that culminates in *Timiti* or the "fire-walking" ceremony, posits the minutiae of the ritual practices as re-enactments of the epic Hindu drama, the *Mahabharata*. His analysis of the *Thaipusam*[9] procession is a re articulation of one of the classic concerns of sociologists: the dialectics between individual and society, structure and agency but refreshingly viewed through the prism of the *Thaipusam* ritual. Babb posits that Hindu culture is largely hierarchical, collective and corporatist and that the idea of egalitarian individualism is not given prominence. However, this

---

9.   This is the Tamil festival in honour of Lord Muruga, the son of Shiva where devotees carry *kavadis* (wooden structures or metal structures supporting pots of milk) for nearly 3km from the Sri Srinivasa Perumal Temple to the Sri Thandayuthapani Temple in Tank Road. The devotees carry the milk offerings in fulfillment of vows made to Muruga or as thanksgiving.

does not mean that the individual does not exist in Hindu culture. Babb theorises that the autonomy of the individual co-exists with group membership in the symbolism as well as rituals of *Thaipusam*. The carrying of the *kavadi*[10] is motivated by personal goals and is the manifestation of a contract between the individual and Muruga[11]. The successful completion of this ritual is the accomplishment of the devotees alone; no one else can do it for them. Thus, *kavadi* carrying is subjective. It is an act of ritual self-definition emphasizing the autonomous self even while the collectivised imagery of *Thaipusam* is also stressed.

The majority of Indians in Singapore are South Indians who tend to practice a brand of Hinduism that is quite different from the 'ideal type' that is the Sanskritic version of Hinduism, taught to Singapore students in Religious Knowledge classes (refer to the textbooks by Dass 1984). Mention should be made of Rajah's (1975) academic exercise, which is one of the earliest works on folk Hinduism in Singapore and manages to capture the highly syncretic nature of Tamil Hindu religious activity in Singapore. Babb (1976b, 199) notes the persistence of mediumship and the 'pragmatic complex' of popular Hinduism, which is "concerned primarily with illness and other types of everyday misfortune" even in a Singaporean cultural milieu that stresses the use of "rational" strategies of dealing with problems. PuruShotam's (1981) detailed ethnographic account of *Navarattiri* or the "Nine-Nights Festival" and Nilavu Mohd Ali's (1985) studies on the village-cultish aspect of South Indian Hinduism as manifested in Mother Goddess worship shed further light on the internal variations within the grand narrative of Hinduism.

Apart from documenting the practice of everyday Hinduism as opposed to the more frequently explored philosophical or structural Hinduism, analyses have emerged that chronicle the changes and adaptations in the Hindu landscape. Neo-Hindu movements have

10. Wooden or metal structures supporting pots of milk that are then offered to the deity, Muruga.
11. Muruga is god of war and the son of Parvathi and Shiva as well as brother to Ganesa, the elephant-headed god. His worship by North Indians is limited; he is considered a god of the Tamils.

featured in the Singapore Hindu landscape since the 1970s. Neo-Hinduism is described as "a reformist, highly intellectualised, and largely deceremonialised version of the Hindu tradition... whose appeal appears to be class-specific, it's main constituency being drawn from Singapore's English-educated elite" (Babb 1976b, 192). Menon (1984) has researched a neo-Hindu movement in Singapore and draws useful distinctions between this variety of Hinduism and the folk Hinduism that Indian immigrants brought to Singapore. Sinha (1985) has an excellent study on the Singapore branches of some of these movements[12].

While stressing the anti-ceremonialism and reformism of the neo-Hindu sects, it should not be forgotten that even the Hindu majority that retains the traditional folk orientation of its religion have had to accommodate to a society that is very different from the Indian homeland. Babb (1976b) notes that the Singapore context does not allow the Hindus to practice the full ritual observances of the Hindu religious calendar that is geared to the rhythms of the agricultural cycle. One of the fundamental concerns in the Hindu religious system is the avoidance of ritual pollution. However in the context of Singapore, this religious concern has to contend with living in a multiethnic and multicaste environment. It is inevitable that the public sphere would not be accommodative to the strict observance of a Hindu way of life, given the poly-ethnic milieu. Even the private arena or the home is not entirely conducive to the religious beliefs and rituals of the Hindus. Chua (1988) presents a compelling case of the modifications to their religious behaviour that the various ethnic groups have had to make in such an urban and highly crowded environment as the Housing Development Board (HDB) estate. For Hindus, activities associated with excretion, menstruation, parturition and death are considered extremely polluting. However, the standardised nature of HDB apartment architecture negates the performance of the "proper" rituals involved in pollution avoidance. For example, in HDB apartments, the kitchen (the room where food is prepared and therefore subject to strict

12. Particularly, the Punjab-based Radhasoami Satasang (Beas) and the Sri Satya Sai Baba Movement (Sinha 1985, 94 -100).

purity maintenance in Hindu cosmology) and the toilet (the site of excretion and therefore of extreme pollution) are together: the toilet even opens out into the kitchen. Given the Hindu belief system, this architectural arrangement is tantamount to maintaining a permanent state of ritual pollution for it brings together two diametrically opposed elements, which must be kept apart in the symbolic universe. Consequently, the sole sacred area, which is protected absolutely from pollution in conformity with traditional rules, is the family shrine (see Sinha 1987 for an excellent treatment of Hinduism as it is practiced in the private domain of the home). The symbolic universe of Hinduism therefore becomes intensely focused on a particular site in the private domain. Cosmology can thus be said to have become concentrated upon a particular architectural site, the prayer room[13]. Hinduism has often been described as not a religion but "a way of life". It is interesting to note how this "way of life" has been adapted to contexts that are not entirely conducive to its retention and maintenance due to the exigencies of a multiethnic society.

The anthropological and sociological data on Hinduism are varied and very valuable. They contribute tremendously to theoretical and ethnographic understanding of religious affiliation as well as the internal diversity within Hinduism. They chronicle the changes that have occurred in the Hindu landscape in Singapore. Sinha's (1997) deconstruction of the "Hindu" label shows a critical bent as well, in the sociology of Indians and Hinduism. Further research in this area can develop from this excellent foundation. The "other" religious affiliations within the Indian category deserve further attention than they have gotten so far. One must be careful not to conflate the "Hindu" and the "Indian" categories. There are interesting religious community studies on Sikhs (Bibijan 1981 and Datt 1966), Indian Muslims (Baguir 1974 and Bibijan 1977a and 1977b) and Indian Christians (Lu 1976 and

---

13.   In HDB apartments, altars or shrines have been constructed to house the representations of the family gods. But more often than not, these gods are housed in the storeroom provided as part of the design of the apartments. These storerooms are remade as prayer rooms.

Stephens 1983). However, more analysis of the dynamic religious situation amidst the Indian category is needed. How do these "other" religious communities interact with the "majority" Hindu community? How do the different languages create variation in the practice of Hinduism? What are the class implications? In recent years, the number of non-Indians such as the Chinese going to Hindu temples, donating money, volunteering their services at these temples and participating in religious occasions such as *Thaipusam* have increased (Sinha 1997). Why is this happening? What do these non-Indians perceive of Hinduism? How does their participation affect the dynamics within Hinduism?

Indians: Economy and Society

What drew Indians voluntarily to this region in the pre-colonial era was trade. Droves of Tamil Muslim and Gujerati traders came to the Malayan Archipelago for trade and ended up greatly involved in the political, social and economic life of the Archipelago. But it was only in the 19th century that the Indian presence in Malaya and Singapore reached significant proportions. Indian indentured emigration was introduced to meet the shortage of labour supply caused by the abolition of slavery in the British Empire in 1833 (Lal 1996). The rubber boom then demanded that this ready supply be maintained. The Indians were considered suitable for plantation work because they were regarded as docile and more amenable to discipline in comparison to the Chinese who were thought to be too independent (Hirschman 1984). Although there is much historical literature on the Indian involvement in the colonial plantation economy (Sandhu 1969, Arasaratnam 1979, and Singh 1982), these are merely documentary. The investigation of the exploitation of Indian labour through colonial capitalism in Singapore and Malaya in sociological or anthropological literature is sparse. More works in the mould of Jan Bremen's (1989) *Taming the Coolie Beast* on the coolie involvement in plantations in the Dutch Netherlands are needed. This comprehensive work explores the emergence of a plantation society and examines the plantation as a mode of capitalist production. Even more interesting is Bremen's investigation of plantation society as an embodiment of colonial order and resistance to such controls.

Some of the most innovative work done on economic history and social science in recent years has been in the field of subaltern studies. While subaltern studies were initiated by a specific group of social scientists and historians working in India, this perspective has gained an impetus as well as importance far beyond its original scope. It has been one of the most important contributions that India has made to global social science. The subaltern perspective is born out of post-colonial thought. It seeks to make visible alternative discourses and histories that have been structurally written out of the dominant narrative of, to put it in Bell Hook's eloquent words, "white, supremacist, capitalist patriarchy" (Hooks 1996). Works by Gayathri Spivak (1994), Ranajit Guha (ed) (1997) and Dipesh Chakarabarty (1989) re-examine the writing of history, using Marxist and Gramscian perspectives. Such perspectives allow for the articulation of discourses that have been subsumed under elite-constructed versions of history and thus posits a site for the generation of critical scholarship.

The coolie system was one of the most important reasons for the presence of numerous Indians in this part of the world. It was a very difficult period in the lives of the Indian immigrants, akin to slavery for the African Americans. Yet apart from works by novelist V.S. Naipaul, not much is known about this system, especially from the perspective of the coolies and as it was practiced in Malaya and Singapore. The coolie system represented a dramatic rupture of previously known social, religious and caste systems. Vijay Mishra (1996) details that the ship that carried the indentured labour to the colonies put paid to any idea of caste purity. In India, there is spatial as well as ritual and social segregation of higher and lower castes so as to minimize contact and thus, ritual pollution for the higher castes. However on the ship, there was neither space nor the institutional support for such segregation and the whole caste system had to be reworked to befit the contingencies of the journey. As the ocean was crossed, some structures became obsolete and people made changes accordingly. While most of the immigrants were sojourners and male, some forms of community structures did develop. New forms of socializations such as "*Jahaji-bhai*" or "ship brotherhood" became common. Marriages between castes that would never have happened in the "homeland" occurred.

Living arrangements that rendered impossible the upholding of most ritual and caste pollution laws posed great challenges and wrought significant changes. "Social interactions during these lengthy sea voyages began a process that led to the re-making of cultural and ethnic identities, to a critical self-reflexivity of the kind missing from the stratified and less mobile institutions of the homeland" (Mishra 1996, 195). Similarly, Indian society in Singapore has been transformed. Yet, there have been very few attempts to theorize or even describe these changes in the local sociological and anthropological literature, again prompting a recourse to literature on Indians of other countries.

Indians who migrated to Singapore and Malaysia had to make many social and ritual changes due to the vagaries of their journey as well as their new abode (both the new country and their plantation quarters). At the same time, there were attempts made to maintain some form of continuity with the structures of their 'homeland' as well. The coolies tried to counter the displacement represented by their journey as well as their indenture through various means.

> It was astonishing what they [the indentured labourers] did bring; but they were going to the end of the world and they came prepared for the wilderness; they brought holy books and astrological almanacs, images, sandalwood, all the paraphernalia of the religious shrines, musical instruments, string beds, plates and jars, even querns, even grinding stones … as it was, they carried India with them and were able to recreate something like their world (V.S. Naipaul quoted in Mishra 1996, 217)

Does Naipaul's observation hold true for Singapore as well? How did the coolies in Singapore re-create "home" in such an "alien" and alienating environment? Such disruption as well as continuation in Indian society is something that sociology and anthropology in Singapore has yet to investigate. There is still a tendency to use official versions of history, without adequate introspection in scholarship on Indians in Singapore. Critical scholarship, re-examining elite-constructed versions of history from phenomenological or subaltern perspectives, have yet to develop sufficiently.

Even though many Indians in Malaya and Singapore under the indenture system were virtually slaves in the plantations, Sandhu (1993) contends that Indians from certain communities figured prominently in entrepreneurial activities especially in wholesale, retail and other small-scale enterprises. Much of the wholesale Asian textile trade of post-war Singapore and Malaya was for several years, largely controlled by the Sindhis and Sikhs. Although their dominance has declined, they are still an active group in this trade and could prove fertile ground for the analysis of developments of networks of trade and commerce as well as Indian entrepreneurship in the pre-industrial era. Money lending is another trade that has seen a large amount of Indian entrepreneurial activity. The *Chettiars*, a South Indian caste group, were dominant in this area for many years. This brings to mind one of the interesting features of Indian society. There are distinct overlaps between one's caste group and one's occupation, though this has declined tremendously with the changes wrought by the modern economy. Some occupational community studies have taken note of this point. Yeo's (1984) study of Bihari dairymen is a case in point. However, Evers and Pavadarayan's (1993) insightful study on the *Chettiars* of Singapore contributes more sociological insight to the dynamics of cultural capital, religious fervour, a tight in-group and economic success. Like the entrepreneurial "ideal type" of Max Weber's classic analysis of the *Protestant Ethic and the Spirit of Capitalism*, the *Chettiars* are postulated to have an "ascetic" framework underpinning their economic pursuits. The *Chettiar* lifestyle is seen to be characterised by strict fiscal and personal discipline: frugality, non-indulgence in worldly pleasures, strict book-keeping, itemization of expenditure and reinvestment of profits. The authors see them as possessing an "inner-worldly type of asceticism", "oriented towards active involvement in the external, material world vis-à-vis economic activity" (Evers and Pavadarayan 1993, 860), thereby resembling Calvinist ethics. However, along with the "asceticism", the authors identify an "ecstatic" element in the *Chettiar* lifestyle which renders any attempt to force a strictly Weberian reading of their economic success problematic. The *Chettiars* are intimately associated with *Thaipusam*: an occasion, which is as much a carnival as it is a religious one. Like the Saturnalia in Ancient Rome and Carnival in

Caribbean and West Indian cultures today, *Thaipusam* is associated with excitement, frenzy and "ecstasy" — seemingly diametrically opposed to the "ascetic" lifestyle of the *Chettiars*. Moreover, while their personal and business affairs are characterised by frugality, *Chettiars* contribute very generously to charities. How is it possible to reconcile these seemingly rank opposites? This fascinating blend of "asceticism", "ecstasy" and "charity" in the *Chettiars* seems to demonstrate the futility of attempts to attribute economic success in Asia to Asian or Confucian values and draw simplistic links between culture, values, and economic success. Such theoretically informed studies about the economy and Indians are however rare.

The economic milieu has changed rapidly over the years. Every other day, there are reports in the newspapers about the "New Economy", "knowledge-based economy" and "information technology". These spell a re-arrangement if not a revolution in the global economy into which Singapore is plugged. Sociological studies could analyze the impact of these global transformations on the Indian community. So far there has not been much emphasis on the economic aspects of the Indian community and this is ripe ground for some reflective sociology. Linking the local aspects of changes within the Singapore Indian community with the global processes of socioeconomic transformation would make for some very interesting analyses.

Indians and Mobility: Sojourners, Immigrants and Diaspora

"Indians are ubiquitous", reported the Calcutta newspaper, *The Statesman* on 5 August 1980 (quoted in Lal 1996, 167). According to this report there are only five countries where Indians have not chosen to stay[14]. It is estimated that almost 8.6 million people of South Asian origin live outside the subcontinent, with Southeast Asia accounting for the highest concentration of South Asian people at 1.86 million (Clarke et al. 1990, 2). The interactions between South Asia and Southeast Asia pre-date the colonial era. There is

---

14. These are Cape Verde Islands, Guinea Bissau, North Korea, Mauritania and Romania (Lal 1996, 167).

much compelling evidence of Indian travellers and traders (together with Arab and Chinese) to many parts of the world (Alvares 1991, Kabbani 1998 and Ghosh 1992). While according to the "Great Tradition" in Hinduism, it is believed that the crossing of the dark ocean, the *kalapani*, signified the loss of caste (Mishra 1996, 195); the Southern Indian traditions especially, had always been maritime ones. In fact, the earliest evidence of Indian presence and influence found in Malaya is in the form of fragmentary religious inscriptions in the *Pallava Grantha* script of the 4th and 5th centuries which denotes a Southern Indian origin (Arasaratnam 1979). These pre-colonial interactions were initiated by Indians for the purpose of trade and occurred with much regularity. However sociological work on such pre-colonial interactions is sorely lacking. One of the most valuable contributions of historical sociology is that it problematises the status quo and declares that "things were not always so". Historical sociology demonstrates that ideas and institutions that are held primordial, sacred and inviolable presently had a beginning, were constructed to a large extent and have political or social agendas embedded in them. Of course, Eric Hobsbawm and Terence Ranger's (1983) *The Invention of Tradition* is the example par excellence of this kind of critical scholarship. More of such historical interrogations of ethnic relations in the past, showing how they were shaped and manipulated by the colonizers as well as the nation-state, would shed valuable light on the state of ethnic relations today.

Some of the most interesting theoretical insights into ethnic and racial studies are being generated by research in migration and diaspora. De-territorialized and globalized ethnicity, multiple and syncretic ethnicities, hyphenated identities and ethnicities on the border are objects of theorizing in current studies in ethnicity (Appadurai 1990, Safran 1991, Gopinath 1995). Even as there are oft-repeated litanies in social discourse acknowledging that Singapore is a nation of immigrants, there have been no serious attempts to understand the various ethnic groups in terms of the global processes of migration. Migration from the Indian sub-continent to Singapore has once again become very visible. On the previous occasion, when Indian movement to this region had been considerable, Indians had arrived to become part of the plantation economy. Now many of them are coming to participate in the "knowledge economy". How can we compare these two epochs of Indian movement and contribution to this region? There should be considerations of whether such comparisons provide productive sites for the generation of theoretical and ethnographic insights.

Mishra (1996, 190) using literary works by writers of the diaspora, posits two types of Indian diaspora: the old one of "exclusivism" to which V.S. Naipaul belongs and the new one of the "border" to which Salman Rushdie belongs. This conceptual dichotomy can be usefully applied to the Singapore situation as well. The "exclusivist" diasporic type could be seen to encompass the majority of Indians in Singapore, those who are designated as the "I" in the CMIO taxonomy. This diaspora of "exclusivism" is made up of people whose journey out of the "homeland" had been final and who cannot understand India any longer. India becomes an area [only] of the imagination but without its memory, the diaspora cannot function. As years pass, India becomes a subject of nostalgia and selected fragments are imbued into the new geographical spaces that the Indian migrants have come to occupy. Siddique and PuruShotam (1982) have actually documented this happening in a geographical space that has been Indianized, Singapore's Little India. While this process is more or less voluntary in the case of other Indian diasporas, in Singapore it is mapped upon the government discourse of origins, homeland, cultural continuity of Asian values and maintenance of racialized spaces. An exploration of this overlap as well as the relationship between India (real and imagined) and Indian Singaporeans would be very interesting. Are Indian Singaporeans part of a diaspora? Is such an idea of diaspora useful for the analysis of Indian society or does it merely alienate, and detract away from the idea of citizenship and full participation in political and civic life?

Mishra's second diasporic type that of the "border" represented by Salman Rushdie may also be of relevance regarding Singapore. In 1990, according to former Minister for National Development, S. Dhanabalan, Singapore's racial balance was to be maintained by attracting overseas Indians (*The Straits Times* 1990, 47). Ten years later, there are significant numbers of highly educated, technology-savvy personnel in residence in Singapore. While they reside in

Singapore, their contacts with India are very pertinent. This is a group of highly skilled, highly mobile workers, who may see Singapore as their new "home" or may treat Singapore simply as a springboard to more favourable economic opportunities in the United States. How is their presence (permanent or temporary) impacting upon Singapore Indian society? What are the dynamics between the descendants of the early immigrants and these newest immigrants? In other words, what are the dynamics between these two diasporic typologies as they are played out in Singapore? While there are sociological studies that acknowledge the immigrant makeup of Singapore Indians (Mani 1977, Siddique and PuruShotam 1982 and Walker 1994), they assume this migration to be of the past and that the Indian community has settled and developed roots. This may be so but the Singapore Indian community is also constituted by routes. Many local Indians are emigrating and many more overseas Indians are immigrating. The dynamics of this movement and restlessness have yet to be incorporated into the sociological literature.

There is a class dimension to all this movement. While the well-educated, high income earners are considered expatriates and can settle here as citizens, there is another group of highly mobile workers that are treated less solicitously. Just like in colonial times, the economic boom in Singapore has generated a huge demand for manual labour. Once again, the source of cheap and docile labour is the Indian subcontinent. While there are some recent works on these workers and their economic positions in Singapore and their countries of origin (Rahman 1999), there is room for more such research. Comparisons between the indentured labour of old and the construction labour of today could generate some theoretical insights on capitalism as well as globalized and ethnicized labour. Like many Indians of the previous immigration boom during the British tenure in Singapore, these new "foreign workers" are also sojourners and largely male. These manual labourers are subject to intense legal, social and sexual discipline. Developing theoretical links between the manual labour of today and that of colonial times may shed light on the processes of marginalization, discipline and power relations that are essential to the preservation of an economic system and the management of labour. Singaporean Indian identities are not only constructed vis-à-vis the "other" racial groups, but also vis-à-vis these workers as well as overseas Indian expatriates. As such, what is the impact of these sojourners and immigrants on local Indian identities? Processes of movement and migration have problematised notions of culture and identity that are embedded in ideas of original homelands and rootedness. As Karl Marx had predicted, long before the globalisation of capital and the transnationalization of labour, "The working men have no country" (quoted in Chakrabarty 1989, 228). Judicious sociological and anthropological analyses must take this into account.

Conclusion

This survey of the historical and anthropological map of Singapore Indian society is not a complete reconnaissance but it has highlighted some of the landmarks on the scholarly terrain. It has reviewed some of the most important and visible works in sociological and anthropological scholarship on Singapore Indian society and argues that such studies have undergone some changes over the years. From the 1950s to the early 1980s, most if not all such works took the concept of "Indian" as a given. They repeated colonial and Orientalist notions of the concept. Many good ethnographies and descriptive studies, some of which have been cited in this survey, did emerge out of this period. Studies on the many cultural, religious, language, caste and occupational variations within the "Indian" community have tremendously enriched the ethnographic landscape of Singapore. These studies do try to incorporate some sociological analysis and do arrive at some vaguely sociological conclusions. They also manage, by their very existence, to criticize essentialised notions of ethnicity. They do demonstrate the tremendous internal variation behind the all-inclusive concept of "Indian". However, theoretically and conceptually, these early studies have nevertheless used social categories such as "Indian" superficially. It is only in the late 1980s and 1990s that a few works have emerged to question such taken for granted theoretical and conceptual notions. The works of PuruShotam (1998) and Sinha (1987, 1997) treat concepts of ethnicity, culture, race, language and religion reflectively. Even as they demonstrate the constructed nature of these concepts and the power dynamics that influence them, these works also exhibit sensitivity to phenomenological issues and subjective experiences. However they are exceptions to the rule, much of Indian sociology still tends to exhibit a dearth of theoretical sophistication. Much of the research in this field remains like the fumbling of the apocryphal blind trio, oblivious to the existence of the pachyderm, but still pondering on its parts.

Furthermore, there has been an identification of some of the problems attending the scholarship on Singapore Indians such as the lack of theoretical and conceptual sophistication. Proposals have been made for the rectification of some of these problems. A critical scholarship on Indian studies should eschew seeing the productions or recreations of ethnicity or Indianness as isolated, monolithic or intensely specific. Issues of ethnicity and race should be linked to the trajectories of transformations from colonial states to post-colonial nation-states and the resultant ideology and myth-making. The true challenge for critical scholarship on race and ethnic theory and politics is to find "ways to disrupt the relationship and presumed fixity of both the universalist and the particularist positions" (Omi and Winant 1994, 157). And this is possible if ethnography, the study of the particular is usefully mapped against the panorama of history. While admitting the centrality of history, there must also be awareness of whose history it is. Alternative histories or alternate readings of history should be consulted as well as constructed.

It is also important not to see ethnicity and race as localized and isolated. They should be linked to global processes and studied in context. How is Indianness being constructed all over the world amidst the information technology boom that has created such demand for Indian labour, unparalleled since colonial times? Current theorizing links race and ethnicity to global capitalism, transnational labour mobilization and worldwide consumption patterns. There is some need to keep abreast of such scholarly developments and incorporate them judiciously.

Finally, there is a need for reflexivity. "Racism is a scholarly exercise", remarked African American Nobel laureate for literature, Toni Morrison in a television interview. It is taught and it is learned. The popular discourse on essential differences and inferiority of the 'other' races was validated by European scientific and academic discourse in the 19th century. According to Harvard palaeontologist and popular science writer, Stephen J. Gould, "Scientists assume that their own shifts in interpretation record only their better understanding of newly discovered facts. They tend to be unaware of their own mental impositions upon the world's messy and ambiguous factuality" (Gould 1997, 6). Therefore, there is a need to be reflective in the use of research tools; that is the concepts, theories and ideas of sociology and anthropology that are fundamental to our research. This is so as to eschew essentialism and promote a critical stance towards ethnicity, race and Indianness.

This essay has emphasized the issues deemed most pertinent to scholarly attention and reviewed issues of culture, religion, and the economy and their impact on the community. It has also suggested areas in the sociology of the Indians, which are seen as fertile grounds for the germination of fresh and innovative scholarship. The mobility demanded and afforded by economic transformations has spelled some interesting changes for the notion of "Indian". This has resulted in the increasing globalization of "Indian" ethnicity and identity, which invites a re-examination of classic sociological concepts such as race, ethnicity and culture. Such a critical outlook coupled with awareness of the current developments in the field of ethnic and racial studies should engender some very interesting and creative scholarship in the field of local Indian sociology.

References

Appadurai, A. (1990) "Disjuncture and Difference in the Global Cultural Economy", *Theory, Culture and Society,* 7(3): 295-309.

Allen, J. de V. (1964) "Two Imperialists: A Study of Sir Frank Swettenham and Sir Hugh Clifford", *Journal of the Malayan Branch of the Royal Asiatic Society,* 37 (1): 41-73.

Alvares, C. (1991) *Decolonizing History,* New York: The Apex Press.

Ang, I. (1993) "To Be or Not to Be Chinese: Diaspora, Culture and Postmodern Ethnicity", *Southeast Asian Journal of Social Science*, 21(1): 1-17.

Arasaratnam, S. (1979) *Indians in Malaysia and Singapore* (Revised Edition), Kuala Lumpur: Oxford University Press.

Babb, L. (1974) "Walking on Flowers in Singapore – a Hindu Festival Cycle", *Sociology Working Papers No. 27*, Dept. of Sociology, National University of Singapore.

Babb, L. (1976a) "Thaipusam in Singapore: Religious Individualism in Hierarchical Culture", *Sociology Working Papers No. 49*, Dept. of Sociology, National University of Singapore.

Babb, L. (1976b) "Patterns of Hinduism", in Riaz Hassan (ed) *Singapore Society in Transition*, Kuala Lumpur: Oxford University Press.

Baguir, Muhammad, bin Md. Ibrahim (1974) *The Tamil Muslim Community in Singapore*, Academic Exercise, Dept. of Sociology, National University of Singapore.

Benjamin, G. (1976) "The Cultural Logic of Singapore's 'Multiracialism'", in Riaz Hassan (ed) *Singapore: Society in Transition*, Kuala Lumpur: Oxford University Press.

Bibijan Ibrahim (1977a) *The Dawoodi Bohra Muslims: Ethnic Boundary Maintenance, With Special Focus on Marriage*, Academic Exercise, Dept. of Sociology, National University of Singapore.

Bibijan Ibrahim (1977b) "Behavioral Malayization Among Some Indian Muslims in Singapore", Tamil *Peravai* (Journal of the Tamil Language Society), National University of Singapore, pp. 99-123.

Bibijan Ibrahim (1981) *A Study of the Sikh Community in Singapore*, Thesis (M.Soc.Sc), Dept. of Sociology, National University of Singapore.

Breman, J. (1989) *Taming The Coolie Beast: Plantation Society and the Colonial Order in Southeast Asia*, Delhi: Oxford University Press.

Brockington, J. (1995) "The Concept of Race in the Mahabharata and Ramayana", in P. Robb (ed) *The Concept of Race in South Asia*, Delhi, Oxford University Press.

Brumann, C. (1999) "Writing for Culture: Why a Successful Concept Should Not Be Discarded", *Current Anthropology,* 40 (Supplement): 1-27.

Chakrabarty, D. (1989) *Rethinking Working-Class History: Bengal 1890-1940*, Princeton: Princeton University Press.

Chua, B. H. (1988) "Adjusting Religious Practices to Different House Forms in Singapore", in *Architecture and Behavior,* 4 (3): 3-25.

Clarke, C., Peach, C. and Vertovec, S. (eds) (1990) *South Asians Overseas: Migration and Ethnicity*, Cambridge: Cambridge University Press.

Cohen, A. P. (1985) *The Symbolic Construction of Community*, London and New York: Tavistock Publications.

Dass, M. (1984) *The Hindu Reader,* Books One and Two, Singapore: Federal Publications.

Datt, S.(1966) *A Sikh Community in Singapore*, Academic Exercise, Dept. of Social Studies, University of Singapore.

Evers, H. D. and Pavadarayan, J. (1993) "Religious Fervour and Economic Success: The Chettiars of Singapore", *Indian Communities in Southeast Asia*, Singapore: Institute of Southeast Asian Studies.

Furnivall, J. S. (1948) *Colonial Policy and Practice: A Comparative Study of Burma and Netherlands India*, Cambridge: Cambridge University Press.

George, R. M. (1997) "'From Expatriate Aristocrat to Immigrant Nobody': South Asian Racial Strategies in the Southern Californian Context", *Diaspora,* 6(1): 31-60.

Ghosh, A. (1992) *In an Antique Land*, London: Granta Books.

Gopinath, G. (1995) "Bombay, U.K., Yuba City: Bhangra Music and the Engendering of Diaspora", *Diaspora,* 4(3): 303-22.

Gould, S. J. (1997) "The Geometer of Race", in E.N. Gates (ed) *The Concept of "Race" in Natural and Social Science,* New York and London: Garland Publishing Inc.

Guha, R. (ed) (1997) *A Subaltern Studies Reader, 1986-1995*, Minneapolis: University of Minnesota Press.

Hirschman, C. (1984) "The Making of Race in Colonial Malaya: Political Economy and Racial Ideology", *Sociological Forum*, 1(2): 330-61.

Hobsbawm, E. and Ranger, T. (eds) (1983) *The Invention of Tradition*, Cambridge and New York: Cambridge University Press.

Hooks, B. (1996) *Killing Rage: Ending Racism*, New York: Henry Holt and Company.

Jaffrelot, C. (1995) "The Idea of the Hindu Race in the Writings of Hindu Nationalist Ideologues in the 1920s and 1930s: A Concept Between Two Cultures", in P. Robb (ed) *The Concept of Race in South Asia*, Delhi: Oxford University Press.

Kabbani, R. (1984) *Europe's Myths of the Orient*, Bloomington: Indiana University Press.

Kupur, A. (1989) *Culture: The Anthropologists' Account*, Cambridge, Massachusetts: Harvard University Press.

Lal, B. V. (1996) "The Odyssey of Indenture: Fragmentation and Reconstruction in the Indian Diaspora", *Diaspora*, 5(2): 167-87.

Lu, L. L. P. (1976) *The Indian Christians: Hierarchy in an Egalitarian Religious Community*, Academic Exercise, Dept. of Sociology, National University of Singapore.

Malik, K. (1996) *The Meaning of Race: Race, History and Culture in Western Society*, Basingstoke, Hants: Macmillan.

Mani, A. (1977) *The Changing Caste-Structure Amongst the Singapore Indians*, Thesis (M.Soc.Sc), Dept of Sociology, National University of Singapore.

Mani, A. and Bala, M. (1991) *The Last Twenty-Five Years*, Singapore: Singapore Tamil Youth's Club.

Mani, A. (1993) "Indians in Singapore Society", in K.S. Sandhu and A. Mani (eds) *Indian Communities in Southeast Asia*, Singapore: Institute of Southeast Asian Studies.

Mathew, M. E. K. (1975) *Marriage Patterns and Community Identity Among Syrian Christians in Singapore*, Academic Exercise, Dept. of Sociology, National University of Singapore.

Mishra, V. (1996) "(B)ordering Naipaul: Indenture History and Diasporic Poetics", *Diaspora*, 5(2): 190-237.

Menon, S. (1984), *An Ethnographic Study of a Neo-Hindu Group*, Academic Exercise, Dept. of Sociology, National University of Singapore.

Menon, S. (1976) *Role of Religious Institutions and Associations in a Malayalee 'Neighbourhood'*, Academic Exercise, Dept. of Sociology, National University of Singapore.

Nash, M. (1989) *The Cauldron of Ethnicity in the Modern World*, Chicago and London: The University of Chicago Press.

Nilavu Mohammed Ali (1985) *Hindu Mother Goddess Worship in Modern Singapore: An Ethnographic Study*, Academic Exercise, Dept. of Sociology, National University of Singapore.

Omi, M. and Winant, H. (1994) *Racial Formations in the US: From the 1960s to the 1990s*, New York: Routledge.

PuruShotam, N. (1981) "Navarathiri: The Celebration of a Hindu Festival", *Tamil Peravai* (Journal of the Tamil Language Society), National University of Singapore.

PuruShotam, N. (1995), "Disciplining Difference: Race in Singapore", *Sociology Working Paper No. 126*, Dept. of Sociology, National University of Singapore.

PuruShotam, N. (1998), *Negotiating Language, Constructing Race: Disciplining Difference in Singapore*, Berlin, New York: Mouton de Gruyter.

Rahman, Mohammad Mizanur (1999) "The Asian Economic Crisis and Migrant Workers: The Bangladeshi Workers in Singapore", *Sociology Working Papers No. 147*, Dept. of Sociology, National University of Singapore.

Rajah, A. (1975) *The Ecological Study of Shrines*, Academic Exercise, Dept. of Sociology, National University of Singapore.

Rajah, G. (1958) *The Ceylon Tamils of Singapore*, Academic Exercise, Dept. of Social Studies, University of Malaya.

Robb, P. (ed) (1995) *The Concept of Race in South Asia*, Delhi: Oxford University Press.

Safran, W. (1991) "Diasporas in Modern Societies: Myths of Homeland and Return", *Diaspora*, 1 (1): 83-99.

Sandhu, K. S. (1969) *Indians in Malaya: Some Aspects of Their Immigration and Settlement*, London: Cambridge University Press.

Sandhu, K. S. (1993) "Indian Immigration and Settlement in Singapore", in K. S. Sandu and A. Mani (eds) *Indian Communities in Southeast Asia*, Singapore: Institute of Southeast Asian Studies.

Sandhu, K.S. and Mani, A. (eds) (1993) *Indian Communities in Southeast Asia*, Singapore: Institute of Southeast Asian Studies.

Saroja Devi (1987) *An Ethnographic Study of an Indian Family Firm*, Academic Exercise, Dept. of Sociology, National University of Singapore.

Shantakumar, G. (1991) "The Indian Population of Singapore: Some Implications for Development", in K.S. Sandhu and A. Mani (eds) *Indian Communities in Southeast Asia*, Singapore: Institute of Southeast Asian Studies.

Siddique, S. and PuruShotam, N. (1982) *Singapore's Little India: Past Present and Future*, Singapore: Institute of Southeast Asian Studies.

Siddique, S. (1990) "The Phenomenology of Ethnicity: A Singapore Case-Study", *Sojourn*, 5(1): 35-62.

Siddique, S. and PuruShotam, N. (1993) "Spouse Selection Patterns in the Singapore Indian Community" in K.S. Sandhu and A. Mani (eds) *Indian Communities in Southeast Asia*, Singapore: Institute of Southeast Asian Studies.

Singh, B. (ed) (1982) *Indians in Southeast Asia*, New Delhi: Sterling Publishers Private Limited.

Sinha, V. (1985) *Modern Religious Movements: Religious and Counter-Religious*, Academic Exercise, Dept. of Sociology, National University of Singapore.

Sinha, V. (1987), *Hinduism in Singapore: A Sociological and Ethnographic Perspective*, Thesis, (M.Soc.Sc), Dept. of Sociology, National University of Singapore.

Sinha, V. (1993) "Hinduism in Contemporary Singapore" in K.S. Sandhu and A. Mani (eds) *Indian Communities in Southeast Asia*, Singapore: Institute of Southeast Asian Studies.

Sinha, V. (1997) "Unpacking the Labels 'Hindu' & 'Hinduism' in Singapore", *Southeast Asian Journal of Social Science*, 25(2): 139-60.

Sinha, V. (2000) "Socio-Cultural Theory and Colonial Encounters: The Discourse on Indigenizing Anthropology in India", *Sociology Working Papers No. 148*, Dept. of Sociology, National University of Singapore.

Spivak, G. (1994) "Subaltern Studies: Deconstructing Historiography", in R. Guha (ed) *Subaltern Studies IV: Writings on South Asian History and Society*, Delhi: Oxford University Press.

Stephens, J. (1983) *Catholic Vellala in Singapore: Origin and Identity*, Academic Exercise, Dept. of Sociology, National University of Singapore.

Stoler, A. (1990) "Making Empire Respectable: The Politics of Race and Sexual Morality in 20th Century Colonial Cultures", in J. Breman (ed), *Imperial Monkey Business: Racial Supremacy in Social Darwinist Theory and Colonial Practice*, Amsterdam: VU University Press.

Straits Times (1990) "Racial Balance 'Will Be Maintained' With Move to Attract Overseas Indians", *The Straits Times*, 23 April, p. 47.

Tambiah, S.J. (1996) *Levelling Crowds: Ethnonationalist Conflicts and Collective Violence in South Asia*, Berkeley: University of California Press.

Tham, S.C. (1982) *Religion and Modernization: A Study of Changing Rituals Among Singapore's Chinese, Malays and Indians*, Singapore: Graham Brash.

Visweswaran, K. (1997) "Diaspora By Design: Flexible Citizenship and South Asians in U.S. Racial Formations", *Diaspora*, 6(1): 5-30.

Walker, A. (ed) (1994) *New Place, Old Ways: Essays on Indian Society and Culture in Modern Singapore,* New Delhi: Hindustan Publishing Corp.

Yeo, C. S. (1984) *A North Indian Community in Singapore: Continuity and Change Among Bihari Dairymen,* Academic Exercise, Dept. of Sociology, National University of Singapore.

12

Who Says What to Whom: Language and Society in Singapore

Laurence Leong Wai Teng

E. Afendras and S. Afendras (1980, 267) noted that academic research in language in Singapore society has been diverse in focus and come from a range of disciplinary backgrounds. Ten years later, much more has been written about language in Singapore, partly because of the institutional growth of the Regional English Language Centre, and the Department of English Language & Literature at the National University of Singapore, and partly because of the burgeoning profession of linguists, applied and theoretical. Combing through the vast output of written material is a feat which is beyond the scope of my survey here.

So many scholars have an interest in language and language issues that sometimes distinctions have been made in order to separate the different kinds of concerns and research questions. Thus, both sociolinguists and sociologists who have an interest in language seek to understand the relationships between language and society. However, sociolinguists try to understand these relationships in order to arrive at a more detailed analysis of the structure of languages and their role in communication, while sociologists try to understand these relationships in order to generate insights about social structure and social relationships (Wardaugh 1992, 13).

Using this distinction, my approach would be that of a sociologist concerned with what languages in various social contexts tell us about the nature of Singapore society. I will ignore the large volume of writings on various aspects of structures of Singapore languages in terms of morphology, phonology and syntax (Crewe 1977, Foley 1988, Tay and Gupta 1983, Tongue 1979), and the role of bilingualism in Singapore's education system (Pakir 1995, Gopinathan 1998). I am more interested in the social rather than the structural aspects of the language (even though the two are interrelated).

The cultural and linguistic heterogeneity of Singapore society is well known. The linguistic diversity has led scholars to ask various questions: how do social groups speaking different languages communicate with each other and what are the prevalent languages in which individuals communicate with each other in various domains? What does linguistic diversity reflect about social structure, particularly ethnic relations? What is the consequence of linguistic diversity in terms of social divisions or conflict, and in terms of national policy?

Accordingly, I will structure my paper along three themes: (1) language and the communication of social groups; (2) language and social structure; and (3) language and political structures. These three themes are in reality related but treated separately for analytical purposes.

Language and the Communication of Social Groups

In the early development of an "indigenous" sociology in Singapore, scholars assumed a separation between theory and facts: facts were all the details and data about social life to be collected, mapped out and made sense of, while theory consisted of abstract frameworks to explain these facts. Facts must be collected first before one could theorize about social phenomena. This was the organising principle that served as the basis for research done by sociologists in the 1970s.

Accordingly, with few exceptions, early sociological studies on Singapore resembled "country reports" that one finds in encyclopaedias and world almanacs. They were mostly descriptive, depicting various dimensions of social life with little attempt to draw theoretical connections with larger issues. Researchers adopted a kind of stock-taking approach: reporting whatever existed in the world "out there" but seldom going beyond that mere reporting.

Stock-taking characterized the first few sociological works on language in Singapore. Thus, Eddie Kuo (1976) began sketching what he called "a sociolinguistic profile" of Singapore. Borrowing from Ferguson (1971), Kuo devised a formula to represent in quantitative and abbreviated terms the linguistic diversity of Singapore society:

$$8L = 5Lmaj \text{ (Sow, Sowi, Soi, So, Vg)} + 3Lmin \text{ (3Vg)},$$

where Language type, designated by capital letters, includes Standard (S) and Vernacular (V) languages; and language functions are designated by lowercase letters: o (official), g (group, or intra-group communication), w (wider communication, or inter-group communication), and i (international communication).

In this formula, there are eight languages in Singapore, consisting of five major and three minor types. The criteria for "major" language includes: (1) spoken as a native language by over 25% of the population or over one million people in the country, (2) official language of the nation, or (3) language of education of over 50% of the secondary school students. Thus, English, Malay, Mandarin and Tamil, which are the four official languages in Singapore are included as "major" languages. In addition, Hokkien which is a predominant language among the Chinese population, the native tongue of 30% of the 1957 population, and understood by about 64% of a 1978 sample study population, is considered as the fifth major language.

English language is "Sowi" because it is official, used in wider and international communication. Malay language is "Sow", being official and used in wider communication (up to 1978, two thirds could understand and communicate in "Bazaar Malay"). Mandarin is "Soi": official and international language (before 1980, Mandarin was not considered a lingua franca language). Tamil is "So", which signifies its only official status. Hokkien is classified as "Vg", a vernacular language, used in group communication.

"Minor" languages are (1) spoken as native language by no more than 25% of the population, but more than 5% or over a hundred thousand people; or (2) used as a medium of instruction above the first years of primary school, with textbooks published in that medium. Here, Kuo lists Teochew, Cantonese and Hainanese as minor languages spoken by about 5-15% of the population as respective native languages. Together, these three minor languages constitute "3Vg", vernaculars used in group communication.

Kuo's formula seems complicated. Kuo's work demonstrates ingenious use of very limited data: secondary sources from the 1957 census (and subsequently, 1978 sample research done by Survey Research Singapore). The 1957 census identified 33 specific mother tongue groups, but since then, the Census Board has not collected fine or rich details about linguistic behaviour or practices. So working on whatever resources available at hand, Kuo paints a sociolinguistic profile in the form of a formula.

On the other hand, formulas simplify complexities. The formula identifies the major and minor languages in Singapore, but offers no information about the degree to which people use or communicate in those languages. Thus, in an updated version, Kuo (1980) relied on the 1978 Survey Research to add detail to the formula. Some of the interesting observations (often overlooked by linguists and policy makers) he makes are: (1) Hokkien is understood by the highest proportion of the population, mainly the Chinese; (2) Malay is understood and used by people from different ethnic backgrounds; (3) There are more Indians who understand Malay than there are Indians who understand Tamil, even though Tamil is decreed officially as the "mother tongue" of Indians.

Kuo's sociolinguistic profile is akin to a snapshot of Singapore society that is not only one-dimensional but also static. Languages and contexts change, and such changes render Kuo's work, while leading in its initial forays, obsolete. In the 1980 paper, Kuo makes comparisons from 1957 and 1978 figures even though the two databases are different. He notices that English language is increasingly used in communication, and the number of Mandarin speakers has also increased. On the other hand, the population segments ("Indians") who understand Tamil have progressively declined.

In the latest 1990 Census data, all ethnic groups have increased their use of English as the main language at home. Among the Chinese, the percentage who use English as a predominant language in the household has doubled from 10.2 in 1980 to 20.6 in

1990. The percentage of Chinese who use Mandarin as the predominant household language has tripled from 13.1% in 1980 to 32.8% in 1990. In 1980, 76.2% of Chinese households use Chinese dialects but this has dropped to 46.2% in 1990. It appears that increasingly more and more Chinese use Mandarin over dialects in their homes. However, dialects continue to be the predominant language used by Chinese households (46.2% in 1990, compared with 20.6% using English, and 32.8% using Mandarin). In a survey done by the Ministry of Information and the Arts with a sample of 430 respondents, 66% of Chinese speak to their parents in dialects, and comparing 1991 with 1993, fewer Chinese students use Mandarin in schools (*The Straits Times*, 4 September 1993).

However, these data, like Kuo's formula, only give us a partial profile of the sociolinguistic situation in Singapore. The census data are based on self-reported and not actual behaviour. Moreover, if we consider the linguistic repertoire of most Singaporeans — the baggage of languages that they carry and use at appropriate situations and contexts — it would consist of a wide variety. Although most Singaporeans are not effectively trilingual in the literate sense of being able to understand, read *and* write in three languages, they have at least some comprehension of words and idioms of various languages, especially Hokkien, Malay and perhaps Mandarin.

The situation in Singapore has been described as "polyglossia", where several languages and varieties of a language exist side by side (Platt 1980, Platt and Weber 1980). Given that the status of English language is high in Singapore, and its functions varied and diverse, the linguistic repertoire of most young Singaporeans include: native (mother tongue) language, and local slang or Singlish. Singlish is a variety of English with syntax and phonemes borrowed from dialects, vernaculars, and lingo (Ho and Platt 1993); in particular, men who serve two or more years of military service often speak a mixture of Hokkien, Malay, "broken" (non-standard) English and military argot.

Generalizations about the patterns of code-switching according to the kinds of domains (settings of home, friendship, education, religion and administration) are difficult to make because of the wide linguistic repertoire and the mutations of language varieties. Whereas Kuo has come up with a formula that offers a useful but simplistic understanding of the sociolinguistic situation in Singapore, Platt (1980) has provided a model, called "Societal Code Selection Matrix" to show under what conditions people try to select the variety of language they use.

This matrix takes into account the polyglossic nature of Singapore's linguistic situation and the wide linguistic repertoire of speakers. Along with complex jargon, Platt uses diagrams that are replete with arrows and notations that ultimately lose the readers. The matrix alerts us to the interaction of variables like repertoire, status of language, domains, and the multilingual context of Singapore society, but in the end has no predictive power. We cannot predict under what precise conditions, what variety of language will be used in communication.

It appears that we cannot make any firm conclusion about code-switching other than the fact that high status varieties of language tend to be used in formal settings. Code-switching depends on individuals in the interaction process and is often haphazard or whimsical. As Bloom (1986, 388) notes, "All speakers switch languages or varieties of languages according to changes in subject matter and social situation, and if all parties to a conversation are reasonably proficient in a number of languages or varieties, they are likely to switch fairly frequently without any particular practical reason at all, but apparently just for the pleasure of switching."

If sociolinguistic formulas are too mechanical and code-switching models are too fuzzy or obscure, then some social-historical material can at least offer some concrete evidence of the role of language in group communication. Combing through the historical sources, David Bloom (1986, 363) concludes that Malay was historically the spoken lingua franca in Singapore, while English was the written lingua franca that cut across various groups. Over the years, with increasing enrolment of students in English-medium schools, the role of Malay as a language that bridged inter-group communication was superseded by English.

Language and Social Structure

Sociologists and sociolinguists are concerned with not just how and through what languages or varieties or languages diverse groups communicate and interact. Sociologists in particular are also concerned with understanding the nature of society in which linguistic groups are comprised. They look at how linguistic divisions in society provide clues to the analysis of social structure in terms of hierarchies, stratification or inequalities.

Gender is one of the many social divisions that an understanding of linguistic patterns can illuminate. An extensive literature on language and sex has appeared in recent years (Lakoff 1990, Kramarae 1981, Spender 1980, Tannen 1990, Thorne & Henley 1975). Researchers have asked whether differences in language use occur between men and women, and if yes, how to make sense of these differences – as expressions of dominance or mere non-equivalences. Here, there is a research lacuna in Singapore. There is no published work on language and gender issues.

"Singlish" — consisting of a variety of Singaporean versions of the English language — has been studied by linguists (Crewe 1977, Foley 1988, Tay and Gupta 1983), but these studies do not sufficiently tap the sociological dimensions such as age or generation. There is some indication that Singlish, which combines syntax and phonemes of local dialects and lingo, tends to be well developed among the younger generation in institutions like the army (where interethnic mixing facilitates the interchange of languages) and popular culture (where local pop songs, cartoons and books of humour play on the oddities and flavour of Singlish).

Since there is a youth dimension to Singlish, such a variety of language spoken by the younger generation may be called "teenage mutant language". Youth, in particular, tend to have a creative capacity to invent, borrow and mix dialects and lingo into a linguistic pastiche that eventually acquires a distinctive cast. One example is "Pig Latin" which transfers the first sound of a word to the position after the last syllable in the word and adding a vowel to the sound. Thus "pig" becomes "ig-pe", "Latin" becomes "atin-le". As yet, there is no published work on Pig Latin in Singapore, but it is used mostly by young people as a secret code to disguise speech so that adults and non-members have no access to this language.

Another aspect of social structure that sociologists have long been interested in is social class. Language varieties exist in all societies, and the different status and prestige attached to particular varieties gives rise to inequality that can often be traced back to social class (Bernstein 1972) or ethnicity (Labov 1972). Bernstein's work, while subject to criticisms, makes theoretical sense of the connections between social class, socialization, language and educational inequality.

In the case of Singapore, research on language and disadvantage has focused on the significant role English-medium education has played in income and occupational mobility (MacDougall and Chew 1976, Clark and Fong 1980, Kuo 1985). The relationship between income and English-language use is long established and confirmed time and time again. Historically, the English language was a key to the doors of economic and political power during the colonial period. In the post-colonial era, the significance of English as the language of commerce, industry, and government provides social mobility to those who can master it. Even in 1990, the census data show that in families with combined monthly income of over S$10,000, over 57% used English as a predominant home language. Among families with less that $999 per month, only 8% used English most of the time; the majority used Mandarin, Malay, Indian and Chinese dialects (*The Straits Times* 1 May 1993).

While it is clear that there is a correlation between income and use of English, the relationship is not linear or simple. Clark and Pang (1980, 169) note that before 1980, there were income differences based on the language stream of one's education, but this relationship held true mostly for those with higher education. Among those with little schooling, it did not matter whether one was English- or Chinese- or Malay-educated; one would end up in low-paying, unskilled jobs anyway.

Moreover, since 1955, more parents have been sending their children to English schools. Over the years, the supply of English-educated workers has outstripped that of other-language workers, the income gap between English-educated and Chinese-educated has narrowed, and the distinction between English and other language streams becomes blurred.

It is interesting to note that research on the link between income and English language in Singapore is based on statistical correlation of available data, and not on theoretical inspiration. These works do not focus on class as an issue: income is a measure of socio-economic status, and the latter is not the same as social class. Social class consists of groups with particular economic or occupational patterns and cultural consumption habits. Correlational studies in Singapore demonstrate that the mastery of English language is associated with higher income but does not provide an explanatory framework to understand the connection between English language, worldview, socialization and social advantage.

Given the proliferation of English schools and the progressive decline (in many cases, death) of other language-stream schools, one may suppose that the link between income and language would progressively become weaker. However, language differences will continue to exist and affect educational performance and life-chances. Following the 1978 Goh Report on Education, schools would track students along certain paths, channelling them into appropriate places. The main means of tracking or streaming is examinations, which includes language competence. At the end of Primary Three, those who score low in points are put into the monolingual stream, from which they proceed to vocational and technical education (Hill and Lian 1995). Streaming now provides the connecting link between language performance and institutionalized inequality through differential education. Much research needs to be done in this area to bear out or test the ideas of Bernstein or Labov.

Sociologists who look at linguistic diversity in order to understand the social structure of Singapore have tended to focus not on social class, but on ethnicity. Part of the reason is that there is more overlap between linguistic communities and ethnic groups than between linguistic communities and class groupings. However, there is disagreement among sociologists over how to study the link between language and ethnicity.

In the positivist camp, Chiew (1980) and Kuo (1980) recognize the multilingual nature of Singapore society and the imperfect overlap with ethnic groups. However, they take for granted the official categories of "Chinese, Malay, Indian and Others" (CMIO) and construct their analyses with these categories of ethnicity as if they were fixed, and represented the real world out there. Chiew argues that in the colonial period, Singapore was a plural society with ethnic groups (CMIO) having their own parallel institutions like schools, religion, and economic specialisation.

Official bilingualism was introduced in schools in 1966 on the basis of English transmitting scientific norms and Mandarin or Malay or Tamil transmitting "Asian" and "cultural" values. Chiew argues that bilingual schools transform parallel institutions into "broker institutions", whereby various ethnic groups share and participate in the same institutions like school curriculum. Chiew believes that bilingualism would foster a spirit of national identity.

On the non-positivist camp, Benjamin (1976) and PuruShotam (1989, 1998) refuse to take ethnicity for granted, seeing ethnic relations as fluid, and tied to language only in a problematic manner. Benjamin in fact deconstructs official ideas of ethnicity and argues that the state's conception of ethnicity is an attempt to shape cultural and social life of the population.

PuruShotam (1987) criticises the CMIO model in which Chinese are expected to study Mandarin, Malay to study Malay, and Indians to study Tamil. She chooses to study the "minority" or "deviant" case of "Indians" whose heterogeneity in terms of caste, language, dress, skin colour, food, and customs, illustrate the complexity of ethnic identity and the contradictions of linguistic ascription. She shows that the bilingual policy in school tends to limit language choices for students studying a second language. Thus a Chinese is expected to learn Mandarin and not Malay or Tamil.

PuruShotam (1989, 517) argues that far from dissolving differences or fostering interethnic communication, bilingualism in Singapore invites insidious comparisons of the unequal statuses of languages. PuruShotam (1998) also takes a Foucauldian perspective in arguing that language policies are mechanisms of "disciplining" differences, pigeonholing ethnic groups into neat boxes according to official pre- and mis-conceptions of the associated language: Mandarin for the Chinese, Tamil for the Indians, Malay for the Malays.

Language and Political Structure

Rubin and Jernudd (1971) have raised the question, "Can languages be planned?" This question appears rhetorical in that most languages do not always evolve willy-nilly out of people's interactions. Some element of conscious intervention is at play in the institutionalization and shaping of languages. In particular, leaders in a political regime make decisions about language. These decisions involve choices among alternatives, and the choices between varieties of languages have political consequences (Weinstein 1983).

There is a large amount of literature on language, politics and power (O'Barr and O'Barr 1976; Kramarae et al. 1984, Lakoff 1990). From the linguistic and communicative point of view, studies tend to look at the power of words to exclude people, to move people, to persuade people into doing something against their wishes. From the political point of view, studies look at language as a divisive political issue, and how multilingual societies engage in and deal with conflict arising from it.

In Singapore, the visible hand of the nation-state is prominent in all areas of social life. A full understanding of Singapore society must take into account the role of the state in the patterning of social structures. The politics of language in Singapore involves not just languages in competition but also the policies and actions of the state that in the first place give rise to such competition.

Language politics in Singapore have been dominated by the status of Mandarin vis-à-vis English. In the writings by Chan (1983), De Souza (1980), and Bloom (1986), there is a tendency to portray language politics as a kind of violent or conflictual drama, with key protagonists being the representatives of Chinese community such as the Chinese Chamber of Commerce, the agitators such as the Chinese school teachers and students who participated in riots, and the government which had to respond to these challenges.

Secondly, these accounts constitute a narrative of events, one following another, and how these events led to policy decisions, and in turn how policy decisions affected various communities. As such a narrative tends to be descriptive and recounting. I will not repeat the events and incidents. I will develop a more theoretical account in the next section.

A Materialist Account of Language in Singapore

The literature on language and society in Singapore tend to be disparate and somewhat theoretical. The theoretical part is excusable on the grounds that in the early development of an indigenous sociology of language, it is important to do "stock-taking", noting how many languages are there in Singapore, how they relate or do not relate to various social institutions and groupings, and how they impact on policies and planning.

In this final section, I want to tie up the three parts by providing some kind of theoretical unity and framework. I call it a "materialist account" of language and society in Singapore since I give more weight to concrete factors than idealist factors as explanatory variables. By "concrete factors" I have in mind economic realities and instrumental reasoning that concern material gains rather than emotional appeasement.

Bourdieu's writings on language (Bourdieu 1991, Bourdieu and Wacquant 1992), which use terminology from economics, inspired me to develop a materialist account. Bourdieu argues that every linguistic act reflects the social conditions of production and reception. On the production side, the speech act reflects the speaker's "habitus", a linguistic competence to speak in a certain way. This linguistic competence is socially defined and unevenly distributed and valorized. Here, power relations and cultural strategies through which social groups manipulate symbolic resources, have given rise to the distinction between standard and vernacular languages.

Standard languages are in fact the product of social processes just like the history of state formation. They are formed and determined by power relations. Standard languages are forms of capital, yielding measurable benefits to those who possess them. They open doors to power, wealth and prestige within societies. Whenever the dominated or disadvantaged speaks with the dominated, his or her linguistic capital is devalued as a "broken" or "non-standard" language. Those who speak the valued, standard language intimidate those who do not, and the latter find school alienating and drop out of school.

On the reception side, the speech act reflects the "linguistic market", that is the perceived audience. How I perceive the audience's response constitutes my anticipation of the "price" my speech will fetch, and this determines how and what I say. The variety of domains (informal settings of home, friendship circles, versus formal settings of school, work and state) constitutes different linguistic markets that give rise to different kinds of speech and code-switching.

Again not everyone can engage in code-switching freely. Bourdieu talks about the "illusion of linguistic communism", the illusion that everyone participates in language as if everyone has access to the sun, air or water. Certain categories of speakers are deprived of the capacity or competence to speak in certain situations. As Bernstein notes, the upper class has a wider range of linguistic repertoire and can shift from one code to another. The lower classes do not have this range of linguistic repertoire and code switching is limited. Thus, well-educated Singaporeans can speak Standard English as well as the devalued Singlish, while those who receive less education are restricted to Singlish and vernaculars.

Symbolically, social groups may compete and fight over language issues in order to secure or preserve the social prestige or "standardness" of their respective languages. But underlying such symbolic or sentimental concerns about language are material motivations and, access to socio-economic goods.

In the political history of the 1950s, it appears that the Chinese sought to protect Chinese language and education on sentimental grounds of group and cultural preservation. However, as Bloom (1986, 365) notes, it was not the entire Chinese community who were concerned with preserving traditional Chinese cultural patterns through the school system. It was the minority of wealthy merchant class, the millionaires in the Chinese Chamber of Commerce who clamoured for the recognition of Mandarin and the significance of Mandarin in preserving traditional Chinese values.

Chinese businesses often operate on the basis of kinship networks. The underlying motive for this campaign and the need to preserve Mandarin may have something to do with the attempt to maintain continuity of these business and trade networks. Rich Chinese merchants are able to afford overseas and English education for their children, but the need to carry on the business and kinship networks that gave rise to their wealth calls forth the emphasis on preserving traditional Chinese values, especially language.

Already in the 1950s, the majority of Chinese parents wanted to send their children to English language schools. Sentiments of identity aside, they recognised the economic benefits of English stream education, and so rates of enrolment in English-streamed schools have progressively increased. Material concerns and instrumental conceptions of English language dictated the choice of English stream education. Preserving Chinese cultural values is an abstract idea while sending one's own children to English schools for future expected returns is an option that is more practical and attractive.

In May 1955, Chinese school students supported bus workers' strikes by engaging in violent protest. The incidents that led to this explosive rebellion are complicated, but it is clear that material concerns were at stake here. Chinese school students were frustrated at being denied the benefits that accrued from English education, such as employment security. Excluded from material advantages, they became easy targets for communist and communalist ideologues. Chinese schools thus became seedbeds of political agitation.

As Bloom (1986, 365) observes, teachers' unions supported Chinese education and schools largely because they were concerned with preserving jobs. Chinese schoolteachers were poorly remunerated: some had to take on private tuition to supplement their meagre incomes. Many had no prospects of promotion or continued employment. It is not surprising that they were involved in violent radical politics.

Today, one continues to hear Chinese spokespersons advocating the importance of Mandarin on sentimental grounds of preserving Chinese cultural roots. These advocates are the loud, vocal minorities within the Chinese community. For the greater majority of Chinese Singaporeans, English is recognised as the language that offers access to economic, political and status goods.

Material motivations also underlie Speak Mandarin campaigns. In 1971, Lee Kuan Yew said, "We must give our children roots in their own language and culture, and also the widest common ground through a second language...Then we shall become more cohesive a people, all rooted in their traditional values, cultures and languages; but effective in English, a key to the advanced technology of the West, from where all our new and more advanced industries come from" (*The Straits Times* 29 April 1971).

"Mr Lee Kuan Yew made repeated pleas last night to Chinese parents to drop dialects at home and speak Mandarin to help lighten the load of their children in school. Mr Lee also made the point that learning and using Mandarin, apart from being culturally worthwhile would also be economically useful because China, after successful implementation of its "Four Modernizations" programme would become a major trading partner — accessible not through Hokkien but Mandarin" (*The Straits Times* 8 September 1979).

The instrumental side of Mandarin again resonates the campaign message of 1993, which is running into the 15th year of promotion of Mandarin. The thrust of the message is that "Mandarin is not just the gateway to understanding Chinese culture; it can help you clinch business deals too" (*The Straits Times* 4 September 1993). Five days after this message was sounded, an advertisement in the English papers came up with the blurb, "Business Mandarin helps you to plug into the China connection".

The materialist interpretation of language in Singapore offers the prediction that if Malaysia and Indonesia are moving faster economically than China and Taiwan, then there will be Speak Malay campaigns. The status of languages in Singapore shifts according to material and political changes in the environment, and linguistic communities engage in civil wars or political contests not so much over sentiments of group identity and culture, as over material spoils.

The "idealist" position of language does not see the instrumental nature of language policies, the economic motivations underlying certain linguistic practices, or the political interests at stake. It emphasises the symbolic value of language, and is exemplified by official discourse on the role of Mandarin in preserving Chinese culture in the face of "Western decadent values" attendant upon modernization.

The idealist view assumes that English is a language of commerce and modernization whilst Mandarin, Malay and Tamil are languages of cultural maintenance and advancement. This view implies ethnic essentialism: that Chinese have to speak Mandarin in order to be culturally Chinese, that Indians have to speak Tamil in order to be culturally Indian, and so forth. Here, the idealist view ignores the impact of globalization on culture and language. Historically, citizens of China and India have travelled widely and are found across the globe, and so there is no one way to being a

Chinese or Indian. The Chinese in Tanzania do not speak the same language as the Chinese in Argentina, and language is only one and not the only means of cultural identity.

Future research in the sociology of language can continue to unravel the ideological underpinnings of language policies, to demystify the somewhat ethnocentric assumptions behind essentialist notions of language and ethnicity, to acknowledge the materialist advantages that both state elites and citizens gain from second language acquisition, and to examine new forms or hybrids of language (eg among young people) emerging in a global and post-modern context.

References

Afendras, E. and Afendras, S. (1980) "A Bibliography of Language in Singapore Society: Trends and Future Directions", in E. Afendras and E. Kuo (eds) *Language and Society in Singapore*, Singapore: Singapore University Press.

Benjamin, G. (1976) "The Cultural Logic of Singapore's 'Multiracialism'", in Riaz Hassan (ed) *Singapore: Society in Transition*, Singapore: Oxford University Press.

Benjamin, G. (1993) Grammar and Polity: "The Cultural and Political Background to Standard Malay", in W. Foley (ed) *The Role of Theory in Language Description*, Berlin: Mouton de Gruyter.

Bernstein, B. (1972) "Social Class, Language and Socialization", in P.P. Giglioli (ed) *Language and Social Context*, Harmondsworth: Penguin.

Bloom, D. (1986) "The English Language and Singapore: A Critical Survey", in B. Kapur (ed) *Singapore Studies: Critical Surveys of the Humanities and Social Sciences*, Singapore: Singapore University Press.

Bourdieu, P. (1991) *Language and Symbolic Power*, Cambridge: Polity.

Bourdieu, P. and Wacquant, L. (1992) *An Invitation to Reflexive Sociology*, Cambridge: Polity.

Chan, H. C. (1983) *Language and Culture in a Multi-ethnic Society*, Unpublished manuscript.

Chiew, S. K. (1980) "Bilingualism and National Identity: A Singapore Case Study", in E. Afendras and E. Kuo (eds) *Language and Society in Singapore*, Singapore: Singapore University Press.

Clark, D. and Pang, E. F. (1980) "Returns to Schooling and Training in Singapore", in E. Afendras and E. Kuo (eds) *Language and Society in Singapore*, Singapore: Singapore University Press.

Crewe, W. J. (ed) (1977) *The English Language in Singapore*, Singapore: Eastern University Press.

De Souza, D. (1980) "The Politics of Language: Language Planning in Singapore", in E. Afendras and E. Kuo (eds) *Language and Society in Singapore*, Singapore: Singapore University Press.

Esman, M. (1990) "Language Policy and Political Community in Southeast Asia", in B. Weinstein (ed) *Language Policy and Political Development*, Norwood, N.J.: Ablex.

Ferguson, C. (1971) "National Sociolingusitic Profile Formulas", in C. Ferguson (ed) *Language Structure and Language Use*, Stanford: Stanford University Press.

Foley, J. A. (1988) "Studies in Singapore English: Looking Back and Looking Forward", in J. Foley (ed) *New Englishes: The Case of Singapore*, Singapore: Singapore University Press.

Gopinathan, S. (ed) (1998) *Language, Society and Education in Singapore*, Singapore: Times Academic Press.

Hardstone, P. and Lock, G. (1980) *Nation-Building in a New State: The Role of the English Language in the Development of a Singapore National Identity*, unpublished manuscript.

Hill, M. and Lian, K. F. (1995) *The Politics of Nation Building and Citizenship in Singapore*, London: Routledge.

Ho, M. L. and Platt, J. (1993) *Dynamics of a Contact Continuum: Singaporean English*, Oxford: Clarendon.

Kramarae, C. (1981) *Women and Men Speaking*, Rowley, Mass.: Newbury House.

Kramarae, C., et al. (eds)(1984) *Language and Power*, Beverly Hills: Sage.

Kuo, E. (1976) "A Sociolinguistic Profile", in Riaz Hassan (ed) *Singapore: Society in Transition*, Singapore: Oxford University Press.

Kuo, E. (1980) "The Sociolinguistic Situation in Singapore: Unity in Diversity", in E. Afendras and E. Kuo (eds) *Language and Society in Singapore*, Singapore: Singapore University Press,

Kuo, E. (1985) "Language and Social Mobility in Singapore", in N. Wolfson and J. Manes (eds) *Language of Inequality*, Berlin: Mouton.

Labov, W. (1972) "The Logic of Nonstandard English", in P.P. Giglioli (ed) *Language and Social Context*, Harmondsworth: Penguin.

Lakoff, R. (1990) *Talking Power*, New York: Basic Books.

MacDougall, J. and Chew, S.F. (1976) "English Language Competence and Occupational Mobility in Singapore", *Pacific Affairs*, 49(2): 294-312.

O'Barr, W. and O'Barr, J. (eds) (1976) *Language and Politics*, Paris: Mouton.

Pakir, A. (1995) "Beginning at the End: Bilingual Education for All in Singapore and Teacher Education", in J.E. Alatis et al. (eds) *Linguistics and the Education of Language Teachers*, Washington, D.C.: Georgetown University Press.

Platt, J. (1980) "Multilingualism, Polyglossia, and Code Selection in Singapore", in E. Afendras and E. Kuo (eds) *Language and Society in Singapore*, Singapore: Singapore University Press.

Platt, J. and Weber, H. (1980) *English in Singapore and Malaysia*, Kuala Lumpur: Oxford University Press.

PuruShotam, N. (1987) *The Social Negotiation of Language in the Singaporean Everyday Life World*, Ph.D. dissertation, Dept. of Sociology, National University of Singapore.

PuruShotam, N. (1989) "Language and Linguistic Policies", in K. Sandhu and P. Wheatley (eds) *Management of Success: The Moulding of Modern Singapore*, Singapore: Institute of Southeast Asian Studies.

PuruShotam, N. (1998) *Negotiating Language, Constructing Race: Disciplining Difference in Singapore*, New York: Mouton de Gruyter.

Rubin, J. and Jernudd, B. (eds) (1971) *Can Languages Be Planned?* Honolulu: University of Hawaii Press.

Spender, D. (1980) *Man Made Language*, London: Routledge.

Tannen, D. (1990) *You Just Don't Understand: Women and Men in Conversation*, New York: William Morrow.

Tay, M. and Gupta, A. (1983) "Towards a Description of Standard Singapore English", in R. Noss (ed) *Varieties of English in Southeast Asia*, Singapore, RELC Anthology Series No. 11.

Thorne, B. and Henley, N. (eds) (1975) *Language and Sex: Difference and Dominance*, Rowley, Mass.: Newbury House.

Tongue, R. (1979) *The English of Singapore and Malaysia*, Singapore: Eastern University Press.

Wardaugh, R. (1992) *An Introduction to Sociolinguistics*, Oxford: Blackwell.

Weinstein, B. (1983) *The Civic Tongue: Political Consequences of Language Choices*, New York: Longman.

13

Religion

Tong Chee Kiong

Early anthropologists, such as Tylor (1871) and Frazer (1890) placed religion at the centre-stage of culture. Similarly, grand theorists Durkheim, Weber, Marx and Freud, devoted much attention to the study of religion. This central, and continuing, emphasis in the study of religion is understandable, given the moral underpinning of all human actions. The task of the sociology of religion is to understand what people believe and how these beliefs bear on the political, economic and cultural activities of the actors. The study of religion seeks to understand human behaviour, particularly how religious ideas shape, and are in turn shaped, by society.

Singapore provides an interesting case study of religion and religious change. It is a multireligious society, and no religion holds a dominant position. Buddhism has the largest group of adherents, but it only accounts for 30.9% of the population. The next largest religion is Taoism, with 22.3% of the population. Islam, whose adherents are primarily ethnic Malays, constitutes 15.3% of the population. 12.8% are Christians and 3.7% are Hindus. Interestingly, a significant 14.5% of Singaporeans claim to have no religion. Over the past 30 years, concomitant with rapid social changes in Singapore, the religious composition of the population has also changed. Shifts in religious affiliations have occurred, and are continuing. Some religions have grown in membership; others show a distinct pattern of decline. For example, the Census of 1931 showed that those who claim adherence to Chinese religion constituted 97.3% of the population. In 1990, this had dropped to

53.2%. At the same time, Christianity registered a growth from 2.7% to over 12.8% in 1990.

This paper will provide a critical review of the literature on religion in Singapore. It will begin with an overview of early religion in Singapore. Given the distinct nature of each of the major religions, the review will offer a comprehensive analysis of each religion, beginning with Chinese religion, followed by Islam, Hinduism, and finally Christianity. In Singapore, most studies have tended to focus on individual religions. Comparative studies of religion and religious change started to appear only in the 1980s. The second section of this paper will look at comparative studies of religion, particularly quantitative survey data. Finally, the conclusion will identify lacunae in the study of religion in Singapore, and suggestions for future research.

Early Religious Life in Singapore

At the point when Sir Stamford Raffles landed in Singapore, it was believed that there existed an *Orang Laut* population of no more than 150 (Song 1967). This community was regarded as having "long been converted to Islam" (Evans 1927). However, other accounts exist. Bartley (1933) suggests that the population was larger, and certainly included Chinese, as there were already gambier plantations owned and cultivated by the Chinese prior to 1819. Bloom (1986) cites some estimated figures: a total population of about 200, consisting of a few *Orang Laut* families ("nominally Mohomedans, but really believing in a sort of fetishism like all untutored peoples"), about a hundred Muslim Malay fisherfolk (thought to have settled on the island in 1811), and a community of about 40 Chinese pepper and gambier cultivators. The Chinese were likely to have adhered to a form of Chinese religion.

As with Islam, archaeological and historical evidence suggests that Buddhism and Chinese religion of some form existed in Singapore prior to Raffles' arrival. Ke (1984) cites eyewitness accounts of the remains of Buddhist sacred architecture on Fort Canning in 1822, suggesting the existence of a pre-Islamic population in Indianized Southeast Asia, including Singapore. A Chinese temple, *Shuntian Gong* (Temple of Submission to Heaven), dedicated to the earth deity

Dabogong (originally in Malabar Street, but currently settled after several moves in Geylang), was first built in 1796, according to an inscription inside the temple. It is believed to be the first Chinese temple in Singapore (Lee et al 1994).

After Raffles' arrival, Chinese religion took root with the arrival of Chinese migrants, mainly from South China. Each dialect group began to establish its own presence and develop its own temples as the Chinese community grew in numbers. The Fujians established their own temples (eg *Hengshan Ting* at Silat Road, established in 1828); the Teochews established *Yuehaiqing Miao* in Phillip Street in 1826; the Cantonese erected *Haichun Fude Si* in 1824; the Hakkas established the *Yinghe Guan* in 1823; and the Hainanese had a *Tianhou* temple on Beach Road in 1857.

Given the European appearance at the time of Singapore's founding, it is to be expected that a Christian presence would soon follow. In 1821, Reverend M. Laurent Marie Joseph Imbert of the Societe des Mission Etrangeres (the French Mission Society), visited Singapore en route to China. His one-week stay in Singapore resulted in a letter to the Bishop, stating that "there were only 12 or 13 Catholics in Singapore, who led a wretched life" (in Buckley 1902; Teixeira 1963).

Aside from the Catholic Church, there are also a great variety of other Christian denominations in Singapore. The earliest non-Catholic Christian presence was the London Missionary Society (LMS), formed by laypersons and missionaries from various denominations in England (Sng 1993). Missionary work started as early as the founding of Singapore in 1819, with the arrival of Samuel Milton that year. He started a school for Malay and Chinese boys. The next missionary to arrive was Claudius H. Thomsen in 1822. He started classes for both Malay boys and girls by 1828. Apart from LMS, the main Protestant denominations established in the 19th century include four main groups — Anglican (1826), Brethren (1864), Presbyterian (1881), and Methodist (1885). Since the turn of the century, various other groups have taken root as well, such as the Seventh Day Adventists (1905), Assembly of God (1926), Lutherans (1927), Salvation Army (1935), Baptists (1937), Bible-Presbyterians (1952), Christian Nationals' Evangelism Commission (1952), and the Church of Jesus Christ of Latter Day Saints (1968) (Tan 1979/80; Hinton 1985; Sng 1993).

Hinduism was brought into Singapore by the Indian immigrants who came as early as 1819 as part of Sir Stamford Raffles' entourage. These later immigrants brought their religion with them and established temples very rapidly. Most of the early immigrants were convicts brought here for construction work (Sandhu 1969), or labourers for the coffee and sugar plantations (Mahajani 1960). In turn, 98% of the labour immigrants were from South India (Sandhu 1969). Given that about 80% of the early Indian migrants into Malaya were Tamils, it follows that Hinduism in Singapore is essentially of a South Indian variety. The remaining 20% of the migrants were Muslims, Sikhs and Christians. The first Hindu temple, located in Bras Basah Road, was believed to be founded by one Naraina Pillay from Penang, in 1819. However, it was soon demolished (Tan 1961/ 62). Another temple was later constructed in 1827, dedicated to the goddess *Mariamman* in South Bridge Road. It stands today as the oldest Hindu temple in Singapore.

Singapore Muslims are primarily of the Shafii School of Law of the Sunni Islamic sect. Adherents to this doctrine are commonly known as orthodox or Sunni Muslims and constitute over 90% of the entire Muslim community today (Farah 1994). As with other Sunnis, Singapore Muslims follow a comprehensive system of community law, the Shariah. Christians are divided among the Catholic Church and a great variety of other Christian denominations, including, for example, mainline Protestant churches (Anglicans, Presbyterians, Methodists and Lutherans), neo-Calvinists (Baptists, Brethrens, and Bible-Presbyterians) as well as other independent churches. Reflecting the South Indian bias in Singapore's Indian population, patterns of Hindu religious practice veer towards South Indian styles in the Republic. These are clearly evident in the way South Indian domestic religious practices, festivals and ceremonial styles prevail over North Indian equivalents. Similarly, there is a predominance of South Indian temples which differ from North Indian ones in design and iconographic style, as well as in separate priesthoods and segregated patronage. Adherents to Islam, Christianity and Hinduism in Singapore sometimes also display evidence of infusion of beliefs and practices with local traditions, for example, animistic beliefs, or are influenced by the religious practices of other world religions.

"Chinese religion", which is used here as a collective term to describe the myriad beliefs adhered to by the majority of the Chinese population, is by far, the most difficult to characterize. The difficulty in characterization is primarily due to the eclecticism of the religion which is reflected in the varied nomenclature adopted to describe it. For example, Elliott (1955) termed it "*shenism*", which he derived from the fact that when asked for their religion, most Chinese would respond with "*bai shen*" (praying to the spirits). Topley (1954, 1956, 1961), who has researched the various Chinese religious practices, institutions and associations in Singapore, termed it the "anonymous religion". Comber (1954, 1955, 1958), in turn, referred to it as the "religion of the masses". More recently, Clammer's (1983) introduction to a volume of works on contemporary Chinese religious practices in Singapore and Malaysia characterized it as "Chinese folk religion". Nyce (1971) similarly adopted that terminology. Wee (1976) has attempted to clarify the status of these various strands of Chinese religions by using Buddhism as an organising base line. She distinguished between Buddhist systems which refer directly to specific Buddhist canonical traditions (Theravada and Mahayana schools) on the one hand; and those which have no direct Buddhist canonical reference, on the other. Of the latter, there are two groups: "*shenism*" (no canonical tradition of any kind); and "sectarianism" (with each sect having its own canonical tradition).

Ancestor worship is also an important element of Chinese religious practices. It has sometimes been described as an extension of filial piety, an important value in Chinese society and strongly grounded in Confucianist thought. Such is the manifestation of mutual care between generations, as much a part of the relationship between the living and the dead, as it should be among the living. In another very important sense, ancestor worship also acts as a "stimulus to morality" (Addison 1925), for the consciousness that the ancestors are watching and will judge and reward or punish one's conduct, and heightens the moral sense of the community. Indeed, Addison (1925) and Hinton (1985) argue that ancestor worship is the most important religious phenomenon in the life of the Chinese. However, it is seldom seen as composing a distinct religion (Tamney and Hassan 1987), and is regarded more as a part of Chinese religious life in general.

Theravada and Mahayana Buddhism are represented in Singapore, the latter far more so than the former. In addition, a Japanese branch of Buddhism, the Soka Association (formerly Nichiren Shoshu Association up till 1992) is also growing in significance (Clammer 1988). Further, there is also Confucianism, even though it is sometimes argued that Confucianism is not a "religion" but a moral code or philosophical system. Leo and Clammer (1983) noted that in Singapore, Confucius is regarded by some as a specific deity in his own right, worshipped apart from other deities and constituting the centre of a specific religious complex.

Chinese Religion

As suggested earlier, Chinese religion, until recently, was the dominant religion, at least in terms of the number of adherents, in Singapore society. Thus, it is not surprising that studies on Chinese religion constitute the main bulk of research on religion in Singapore. There are, however, several major gaps in the literature.

A systematic and comprehensive study on Chinese religion in Singapore is still unavailable. Early studies dealt primarily with Chinese customary practices and festivals. Interestingly, these early works were actually published by Chinese scholars, and written primarily in Chinese. For example, Han Wai Toon (1940) wrote on the *Tuapekong* cult in Singapore; and Chu Chih Chin (1950) described rituals surrounding *Tien Fei*, the Chinese sea goddess. In fact, the *Journal of South Seas Society* regularly published articles on Chinese religions. These were case-studies of rituals. Written by non-anthropologists, they were primarily descriptive, unsystematic, and contained many personal opinions and anecdotes.

Majorie Topley was one of the first professional anthropologists to conduct systematic fieldwork in Singapore. She published a series of articles on a wide variety of topics, ranging from the curing of illness, birth rituals, to vegetarian houses. For example, in *Chinese Women Vegetarian Houses in Singapore* (1954), Topley provided detailed ethnographic descriptions of a small, but significant group of women who intentionally chose not to marry but organised themselves on a "tribal" basis, as "vegetarian houses". Using a functional perspective, she saw vegetarian houses as satisfying the need for security in old age, that is, they are basically "death benefit" societies for arranging funerals, maintaining burial grounds and looking after the "soul tablets". One of her more interesting observations is the belief among these women that by repeating the name of "Amida" on their deathbeds, they are guaranteed rebirth, in the assurance of becoming men (as there are no women in the "Perfect Land"). The symbolism has gender implications but, unfortunately, Topley did not take the analysis any further. In fact, one of the features of Topley's work was its ethnographic detail, to the extent of an itemised description and count of food and other offerings made to the spirits. However, her work lacked systematic analysis, other than the occasional functionalist comments. Even so, it is a useful and important documentation of the religious practices of the Chinese in early Singapore and provides a reference point for more recent work. For example, in *Chinese Religion and Religious Institutions in Singapore* (1956), Topley described and categorised existing Chinese religious institutions, including temples, monasteries, nunneries, vegetarian houses and clan temples. In addition, she provided a broad-based, if brief, description of the historical development of Chinese religion and the origins of sectarian movements such as the Pure-Land and Chan Buddhism. In the same vein, Topley (1951) wrote on rituals and mythology and charms.

Further contributions to the early study of Chinese religion in Singapore can be found in the work of Leon Comber. Although not an academic by training, but an officer in the Government of the Federation of Malaya, he was a keen observer of Chinese religious rituals and practices and published several books on Chinese religion in Singapore in the 1950s and 1960s. For example, *Chinese Ancestor Worship in Malaya* (1954) provided a description of Chinese funerary rituals, from the Preparation for the journey, Paraphernalia of departure, the Journey, Geomancy and Fengshui, Funeral processions, and finally Mourning rites. It includes a somewhat simplistic discussion of the religious aspects of Chinese society. The list of 20 plates is particularly useful as archival material.

Comber's description of a single funeral does not take into account regional and dialect variations or gender differentiation, important features of Chinese funerals. The book appeals to a popular audience but is weak on scholarship. This is true for his other book, *Chinese Temples in Singapore* (1958), which is a short description of various temples in Singapore, including famous temples like the *Thiam Hock Keng* in Telok Ayer, the *Shuang Lin* Temple in Kim Keat Road; and lesser known temples like the *Tou Mu Kung* in Serangoon and *Lin Shan Min* in Bukit Timah Road. In addition, Comber devotes space to a discussion of the popular origins of various gods, such as *Kuanyin, Kuankung, Santaizi* and *Toa Pek Kong*, which he draws from secondary sources. Comber estimated that in 1957, there were about 500 temples in Singapore; a figure that is difficult to verify as he does not define what a temple is. Moreover, the nature of Chinese religion suggests that many temples may be "home-based" and not registered.

In contrast to Comber's largely "anecdotal methods", J.A. Elliot (1955) provided the most systematic account to date of spirit-medium cults in Singapore. He gave a vivid description of the theology and rituals (with accompanying illustrations) of the various types of spirit-medium cults, and delved into divination, myths and theatre. It also included a section on Sino-Malay cults as well as his assessment of the future of spirit-mediumship in Singapore. A reader will benefit from Elliot's systematic and detailed discussion of the rituals, religious specialists, ritual paraphernalia, and organisational structure of Chinese spirit mediumship. He suggested that spirit-mediumship is essentially temple-based, as a medium cannot operate easily without the help of other individuals or premises approximating a temple.

Elliot's study has been criticised for not clearly spelling out what is meant by systematized religion in Chinese society and glossing over the role of systematized religion. However, it is true that Elliot only examined spirit-cults, a form of sectarian movement in Chinese religion and does not deal with the relationship between spirit-cults, (ad hoc "magical" practices of Chinese religion) and the larger religious orientation of the Chinese. In a separate paper, the *Significance of Religion among the Overseas Chinese* (1951), Elliot wrote a short, impressionistic paper on changes in the religious practices of the Chinese in Singapore. He argued that the urban nature of Singapore society had led to changes in kinship and social organizational patterns, resulting in changes to religious practices. Moreover, the migrant experience of the Chinese has led to an attenuation of the cult of ancestor worship. He noted the impact of a modernizing Singapore on Chinese religion, such as the ignorance of the young regarding Chinese religious practices and the trend, which became obvious in the 1970s, towards increasing conversion to Christianity. Elliot's work on spirit-cults has become the standard reference for scholars working on sectarianism, and has resulted in a wide range of papers on the topic.

I have left the most important scholar of this period last, to give ample treatment to his immense contribution to Sinology, and to Chinese religion in particular. Maurice Freedman is the author of three books on the Chinese: a study of family and kinship in Singapore and two studies of lineage organizations in Southeastern China. His more important articles were later compiled into a single volume selected by G. William Skinner (Freedman 1979).

Freedman was primarily interested in the relationship between kinship and religion: "It is clear that both the domestic and hall cults throw certain organizational principles of lineage into relief and expressed ideas central to the competition within, and the unity of the lineage communities" (1966, 118). He stressed the role of filial piety in the understanding of Chinese ancestor worship:

> Filial piety is a duty for the children, who owe their parents obedience for the gift of life. A man's loyalty to the interests and wishes of his father is supposed to outweigh all other loyalties and attachments. The supreme act of filial piety owed by the sons is the performance of the mortuary and funeral ceremonies of the parents. These ceremonies are the first step in the transformation of parents into ancestor spirits, and the worship of the ancestors is in essence, the ritualization of filial piety (1965, 148).

Freedman raised the important dualism between the cult of immediate jural superiors and the cult of descent group. The domestic cult, according to Freedman, revolves around tablets of the recently dead, which are worshiped to preserve the memory of the dead, to serve their needs, and to satisfy the demands of their slight authority. Worship of each tablet continues in this way for three or four generations. Then the tablet is destroyed and its place in the domestic cult comes to an end. Thus, in the cult of jural superiors, the care and commemoration of forebears are done for their own sake and revolves around the family.

Another tablet may be made and placed in the lineage ancestral hall. Here, where the most remote ancestors are enshrined, men conduct all worship and the tablets represent agnatic ascendants in an abstract sense, not well-remembered fathers and grandfathers. The cult of descent group is "a set of rites linking together all the agnatic descendants of a given forebear" (1966, 133). It is associated with extrafamilial kin groups, clans, lineages and lineage segments. Freedman suggests that whereas the domestic cult was very nearly universal, the cult of descent groups was absent wherever lineages were absent. He argues that in Singapore, the cult of ancestor worship, in this sense, is not practised. What is practised is a kind of "memorialism", a "commemoration of forebears as it were for their own sake" (1966, 153).

Freedman also suggested a close relationship between ancestor worship and geomancy, arguing that while the cult has to do with the worship of ancestors, geomancy relates to manipulation of the ancestors: "Men use their ancestors as a media for the attainment of worldly desires ... the tables are turned: descendants strive to force their ancestors to convey good fortune, making puppets of forebears and dominating the dominators" (1979, 298). Freedman's ideas on the passivity of ancestors in geomancy are related to his notion that Chinese ancestors are generally benevolent and benign: "They are essentially benign and considerate of their issue. Before taking action against their descendants, they need to be provoked; capricious behaviour is certainly alien to their benevolent and protective nature" (1979, 303). Although it is true that the Chinese in Singapore perceived ancestors as generally helpful, contrary to Freedman, ancestors are also seen as capable of malicious behaviour and are apt to initiate punishment.

Freedman's interest is primarily sociological, to the degree that he tries to use ethnographic facts to illustrate relevant structural principles and examine how those rules and principles shape social interaction. His approach is basically functionalist, influenced by the works of Evans-Pritchard and Meyer Fortes. Freedman has had a profound influence on the direction of research in Chinese anthropology. One major criticism of Freedman is that his conclusions, because they are reconstructions based on secondary literature, do not always reflect the complexities and nuances of the practice of Chinese religion. Except for his work in Singapore and a short stay in Hong Kong, he himself did very little fieldwork. Even though his study, *Lineage Organizations in Southeastern China*, has been praised by Skinner as revealing an exceptional skill for recreating social institutions from myriad facts and clues, "arm-chair anthropology" has its inherent problems. Freedman's most important contribution is that he has raised relevant issues that have been taken up, confirmed or revised by later scholars based on more accurate ethnographic information.

To conclude this section, it is possible to discern several major themes. First, early studies, with few exceptions, are largely descriptive. They were primarily undertaken by anthropologists rather than sociologists. Sociologists did not really become interested in religion in Singapore until the 1970s and 1980s. Thus, much of the material was based on fieldwork such as case studies of particular rituals. They are important in providing a baseline for future research. Unfortunately, there are no broad strokes of the painter's brush in documenting the practices of the early Chinese, in the tradition of DeGroot (1892-1910) and his massive six-volume work on the religion of the Chinese in Xiamen, or Justus Doolittle's (1865) three volumes on the life of the Chinese. We have only snapshots of ritual life in Singapore. This has had an adverse effect on the contemporary study of Chinese religion. For example, it is generally believed that there has been a decline in the practice of traditional Chinese rituals in modern Singapore. But, without a reference point, it is difficult to assess the extent of the decline or whether it is a misconception. In fact, it is only in recent years that quantitative surveys have been conducted to assess religious trends in Singapore society.

The work of anthropologists who study particular rituals or religious organisations have continued. For example, the interest generated by Elliot's examination of spirit mediumship has resulted in several studies on sectarian spirit-cult activities. Heinze (1983) studied the practice of "plancette-writing" in Singapore. Her fieldwork, based primarily on the study of the *World Red Swastika Society*, looked at the history and development of this organization. She concluded that while the "structural-symbolic" dimensions, by which I think she meant the rituals and beliefs of this group, have not changed, the socio-cultural have.

Ju (1983) examined a spirit-medium cult *(Sanshan Linfa Xianfa Zongtan)* situated in a Housing Development Board (HDB) estate and provided a detailed description of the "house-temple" and the beliefs and rituals of this cult. An interesting observation regarding this cult is that, unlike most spirit-medium groups which are organised as individual-based temples, each independent of one another, the *Xianfa* cult operates a network of temples, with branches and a parent organisation. It possesses an organized structure, a system of membership registration, and a structured training programme for acquiring and mastering the art of *Xianfa*. In contrast with the "normal" spirit-medium cults, which are basically ad-hoc patron-client relationships, *Xianfa* operates more as a community of believers. This type of spirit-cult have also been observed by Tan Chee Beng (1985) for the *te-qiao* group, and Young (1990) and Heinz (1983) for the World Red Swastika Society. This type of sectarian community based on the idea of spirit-possession is fascinating and requires more analysis.

Tong (1989) also examined the idea of spirit mediumship, but the interest was not on the belief and rituals of spirit-mediumship but how this sectarian practice of Chinese mediumship revealed the nature of the relationship between power and knowledge in Chinese society. Drawing on several sources, including Elliot, Freedman and Ju, as well as participant fieldwork, he argued that the Chinese idea of power is linked to the control of rituals as well as a body of sacred knowledge that is only available to the religious specialists.

It is often argued that Confucianism is not a religion, but a philosophical system. Leo and Clammer (1983), however, suggested that Confucius can and has become, a component of syncretic folk religion through his incorporation as a specific deity or *shen* in the Chinese religious pantheon. They argued that the origins of religious Confucianism resulted when a spirit medium was possessed by a spirit who claimed to be Confucius, passed through Singapore on a world tour to visit his students. Consequent to this possession, there was the development of "Confucian" priests.

These temples are believed to be especially efficacious for getting good examination results if offerings of food and money are made to them. Thus, Leo and Clammer argued that Confucianism should not be regarded as a simple homogenous set of beliefs, and that the division between philosophy and religion is rarely clear in Chinese thought.

They however did not provide sufficient evidence whether it is part of the institutional religion or merely the result of an enterprising spirit-medium. It should be noted that spirit-mediums invoke a large and sundry source of deities/gods for their purposes, with temples having images of Mohammed and the Virgin Mary, even spirit possessions by Jesus Christ. These, however, are ad hoc in nature and do not necessarily mean that these deities/gods have entered the Chinese pantheon or religious ideology.

Chinese Religions: Recent Works

More recent works on Chinese religion have continued on this trajectory of ethnographic, anthropological approach. However, one main difference, compared to the earlier works, has been the entrance of Singaporean anthropologists who have returned from graduate programmes overseas. One of these is Vivienne Wee's research on the rituals and beliefs of the Chinese. Wee (1976) was centrally concerned with the disparity between "canonical" and "practised" religion. Noting that the label "Buddhism" used in Singapore did not correspond with those prescribed in Buddhist literature, but consists of a range of beliefs tied to syncretic Chinese religions, including Buddhism, Taoism, Confucianism, ancestor worship and folk beliefs, Wee set up a classification of the various religious practices, using factors such as religious personnel, temple architecture, social organisation, theology and belief systems. Buddhism in Singapore was a fluid and dynamic term which can encompass canonical Theravada and Mahayana forms as well as Chinese folk religions. While this syncretism was not unique to Singapore and probably true of all societies which had a history of Chinese emigration, what was interesting about Singapore Buddhism is its direct linkage to changes in Singapore society. This work is based on an unpublished thesis submitted to the University of Singapore. In it, Wee (1976) attempts to set out the organizing principles of the ritual and belief systems of Chinese religion.

While Wee's treatment was more general, Tong Chee Kiong (1987) examined a specific aspect of Chinese religion, the idea of Chinese death rituals. He was fascinated by the readiness of a supposedly pragmatic people to incur huge expenses in the enactment of death rituals. Based on fieldwork, Tong used a cultural analysis of the symbols of death — flesh, blood, bones, souls, time, numbers, food and money — to examine Chinese perception of death and how they cope with its eventuality. An examination of the interrelationship between death rituals and the socio-economic value system of Chinese society, particularly kinship and economic network, revealed a whole range of organizing principles that operate within the larger social context.

Tong argued that no single factor can exclusively account for the desire to enact elaborate death rituals. Instead, a range of factors, including the observance of rules of descent, subscription to ethical imperatives, sense of duty and obligations, desire for social conformity, fulfilment of calculated self-interest, elevation of social status, and the management of death pollution, combine, in varying degrees, to act upon the Chinese to ensure ritual performance. The explanation lies in a combination of ideal and material interests, a fine balance between the desire for personal benefits and a desire for the "good" society.

Based on the above review, some general observations can be made on the study of Chinese religion in Singapore. First, the majority of studies have been on specific rituals or a particular sectarian movement, especially spirit-medium cults in Singapore. This is understandable as most studies employ anthropological methods, which emphasize participant observation and is most appropriate to closed homogenous groups or bounded religious rituals. Except for Wee (1977) and Tong (1987), there were few attempts to relate the specific focus of the particular set of rituals to the wider arena of Chinese religion or the larger issue of Chinese culture and society. In this sense, we have not made much progress from the seminal works of Maurice Freedman. While Freedman himself did little fieldwork, he attempted broad theoretical generalizations about Chinese religion and culture which are yet to be tested empirically. Questions regarding the nature and boundaries of Chinese religion and the relationship between folk and canonical religions remain unanswered. Secondly, most studies have tended to concentrate on religion in Singapore. How these religions were adapted and transformed, and how they differ from practices in China, remain unanswered. A history of Chinese religion in Singapore, in the tradition of the great Indologists, is needed. This is especially critical, given the transplanting of religion from China, and its transformation in Singapore. Of course, part of the problem is that anthropologists are inherently more interested in the folk or "little" traditions. Contrary to popular belief that Chinese religion is a folk tradition, there is in fact a large corpus of religious text, whose analysis will add to our understanding of Chinese religion. (See Rawski 1988 for a discussion of this, and how texts can be usefully analyzed). This may explain why the study of the canonical traditions of Chinese religion is almost non-existent in Singapore. Thus, while Buddhism is a major religious tradition in Singapore, little systematic research has been conducted. Wee's "Buddhism in Singapore" is in fact about popular religion. Similarly, there are few studies of canonical Taoism in Singapore, although some research have been carried out on philosophical Confucianism (see for example, Tu 1984). There are also few studies, Yip's (1958) work on Theravada Buddhism in Singapore is the exception.

Chinese religion is, of course, marked by pluralism. It is not simply the three great traditions of Buddhism, Confucianism, and Taoism, but also includes folk beliefs, customs and ancestor worship. Moreover, in Buddhism, for example, we find many sects, including Mahayana, Theravada, *Pure Land* and *Chan* coexisting, and intermingling in Singapore society. A study of the interrelationship and interaction of these various traditions which will facilitate an overview of Chinese religion in Singapore is the next task. In this sense, despite the large number of studies, many gaps remain, and the study of Chinese religion remains in sociological infancy.

Islam

In identifying papers for this review, it became clear that there is a significant gap in the study of Islam in Singapore. With its long history in Singapore and almost 350,000 believers today, there are, in fact, very few studies of Islam. The majority of studies have concentrated on kinship, marriage or economic aspects of Malay society. Of course, given the relationship between religion, culture, and politics for the Muslims, most studies, invariably, if often indirectly, make reference to Islam in Singapore (see for example, Djamour (1959), Li (1986).) Thus, while Djamour was primarily interested in Malay kinship and marriage, she devoted a section to Islam. One of her more interesting findings was that while a great many Malays profess Islam, only a small proportion of Malays pray five times a day or fasted for the whole month of Ramadan (Djamour 1959, 15). Unfortunately, she did not analytically pursue this discrepancy between stated belief and actual behaviour.

Similarly, she noted that for the Malays in Singapore, while there was strict adherence to taboos regarding eating pork and alcohol; in actual practice, religious adherence is comparatively mild, compared to the Malay States (present Malaysia), Arabia and Middle-Eastern countries. For example, she claimed that only a handful of believers understand the meaning of prayer and the precepts of Islam. Furthermore, the knowledge of the Koranic tradition is rudimentary and attendance at mosques is generally low (Djamour 1959, 16). However, it should be pointed out that Djamour did not provide any figures or other empirical evidence to support these observations.

One of the early works that treats Malay religion directly was Blagden's *Notes on Folk lore and Popular Religion of the Malays* (1900). Blagden was a colonial civil servant, not an anthropologist. He provided a most impressionistic idea of folk practices in the 1900s, making a distinction between folk (*adat*) beliefs and Islam (at that time, termed by colonial administrators as Muhammaden), and proceeded to document the various types of folk beliefs, including the beliefs in *jin*, the role of the *kramat* and religious functionaries like the *pawang* and the taboos associated with agriculture. Making a clear demarcation between traditional beliefs (*adat*) and canonical Islam, he declared that he found it strange that the Malays do not comprehend the obvious inconsistencies between his professed religion and traditional ritual behaviour. It should be noted that most studies on the relationship between traditional beliefs and canonical religion view the two as separate systems. This is true even for more recent studies. Theoretical developments in the study of religion (see Kirsch 1976), however, no longer see the two as separate, but rather focus on continuities and interrelationships.

Another area of interest has been on Islamic law, particularly the analysis of differences between Islamic and British laws, as well as the administration of Muslim Laws in Singapore. For example, Djamour described the various types of Muslim divorces, including *cherai biasa* (ordinary divorce), *talak* (divorce in which a spouse breaks the condition of marriage), *khula* (divorce by redemption), *fasah* (judicial dissolution of marriage) as well as *rojo* (revocation of divorce). She also discussed the background of the Shariah Court and the appointments of *kathis*. Djamour pointed to the problem of high divorce rates (59.9% in 1950) and suggested that part of the explanation was related to the nature of Muslim religion/culture; especially the practice of a man's right to repudiate wives and the weakness of the institutions of marriage and the family (1959, 179). Moreover, reforms were difficult because of resistance from traditional religious leaders who used Islam to legitimize their position regarding polygyny and divorce, as well as the difficulties of applying the Women's Charter. Interestingly, divorce rates started to decline rapidly after 1960s, (25.7% in 1961) partly through government intervention and the enactment of the 1957 Ordinance regulating the Shariah Court.

While Djamour is more sociological, Hooker (1984) approached the issue of religion and law from a legalistic perspective. In *Islamic Law in Southeast Asia*, Hooker devoted a chapter to the Straits Settlements and Singapore. The work is primarily historical, but the study is sociologically interesting in showing the relationship between law and society. Hooker began with the premise that one cannot understand Islamic laws in Singapore without seeing its historical and social linkages to the British (colonial) legal system. He proceeded to cite a series of case laws to demonstrate the inconsistencies between British and Islamic laws and the inconsistent interpretations given by the British courts. To him, the problem arose because both sets of laws are exclusivistic:

> Islam is an exclusive religion and its laws are equally
> exclusive; indeed, the Sharia is at the heart of Islam and it can
> be nothing other than exclusive (Hooker 1984, 118).

Given this exclusivity, he asked, "How does one ascertain the proper law to decide a conflict of principles between the tenets of Islam and the laws of the State?" The simple answer was that there was none. He then proceeded to look at the celebrated Hertogh case, and how a conflict in the ideological bases of two sets of laws resulted in riots and the loss of lives. This study, while primarily historical in nature and often couched in legalistic terminologies, provides interesting insights on Islam and society in Singapore.

This trajectory is continued by Siddique (1986) who discussed the institutionalization of Islam in Singapore through laws such as the Administration of Muslim Law Act (1966) and the setting up of the *Maglis Ugama Islam* Singapore (MUIS) in 1968. Taking a broader historical perspective, she saw these developments as stages in the evolution of Muslim legal and bureaucratic history in Singapore. Like Djamour and Hooker, Siddique pointed to the demarcation and conflict between Muslim substantive laws (*fiqh*) and British law. She saw several important markers in the development of Muslim laws in Singapore: the Ordinance of 1957, the setting up of Administration of Muslim Law Act (ALMA) and *Maglis Ugama Islam* Singapore (MUIS) in the late 1960s, the appointment of a Mufti who heads the Fatwa Committee, the establishment of Mendaki, the centralisation of pilgrimage (1975) and finally, the setting up the Mosque Building Fund to erect new mosques in HDB New Towns.

Another area of research is Islamic reformism. Peacock analysed Muslim reformism as part of a larger study on reformism in Southeast Asia. Using a survey questionnaire, he sought to understand the nature and extent of the *Kaum Muda* movement, particularly groups like the *Muhammadijahs* and *Ahmadiyya*. He arrived at several interesting findings:

1. Islamic Reformism is not prominent as an organized movement in Singapore;
2. Singapore Muslims tend to hold on to the main pillars of faith, Omnipotence of God, Mohammed as Prophet, Quaran

as sacred, and the Obligations of daily prayer and attendance at mosques;

3. Singapore Muslims retain, to varying degrees, animistic customs, such as ideas of *semangat* (spiritual energy), *kramats* (holy shrines) and *hantus* (ghosts and spirits). But they are quite aware of the distinction between *adat* (customs) and *ugama* (religion); and

4. Singapore reformists tend more towards a "Protestant" style of direct communication with God, high-status white collar employment, and are patrist (patrilocal, patrifocal, and patrilineal family patterns) (Peacock 1978, 174).

In addition, Peacock discussed the tension between Islamic reformers and the bureaucrats and traditional religious leaders.

Peacock's study is significant because he attempted a quantitative analysis of Islam in Singapore. The study, however, suffers from poor research methodology as well as his emphasis on psychological explanations. Peacock failed to properly distinguish between "reformism" and "progressivism". Thus, Peacock is unable to explain why Singapore Malays do not display progressivism as might be expected from their education and urbanity whereas in Kedah, the reverse is true.

Another area of research that has dominated the study of Islam in Singapore is the relationship between culture and economic development, in particular the interest in various explanations for the supposed economic backwardness of the Malay. (See, for example, Alatas 1977, Bedlington 1974, Betts 1975, Clammer 1978.) The most recent study in this debate is Li (1986). She explored the relationship between forms of cultural practices in the Malay household and community and the economic structure of Singapore. It is a detailed historical ethnography that attempts to integrate both cultural and materialist explanations.

It is obvious that there are several major gaps in the study of Islam in Singapore. It is not an exaggeration to say that there has not been a systematic study of Islam in Singapore. I say this because the majority of studies in Singapore on Islam have tended to fuse religion, culture, and community into a single category. While it is true that Islam cannot be bounded as a "religion" in the narrow sense of the term, that is, as a set of doctrines binding the individual (Milner 1983), it is also necessary to examine religion as an independent system first, and then look at its relationship with identity, culture, and community. This is particularly relevant, given the rapid social changes that have occurred in Singapore society.

Most studies of Islam in Singapore have normally been part of a larger study of Islam in Southeast Asia (eg Hooker 1983, Peacock 1978). Because of this, the treatment is, by necessity, brief, given the more dynamic interest in the larger Muslim societies of Malaysia and Indonesia; as well as problems of Islamic resurgence in Southern Thailand and Philippines. There is a considerable body of literature on Islam in these countries. Islam, its history, development and ideology, to quote Siddique, is unique, with its own set of historical circumstances. Muslims in Singapore are a minority, compared to Malaysia and Indonesia. This fact alone suggests that Islam and its relationship to society in Singapore must be different. A comprehensive study of Islam in Singapore, looking at its historical development, theology, rituals, and its relations to the state, and society, is sorely needed.

Given the pace of development in Singapore society, the changes in Islamic beliefs and rituals and the linkages with Malay community warrants investigation. What is the impact of modernization on traditional religious beliefs? How has urban renewal, and the disappearance of the *kampong* affected Muslim identity and religion? If, as Peacock argued, that Malays value communal solidarity, personified in village life, then what are the consequences of the disappearance of these villages in Singapore?

It is clear that there are tensions within the Malay community; traditionalists versus reformists, fundamentalists versus moderates, and English-educated versus the Malay-educated. Tong (1989) for example, suggested that in Singapore, a distinction in Islam or religion in general should be made between fundamentalism and radicalism. However, very little is known about the degree and extent of religious fundamentalism and sectarianism in Singapore. Islam can become the arena where the social tensions are contested and revealed. Again, these require further study and analysis.

Hinduism

The literature on Hinduism in Singapore is sparse and sporadic. Of the four religions surveyed in this review, it has received the least treatment. In fact, there is probably more unpublished (but available) material, in the form of academic exercises and master's theses than published works (eg Rajah 1976, Sinha 1987). As such, in this section, I will also be reviewing some of the more important unpublished works.

One of the earliest publications available is, interesting enough, in the National Geographic Magazine, on the Fire-Walking (*Timithi*) ceremony (Lewis 1931). Another early work is Mialaret (1969) on Hindu temples in Singapore. These are primarily descriptive pieces, with little sociological analysis. The first available sociological work is Babb (1974, 1975, 1975a, 1976), who wrote on Hindu rituals in Singapore. An anthropologist by training, the four papers he wrote were "Walking as Flowers" (1975) Mediumship (1974), *Thaipusam* (1975a), and an overview, *Patterns of Hinduism in Singapore* (1976), where he examined the evolving features of Hinduism in Singapore and how a basically agrarian religion adapted to a highly urbanised, rapidly changing social environment.

He suggested that the diversity of Hindu traditions in Singapore is linked to the different ethnic and regional backgrounds of the migrant Indians. As expected, Babb found that Hinduism in Singapore was very different from Hinduism in India. While there was still segregation between the northern and southern Indians in their patterns of religious practices (mostly due to linguistic and philosophical differences) he noted that Singapore society itself was a constraining influence on Hinduism. Moreover, caste or caste hierarchy was de-emphasized, especially during the performance of religious rituals. Despite these changes, Hindu rituals continued to fulfil important functions for the Indians in Singapore. Interestingly, he found that the practice of taking vows and the reliance on spirit mediums were still deeply entrenched in Singapore, among both the young and the old.

In a separate paper, he looked specifically at Hindu mediumship through a comparison of four spirit-medium temples. This is not an ethnographic study; there is little description of the temples or rituals, but rather a study of the variations in ritual ideology. There are two main themes in the paper. First, Babb suggested that the most salient feature of Hindu mediumship fitted the broader patterns of Hindu beliefs and practices, that is, the highly particularized religious interests of individuals and the abstract conceptions of divine power found in spirit-mediumship was found in the religious system of Hinduism as a whole. While it is true that the ideology of mediumship must invariably be related to Hinduism, I am not convinced that the two fit exactly. Clearly, mediumship falls into the realm of magic, and while the recent literature on the relationship between magic and religion suggests new ways of looking at the problem, the fit is not simple, as they have different starting points (see Tambiah 1992). This problem becomes obvious when Babb argued that like Hinduism, mediums have temples. But, medium temples are, by and large, periphery to the mainstream temples of Hinduism in Singapore, and perform different functions.

These problems arise because Babb subscribes to psychological explanations for religious behaviour. For example, he ascribed the popularity of public ceremonies to their therapeutic and palliative effects on individuals. In the same way, he argued that Hindu practices are concerned with the fears, hopes, and desires of individuals, and to help them cope with life: "… (the) contexts in which religious symbols are brought directly to bear on the problems which ariseout of the unique circumstances of each person's life (1976, 203).

In contrast, Cooper and Kumar attempted a more sociological analysis of Hindu religion, with the ambitious aim of putting analytical order to the confusing variety of Indian-Hindu ceremonies by developing a typological model based on location of ritual action, participation, and the degree of social differentiation involved. At the same time, it hoped to link changes in the form of religious ceremonies with ethnic identity changes among Singaporean Indian-Hindus. Looking primarily at calendrical rituals of the South Indian, and drawing on the theories of van Gennep on rites of passage and Turner on liminality and communitas, Cooper and Kumar saw *Thaipusam* as anti-structure, where caste, age, and gender categories are temporarily suspended. In *Thaipusam* and *Timithi* (fire-walking ritual), caste and regional groupings are basically set-aside, and the greater Indian-Hindu identity takes precedence. This is an interesting idea, but begs for more examples and clearer analysis. Cooper and Kumar does not explain why there is a need to establish a greater Indian-Hindu identity. The paper also attempted to distinguish ceremonies that take place in the streets/temples and home-based worship. They suggested that temple worship involves abandoning the normal patterns of structural differentiations (anti-structure) while rituals at home tend to reaffirm structural differentiations. Again, an interesting idea but the paper does not provide sufficient evidence to support this assertion.

An interesting publication, from an anthropological perspective, is a book edited by Anthony Walker (1994), *New Place, Old Ways: Essays on Indian Society and Culture in Modern Singapore*. The edited book is a collection of revised academic exercises by Honours students in the Department of Sociology, National University of Singapore. In relation to Hinduism, Nilarn Ali records the rituals, paraphernalia and devotees associated with the cult of mother goddess worships on four Hindu temples in Singapore.

Similar to Chinese religion, the bulk of studies of Hinduism in Singapore are ethnographic. For example, Rajah (1976) focused on the ecology of shrines; Manokara (1979) on growth and decay in two Hindu temples in Singapore; and PuruShotam (1985) on the celebration of *Navarathri*. Sinha (1997) examined the broader aspects of Hinduism, including its rituals and theology, changing features, and its relations with the socio-cultural landscape of Singapore society. In "Unpacking the Labels 'Hindu' and 'Hinduism' in Singapore" (1997), Sinha problematised taken–for-granted terms such as "Hindus" and "Hinduism" in Singapore. She argued that for many Singaporean Hindus, there was a great deal of uncertainty when it came to articulating the exact parameters of a "Hindu identity". This was particularly true of younger Hindus, suggesting the existence of inter-generational differences in attitude. In her unpublished Master's dissertation, *Hinduism in Singapore: A Sociological and Ethnographic Perspective* (1987) Sinha also examined the place of Hinduism in Singapore society. She traced the historical development of Hinduism in Singapore and tried to explicate its socio-cultural features, looking especially at class and caste backgrounds. The thesis also examined the attempts by various groups, such as the Hindu Centre, to reform Hinduism in Singapore. In a later paper, she focused on religious specialists. Sinha (1989) observed the growing popularity among Singapore Hindus of the notion that Brahmin priests are necessary to direct ritual behaviour and the increasing popularity of temples and temple-worship in the lives of Hindus in Singapore.

From the review above, it is clear that Hinduism in Singapore is largely underresearched. Like Islam, a comprehensive analysis of Hinduism, its history, ideology, rituals and adaptation is required.

Christianity

Christianity is a minority, albeit important, religion in Singapore. In 2000, Christians accounted for about 13% of the population. Yet, with the exception of Chinese religion, much of the literature of religion in Singapore has focused on Christianity. There may be several reasons for this. First, Christianity has a long history in Singapore. Being a former British Colony, Christianity was brought in together with colonial rule. In fact, the first Roman Catholic Church was built as early as 1833 and the Saint Andrew's Cathedral in 1836. The early Protestant missionaries actually had their sights on China and the headquarters in Singapore were supposed to be only temporary. (Turnbull 1989, 606). Missionary schools were set up in Singapore in 1822, and by 1829, there were already four such schools. In Singapore, missionary work had always been linked to education and the educated class. Initially, churches catered primarily to Europeans and some Babas who, together with adopting western customs and sports, also became Christians. As such, in 1931, only 2% of Chinese considered themselves Christians. The period of rapid growth began in the 1950s, and by 1980, over 10% of the population were Christians.

Early studies on Christianity in Singapore, however, did not address these trends. Rather, they tend to concentrate on the history of churches in Singapore. Greer (1959), for example, documented the history of the Presbyterian Church in Singapore. Teixeira (1963) traced the development of the Portuguese Mission in Malacca and Singapore, while Doraisamy (1985) looked at the history of the Methodist Church in Singapore.

Another interesting trend is the number of studies conducted by theologians and church leaders. While many of these adopt sociological techniques (see for example, Sng and You 1982, Hinton 1985), they are more accurately classified as religious sociology rather than the sociology of religion. The distinction is a fine, but important one. Religious sociologists, while using the same techniques as sociologists, carry out their study as a means to a religious end, while a sociologist's major professional interest is in the study of religion as a social and cultural phenomenon (Robertson 1970, 11). Even so, their studies warrant review as they contribute to our understanding of religion and the religious situation in Singapore. For example, Sng and You's, *Religious Trends in Singapore; with special reference to Christianity* (1982) used a survey questionnaire, administered to church members, to examine the socioeconomic background of Christians in Singapore. Further, it attempted to provide a more in-depth analysis of secondary data derived from the 1980 Census data. As the title suggests, it is primarily interested in explaining how the data related to the church and Christianity. Thus, the last two chapters are actually titled "Areas of Concern and Challenge" and "Prospects". Similar types of research include Finnell's (1986) survey of 218 Baptists.

In *Growing Churches, Singapore Style*, Hinton (1985) sought to explain the growth of Christianity in Singapore. He argued that, in Singapore, anomie is on the increase and people increasingly withdraw into their private world. They become inward-looking, impersonal, individualistic, apathetic and increasingly insecure. But Hinton does not provide any real evidence, whether quantitative or qualitative, that anomie is on the rise, or why, even if people are anomic, they would turn to Christianity. While Hinton suggested in his published work, *Growing Churches*, that there is an increase in anomie in Singapore, his own field-data in his unpublished thesis, *Twelve Churches Study*, indicate that only 18% of his sample cited crisis as the reason for conversion to Christianity. The most important factor, in his study, is the search for a true religion (41%).

This lack of empirical evidence and sweeping generalizations is exemplified in his analysis of why there are more women than men in churches. He suggested that it was because women are, traditionally, more active religiously, and when they lose confidence in traditional religion, they actively seek an alternative; whereas males, who allow females to carry out the family religion on their behalf, more easily slip from passive belief to passive agnosticism. This again is an example of piecemeal explanations that are not supported by other evidence. Hinton has clearly misunderstood the nature of Chinese religion in the Chinese household and failed to consider the difference between public and private rituals in Chinese society. It should also be noted here that most sociological studies have found that anomie is not an effective indicator of religiosity or religious participation. See for example, Carr and Hauser (1976), Dean (1974), and Photiadis and Johnson (1963).

One of the few large-scale sociological studies of Christianity in Singapore is Tong (1988). Using a random survey of 1025 households living in HDB estates, together with a large number of qualitative interviews, he attempted to document trends in religious conversion and participation in Singapore, and provided an explanation for this phenomenon. In *Religious Conversion and Revivalism: A Study of Christianity in Singapore* (1988), Tong sought to ascertain the extent to which Chinese Singaporeans have switched from their traditional and indigenous religions to other religions, particularly Christianity. Second, he examined whether there was a process of religious revivalism in Singapore, and if there was, what were the factors that accounted for religious revivalism.

The study found that there had been a substantial increase in the number of Christians in Singapore, especially among the Protestants and, to a lesser extent, among the Catholics too. Interestingly, he found that the growth in Christianity happened within a specific socio-demographic sector of the population. These people, younger, better educated, from an English-stream, and with higher socio-economic status, had experienced an attitudinal shift, moving away from traditional Chinese ritual practices which they considered to be "illogical" and "irrational" to a belief system which they perceived to be more "rational". Tong termed this the "intellectualisation" of religion in Singapore (Tong 1997). In this context, conversion to Christianity has to do with some push factors, such as the nature of traditional Chinese religion, and certain pull factors, such as the nature of Christianity and the linkage between religion and the educational system in Singapore society.

The study also found that Christianity in Singapore had undergone a certain degree of religious revivalism. In terms of religious beliefs, faith in the tenets of Christianity was high. In addition, there was a distinct trend in religious commitment relative to age. The younger and newer Christians register the strongest religious commitment.

Quantitative Studies

Following on the discussion of Tong, this section examines the quantitative studies conducted on religion in Singapore. As noted earlier, most publications on religion in Singapore have been ethnographic, carried out primarily by anthropologists. In recent years, we see the growing interest of sociologists in the study of religion in Singapore.

There were earlier attempts at collecting quantitative data. For example, Tamney (n.d.) carried out several surveys administered to undergraduates of the then University of Singapore. But, given the unrepresentativeness of the sample, the usefulness of the findings were limited.

Other quantitative studies included Finnell (1986), Tamney and Hassan (1987). While important, these studies suffer from the fact that in most cases, the samples were too small or flawed and did not allow for statistical generalizations. For instance, Finnell used only 218 returned questionnaires, and Tamney and Hassan had only 15 family case studies. Similarly, Tham (1985) had only 300 respondents (180 Chinese, 80 Malays, and 40 Indians). Tham mentioned that his respondents were chosen at random, but from his description of the sampling procedure, it is more likely a non-probability quota sampling based on considerations like occupation, marital and family status, as well as age. Moreover, because he focuses on the ritual practices of three separate communities, the attention given to any one community is, by necessity limited, and further exacerbates the problem of the small sampling size. For example, his analysis on the Indians was based on a sample of only 40 respondents.

It is clear that for a proper understanding of religious trends in Singapore, more rigorous sampling techniques are needed. Even so,

Tham's work is important because it is one of the few that attempted a comparative analysis of the main religions of Singapore, rather than the study of a single community or religion.

The first extensive set of data available for the whole population was the 1980 Census of the Population. Prior to 1980, the only other censuses which reported data on religion were those collected in 1921 and 1931. These censuses provided statistics on the religion of the Chinese and Indians only, since all Malays are assumed to be Muslim. Also, those who did not claim adherence to any religion were excluded.

There are, of course, limitations in the use of census data, particularly in relation to the study of religion. For example, censuses only record religious affiliation as claimed by the individual and there is no way to verify the accuracy of this claim. Hence, the data does not allow an in-depth look into religiosity or religious practices. Moreover, the 1980 Census collected data on only one variable, religious affiliation. Even so, the Census provided the first comprehensive view of the religious affiliation of the whole population and a wealth of information when cross-tabulated with other socio-demographic variables (see Kuo 1987). It will also serve as a benchmark for future studies on religion in Singapore.

By the mid 1980s, it was clear that the data from the 1980 census needed updating, given the significant religious changes and the rise of fundamentalism and revivalism among some religions in Singapore. Two major surveys were conducted. Kuo and Quah (1988) covered a random sample of 1,015 persons aged 15 and above while Tong (1988) used a three-staged stratified random sample of 1025 households living in HDB Estates. Kuo and Quah's survey was very extensive, covering, not just religious affiliation and participation, but included several scales to measure: faith, anomie, and alienation.

Religion and Social Change

In the study of religion in Singapore, there have been two major areas of concern: the adaptation of indigenous practices to main canonical traditions, such as Christianity, Buddhism, and Hinduism, and the changing patterns of religious affiliations and conversion. This is understandable as Singapore society has undergone, and continues to undergo, rapid social changes. Particularly in the last 25 years, there have been immense transformations in the socio-cultural, political and economic milieu in Singapore society. These have necessitated adaptations and modifications in religion. Thus, one of the areas where there have been several studies is whether, because of modernization, westernization, and industrialization, we are witnessing the secularization of religion. Theoretically, secularization, a concept developed to characterize western society, suggests that as society modernizes, sectors of society are increasingly removed from the domination of religious institutions and symbols, given the rise of empiricist thinking and the differentiation of roles and functions within society (see for example Wilson 1969, Martin 1978). How applicable is the secularization hypothesis to "Asian" belief systems, such as Buddhism, Islam, Hinduism, or traditional Chinese religions?

The literature on this issue offers different conclusions. Chen (1976, 23, 24), for instance, suggested that the rapid modernization of Singapore's technological and institutional systems, as well as rapid economic growth in the sixties and seventies, have led to the introduction of new values, some compatible, others in conflict, with traditional values. Among the values identified by Chen as contentious were solidarity (traditional) versus mobility (new), mutual aid versus materialism and individualism, and the declining emphasis on traditional values, such as filial piety. Tham (1985, 17) argued that changes in the economic and institutional systems, including the institutionalization of the English language and the development of an open, capitalist economy have provided greater impetus to the adoption of western "traditions" and values at the expense of local language, cultures, and moral/ethical values. This has resulted in greater individuation and privatization of ritual practices of the various religions and the selective retention of rituals centred on the individual rather than the group. While religion may still be relevant, its role has changed from one of strengthening the group to one of helping the individual. It is interesting to note that these arguments are new. In fact, as early as the 1950s and 60s Topley and Elliot already suggested that religious beliefs and practices were on the decline. (Topley 1956, Elliot 1951).

More recent studies, however, have suggested otherwise. One of the most consistent critics of the secularization hypothesis in Singapore is Clammer, who claimed that religious sentiments in Singapore is experiencing a revival rather than decline (1991). (For a theoretical debate of secularization and Asian religion, see Clammer 1991, 109-20). Similarly, Tong, Ho and Lin, (1989) found that in present-day Singapore, the practice of traditional Chinese rituals remains essentially high. For example, over 98.9% of Chinese Singaporeans reported that they participate in Chinese New Year rituals; over 70% prefers to follow Chinese religion, and over 90% claim that they burn joss sticks and offer food when performing rituals at home. It would be difficult to argue that there has been a serious erosion of traditional religious practices among the Chinese in Singapore. However, it is also obvious, as the data suggest, that there have been changes in the beliefs and rituals. Many rituals have undergone a process of simplification and adaptation to make them more applicable to life in modern society. There is also a general reduction in the length of time required for the performance of traditional rituals (Tong 1987). Similarly, for Hinduism Babb (1976), Cooper (1979), and Sinha (1997), also confirmed that the extent of practice of traditional rituals remains essentially high and did not show signs of decline.

Conclusion

This paper has reviewed over one hundred and fifty years of literature on the study of religion in Singapore. While there have been many significant contributions, it is clear that there are still major gaps that require further work. In the study of Chinese religion, for example, most studies have focused on specific rituals or festivals. The relationship between folk and canonical religions remains unanswered. While Buddhism is the largest religion on Singapore, it remains, other than a few articles, fundamentally understudied. In fact, a systematic and comprehensive study of Chinese religion in Singapore, its history, rituals, ideology, adaptation and relationship with large Chinese society, is still waiting to be written.

Christianity is better documented by virtue of the fact that the early followers were of the educated Anglophone community who kept records of their activities. Even so, there are still many gaps. Early studies were primarily on church histories, with minimal sociological analysis. This did not really develop until the 1970s and 80s. While there have been several large scale studies of religion and religious change, one that analyses the nature of Christianity in Singapore is still waiting to be written. This is especially important in order to understand the reasons for the popularity and rapid growth of Christianity in Singapore. How do we account for the massive conversion to Christianity? Clearly, there must have been adaptations and modifications in the rituals and especially, the belief systems to attract non-believers. For example, unlike in the West, baptism as a mark of conversion or reaffirmation of belief is not widely practised in Singapore. I believe this has something to do with the attitude of Chinese parents who may be willing to allow their children to practise Christianity, but see baptism as a denial of family and ethnicity. This is just one example of local adaptive strategy in a world religion.

The review has also noted the dearth of material on Islam and Hinduism in Singapore. In Islam, studies have tended to focus on areas like kinship, marriage and law; a book focusing on Islam is needed. In addition, the changing social features of Islam in Singapore should be addressed. Like Chinese religion, studies on Hinduism in Singapore have tended to focus on specific rituals and sectarian groups, rather than a comprehensive overview.

Singapore, with its multi-religious population and features of religious change provides a fascinating laboratory for the sociological analysis of religion. While there have been many empirical studies, not much have been done in terms of theorizing. Three areas will yield especially fruitful results. First, as discussed, Singapore society has been radically transformed in the last 25 years. These socioeconomic and structural changes have had a significant impact on the religious landscape, for example in the religious composition of Singaporeans. It has also resulted in modifications and adaptations in both beliefs and rituals of the adherents. There has been an abbreviation and privatization of rituals. Tong (1989) argues that there is a process of "intellectualization" of religion, where religions that are primarily oral in tradition, such as folk Taoism, attempts to create a canonical context in order to raise its social status. Similarly, he observed a process of, in a Weberian sense, a rational attempt at demystification of religious ideology, stripping away what is perceived to be superstitions and folk beliefs to achieve a "true" religion. These observations must be further developed for it has important theoretical implications and should be sensitive to the fact that theorising on the relationship between modernity, social change and religion is based on western society. There is a necessity to develop an Asian perspective, as the process of modernization and the nature of Asian religions, such as Chinese religion and Hinduism, are quite different from the West.

In Singapore, the state is present in most areas of everyday life. It attempts to manage, through social engineering, every aspect of social life, whether it be encouraging population growth, getting graduate women to marry, or keeping Singapore clean. This presence extends to religion, including the institutionalization of religious education in schools, the enactment of the Religious Harmony Bill, and the setting up of the Presidential Council on Religious Harmony. While there have been a few studies in this area (see Tamney 1992, Kuah 1991), it is largely unexplored. Further research and analyses, using Singapore as a case study, will yield interesting insights and new ways of conceptualizing the relationship between religion and the state.

The study of religion in Singapore has yielded a pool of sociological knowledge. Much, however, remains to be done. There is a need for long-term and integrated data collection and comparative studies. Undoubtedly, there are many exciting possibilities that await scholars and students in the study of religion in Singapore.

References

Abdul Rahman Mohamed Said (1976) "Tarekats in Singapore: an Ethnographic Study", Academic Exercise, Singapore: Dept. of Sociology, University of Singapore.

Abu Bakar bin Hashim (1985) *Shariah and Social Order: The Singapore Experience*, Shariah Law Journal, Kuala Lumpur: International Islamic University, November.

Addison, J. T. (1925) *Chinese Ancestor Worship: A Study of its Meaning and its Relations with Christianity*, London: The Church Literature Committee and S. P. C. K.

Ahmad bin Mohamed Ibrahim (1965) *The Legal Status of the Muslims in Singapore*, Singapore: Malayan Law Journal.

Alatas, Hussein Syed (1977) *The Myth of the Lazy Native: A Study of the Image of the Malays, Filipinos and Javanese from the 16th to the 20th Century and its Function in the Ideology of Colonial Capitalism*, London: F. Cass.

Alwi bin Sheikh Alhady (1962) *Malay Customs and Traditions*, Singapore: Eastern University Press.

Babb, L. A. (1974) "Hindu Mediumship in Singapore", *Southeast Asian Journal of Social Science*, 2(1-2): 29-43.

Babb, L. A. (1975a) "Walking on Flowers in Singapore-Hindu Festival Cycle", *Ekistics*, 39(234): 332-38.

Babb, L. A. (1975b) "Thaipusam in Singapore: Religious Individualism in a Hierarchical Culture", Sociology Working Paper No. 49, Dept. of Sociology, University of Singapore.

Babb, L. A. (1976) "Pattern of Hinduism", R. Hassan (ed) *Singapore Society in Transition*, Kuala Lumpur: Oxford University Press.

Baines, H. W. (1960) "The Church in Singapore and Malaya, 1949-1960", *East West Review*, 26: 113-21.

Bartley, W. (1933) "Population of Singapore in 1819", *Journal of the Malayan Branch of the Royal Asiatic Society*, XI: 177.

Bedington, S. S. (1974) *The Singapore Malay Community: the Politics of State Integration*, Ithaca NY: Cornell University, Southeast Asia Programme.

Bell, H. F. (1968) *Religion Through the Ages: An Anthology*, New York: Greenwood Press.

Betts, R. F. (1975) *The False Dawn: European Imperialism in the Nineteenth Century*, Minneapolis: University of Minnesota Press.

Bloom, D. (1986) "The English Language and Singapore: A Critical Survey", in B.K. Kapur (ed) *Singapore Studies: Critical Surveys of the Humanities and Social Sciences*, Singapore: Singapore University Press.

Blagden, C. O. (1900) "Notes on Folklore and Popular Region of the Malays (Preface)", in W.W. Skeat, *Malay Magic: Being an Introduction to the Folklore and Popular Religion of the Malay Peninsula*, London: Macmillan.

Buckley, C. B. (1902) *An Anecdotal History of Old Times in Singapore*, Singapore: Fraser and Neave Ltd. All page references are to the 1984 edition published in Singapore by Oxford University Press.

Carr, L. and Hauser, W. (1976) "Anomie and Religiosity", *Journal for the Scientific Study of Religion*, 13 (4): 105-16.

Chatfield, G. A. (1962) *The Religions and Festivals of Singapore*, Singapore: D. Moore for Eastern Universities Press.

Chen P. (1976) "Asian Values in a Modernising Society: A Sociological Perspective", in R. Hassan (ed) *Singapore Society in Transition*, Kuala Lumpur: Oxford University Press.

Chessman, H. A. R. (1947) "The Presbyterian Church in Malay", *British Malaya*, October, 276-77.

Choong, K. C. (1983) "Chinese Divination", in J.R. Clammer (ed) *Studies in Chinese Folk Religion in Singapore and Malaysia*, Contributions of Southeast Asian Ethnography, No. 2.

Chu, C. C. (1950) "Notes on Tien Fei", *The Hokkien Sea Goddess*, 6(11) Part 1.

Clammer, J. (1978a) *The Social Structure of Religion: A Sociological Study of Christianity in Singapore*, Dept. of Sociology, University of Singapore, Institute for the Study of Religion and Society in Singapore and Malaysia.

Clammer, J. (1978b) *Islam and Capitalism in Southeast Asia*, Sociology Working Paper No. 63, Dept. of Sociology, National University of Singapore.

Clammer, J. (1983) *Studies in Chinese Folk Religion in Singapore and Malaysia*, Contributions to Southeast Asian Ethnography, No. 2.

Clammer, J. (1987) *Studies in Chinese Folk Religion in Singapore and Malaysia*, Bijdragen tot de Taal-, Land-en Volkenkunde, 143 (4).

Clammer, J. (1988) "Singapore's Buddhists Chant a Modern Mantra", *Far Eastern Economic Review*, 29: 26-27.

Clammer, J. (1991) *The Sociology of Singapore Religion: Studies in Christianity and Chinese Culture*, Singapore: Chopmen Publishers.

Clammer, J. (1993) "Religious Pluralism and Chinese Beliefs in Singapore", in H.T. Cheu (ed) *Chinese Beliefs and Practices in Southeast Asia*, Malaysia: Pelanduk Publications.

Comber, L. (1954) *Chinese Ancestor Worship in Malaya*, Singapore: Donald Moore.

Comber, L. (1955) *Chinese Magic and Superstition in Malaya and Singapore*, Singapore: Donald Moore.

Comber, L. (1958) *Chinese Temples in Singapore*, Singapore: Eastern University Press.

Cooper, R. G. and Kumar, R.R. (1979) "Anti-structure and Ethnic Identity Change: An Evaluation of Changing Emphases in Indian Hindu Calendrical Ceremonies in Singapore", *Journal of Sociology and Psychology*, 2.

Dean, D. G. (1974) "Anomie, Powerlessness, and Religious Participation", *Journal for the Scientific Study of Religion*, 13(4): 497-502.

DeGroot, J. J. M. (1892-1910) *The Religious System of China*, London: E.J. Brill, 6 Vols.

Djamour, J. (1959) *Malay Kinship and Marriage in Singapore*, London: The Athlone Press, University of London.

Djamour, J. (1966) *The Muslim Matrimonial Court of Singapore*, New York: The Athlone Press.

Doolittle, J. (1865) *Social Life of the Chinese*, London: Sampson Low and Marston.

Doraisamy, T. R. (ed) (1985) *Forever Beginning: One Hundred Years of Methodism in Singapore*, Singapore: The Methodist Church in Singapore.

Doraisamy, T. R. (1982) *The March of Methodism in Singapore and Malaysia, 1885-1980*, Singapore: Methodist Book Room.

Elliot, A. J. A. (1955) *Chinese Spirit-medium Cults in Singapore,* London: Royal Anthropological Institute.

Elliot, A. J. A. (1951) "The Significance of Religion among the Overseas Chinese", *Annual of the China Society of Singapore*, pp. 28-32.

Evans, I. H. N. (1927) *Papers on the Ethnology and Archaeology of Malay Peninsular,* Cambridge: Cambridge University Press.

Farah, C. E. (1994) *Islam: Beliefs and Observances*, New York: Barron's.

Finnell, D. ((1986) *Evangelism in Singapore: A Research Analysis among Baptists*, Singapore: Singapore Baptist Book Store.

Frazer, J. G. (1890) *The Golden Bough*, London: MacMillan.

Freedman, M. (1965) *Lineage Organisation in Southeastern China*, London: Athlone Press.

Freedman, M. (1966) *Chinese Lineage and Society: Fukien and Kwangtung*, London: Athlone Press.

Freedman, M. (1967a) *Social Organisation*, London: F. Cass.

Freedman, M. (1967b) *Rites and Duties, or, Chinese Marriage: An Inaugural Lecture*, London: London School of Economics and Political Science.

Freedman, M. (1970) *Family and Kinship in Chinese Society*, Stanford: Stanford University Press.

Freedman, M. (1979) *The Study of Chinese Society,* Stanford: Stanford University Press.

Freedman, M. and Topley, M. (1961) "Religion and Social Realignment among the Chinese in Singapore", *Journal of Asian Studies*, 21: 3-23.

Gamba, C. (1966) "Chinese Associations in Singapore", *Journal of the Malayan Branch of the Royal Asiatic Society*, 39: 123-68.

Geertz, C. (1973) *The Interpretation of Culture*, New York: Basic Books.

Greer, R. M. (1959) *A History of the Presbyterian Church in Singapore*, Compiled for the Church centenary, 26 October 1956, Singapore: Malaya Publishing House.

Han, W. T. (1940) *Research on Tuapekong*, 1(2) Part 2.

Harcus, Rev. Dr. Drummond (1955) *History of the Presbyterian Church in Malaya* (27th Annual Lecture of the Presbyterian Historical Society in England) The Presbyterian Historical Society of England, London.

Hassan, R. (1970) "The Religious Factor in Inter-ethnic Marriage in Singapore", *Sedar,* (Journal of University of Singapore Muslim Society) pp. 47-52.

Heinze, R. I. (1979a) "Social Implications of the Relationships between Mediums, Entourage, and Clients in Singapore Today", *Southeast Asian Journal of Social Science*, 7 (1-2): 60-80.

Heinze, R. I. (1979b) "Mediumship in Singapore Today", *Journal of Sociology and Psychology,* Vol. 2.

Heinze, R. I. (1981) "The Nine Imperial Gods in Singapore", *Asian Folklore Studies*, 40: 151-71.

Heinze, R. I. (1983) "Automatic Writing in Singapore", in J.R. Clammer (ed) *Studies in Chinese Folk Religion in Singapore and Malaysia*, Contributions to Southeast Asian Ethnography, No. 2.

Hinton, K. (1982) *Twelve Churches Study*, unpublished manuscript.

Hinton, K. (1985) *Growing Churches Singapore Style: Ministry in an Urban Context*, Singapore: Overseas Missionary Fellowship.

Hooker, M. B. (1983) *Islam in Southeast Asia*, Leiden: E.J Brill.

Hooker, M. B. (1984) *Islamic Law in Southeast Asia*, Singapore: Oxford University Press.

Ju, S.H. (1983) "Chinese Spirit Mediums in Singapore: An Ethnographic Survey", in J.R. Clammer (ed) *Studies in Chinese Folk Religion in Singapore and Malaysia*, Contributions of Southeast Asian Ethnography, No. 2.

Ke, Z. Y. (1984) "What was it Crawford saw on Fort Canning?", *Heritage*, 6, Singapore: National Museum.

Khoo, C. K. (1981) *Census of Population, 1980*, Singapore; *Release No. 9: Religion and Fertility*, Singapore: Dept. of Statistics.

Kirsch, A. T. (1976) "Theravada Buddhism in Southeast Asia", *Journal of Asian Studies*, Vol XXXV.

Kuah, K. E.(1991) "State and Religion: Buddhism and Nation-Building in Singapore", *Pacific Viewpoint*, 32(1).

Kuo, E. C. Y. (1987) *Religion in Singapore: An Analysis of the 1980 Census Data*, Singapore: Ministry of Community Development.

Kuo, E. C. Y., and Quah, J. (1988) *Religion in Singapore: Report of a National Survey*, Singapore: Ministry of Community Development.

Kuo, E. C. Y., Quah, J. and Tong, C. K. (1988) *Religion and Religious Revivalism in Singapore*, Singapore: Ministry of Community Development.

Kuo, E. C. Y. and Tong, C. K. (1995) *Religion in Singapore*, Singapore: SNP Publishers.

Lau, K. E. (1994) *Singapore Census of Population, 1990, Release No 69: Religion, Childcare and Leisure Activities*, Singapore: Dept. of Statistics.

Lee C. Y., Chan, A. K. L., and Tsu, T. Y. H. (1994) *Taoism: Outlines of a Chinese Religious Tradition*, Singapore: Taoist Federation.

Lee, F. G. (1963) *The Catholic Church in Malaya*, Singapore: D. Moore for Eastern University Press.

Leo, J. B. and Clammer, J. (1983) "Confucianism as Folk Religion in Singapore: A Note", in J.R. Clammer (ed) *Studies in Chinese Folk Religion in Singapore and Malaysia*, Contributions to Southeast Asian Ethnography, No. 2.

Lewis, (1931) "Timithi: Firewalking Ceremony", *National Geographic*.

Li, T. (1986) *Cultural and Economic Change in the Singaporean – Malay Community*, Cambridge: University of Cambridge.

Ling, T. O. (1987) *Buddhism, Confucianism and the Secular State in Singapore*, Singapore: Dept. of Sociology, National University of Singapore, Working Paper No. 79.

Loh, K. A. (1963) *Fifty Years of the Anglican Church in Singapore Island, 1909-1959*, Singapore: Singapore University, Dept. of History.

Ma'arof Salleh (1977) "Aspects of Dakwah in Singapore", *Sedar '75-'77*, (Journal of the University of Singapore Muslim Society), pp.18-25.

Mahajani, U. (1960) *The Role of the Indian Minorities in Burma and Malaysia*, Bombay: Vora.

Manokara, S. (1979) *Growth and Decay: A Study of Change in the Hindu Temples in Singapore*, Academic Exercise, Singapore: Dept. of Sociology, University of Singapore.

Mansor Haji Sukaimi (1983) *Dynamic Functions of Mosques: the Singapore Experience*, Singapore: MUIS.

Marriott, H. (1911) *Census Report of the Straits Settlements 1911*, Singapore.

Martin, D. (1978) *The Dilemmas of Contemporary Religion*, Oxford: B. Blackwell.

Mathes, J. (1982) "Religious Change and the Modernization Process: the Case of Singapore", *Southeast Asian Journal of Social Science*, 10 (2).

Melati Haji Salleh (1979) *Mosques in Singapore*, Academic Exercise, Singapore: University of Singapore, School of Architecture.

Mialeret, J. P. (1969) *Hinduism in Singapore: A Guide to the Hindu Temples of Singapore*, Singapore: Asia Pacific Press.

Milner, A. C. (1983) *Kerajaan: Malay Political Culture on the Eve of Colonial Rule*, Tucson, Arizona: published for the Association of Asian Studies by the University of Arizona Press.

Muhammed Zain bin Mahmood (1959) *A Study of Keramat Worship* (with special reference on Singapore), Academic Exercise, Singapore: University of Malaya.

Mutalib, Hussin (1996) "Islamic Education in Singapore: Present Trends and Challenges for the Future", *Journal of Muslim Minority Affairs,* 16(2).

Nathan, J. E. (1922) *The Census of British Malaya 1921*, London: Dunstable & Watford.

Ng, S. H. C. (1983) "The Sam Poh Neo Neo Keramat: A Study of a Baba Chinese Temple", in J.R. Clammer (ed) *Studies in Chinese Folk Religion in Singapore and Malaysia*, Contributions to Southeast Asian Ethnography, No. 2.

Nyce, R. (1971) "Chinese Folk Religion in Malaysia and Singapore", *The Southeast Asian Journal of Theology,* 12 (Spring): 81-91.

Peacock, J. L. (1978) *Muslim Puritans: Reformist Psychology in Southeast Asian Islam*, Berkeley: University of California Press.

Photiadis, J. and Johnson, A. (1963) "Orthodoxy, Church Participation, and Authorianism", *American Journal of Sociology*, 69: 224-48.

PuruShotam, N. (1985) "Navarathri: The Celebration of a Hindu Festive in the Sri Dandayuthapani Temple, Singapore, 1973", *Heritage*, 7: 1-20.

Raj, K. R. (1978/79) *Public and Private Rituals: An Interpretation of India Ceremonies in Singapore*, Academic Exercise, Singapore: Dept. of Sociology, University of Singapore.

Rajah, A. (1976) *The Ecological Study of Shrines*, B.Soc.Sci. Hons., Academic Exercise, Dept. of Sociology, University of Singapore.

Rawski, E. (1988) *Death Ritual in Late Imperial and Modern China*, Berkeley: University of California Press.

Robertson, R. (1970) *The Sociological Interpretation of Religion*, Oxford: Blackwell.

Roff, W. R. (1964) "The Malay-Muslim World of Singapore in the Late 19th Century", *Journal of Asian Studies*, 24(1): 75-90.

Sakai, T. (1981) "Some Aspects of Chinese Religious Practices and Customs in Singapore and Malaysia", *Journal of Southeast Asian Studies*, 12(1): 133-41.

Sandhu, K. S. (1969) *Indians in Malaya: Some Aspects of their Immigration and Settlement*, London: Cambridge University Press.

Shan, V. L. T. (1995) "Specializing in Death: The Case of the Chinese in Singapore", *Southeast Asian Journal of Social Science*, 23 (2).

Skeat, W. W. (1990) *Malay Magic: Being an Introduction to the Folklore and Popular Religion of the Malay Peninsula*, London: Macmillan.

Siddique, S. (1986) "The Administration of Islam in Singapore", in Taufik Abdullah and Sharon Siddique (eds) *Islam and Society in Southeast Asia*, Singapore: Institute of Southeast Asian Studies.

Sinha, V. (1987/88) *Hinduism in Singapore: A Sociological and Ethnographic Perspective*, unpublished M.Soc.Sci., Singapore: Dept. of Sociology, National University of Singapore.

Sinha, V. (1989) "Locating Religious Specialists in Singapore's Hindu Nexuses", *Contributions to Southeast Asian Ethnography*, No. 8, pp. 87-110.

Sinha, V. (1997) "Unpacking the Label 'Hindu' and 'Hinduism' in Singapore", *Southeast Asian Journal of Social Science*, 25(2): 139-60.

Sng, B. E. K. (1993) *In His Good Time: The Story of the Church in Singapore, 1819-1992*, 2nd edition, Singapore: Graduate's Christian Fellowship.

Sng, B. E. K. and You, P.S. (1982) *Religious Trends in Singapore with Special Reference to Christianity*, Singapore: Graduates' Christian Fellowship and Fellowship of Evangelical Students.

Song, O. S. (1967) *One Hundred Years of the Chinese in Singapore*, Singapore: University of Malaya Press.

Tambiah, S. J. (1992) *Buddhism Betrayed?: Religion, Politics and Violence in Sri Lanka*, Chicago: University of Chicago Press.

Tamney, J. B. (1970) "Islam and Community", *Sedar*, 2: 17-26.

Tamney, J. B. (1973) "The Scarcity of Identity: the Relation between Religious Identity and National Identity", in H.D. Evers (ed) *Modernization in Southeast Asia*, Kuala Lumpur: Oxford University Press .

Tamney, J. B. (1988) "Religion and the State in Singapore", *Journal of Church and State*, 30(1): 109-28.

Tamney, J. B. (1992) "Conservative Government and Support for the Religious Institution in Singapore: An Uneasy Alliance", *Sociological Analysis*, 53(2).

Tamney, J. B. (n.d.) "An Analysis of the Decline of Allegiance of Chinese Religions: A Comparison of University Students and their Parents", in R. Hassan and J.B. Tamney (eds) *Analysis of An Asian Society*, unpublished.

Tamney, J. B and Hassan, R. (1987) *Religious Switching in Singapore: A Study of Religious Mobility*, Singapore: Select Books Pte Ltd for the Flinders University of South Australia, Asian Studies Discipline.

Tan, C. B. (1985) *The Development and Distinction of Dejiao Associations in Malaysia and Singapore: A Study on a Chinese Religious Organization*, Singapore: Institute of Southeast Asian Studies.

Tan, K. C. (1979/80) *Church Architecture in Singapore since 1950*, unpublished Academic Exercise, Singapore: School of Architecture, University of Singapore.

Tan, R. (1961/62) *The Cultural Landscape of Singapore: A Study of the Growth and Distribution of the Religious Institutions on the Island (1819-1961)*, unpublished Academic Exercise, Singapore: Dept. of Geography, University of Malaya.

Teixeira, M. (1961-63) *The Portuguese Missions in Malacca and Singapore (1511-1958)*, Lisbon: Agencia Geraldo-Ultramar, 3 Vols.

Tham, S. C. (1985) *Religion and Modernization: A Study of Changing Rituals among Singapore's Chinese, Malays and Indians*, Singapore: Graham Brash.

Tong, C. K. (1987) *Dangerous Blood, Refined Souls: Death Rituals among the Chinese in Singapore*, Cornell University: Ph.D. Dissertation.

Tong, C. K. (1988) *Trends in Traditional Chinese Religion in Singapore*, Singapore: Ministry of Community Development.

Tong, C. K. (1989a) *Religious Conversion and Revivalism: A Study of Christianity in Singapore*, Singapore: Ministry of Community Development.

Tong, C. K. (1989b) *Child Diviners [dangki]: Religious Knowledge and Power among the Chinese in Singapore*, Contributions to Southeast Asian Ethnography, No. 8.

Tong, C. K. (1997) "The Rationalization of Religion in Singapore", in J. H. Ong, C. K. Tong and E. S. Tan (eds) *Understanding Singapore Society*, Singapore: Times Academic Press.

Tong, C. K., Ho, K. C. and Lin, T. K. (1989) *Chinese Customs and Rites in Singapore: a Report of the Survey*, Singapore: Federation of Chinese Clan Associations.

Topley, M. (1951) "Some Occasional Rites Performed by the Singapore Cantonese", *Journal of the Malayan Branch of the Royal Asiatic Society*, XXIV, Pt. III: 120-44.

Topley, M. (1954a) "Chinese Rites for the Repose of the Soul", *Journal of the Malayan Branch of the Royal Asiatic Society*, XXXVII, Pt. 1.

Topley, M. (1954b) "Chinese Women's Vegetarian Houses in Singapore", *Journal of the Malayan Branch of the Royal Asiatic Society*, Pt 1 (May): 57-67.

Topley, M. (1955) "Ghost Marriages among the Singapore Chinese", *Man*, LV: 29-30.

Topley, M. (1956) "Chinese Religion and Religious Institutions in Singapore", *Journal of the Malayan Branch of the Royal Asiatic Society*, 29 (1): 70-118.

Topley, M. (1961) "The Emergence and Social Function of Chinese Religious Associations in Singapore", *Comparative Studies in Society and History*, III, 289-314.

Tu, W. M. (1984) *Confucian Ethics Today: the Singapore Challenge*, Singapore: Curriculum Development Institute of Singapore, Federal Publications.

Turnbull, C.M. (1989) *A History of Singapore 1819 – 1988*, Singapore: Oxford University Press.

Tylor, E. B. (1929) *Primitive Culture*, London: John Murray.

Vlieland, C. A. (1932) *British Malaya: A Report on the 1931 Census and Certain Problems of Vital Statistics*, London: Crown Agents for the Colonies.

Walker, A. (ed) (1994) *New Place, Old Ways: Essays on Indian Society and Culture in Modern Singapore*, Academic Exercise, Dept. of Sociology, National University of Singapore.

Wee, V. (1977) *Religion and Ritual among the Chinese of Singapore: An Ethnographic Study*, M.Soc.Sci Thesis, University of Singapore: Dept. of Sociology.

Wee, V. (1976) "Buddhism in Singapore", in R. Hassan (ed) *Singapore Society in Transition*, Kuala Lumpur: Oxford University Press.

Weyland, P. (1990) "International Muslim Networks and Islam in Singapore", *Sojourn*, 5(2): 219-54.

Wilson, B. R. (1969) *Religion in Secular Society*, Harmondsworth: Penguin.

Yip, P. L. (1958) *The Taai Paak Kung Chinese Temple*, Singapore: A study of the Social and Economic position of a Chinese Temple in Singapore; whence its funds are derived; how it is administrated; what functions it performs for the community, University of Malaya, Dept. of Social Studies, Academic Exercise.

Young, R.F. (1990) *Pavilioned in Splendour: Interregional and Intersectarian Dynamics in a Singapore Planchette Society*, Contribution to Southeast Asian Ethnography, No. 9.

14

Crime and Deviance

Narayanan Ganapathy

...Academic debate has both an interior and exterior history. The interior history is the interchange between scholars buttressed by the material strength of departmental hierarchies and the underpinning of publishing outlets, together with access to external funding. But however autonomous this academic debate is considered to be by many of its participants, the interior dialogue is propelled by the exterior world. The dominant ideas of a period, whether establishment or radical; the social problems of a particular society; the government in power and the political possibilities existing in a society – all shape the interior discourse of the academic. Nowhere is this more evident than in criminology and the sociology of law. Exterior problems of crime, of law-making, of political options and current ideas, all profoundly shape the theories emanating from the interior world of academic criminology and legal scholarship... (Young 1994, 71).

In Singapore, criminological research undertaken in the Sociology Department of the National University of Singapore (NUS), and contained in journal articles, consultancy works commissioned by the Ministry of Home Affairs, and other publications, has clustered around three main areas. These relatively distinct areas consist largely of research done on **Chinese secret societies** (Wynne 1941, Comber 1959, Buckley 1965, Blythe, 1969, Mak 1973, 1981, Trocki 1990, Long and Chiew 1981, Chiew, 1983, Narayanan 1994), **drug**

abuse (Hanam 1973, 1976, Wan and Yong, 1973, Ong 1975a, Lee 1973, Lee 1977, Teo 1989, Ong 1989, Mak 1990, Yahya 1991) and **crime prevention** (Ong 1976, Mak 1987, Pakiam and Lim 1983, Quah and Quah 1987, Austin 1989, Ong 1989, Quah 1994). The re-emergence of the problem of the secret societies after the Second World War (Narayanan 1994), and an increase in drug abuse and criminal activities among the youth in the 1970s due to a perceived influence of a decadent Western culture (Goh 1979) are identifiable factors which have directed research interests to these areas.[1]

It is equally important to recognize that specific theories emanating from such research and from the interior world of academic criminology and sociology of deviance were also influenced by the kind of exterior history indicated by Young (1994). None of this is to suggest a relativism of theory but rather it is to point to its reflexivity, to the reality that theory emerges out of certain social and political conditions, and that each theory maintains a certain understanding of the criminal or the crime event. Thus the sociology of deviance and criminology are not one coherent discipline but a collection of independent, albeit conflicting versions of sociology in general and theories of crime in particular (Downes and Rock 1995). From the early

1. During the Japanese Occupation 1942-45, all secret societies went underground because of persecution by the Japanese authorities. They returned full force after liberation. The Banishment Ordinance and the Societies Ordinance which previously empowered the British authorities to suppress the secret societies were largely ineffective. A record number of initiation rites were known to be held. The British then decided to use the Emergency Regulations, which were used to suppress Communist insurrections, against the secret societies. In the drug scene, there was an increasingly disturbing trend from 1974 onwards. The number of drug addicts rose from 2203 in 1970 to 7725 in 1977 (Ong 1989). The age pattern of addicts also changed. Of the 1,865 arrested addicts in 1970, over 80% were more than 40 years old (*The Straits Times* 27 March 1971) and majority were opium addicts. But of those below 30 years of age the percentage rose rapidly from about 20% of total drug population in 1971 to about 89.4% in 1977. Influences from the West such as hippie culture were blamed for the rising number of young addicts from all social classes (*The Straits Times* 6 April 1972, 29 October 1972, 25 June 1973).

criminologies of Beccaria and Lombroso, and later Durkheimian sociology and structural functionalism, through social control theory, labelling theory, New Criminology, to the re-emergence of new and idealistic forms of neo-classicism — the new Administrative Criminology — we find an unceasing competition between two equally abstract images of the criminal and hence of humanity: on the one hand the moral actor, freely choosing crime, and on the other the automaton, the person who has lost control and is beset by forces within or external to him or her (Young 1994, 67).[2]

It is against such a backdrop that this chapter attempts to highlight and understand some of the basic approaches and theoretical perspectives that have come to characterize much of the work done in the field of criminology and sociology of deviance in Singapore. I also hope to convey something of the excitement associated with the development of various theories, methodologies and concepts, using selected relevant Singapore examples and research findings.

Distinguishing Sociology of Deviance from Criminology

So far, the distinction between sociology of deviance and criminology has not been made and they have been treated as two separate academic enterprises each specializing in a core area; the former being concerned with deviance and the latter solely with crime. Deviance is the term we use to identify categories of acts or persons, which violate the social norms or rules of a particular social group or of society at large. The concept of deviance may not only be applied to aspects of bizarre and

---

2.   These two images of the criminal have influenced the criminologist to assume partiality. This may involve taking the criminal at one point of time (maybe at the point of arrest) and denying past circumstances; or taking into account his previous convictions and ignoring the criminal's present crime and circumstances; or exemplifying the macrostructure of society as in the formulation and operations of the criminal justice system and pay less attention to the criminal as an individual moral being. See Young, J. (1994) *Incessant Chatter: Recent Paradigms in Criminology* p. 70.

unusual behaviour as in the study of "nuts, sluts and perverts" (Liazos 1972) but may encompass any violation of the social rule, however, minor it may be. The concept of social rule refers to expected and desirable patterns of conduct or behaviour, and such normative behaviour is generally understood to include both proscriptive and prescriptive elements (Gidlow 1982). Usually, variations in normative expectations are linked to variations in social "positions" or social "roles" (Cohen 1966, 12).

At the outset it must be noted that the recognition of deviance is inherently political, because it depends on the power of some groups or some members of a particular group, or institution in society to maintain the definition of deviance over less powerful groups or members who are so defined. Deviance situations seem to arise when (and to the extent that) people who are in a position to impose their judgements find other people's behaviour in one way or another "unsettling" (Suchar 1978, 1). Schur recognizes that deviance is an inherently political issue since by definition it involves modes of disvaluing and discrediting, and emphasises that the designation and deviantizing of individuals involves the exercise and subsequent distribution of power (1980, 25-26). As such, at both the individual and collective levels, all deviance situations must centre on the distribution of power. As Schur (1980, 7) states: "... Power, of any sort, is more like a process than an object. From that standpoint, it tends to operate as both cause and effect. Deviance outcomes (individual or collective) thus both reflect and determine configurations of power." Indeed, in a sense it is only by observing their success   which we then attribute to the exercise of pre-existing power — that we can determine who the powerful really are. The process of social labelling, therefore, points to one of the most vexatious questions in sociology, that is, to what extent social rules are "shared" by all members of a society, especially when the societies in question are composed of diverse class and ethnic cultures.

Crime, on the other hand, refers to that form of rule breaking which is recognised by the State, defined by the criminal law and legal statutes, and processed by judicial institutions. It is a feature of crime that appropriate punishments are exacted upon the offender(s) by the State. Some acts which are widely regarded as deviant may also be criminal acts — burglary and rape for instance

— while other acts which may be widely defined as deviant are not currently in many societies defined as criminal. A good example would be adultery. Thus as a broad generalization we can say that all crime is deviant, but not all deviance is crime: or in other words, that crime is a subset of deviance.

Sociology of deviance, therefore, has been distinguished from criminology in three general aspects.[3] First, criminology has been mainly concerned with the infraction of the criminal law and legal norms, while research into deviance has looked at a broad range of socially unacceptable departures from "normality" which may include sexual orientations of a gay community, transvestism and alcohol abuse. Second, there is a tendency for criminologists to concentrate on institutionalised populations — those convicted of offences, prisoners, juveniles in remand homes, and others "inside". Sociology of deviance insists that deviance is "out there", and often in unexpected places. It also opens up the question of other forms of social control besides the law such as family, neighbourhood organizations, government bureaucracies and places of worship, but without formally defining and labelling persons as criminal. Third, in looking for causes of crime, some approaches in criminology have tended to see crime as an objective phenomenon, measured by rates of offending and such statistics as court convictions and police records. The sociology of deviance, by contrast, would argue that at least some forms of deviant behaviour are made visible by the very process of imposing social control on less powerful social groups. Activities which might previously have gone unnoticed or have been regarded as trivial become amplified and take on a more permanent quality when they become the subject of widespread social concern and media attention.

Although there are certain discriminating features distinguishing sociology of deviance from criminology, it can be argued that the overlap between the two fields of study is almost complete if one is to examine the subject matter of the so-called "traditional" or "normative" theories of deviance and "orthodox" criminology (Hirschi 1969, Gidlow 1982). Both tend to focus on

3.   See David Downes and Paul Rock (1995) *Understanding Deviance*, Oxford, Clarendon Press, pp. 17-21.

the motivation of offenders in the commission of crime, principally concentrating on the motivation of juvenile and adult criminal offending. The question of why do they commit crime which had been the defining feature of "strain", subcultural and social control theories also points to an implicit recognition that crime "exists" as an objective phenomenon, a point which was earlier identified to mark the departure of criminology from the sociology of deviance.

Explaining Crime and Deviance Sociologically

Most studies of deviant behaviour in Singapore have been of criminally-deviant behaviour. This emphasis is largely explicable in terms of the tight hold which the "traditional" theories of deviance and orthodox criminology — theories of deviant motivation – had on shaping the development of theoretical perspectives in academic research as well as in consultancy works submitted to the Ministry of Home Affairs. The defining feature of most criminological studies in Singapore, therefore, tended to concentrate on rule violation (normative theories) rather than on rule application (labelling perspective) or rule formation (New Criminology). In this section, I intend to examine work done in the respective areas of study and also highlight significant theoretical developments in the international scene that are relevant to the local research.

Normative Theories

Of the theories in the normative tradition, social control theory assumes a distinct prominence in the local literature on crime and deviance. Perhaps a notable reason for this is the political elite's overwhelmingly Hobbesian view of its citizens — that human beings by "nature" are both asocial and anti-social — which provides the fundamental justification for the need to strengthen formal laws and to "widen the net".[4] Social control theory attempts to make conformity rather than deviance problematic. It differs from the

---

4.   This Hobbesian view of the citizens has been the baseline for justifying the legislative powers of the Internal Security Act and the Criminal Law

other two theories in the normative tradition, strain and culture-conflict, in this aspect. Control theory posits that the task of theory is not to explain deviance but to account for conformity on the understanding that human beings are basically asocial and selfish. This gives rise to the notion of social contract in social control theory which can be traced back through Durkheim to Hobbes and to Aristotle: "It is in the nature of men not to be satisfied... The fact is that the greatest crimes are caused by excess and not by necessity" (Aristotle, *Politics*, quoted in McDonald 1976). Similarly, Durkheim wrote in *Suicide*: "it is not human nature which can assign the variable limits necessary to our needs. They are thus unlimited so far as they depend on the individual alone. Irrespective of any external regulatory force, our capacity for feeling is in itself an insatiable and bottomless abyss" (Durkheim 1952, 247). Arising from Durkheim's assertion then is the central question of not why do they commit crime but why do we not commit crime. Hirschi, a major proponent of control theory, writes: "According to control or bond theories a person is free to commit delinquent acts because his [sic] ties to the conventional order have somehow been broken" (1969, 3), and elements of the conventional order or social bond are attachment, commitment, involvement and belief.

A central feature of social control theory is the relative importance it gives to the family as a causative factor in delinquency. "The family is considered to be the single factor most important in exercising social control over the adolescent" (Nye 1964, 19). One of the most celebrated pieces of empirical research, using longitudinal designs, which indicated the important influence of early family socialization and family circumstances

(Temporary Provisions) Act of 1955, Chapter 67 (1985 ed) which allow the police to detain a person without trial for a maximum of two years. Typically, the possibility of another September 1964 race riot that killed 13 and injured more than 100, the 1969 race riots, and the "Marxist conspiracy" of May 1987, were frequently cited to justify the importance and relevance of these laws, albeit their draconian powers. The achievement of a "no-riot" situation in modern Singapore or "inactive procommunist movements" has been attributed to these laws — implying that Singaporeans are prone to deviate if there are no such laws.

is provided by the *Cambridge Study of Delinquent Development* (West 1982). A central aspect of its findings relates to the identification of five clusters of items which have some statistical relationship to subsequent delinquency. They are: coming from a low income family; coming from large sized family; having parents considered by social workers to have performed their child rearing practices unsatisfactorily; having below average intelligence; and having a parent with a criminal record (West 1982, West and Farrington 1973, 1977).

Incidentally social policies on the family in Singapore have been designed to restrict the size of the working class family in particular, for example, by way of providing a cash grant for women who agreed to undergo sterilization, and the condition that parents must agree to have no more than two children before they qualify for assistance under the Small Families Improvement Scheme (Hill and Lian 1995, 153-4). In fact, the introduction of the Small Families Improvement Scheme was the result of a concern expressed by Prime Minister Goh in 1993 that most dropouts from the educational system — about 1.7% of the total cohort (*The Straits Times* 16 August 1993) — are from large families, living in a one- or two-room Housing and Development Board (HDB) flat, and having parents who had not attended secondary school (Hill and Lian 1995, 153). Limiting the size of the working class family also reflects a greater concern on the part of the Singapore State that as mediator of moral values between the State and the family, it is the middle-class or bourgeois family rather than the working class family that will play a more effective role (Berger and Berger 1983, 189 quoted in Hill and Lian 1995, 157).

Empirical research and theoretical debate on crime and deviance in Singapore, therefore, has relied extensively on social control theory. Not only because of its common sense appeal and greater explanatory power, but more so of its alignment with the political and social persuasion of the State in emphasizing macro-sociological (formal control systems) and more importantly, micro-sociological (informal control systems) factors, particularly the family being a source of moral values (Hill and Lian 1995, 156), in promoting conformity in society. "The family has been called upon to preserve the traditional cultural values and bear the responsibility for socializing the children in the virtues of the 'rugged society'" (Kuo and Wong 1979, 11). Clearly, the State wants to ensure the preservation of the family unit whose role is clearly defined in the White Paper on *Shared Values* (1991, 3): The family is seen as the 'fundamental building block out of which larger social structures can be stably constructed'. Abdullah Tarmugi, Minister of Community Development and Minister-in-charge of Muslim Affairs outlined the importance of maintaining the family as a source of inculcating good moral values in children (1995, 99):

> Our families' strength and cohesiveness draw much from the traditional values that the various communities in Singapore hold and cherish. These values served us well over the past decades. We are therefore mindful that our traditional values and institutions should not be eroded by external influences and lifestyles which diminish the importance of the traditional family and encourage nonchalance towards sexual morality.

Alternative lifestyles largely defined in western cultural terms, deficiency in "Asian" values in the homes, inadequate socialization, ineffective child rearing practices, lack of parental supervision of children at home, absence of good role models in the family, casual sexual relationships and single parenthood are all seen to undermine the stability and structure of the "traditional" family unit which is in turn perceived to be the cause of delinquency. These factors relate to what Harriet Wilson calls aspects of "chaperonage" — relating to "strict" rather than "permissive" standards of morality (Wilson 1980, Wilson and Herbert 1978, 176).

As early as in 1958, Benjamin Williams in his investigation into the profile of a *Habitual Offender* found that the single most important factor contributing to a present recidivist re-offending was the quality of relationships which an offender experienced in the home before committing crime and after serving a sentence. These findings that the family as an important control variable in the explanation of juvenile and adult criminal offending were also evident in a range of ' other research: *Social Aspects of Drug Abuse Amongst Young People* (Vasoo 1973), *The Drug Scene in Singapore* (Hanam 1973), *Profiles of Delinquents in Singapore* (Ngien 1977), *Vandals and Vandalism in*

Singapore (Fatt 1978), *A Study on the Psychosocial Characteristics of Male Inhalant Abusers in Singapore* (Teo 1989), *Crimes Against Property in Singapore* (Wong 1985) and *Academic Achievement, School Adjustment and Delinquency Process* (Miao and Kong 1971). It is interesting to note that the first few studies on female delinquency, Woon's *Drug Abuse Among Female Addicts* (1976), Cheow's *Delinquent Girl in Singapore* (1959) and Kwa's and PuruShotam's (1974) *Female Delinquency in the Light of the Quality of the Adolescent's Home Background* had similarly used social control variables in explaining the etiology of female crime. For example, Kwa and PuruShotam used variables like size of the family, controls in the home, parent-child relationship, and level of disorganization in the family (ie a broken home) to establish a causal relationship between these variables and delinquency production, and came to a conclusion that "more non-delinquents than delinquents came from homes characterized by a quality of family life that is better" (1974, 67-8).

There is an extension of the idea of the family being a "cause" of female delinquency by later feminist criminologists elsewhere as well (Heidensohn 1987, Carlen and Worrall 1987). But they have provided a gendered analysis of the "problem" by locating its source in the role of informal social control within the family network and the social processes generating and amplifying deviance among female delinquents, leading to a much higher risk of institutionalization by the predominantly male moral entrepreneurs (Smart 1977, 1990, Heidensohn 1987). "There is a sexually stratified inverse relationship between structurally differentiated processes of social control such that women are more frequently the instruments and objects of informal social controls" (Hagan, Simpson and Gillis 1979).

The appeal of social control theory in Singapore does not only lie in its explanatory and predictive model of delinquency (Jupp 1989, 44) but in the way it lends itself to the technology of crime control and prevention within the tradition of *Right Realism* and *Administrative Criminology*[5]. In the right realist criminology, the work of James Q Wilson, the author of best selling book *Thinking*

---

5. For a detailed discussion on the two paradigms, see Young, J. (1994) *Incessant Chatter: Recent Paradigms in Criminology*, pp. 91-102.

about Crime (1975) is clearly evident. Wilson has developed an influential position on the relationship between policing and crime. He argues that policing is effective not through a direct effect on the control of crime, but rather in facilitating the maintenance of social order. Furthermore, if disorderly behaviour, for example, that of public drunkenness or rowdy youth, is not controlled the neighbourhood enters a spiral of decline in which law-abiding citizens emigrate from the area, informal social controls weaken, and crime itself begins to rise. Police involvement in 'order maintenance' facilitates, in the long run, the process of crime control.

Wilson thus sees informal social control as the most powerful form of social control, and the police role is, so as to speak, to jump-start the informal social control system in areas where it has broken down. Police presence facilitates the growth of informal neighbourhood controls on crime by giving the area a general sense of security. A significant statement, which Wilson makes, is that the interest of order overrides those of justice — it is better to remove a recidivist from society proportionally to his/her criminal record than to judge them according to his/her last crime. This is one of the guiding principles of sentencing in Singapore (see Chief Justice's comments: *The Straits Times* 11 March 1997).[6]

The literature on crime control and crime prevention in Singapore clearly highlights the role played by the informal social control system in the overall crime prevention strategy. In his discussion on community security, Ong (1989) demonstrates that even historically during the period of colonial rule, the British had in fact used a device which essentially made the community

---

6.   In *Public Prosecutor V. Mohamed Jais Bin Arsal* (DAC 2399 of 1995 and DAC 2116 of 1995 {Mag. App. 71/95/01}), the District Judge sentenced the accused to seven years of preventive detention for committing theft of cash of $15, one box of cigarette valued at $5 and some personal documents, a total value of $20. The usual sentence for a case of simple theft of $20 by a first offender is only a caution being administered by the police but since the accused in this case had a list of previous convictions mainly for theft, he was committed to seven years preventive detention. The notion of preventive detention, detention without trial, points to an overriding interest of order over justice.

responsible for a large part of its own security. They achieved this through the appointment or recognition of community headmen who were often linked to the Triad societies. A vivid illustration of this is the technique adopted by the Governor in the 1860s to quell rioting among the Chinese secret societies:

> The only way in which Cavenagh and his colleagues could hold the societies in check when trouble broke out was to swear in their leaders as special constables and parade them up and down in order, as Cavenagh says with a nice irony, 'to entice them to take a warm personal interest in the preservation of the peace' (Freedman 1960, 31).

The Chinese community, to a large extent, had its own institutions and organizations for facilitating social control, and the connection with Triad societies provided much of the manpower and muscle power to exercise the function of social control. Not only the British depended on these internal communal controls to bolster their own limited policing resources but "within the early Singaporean Chinese community these tightly knit networks of individuals, each fulfilling obligations to and having expectations of the other, defined the meaning of community security" (Ong 1989, 940).

Austin (1989) argues that although the lifestyle in early kampongs lacked modern physical comfort and proper hygiene, extended families were able to live in close proximity. Neighbourhoods were held tightly together by bonds of dialect, nationality, race, and religion, all ties which provided substantial mutual support. More importantly, they engendered a sense of community identity, mutual assistance among neighbours, and local community security (Hassan 1976, 249-68, Chen and Tai 1977, 65-73). Disputes were dealt with at the kampong and neighbourhood levels with less reliance on formal law and government intervention. Austin (1989) and Ong (1984) point out that there was a breakdown of neighbourhood cohesion and support patterns associated with the earlier kampongs because of the relocation of the population to high-rise HDB flats. This had led, according to them, to the increase in Singapore's overall crime rate between mid-1970 and 1980.

Thus, the origins of community policing with an emphasis on a service-oriented policing style and on rejuvenating the community, saw the establishment of Neighbourhood Police Post system in 1983 (Quah and Quah 1987); the Neighbourhood Watch scheme in 1981 and later the Neighbourhood Watch Zone in 1997 (*The Sunday Times* 27 April 1997); Crime Prevention Committees involving the residential, commercial and industrial sectors (Quah 1994); Police Boy's Clubs; and the network of Residents' Committees as a link between the Neighbourhood Police Post system and the Prime Minister's Office (Austin 1989, 920). These developments point to the importance and recognition of the joint-partnership between the formal and informal social control systems in preventing crime. That Singapore today is a prototype of an orderly society is evident in light of its comparatively much lower crime rates than those found in many other societies (Austin 1989, Buendia 1989, Ong 1989, Quah 1994).

An interesting observation, which can be made from the local literature on crime prevention, is the shift of focus from identifying the social causes of crime to an emphasis on situational determinants of crime. Within Administrative Criminology the concept of situational crime prevention and rational choice theory side step the etiological crisis by suggesting that the causes of crime are either relatively unimportant or politically impossible to tackle (Young 1994, 91). The question becomes that of the most cost-effective way of securing control intervention, with an emphasis on the purely technical, cost-benefit ratio aspects of crime: the opportunities for crime available in the environment, and the risks attached to criminal activity (Downes and Rock 1995, 253). They are not just based on a mechanistic manipulation of the environment but on the concept of the offender making rational choices. For Administrative Criminology, the flaw of all previous criminology is seen as being pervaded by a "dispositional bias" (Clarke 1980, 136): a search for causes which dispose people to commit crime, whether these be social factors, as in positivism, or administrative labels, as in labelling theory (Young 1994, 93). This "dispositional" bias of earlier theories tends to negate the fact that most crimes are opportunistic. The immediate stress of Administrative Criminology, by contrast, is the notion that the occurrence of a crime event can be prevented by structural barriers:

for example, steering locks in cars, better locks and bolts in houses, better lighting, greater surveillance from, for example, Neighbourhood Watch schemes, a Neighbourhood Police Post system, beat policing and mobile police patrols. It emphasizes the actual spatial nature of crime, in terms of both opportunities and surveillance. Administrative Criminology at this juncture coalesces with the two main concerns of Environmental Criminology: first, explaining the spatial distribution of offences and second, explaining the spatial distribution of offenders (Bottoms 1994, 586-7). Bottoms argues that crime and criminality are highly geographically skewed, and an understanding of this uneven distribution in terms of time and space is of crucial importance both to the explanation of crimes as well as to the social production of offenders (1994, 586).[7]

In his article on *Crime Prevention: Singapore Style* Quah (1994) outlines the importance of this situational approach. The philosophy of the Singapore Police Force (SPF) towards crime prevention is victim-oriented in that "if the risk of apprehension is increased by hardening the site and thus limiting the opportunity, then criminal desire will be lessened" (Ong 1984, 13), and therefore, it is concerned with the "anticipation, recognition and appraisal of crime risk, and the

7. "Environmental Criminology" provides a generic description of the relationship between place, crime, and offending. Brantingham and Brantingham (1988, 7) define Environmental Criminology as such: "A crime is a complex event. A crime occurs when four things are in concurrence: a law, an offender, a target, and a place. Without a law there is no crime. Without an offender, someone who breaks the law, there is no crime. Without some object, target, or victim, there is no crime. Without a place in time and space where the other three come together, there is no crime. These four elements – law, the offender, the target, and the place-can be characterized as the four dimensions of crime. Environmental criminology is the study of the fourth dimension of crime". Also see Bottoms, Anthony and Wiles, Paul (19%) "Explanations of Crime and Place" in Muncie John, McLaughlin Eugene and Langan Mary (eds) *Criminological Perspectives: A Reader*, London, Sage Publications, for detailed discussion on the theoretical relevance of Anthony Gidden's (1984) "theory of structuration" for environmental criminology.

initiation of action to remove or reduce those risks" (Ong 1984, 13). Residential, commercial and industrial, youth, and "removable property" are the four functional areas that have been identified by the SPF for the implementation of the crime prevention programmes (Quah 1994, 157).

The concern with predatory crimes, a major component in the situational crime prevention approach, is manifested in the consultancy work carried out by Ong (1976). His study attempts to construct the patterns of housebreaking, thefts and robberies in HDB estates. It revealed that housebreaking into the first five floor levels accounted for over 60% of incidents in a high-rise block. Mak (1992) formulates the Structure of Timing by incorporating Oscar Newman's (1972)[8] concept of defensible space and the Routine Approach theorists' (Cohen and Felson 1979)[9] components of capable guardianship and suitability of targets to explain the occurrence of a crime event. The importance placed on the situational crime prevention approach is also apparent from a survey report submitted to the Ministry of Home Affairs assessing the public's preventive behaviour towards crime (Chang, Mak and Ong 1982). What situational crime prevention does is to "normalize" both the occurrence and activity of crime: crime is there and always will be. What is needed therefore is a strategy for how best to prevent its occurrence. As the responsibility to prevent crime falls on the victims or potential victims (or on all law-abiding citizens), there is also a tendency to privatize one's own security. "Normalization of crime" leads to a "privatisation of security" (Young 1992, 59). This points to a phenomenon where crime is accepted as a "normal" part of everyday life, the role of the police is restricted to that of solving high-

---

8. Newman, Oscar (1972) *Defensible Space: Crime Prevention Through the Urban Design*, London, Architectural Press. This work is among the most important literature defining the relationship between architectural design and crime.

9. The central hypothesis of routine activities theory is that "the probability that a violation will occur at any specific time and place might be taken as a function of the convergence of likely offenders and suitable targets in the absence of capable guardians" (Cohen and Felson 1979, 589).

profile serious crime and offering crime prevention advice, the relevant authorities (like the HDB and Town Councils) should be responsible for "designing out" crime, and the "active citizen must become a major player in crime control by making his or her home more secure and by becoming involved in Neighbourhood Watch schemes" (*The Straits Times* 13 June 1997 and 23 June 1997).[10]

Subcultural Studies

A few local studies on the phenomenon of gangs and delinquent youth subcultures in Singapore (Mak 1981, Wee 1985, Man 1991, Yahya 1991, Noordin 1992) have conceptualized their analysis within a subcultural and "strain" theoretical framework. Mak for example, has provided two excellent ethnographic studies on secret societies in Malaya and Singapore. The first, *The Forgotten and Rejected Community — A Sociological Study of Chinese Secret Societies in Singapore and Western Malaysia* (1973), is an unpublished working paper. It contained some first-hand experience of the researcher with secret society members, and described the significance of initiation ceremonies and rite practices in imparting the value system to newly initiated members within the parameter of a criminal subculture. In a related work, *Sociology of Secret Societies — A Study of Chinese Secret Societies in*

---

10.   Some of the publications of the Crime Prevention Office of the Public Affairs Department, SPF, reveal an increasing trend towards stressing the importance of a situational crime prevention approach. Title of publications like "Break-in: How to Prevent it", "Save Your Motorcycle", "Don't Get Robbed", "Snatch Theft - Prevent it Before It Happens to You" and "Crime Prevention — Do You Know How to Prevent It" essentially emphasize victim-responsibility. These are some preventive measures suggested by the police when "walking" — avoid carrying a large amount of cash; avoid wearing excessive jewellery; avoid taking short cuts through backlanes or other lonely place; use crowded places; carry a shrill or police whistle with you and use it to deter the robber or to attract the attention of passer-by should anyone attempt to rob or hurt you; and don't accept car rides from strangers. In other words, crime prevention activity becomes an integral part of routine activity in response to the 'normalisation' process that crime is itself a normal part of that activity.

Singapore and Peninsula Malaysia (1981), Mak had incorporated Merton's (1938) typology of classifying anomic deviant solutions and Cloward and Ohlin's (1961) concept of illegitimate opportunity structures to understand the phenomenon of gang recruitment, membership and activities.

Subcultural theories were also used to understand the formation of drug subcultures and youth subcultures like the "Mat Rockers" (Noordin 1992). Using a "sequential-model" (Becker 1963) and theoretical sampling (Glaser and Strauss 1967), Yahya (1991) detailed the social processes of how Malay youths became drug abusers, and identified some of the motives and rationalizations (similar to Sutherland's theory of differential association)[11], and Syke's and Matza's techniques of neutralization[12] that were commonly used by the participants to sustain their drug activities. An important contribution of the study was the recognition of how otherwise positive cultural features of the Malay community — the emphasis on a closely knit familial network and in-group solidarity — act as catalysts in the formation of a delinquent drug subculture since the essential group structure needed for the formation of a drug subculture has already been laid. Also the in-group solidarity tends to facilitate the learning process of becoming a member of a deviant subculture, for example, learning to smoke from the self-made pipe, to use the syringe, or even in achieving the desired level of being "high". Similar findings indicating the role of culture in the formation of a delinquent subculture were also evident in Murphy's (1963) study in which he investigated the problem of juvenile delinquency in the Chinese, Malay and Indian communities in Singapore.

An interesting feature of these subcultural studies, with the exception of Mak's study on secret societies, were the attempts of the researchers to locate the origin of deviance within the family — an apparent reliance on the anchor point of social control theory. Although research on "Marina Kids", Malay Drug

---

11. See Sutherland, E. (1947) *Principles of Criminology*, 4th edition, Philadelphia: Lippincott.
12. See Sykes, G. and Matza, D. (1957), "Techniques of Neutralization: A Theory of Delinquency", *American Sociological Review*, 22: 664-70.

subculture and "Mat Rockers" contained some very rich and interesting details on the phenomenon of delinquent subcultures, these studies have tended to turn to the family and informal social network for individualised explanations as to why members join subcultures. Factors like poor parenting skills, poor parent-child relationships, lack of supervision over the children, an inadequate or negative socialisation process, and transmission of an incompatible value and moral system to that of mainstream society were frequently cited in the studies as possible causes. The origin of deviance is once again rooted within the common sense explanations of social control theory.

Clearly, Cohen's (1955) study of lower-class delinquent subcultures contained elements of social control within the family and neighbourhood as determining the production of subcultures. But any subcultural study must also recognize that the crucial condition for the emergence of new subcultural forms is the existence, "in effective interaction with one another, of a number of actors with similar problems of adjustment" (Cohen 1955, 59). Subcultures are about "lived realities" (Young 1979), and are concerned with the material and non-material problems which particular groups of people experience in terms of the major social axes of age, class, gender, and race, and spatially within their locality (Young 1994). It is these structural parameters which give rise to subcultures. Subcultures are problem-solving devices which constantly arise as people in specific groups attempt to solve **structural** problems they face. Crime and deviance are forms of subcultural adaptations which occur where material circumstances block cultural aspirations and where non-criminal alternatives are absent or less attractive (Young 1994). In contrast to social control theory which offers an individualized explanation of delinquency and its almost positivistic portrayal of the association between the quality of the family environment and delinquency (Cohen 1981), subcultural theories on the other hand attempt to understand how subcultures are expressions of structural circumstances. Subcultures highlight the reality of the human predicament in the construction of choices but in determinate circumstances.

Labelling Perspective

A few local studies, particularly Academic Exercises (Honours theses) in NUS, using the labelling perspective have been largely responsible for loosening the criminological focus of the sociology of deviance by initiating a movement away from an obsession with criminal offending towards recognition that criminal and deviant behaviours are not synonymous (Gidlow 1982). A large number of behaviours, for example, breaches of social etiquette and sexual "deviance", and social statuses like that of a prostitute are commonly regarded as "deviant" but are not legally sanctioned (Bottomley 1979). Following Becker (1963), labelling theorists argue that rule breaking and deviance are not synonymous and that "deviance" is a "label" applied by an audience to real or imputed acts of rule breaking. They are concerned with how conforming members of society play a dominant role (especially seen from a political stance) in establishing and enforcing rules to which members are expected to conform, and in imputing deviant characters to those who violate these rules. As Kitsuse points out, "The critical feature of the deviant-defining process is not the behaviour of individuals who are defined as deviant; but rather the interpretations others make of their behaviours, whatever those behaviours may be" (1962, 255).

The process of societal reaction to a real or imputed act of rule-breaking, be that reaction of an interpersonal or collective, informal or formal kind, has an important influence on the formation of a deviant character or identity. To labelling theorists, the study of social processes (Rock 1973, 18) by which social rules are applied and deviant statuses are conferred are of greater sociological interest than the explanation of rule-breaking *per se.*

Some of the excellent works on the local scene — *A Sociological Study of Transvestism in Singapore* (Tan 1979), *Stigmatisation, Self-image and Secrecy in the Gay Community* (Leong 1982), *Prostitution and Stigmatisation: Perspectives on Deviance* (Chan 1987), *Lesbianism in Singapore* (Low 1993), *Recognising Strangers: Gay Cruising in the City* (Low 1995) — have clearly demonstrated the role of social processes in contributing to the formation and maintenance of a "deviant" identity or "deviant" career. Leong (1982), for example, using the "qualitative sociologies" of phenomenology and symbolic interactionism in his study of male homosexuals, has illustrated how stigmatization of the homosexuals by the "straight community" leads to a construction of the male homosexual identity and role, and how this conception of the self helps the male homosexual to preserve his identity within the gay community. Similarly, Low (1993) revealed how women come to construct and maintain their lesbian activities through interaction and participation in various social setting, especially in romantic and sexual ones. The lesbian identity is seen as a fluid aspect of an individual's life which is being shaped and re-shaped according to respective social situations.

Thus far, it will be seen that labelling theory offers a caution against the methodological excesses of traditional sociological theories of deviance, particularly against the assumption that the facts of rule-breaking are contained in information about those who have been ascribed a criminal label (Gidlow 1982, 338). Besides its methodological caution, labelling theory offers a theoretical justification for adopting a sceptical attitude towards traditional theories of deviance by taking on the debunking — says who? — motif of sociology (Berger 1966, 51), and implicitly or explicitly recognizing how conforming members and social control agents in actual fact manufacture and amplify deviance (Young 1971). A local study on the "Breakdancers" points to this phenomenon, showing how the police who were given the task of controlling the problem of breakdancers in the Orchard Road area, in fact amplified the problem to an extent where even other conforming citizens wanted to become breakdancers solely because of the attention the breakdancers received from the social control agents, ie the police (Wee 1985).

Therefore, it could be suggested that although labelling theory has loosened the criminological obsession of the traditional theories of sociology of deviance, it has not completely lost interest in the operations of the criminal justice system, recognizing that the experience of formal sanctioning, criminal prosecution and conviction is an important step in the attribution of a criminally deviant character. Using Lemert's conception of "primary" and "secondary" deviation, a few local studies — *Recidivism among Drug Addicts in Singapore* (Chua 1980), *Recidivism among Drug Users* (Lee 1977), *Adjustment of Ex- prisoners* (Ong 1986) — have examined how the criminal's experience of societal reaction, of stigmatization, punishment, segregation and social control (Lemert 1972, 225) have a definite causal significance in forming a criminal life-style and identity. As Ong (1986, 66) puts it:

> stigma is expressed firstly in the way the ex-prisoner feels about himself and the society in general. He views himself negatively, develops a low self-image, shuns away from the world, feels that the society is against him. Stigmatization is also expressed in the way the society discriminates against him. Discrimination by the society can take the form of total ostracism and rejection, avoidance, unkind treatment like sarcasm, humiliation, mockery, criticism and suspicion.

The criminal status becomes a master status overriding all other statuses in determining how others respond to the criminal and a significant feature of the deviantizing process in our culture is that it is almost irreversible. Official processing of an individual from the status of a suspect (at the time of arrest), through the criminal trial after being charged with the particular offence, upon conviction, and eventually upon release after serving sentence, depicts dramatically the processed individual's abrupt and substantial change in status. Garfinkel (1956) refers to these processes as "status degradation ceremonies".

Here, there is an interesting link between social control theory and labelling theory. The relationship between them is much more defined in cultures which rely heavily on punishment, exclusion and stigma for social control (Braithwaite 1989, 18); Singapore society being a good example. This is to say that the emphasis and reliance on social control locks the criminal into an indelible role, and impedes effective reintegration (Braithwaite 1989). There is a substantial body of evidence to support this fairly straightforward prediction, the most persuasive of all is provided by the *Cambridge Longitudinal Study of Delinquency Development* (West and Farrington 1977, 162). West and Farrington discovered that boys who were apprehended for and convicted of delinquent offences became more delinquent than boys who were equally delinquent to begin with but who escaped apprehension. The Cambridge Study perhaps amounts to the most convincing empirical support for radical non-intervention, for the notion that juveniles who are "helped" by the juvenile justice system turned out worse. The result is that these studies fostered a sense of justifiable cynicism, especially in the 1960s and 1970s, about a variety of rehabilitative and punitive measures which amounted to net-widening without any reason for believing that crime itself would be reduced. A wholesome liberal tolerance of diversity was encouraged; the community learned of the dangers of overreacting to deviance that might be transient if left alone (Braithwaite 1989, 20).

Despite the sociological excitement which is associated with the labelling perspective, the application of labelling theory in Singapore has rested largely on impressionistic, circumstantial and anecdotal evidence. Besides the few studies mentioned above, there is no evidence of a longitudinal study being carried out in Singapore to assess, for example, the effect of formal processing by the criminal justice system on delinquents and ex-convicted adults. A reason why labelling theory did not assume prominence in Singapore could be due to the fact that it does not in any way lend itself to the technology of crime control and crime prevention, a chief priority of the government (Quah 1994). Although an understanding of the implications of negative labelling would help curb recidivism amongst ex-prisoners and those who have been officially processed by the criminal justice system, it is unlikely that the custodians of the criminal justice system would want to acknowledge the cynicism and suspicion which the labelling perspective fosters in relation to the role and function of the formal social control agents. Comparatively, the appeal of social control vis-à-vis other criminological theories can be easily comprehended and appreciated.

Another reason could be due to the fact that the labelling perspective has fostered a debilitating nihilism that gave no advice about the limits of tolerating diversity (or deviance) in the first place. Braithwaite states (1989, 20):

> Would it really be counterproductive to label as criminal a drug manufacturer who bribed a health minister to have a ban lifted on a profitable pharmaceutical, or to label a rapist as criminal? If 'moral panic' over petty juvenile offending was anathema to liberal labelists, was moral apathy over some forms

of sexual abuse of women and white-collar crime equally a cause for celebration? While tolerance of diversity is important for avoiding the excesses of counterproductive cracking down on petty deviance, intolerance of diversity is also critical for crime control. Societies imbued with the ideology of labelling theory will be excessively apathetic about non-trivial crime; to be effective against crime, societies need to be interventionist in a communitarian sense, to be intolerant of crime in a way that is both spiteful and forgiving.

Perhaps the bulk of the criticisms levelled at labelling theory have been advanced by the New Criminologists (Taylor, Walton and Young 1973) whose work I will examine next.

New Criminology

Inspired by the work of Karl Marx, the New Criminologists place the study of crime and deviance within the context of the conflicts and contradictions of capitalist societies. They all mark a shift away from asking behavioural questions — what initially causes an individual to commit a deviant act? — to posing definitional and structural questions — why does an act come to be defined as deviant? Who enforces such definitions and in whose interests? Thus, one of the main limitations of labelling theory, as claimed by the New Criminologists, is that the labelling theorists' concentration on "micro-world" encounters between deviants and bureaucratic functionaries tend to neglect the study of the structural processes by which powerful groups are able to gain the authority to impose definitions of deviance upon others. In other words, the labelling perspective lacks an adequate theory of power (Muncie and Fitzgerald 1981, 420) to explain the relationship between crime, law and the state (Hall and Scraton 1981).

According to the New Criminologists, the criminal law in capitalist society is used to protect and enhance the interests of the bourgeoisie and to punish attempts of the working class to subvert the existing relationship of exploitation (Quinney 1975, 192). Numerous researchers (for example Chambliss 1964, 1984, Duster 1970, Hall 1952, Hall et al. 1978, Hall and Scraton 1981) have produced evidence consistent with the view that criminal law categories are ideological reflections of the interests of particular powerful groups. As such, "criminal law categories are resources, tools, instruments, designed and then used to criminalize, demoralize, incapacitate, fracture and sometimes eliminate those problem positions perceived by the powerful to be potentially or actually threatening the existing distribution of power, wealth, and privilege. They constitute one, and only one way by which social control over subordinate, but 'resisting', populations is exercised" (Box 1983, 7). The velvet glove of the soft, ideological machine of social control contains within it an iron fist of coercion. The various institutions of society, whether primarily ideological (the school and mass media) or coercive (the criminal justice system) are organized into a functioning whole aimed at perpetuating the present social and political order (Young 1994, 82).

Seen from a New Criminology perspective there is nothing inherently "pathological" about deviant or criminal behaviour, for in an inequitable society property crime appears as a normal, rational and conscious attempt to amass property in the absence of alternative means (Taylor, Walton and Young 1975, 34). Deviant behaviour becomes a threat to class rule when it becomes "politicized", when it is used systematically to attack the weak points of capitalist domination, to increase the visibility of capitalist exploitation and to raise working class consciousness.

It is difficult to identify any groups in Singapore which are expressly committed to the use of criminal behaviour to further any political or economic ends. Although some minority street corner gangs have used gang names like "Black Power", "Black Panther", "Chicago Indians", *"Satu Hati"* and *"Makal Power"*[13]

---

13. In a joint paper presented by Narayanan Ganapathy and Superintendent of Police Vendesan Somo, it was revealed that minority gangs use names like *"Satu Hati"* (a Malay word signifying a sense of solidarity and collective strength among Malay youths. This term is also used by some Indian gang members), and *"Makal Power"* (Tamil word meaning "Peoples' Power". The term is used commonly by working class Tamil youths to suggest the strength of one's street corner gang). The study also revealed that most fights occur among members who share similar demographic characteristics, suggesting that the conflict is intra-class than inter-class – as what Jock Young (1994) has termed as the "moral symmetry of offenders and victims".

(Narayanan 1994), the names were basically used to symbolize the solidarity of group strength. There is no evidence to suggest that the gang activities carried a political message, and members interviewed were unaware of the implications and ideology of the names used (Narayanan 1993).

Certainly, systematic studies of deviance in Singapore from a "pure" Marxist standpoint are absent. This could be due to the perception amongst politicians and the wider public that that there are no distinct class differences in Singapore (Noordin 1992) to excite a Marxist analysis. Further there is also a perception among practitioners in the criminal justice system that there is no clear-cut evidence of a possible association between class and crime. Usually, any perceived association tends to be defined in terms of variables of ethnicity and/or race due to the fact that ethnic categorization seems to be more defined and visible in Singapore (Benjamin 1976). However, there seems to be a dearth of research covering this aspect in the study of crime and deviance in Singapore, and research efforts must be directed to this aspect. Furthermore it is also possible for the State to depoliticize any criminal activity of some of these criminal gangs and of property offenders by merely projecting them, via the mass media, as constituting the "crime problem", thus deflecting attention from the wider structural, economic, political and social problems generated by the capitalist mode of production. The State whilst maintaining its legitimacy protects the capitalist mode of production by appearing to take action against the "criminal class" on behalf of all "respectable" citizens. Kelsey's (1980) work on gangs, for example, illustrates how the potential "spread" of dissatisfaction which occurs when a capitalist economy is in crisis is prevented by the "criminalization" of that "dissatisfaction", by presenting it as a "law and order" issue to a frightened and receptive public (1980, 5), and hence concealing the crisis of legitimacy it embodies.

Nevertheless, there are a few studies which contain elements of a class analysis. For example in his article *Crime and Control*, Austin (1989) argues that a conflict-theory approach (Chambliss 1984) may yield some worthwhile insights into the government's use of law and control, and how they tend to "benefit the middle and elite classes and yet be a detriment or misfortune to the lower classes" (1989, 923) especially since the jury system has been discontinued (Clutterbuck

1985). Austin states, "…laws against littering may benefit society, but the street worker, for instance, labouring under the equatorial sun may find it more difficult to avoid tossing a cigarette or spitting than would the white-collar worker in an air-conditioned office" (1989, 924). But such an analysis of the law points to the inherent nature of the processes of law itself — that how impartial the formulation, implementation and enforcement of the law is, the differential impact of the law on various classes or in terms of race, ethnicity and gender remains an inevitable and integral consequence.

Methodologically speaking, one does not have to be necessarily a Marxist in order to appreciate the theoretical conceptualization of the relationship between crime and criminal justice, on the one hand, and the State, social structure and historical transitions on the other (Jupp 1989). Although the major proponents of the theories of crime and deviance before the New Criminologists — strain, subcultural, social control and labelling — have been guilty of being "zookeepers of deviance" (Gouldner 1968) — meaning that their analysis of crime and deviance had been both ahistorical and astructural — these theories, explicitly or implicitly, contain the class/structure input. For example, Merton's anomie of the disadvantaged which is largely concerned with relative deprivation, and Young's anomie of the advantaged, which is often a product of a limitless pursuit of money, status, and power (Young 1979, Taylor 1990) tended to focus on the different types of crime committed by respectively the lower working class and the upper middle class. Cohen's analysis of lower class delinquent subcultures is again clearly a function of the class/structure equation. Similarly, in relation to the social control theory, Wilson writes,

> the essential point of our findings is the very close association of lax parenting methods with severe social handicap… If these factors are ignored, and parental laxness is seen instead as an "attitude" which by education or by punitive measures can be shifted, then our findings are being misinterpreted. It is the position of the most disadvantaged groups in society, and not the individual, which needs improvement in the first place (1980, 233-4).

In such an analysis, a control theory of delinquency is combined with a strong sense of structural context (Downes and Rock 1995, 251) — a baseline of the Marxist analysis of crime and deviance.

In short, the development of criminology and sociology of deviance has not been characterized by theoretical or methodological unity. There have been variations in the degree of emphasis given to positivist explanations in causal terms and in the degree of emphasis given to different units and level of analysis. The latter has seen shifts from a concern with individual crime and criminality to an interest in social groups and social structures within which crime is committed. However, whatever corners that have been turned, criminology and sociology of deviance have developed by interactions between theory and the data generated by methods of investigation (Jupp 1989, 5). On one hand, methods that come to be used in a criminological investigation have implications for the way in which problems are conceptualized and for the type of explanations employed — for example, researchers relying on official statistics would be inclined to believe that crime is largely a problem of lower socioeconomic status groups, the working class, or ethnic minorities (Gidlow 1982). On the other hand, problems and theories of criminology and sociology of deviance have implications for the kinds of methods that come to be used — for example, some of the local research that has been done on homosexuality and prostitution (Leong 1982, Chan 1987) have relied on qualitative methods of observation that allowed a detailed insight into the activities of their subjects, and were unlikely to be captured by quantitative research methods such as surveys. Broadly, it can be argued that different theoretical positions seem to have preferences as to the method employed because of the types of data collected, the level and unit of analysis used and the degree of primacy given to the search for causes (Jupp 1989, 4).

In the following section, an overview of the sources of data that are available to researchers and students in Singapore will be examined, and the relationship between particular theoretical positions and methods is elicited. Particular attention will also be given to address the problem of official statistics on crime since most research on crime in Singapore have extensively, and almost uncritically, relied on official statistics to conceptualise their research problems.

Sources of Data

Crime data for research purposes are normally available from two principal channels: official and non-official (Jupp 1989). Non-official data include those gathered via other methods of data collection, for example social surveys, participant observation or life interviews. Those embarking on these forms of data collection on crime (or deviance) in Singapore are usually Honours students doing research for their Academic Exercises and University staff from the sociology or psychology departments. These forms of data are known as **primary** data. Official data on crime, which is compiled and supplied by the Criminal Investigation Department (CID), represent key sources of **secondary** data. They include data on two aspects of crime and criminal activity. First, statistics are provided on the number of seizable offences[14] **recorded** by the police, and second, statistics are provided on known offenders. The CID, however, has ceased publicising its annual *Statistical Report on Crime in Singapore* since 1986. Information related to crime and criminal justice system may also be obtained from the following list of publications (with the years of publication inserted).

Statistical Report on Crime in Singapore (1973 -1986)
National Crime Prevention Council (1983 - 1999)
Police Life (1976-1999)
Police Life Annual (1977-1999)
Singapore Anti-Narcotics Association (SANA), Annual Report (1974-1999)
Singapore Aftercare Association – Proceedings of the Seminar on Crime and Society (1970)
Singapore Police Journal (1971 - 1979)
Singapore Prison Service Magazine (1948-1999)

14.   Seizable offences refer to those offences for which the police can arrest the offender or any suspect without a police warrant, no bail can be posted on right. It usually includes offences against person and property like murder, rape, outraging of modesty, kidnapping, motor vehicle theft, and robbery.

Problems of Official Statistics

Criminological research in Singapore has, to a large extent, relied on official statistics to provide the empirical data. This is due to the fact that most research on crime has used traditional theories — theories of deviant motivation — to understand the crime problem. Most "traditional" theories of crime were formulated at a time when it was assumed that criminal offending (and by implication forms of deviant behaviour) was largely a problem of lower socioeconomic status groups, the "working class", or ethnic minority groups (Gidlow 1982). The reliance of most local research on "facts" — official statistics — confirms that this was indeed the case. Therefore, it is important to note that the reliance on both "traditional" normative theories and official statistics implicitly suggest that "crime" and a "criminal class" exist as an objective phenomenon which can be measured validly by the collection and analysis of statistics on crime, and of data derived from the arrested (or convicted) population respectively.

It is also interesting to note that consultancy works such as *A Profile of Secret Society Gangsters in Singapore* (Chiew 1983*), A Study on the Profile of Chinese Secret Society Members* (Long and Chiew 1981), A *Profile of the Criminal in Singapore* (Ong 1975b) submitted to the Ministry of Home Affairs seem to suggest that there is a particular "criminal type" — a vague variant of the individualist positivism of Cesare Lombroso. Although it appears that such profiling facilitates the detection and apprehension of "criminals", or potential "criminals", such theorizing about the "criminal" is clearly antithetical to a sociological understanding of crime and deviance as a social and political construct. As Erickson has properly emphasised, "Sociologically... the critical variable is the social audience which eventually decides whether or not any given action or actions will become a visible case of deviation" (1966, 308).[15]

Attempts must be made to deconstruct official statistics to make them suspect. Overseas studies using "self-reporting" (see for example

---

15. The already classic statement by Becker (l963) laid the groundwork for recognising that deviance in fact is "produced" or "constructed" through social processes: "... social groups create deviance by making the rules whose infraction constitutes deviance, and by applying these rules to particular

Clarke and Trifft 1966, Hirschi 1969, McDonald 1969, West and Farrington 1973) and "victim-reporting" techniques (see Hough and Mayhew 1983 on *British Crime Survey*) lend support to an important conclusion that for most categories of offending the numbers of offences officially recorded considerably under-estimate the numbers of offences actually committed. The gap between official recording of crime by the police and the actual incidence of crime at any given time is known as the "dark figure of crime". The "dark figure of crime" includes those offences which are known but not reported to the police especially in cases of sexual offences; offences which are reported but not officially recorded by the police, since a police officer arriving at the scene of crime may apply his/her discretion to administer a caution instead of arresting the offender. Police intervention (or non-intervention) in situations of domestic violence is a good example[16]. The "dark figure" may also refer to those offences not known to the police or public. A recent recognition of this "dark figure" has driven the Singapore Police Force to introduce its new slogan "Low Crime Does Not Mean NO Crime". In the context of such a discussion, Jock Young points to a "square of crime" referring to the understanding between the police and other agencies of social control, the public, the offender, and the victim, and how the relationship between the four corners of the square determine crime rates (Young 1987, 1992). For example, the police and agency response to victims greatly affects the actual impact of victimization and, in certain instances such as rape and sexual assault, can even involve what has been termed "secondary victimization" — where the victim is further stigmatized by the courts. All of this, particularly in terms of willingness to report crime to the police, affects the official crime statistics and the possibilities of clear-up. Similarly, in the case of burglary, close

---

people and labelling them as outsiders. From this point of view, deviance is not a quality of the act the person commits, but rather a consequence of the application by others of rules and sanctions to an 'offender'. The deviant is one to whom that label has successfully been applied; deviant behaviour is behaviour that people so label" (Becker 1963, 9).

16. See Hanmer, J., Radford, J. and Stanko, E. (1989) *Women, Policing and Male Violence*, London: Routledge.

relationship between the offender and certain sections of the public may occur in terms of purchasing stolen goods from the offender within the "hidden" or "black" economy which may greatly succour and encourage criminal activities.

Apart from the technical shortcomings that are integral to the compilation of official statistics, the institutionalist and radical approaches[17] derived from the theoretical critiques of sociological positivism (Jupp 1989) caution against the positivist use of official statistics[18]. The institutionalist approach argues that too much weight is given to official statistics as objective indicators of attributes of society and not sufficient to the way in which crime statistics are socially constructed. The emphasis is upon the crime statistics as the outcome of everyday interactions between deviance (or potential deviance) and law enforcement officers. Statistics are seen as products of the criminal justice system in general, and specifically as indicators of the activities of those who work within it. In this sense, official statistics are not accurate measures of crime upon which to base causal explanations, but representations of individual and institutional policies and practices (Kitsuse and Cicourel 1963, 135) and informal norms of "cop culture" (Holdaway 1983). Rate-producing actions may be the result of formal policy-making edicts — for example, when the Traffic Police department sets up additional road blocks during festive seasons to monitor drink-driving, and the recent inauguration of the Neighbourhood Watch Zone Scheme which may affect public tolerance of offending.

The radical approach drawing its strength from "New Criminology" points to the role of the state and its crime-control operators (including incidentally its crime-research apparatus) in so

17. For a detailed discussion, see Jupp, V. (1989) *Methods of Criminological Investigation*, pp. 92-101.
18. Both the attempts to measure the extent of crime and also to provide explanations of variations in the rates of crime have been influenced by positivism. Durkheim argued for the use of statistics as indices of "social facts". This methodological approach was expressed in *Suicide*. The later Chicago sociologists of the 1920s and 1930s used crime statistics to delineate "natural" areas of crime, and also by those concerned with the epidemiological aspects of crime and criminal activity.

far as the state is viewed as a mere agent of the propertied class (Taylor, Walton and Young 1975, Hall et al. 1978). Within this framework, official data reflect patterns of crime and patterns of criminalization as structurally induced.

Statistics are not viewed as the composite of a wide range of everyday interactions but as the outcome of class relations in society at any given time. It is because official statistics are outcomes of class relations that offences committed by the poor, the unskilled and members of the working class are more likely to come to official attention and to result in successful prosecution. "Crimes of the powerful" (Pearce 1976, Box 1983) are under-represented either because their actions are not criminalized or because they can avoid detection and prosecution (Jupp 1989, 99).

Local studies that have come to rely on official statistics do not critically address the social processes by which official statistics come to be socially constructed, or the implied theoretical and methodological assumptions characterizing the relationship between official statistics and "traditional" theories of deviant motivation. Researchers are too ready to develop and test hypotheses from official data. Research on the nature of differential policing, particularly on the geographical and social distribution of patrolling as manifested in their "stop and search" practices and the structural-situational factors involved in making arrests remain a "black hole" of knowledge which otherwise would allow a critical appreciation of the construction of official statistics. We have yet to build up alternative sources of data against which official statistics might be compared and evaluated.

Conclusion: Future of the Sociology of Deviance and Criminology in Singapore

It will become evident from the above that the sociology of deviance and criminology in Singapore has hitherto been characterized by a narrow theoretical and methodological focus. Much of the research work done on crime and deviance tends to be centred around three distinctive areas: Chinese secret societies, drug abuse, and crime prevention.

Theoretically, with the exception of a few studies using the labelling perspective (eg Leong 1982, Chan 1987, Low 1993, Low

1995), most studies which have so far been conducted fall within the category of "traditional" or "normative" theories of deviance. They attempt to shed light on, and explain, the motivation behind criminally deviant behaviour. In this respect the overlap between the sociology of deviance and criminology is almost complete as the subject matter of both disciplines tend to focus on the motivation of offenders, principally concentrating on the motivation of juvenile and adult criminal offending. Of the normative theories, social control theory assumes a distinct prominence in the research works. As pointed out in the chapter, the attraction of social control theory does not only lie in its common sense appeal and greater explanatory power but more so in its alignment with the political and social persuasion of the State in emphasizing macro-sociological (like the criminal justice system and State bureaucracies) and more importantly, micro-sociological factors (like the family, schools and neighbourhood) in promoting conformity in society. The perceived relevance of social control theory to crime control and prevention is an added feature. The social control explanation is likely to continue to assume a central position in criminological research in view of the claimed increase in teen gang activities and youth crime in Singapore (*The Sunday Times* 16 March 1997 and *The Straits Times* 12 February 1996, 9 July 1996, 17 March 1997). Media reports, social workers and police spokespersons are always too ready to point the accusing figure at the family — lack of quality of family life, lack of parental discipline, inconsistent parenting skills, absence of effective role models — whenever a teenager is involved in any illicit or criminal activities (*The Straits Times* 25 May 1997).

Whatever potential the explanatory power of social control theory has, especially with its focus on the family as cause of delinquency, researchers in crime and deviance must pay equal attention to the importance of other factors impinging on it — of class, race, gender and environment — than treating the family as an independent microcosm. As a consequence of relying on traditional theories of deviance and crime, most, if not all, research on the area have sought to explain "street" blue-collar rather than "suite" white-collar crimes and has thus selectively studied crimes that are disproportionately committed by members of low socio-economic status groups. In doing so, local criminological research has reinforced the traditional biases of criminology and sociology of deviance (Box 1983). Official statistics obtained from the CID and other law enforcement agencies such as the Central Narcotics Bureau (Yahya 1991) confirm that our (official) "crime problem" is often caused by young males with low education, usually holding a low paid or odd job and almost certainly from a lower working class background.

Methodologically too, the narrowness of focus is even more marked with most researchers abdicating the responsibility for developing sociologically appropriate methodologies in favour of using available published data on crime and delinquency. Attempts to develop and test hypotheses from official data too readily overlook the social processes involved in the compilation of the statistics. Researchers also need to develop a facility with methods other than those that stem from the heavily statistical social survey tradition and its implicit positivism. A few of the unpublished academic exercises (cited under the section "Labelling Perspective") have been successful in punctuating the "methodological monotony" by injecting the qualitative sociologies of phenomenology and interactionism. The researcher in crime and deviance at times needs to be a "deviant" him- or herself by stepping out of the traditional theoretical and methodological boundaries to capture and practise the sociological imagination (Mills 1970, 5).

References

Abdullah, Tarmugi (1995) "Singapore's Approach to Social Development", *Speeches,* 19(2): 88-92.

Austin, W. T.(1989) "Crime and Its Control", in K.S. Sandhu and P. Wheatley (eds) *Management of Success,* Singapore: Institute of Southeast Asian Studies.

Becker, H. (1963) *Outsiders: Studies in the Sociology of Deviance,* New York: Free Press.

Benjamin, G. (1976) "The Cultural Logic of Singapore's 'Multiculturalism'", in R. Hassan (ed) *Singapore: A Society in Transition,* Kuala Lumpur: Oxford University Press.

Berger, P. (1966) *Invitation to Sociology*, Harmondsworth: Penguin.

Berger, P. and Berger, B. (1983) *The War Over the Family: Capturing the Middle Ground*, London: Hutchinson.

Blythe, W. (1969) *The Impact of Chinese Secret Societies in Malaya*, London: Oxford University Press.

Bottomley, A. K. (1979) *Criminology in Focus*, Oxford: Martin Robertson.

Bottoms, A. E. (1994) "Environmental Criminology", in M. Maguire, R. Morgan and R. Reiner (eds) *Oxford Handbook of Criminology*, Oxford: Clarendon Press.

Bottoms, A. E. and Wiles, P. (1996) "Explanations of Crime and Place", in J. Muncie, E. McLaughlin and M. Langan (eds) *Criminological Perspectives: A Reader*, London: Sage.

Box, S. (1983) *Power, Crime and Mystification*, London: Tavistock Publications.

Braithwaite, J. (1989) *Crime, Shame and Reintegration*, Cambridge: Cambridge University Press.

Brantingham, P. J. and Brantingham, P. L. (1981) *Environmental Criminology*, Beverley Hills: Sage.

Buckely, C. B. (1965) *An Anecdotal History of Old Times in Singapore 1819-1867*, Kuala Lumpur: Oxford University Press.

Buendia, H. G. (1989) *Urban Crime: Global Trends and Policies*, Tokyo: United Nations.

Carlen, P. and Worrall, A. (1987) *Gender, Crime and Justice*, London: Milton Keynes.

Chambliss, W. J. (1964) "A Sociological Analysis of the Law of Vagrancy", *Social Problems*, 12: 46-67.

Chambliss, W. J. (1978) "The Criminalization of Conduct", in H.L. Ross (ed) *Law and Deviance*, London: Sage.

Chambliss, W. J. (1984) *Criminal Law in Action*, New York: Wiley & Sons.

Chan, J. (1987) *Prostitution and Stigmatisation: Perspectives in Deviance*, Unpublished Academic Exercise, Dept. of Sociology, National University of Singapore.

Chang, C. T., Mak, L. F. and Ong, J. H. (1982) *Crime Prevention Behaviour and Attitudes of the Public in Singapore*, Report submitted to the Singapore Police Force.

Chen, P. S. and Tal, C. L. (1977) *Social Ecology of Singapore*, Singapore: Federal Publications.

Cheow, L. Y. (1959) *The Delinquent Girl in Singapore*, Unpublished Academic Exercise, Dept. of Social Studies, University of Malaya, Singapore.

Chiew, S. K. (1983) "A Profile of Secret Society Gangsters in Singapore", in Proceedings of the Second Asian-Pacific Conference of Juvenile Delinquency, Seoul, Cultural and Social Centre for the Asian and Pacific Region.

Chua, K. T. (1980) *Recidivism Among Drug Addicts in Singapore*, Unpublished Academic Exercise, Dept. of Sociology, University of Singapore.

Clarke, R. (1980) "Situational Crime Prevention: Theory and Practice", *British Journal of Criminology*, 20(2): 136-47.

Clarke, J. P. and Trifft, L. L. (1966) "Polygraph and the Interview Validation of Self-reported Deviant Behaviour", *American Sociological Review*, 31(1): 516-23.

Cloward, R. and Ohlin, L. (1961) *Delinquency and Opportunity: A Theory of Delinquent Gangs*, London: Routledge.

Clutterbuck, R. (1985) *Conflict and Violence in Singapore and Malaysia 1945-1983*, Singapore: Graham Brash.

Cohen, A. (1955) *Delinquent Boys: The Culture of the Gangs*, Chicago: Free Press.

Cohen, A. (1966) *Deviance and Social Control*, New Jersey: Prentice-Hall.

Cohen, S. (1981) "Criminology and the Sociology of Deviance", in M. Fitzgerald, G. McLennan, and J. Pawson (eds) *Crime and Society: Readings in History and Theory*, London: Routledge and Kegan Paul.

Cohen, A. K. and Felson, M. (1979) "Social Change and Crime Rate Trends: A Routine Activity Approach", *American Sociological Review*, 44: 588-608.

Comber, L. (1959) *Chinese Secret Societies in Malaya*, London: Augustin.

Downes, D. and Rock, P. (1995) *Understanding Deviance: A Guide to the Sociology of Crime and Rule-Breaking*, Oxford: Clarendon Press.

Durkheim, E. (1952) *Suicide: A Study in Sociology*, London: Routledge and Kegan Paul.

Duster, T. (1970) *The Legislation of Morality*, New York: Dutton.

Erickson, K. T. (1966) "Notes on the Sociology of Deviance", *Social Problems*, 9: 307-14.

Fatt, Y. T. (1978) *Vandals and Vandalism in Singapore*, Unpublished Academic Exercise, Dept. of Sociology, University of Singapore.

Freedman, M. (1960) "Immigrants and Associations: Chinese in Nineteenth Century Singapore", *Comparative Studies in Society and History*, 3 (1): 25-48.

Garfinkel, H. (1956) "Conditions for Successful Degradation Ceremonies", *American Journal of Sociology*, 61: 420-24.

Giddens, A. (1984) *The Constitution of Society*, Cambridge: Polity.

Gidlow, B. (1982) "Deviance" in P. Spoonley, D. Pearson and S. Ian (eds) *New Zealand: Sociological Perspectives*, Palmerston North: Dunmore Press.

Glaser, B. and Strauss, A. L. (1967) *The Discovery of Grounded Theory*, Chicago: Aldine.

Goh, K. S. [and The Educational Team] (1979) *Report on the Ministry of Education 1978*, Singapore: Government of Singapore.

Gouldner, A. (1968) "The Sociologist as Partisan", *American Sociologist*, 3: 103-16.

Reprinted in Gouldner, A. (1973*) For Sociology. Renewal and Critique in Sociology Today*, London: Allen Lane.

Hagan, J., Simpson, J. and Gillis, A. (1979) "The Sexual Stratification of Social Control: A Gender Based Perspective on Crime and Delinquency", *British Journal of Sociology*, 30: 25-38.

Hall, J. (1952) *Theft, Law and Society*, Indianapolis: Bobbs-Merrill.

Hall, S., Critcher, C., Jefferson, T., Clarke, J. and Roberts, B. (1978) *Policing the Crisis: Mugging the State and Law and Order*, London: Macmillan.

Hall, S. and Scraton, P. (1981) "Law, Class and Control" in M. Fitzgerald, G. McLennan, and J. Pawson (eds) *Crime and Society: Reading in History and Theory*, London: Routledge and Kegan Paul.

Hanmer, J., Radford, J. and Stanko, E. A. (1989) *Women, Policing and Male Violence*, London: Routledge.

Hanam, J. (1973) "The Drug Scene in Singapore", in S.K. Lee and T.C. Choa (eds) *Drug Misuse in Singapore*, Singapore: Singapore Medical Association, pp. 3-6.

Hanam, J. (1976) "Our Problem", in Singapore Anti-Narcotics Association (ed) *Conquer Drug Abuse Now*, Singapore: Singapore Anti-Narcotics Association, pp. 4-6.

Hassan, R. (1976) *Singapore: Society in Transition*, Kuala Lumpur: Oxford University Press.

Heidensohn, F. (1987) "Women and Crime: Questions for Criminology", in P. Carlen and A. Worrall (eds) *Gender, Crime and Justice*, Milton Keynes, England: Open University Press.

Hill, M. and Lian, K.F. (1995) *The Politics of Nation Building and Citizenship in Singapore*, London: Routledge.

Hirschi, T. (1969) *Causes of Delinquency*, Berkeley: University of California Press.

Holdaway, S. (1983) *Inside the British Police*, Oxford: Blackwell.

Hough, M. and Mayhew, P. (1983) *The British Crime Survey: First Report*, Home Office Research Study No. 76, London: HMSO.

Jupp, V. (1989) *Methods of Criminological Research*, London: Routledge.

Kelsey, J. (1980) *Hegemony in Crisis: A Case Study of the Maori Gang Crisis in 1979*, Marxist Political Economy Conference.

Kitsuse, J. (1962) "Societal Reactions to Deviance: Problems of Theory and Method", *Social Problems*, 9: 247-56.

Kitsuse, J. and Cicourel, A. V. (1963) "A Note on the Use of Official Statistics", *Social Problems*, 2: 131-9.

Kuo, E. C. Y. and Wong, A. K. (1979) *The Family in Contemporary Singapore*, Singapore: Singapore University Press.

Kwa, K. H and PuruShotam, S. (1974) *Female Delinquents in the Light of the Quality of the Adolescents Home Background: A Comparison Between Delinquents and Non-Delinquents*, Unpublished Academic Exercise, Dept. of Sociology, University of Singapore.

Lee, S. H. (1973) *Some Aspects of Student Drug Abuse*, Unpublished Academic Exercise, Dept. of Sociology, University of Singapore.

Lee, S. W. (1977) *Recidivism Among Drug Users: A Case Study*, Unpublished Academic Exercise, Dept. of Sociology, National University of Singapore.

Lemert, E. M. (1972) *Human Deviance, Social Problems and Social Control*, New Jersey: Prentice-Hall.

Leong, W. T. (1982) *Stigmatisation, Self-image and Secrecy in the Gay Community*, Unpublished Academic Exercise, Dept. of Sociology, National University of Singapore.

Liazos, A. (1972) "The Poverty of the Sociology of Deviance: Nuts, Sluts and Preverts", *Social Problems*, 20(1): 102-20.

Long, F. Y. and Chiew, S. K. (1981) *A Study on the Profile of Chinese Secret Society Members*, Report submitted to the Ministry of Home Affairs.

Low, S. (1993) *Lesbianism in Singapore*, Unpublished Academic Exercise, Dept. of Sociology, National University of Singapore.

Low, K. H. (1995) *Recognising Strangers: Gay Cruising in the City*, Unpublished Academic Exercise, Dept. of Sociology, National University of Singapore.

Mak, L. F. (1973) *The Forgotten and Rejected Community – A Sociological Study of Chinese Secret Societies in Singapore and Western Malaysia*, Unpublished Working Papers, Dept. of Sociology, University of Singapore.

Mak, L. F. (1981) *The Sociology of Chinese Secret Societies – A Study of Chinese Secret Societies in Singapore and Peninsular Malaysia*, Oxford: Oxford University Press.

Mak, L. F. (1987) "Private and Public High Rise Housing and Fear of Victimisation", *Chinese Journal of Sociology*, 1: 133-48.

Mak, L. F. (1990) *Report on Drug Addiction in Singapore*, Report submitted to the Ministry of Home Affairs.

Mak, L. F. (1992) *Keti Yu Chituan Fanchui* (Individual Criminality and Organised Crime), Taipei: Chuliu Press.

Man, Y. C. (1991) *A Sociological Study of the Marina Kids*, Unpublished Academic Exercise, Dept of Sociology, National University of Singapore.

Matza, D. (1964) *Delinquency and Drift*, New York: John Wiley.

McDonald, L. (1969) *Social Class and Delinquency*, London: Faber.

McDonald, L. (1976) *Sociology of Law and Order*, London: Faber.

Merton, R. (1938) "Social Structure and Anomie", *American Sociological Review*, 3(1): 672-82.

Miao, S.M. and Kong, G. L. (1971) *Academic Achievement, School Adjustment and Delinquency Process in a Housing Estate School*, Unpublished Academic Exercise, Dept. of Sociology, University of Singapore.

Mills, C. W. (1970) *The Sociological Imagination*, Harmondsworth: Penguin.

Murphy, H. B. M. (1963) "Juvenile Delinquency in Singapore", *Journal of Social Psychology*, 61: 201-31.

Muncie, M. and Fitzgerald, M. (1981) "Humanising the Deviant; Affinity and Affiliation Theories", in M. Fitzgerald, G. McLennan and J. Pawson (eds) *Crime and Society: Readings in History and Theory*, London: Routledge and Kegan Paul.

Narayanan, G. and Somo Vendesan (1993) *Indian Gangs in Singapore*, Paper presented at the '93 Biennial Seminar/Conference Organised by the Tamil Language Society of the National University of Singapore (NUS), NUS, 15 August 1993.

Narayanan G. (1994) *The Development of Criminal Policies in the Suppression of Chinese Secret Societies in Singapore*, Unpublished Masters Thesis, Dept. of Law, Brunel University, United Kingdom.

National Crime Prevention Council (1984-1999), Singapore: The Council.

Newman, 0. (1972) *Defensible Space: Crime Prevention Through Urban Design*, London: Architectural Press.

Ngien, S. I. (1977) *Profiles of Delinquents in Singapore*, Unpublished Academic Exercise, Dept. of Sociology, University of Singapore.

Noordin, S. (1992) *Mat Rokers: An Insight into a Malay Youth Subculture*, Unpublished Academic Exercise, Dept. of Sociology, National University of Singapore.

Nye, I. F. (1964) *Family Relationships and Delinquent Behaviour*, New York: John Wiley and Sons.

Ong, J. H. (1975a) *The Problem of Drug Abuse among Singapore Youths*, Report Submitted to the Ministry of Home Affairs.

Ong, J. H. (1975b) *A Profile of the Criminal in Singapore*, Report submitted to the CIU/CID.

Ong, J. H. (1976) *Criminal Patterns of Housebreaking and Thefts and Robberies with Special Emphasis on Crimes in HDB Estates*, Report submitted to CIU/CID.

Ong, J. H. (1989) "Community Security", in K.S. Sandhu and P. Wheatley (eds) *Management of Success*, Singapore: Institute of Southeast Asian Studies.

Ong, T. H. (1989) *Drug Abuse in Singapore*, Singapore: Hillview Press.

Ong, S. C. (1984) *Crime Trends and Crime Prevention Strategies in Singapore*, Paper Presented at the UNU-UNAFEI International Expert Meeting in Tokyo, 29-31 May.

Ong, K. K. (1986) *Adjustment of Ex-Prisoners*, Unpublished Academic Exercise, Dept. of Sociology, National University of Singapore.

Pakiam, J. E. and Lim, M. (1983) "Temporal Patterns of Crime in Singapore", *International Journal of Comparative and Applied Criminal Justice*, 7(2).

Pearce, F. (1976) *Crimes of the Powerful*, London: Pluto Press.

Police Life (1976-2000), Singapore: Singapore Police Force.

Police Life Annual (1976-1999), Singapore: Singapore Police Force.

Public Prosecutor v Mohamed Jais Bin Arsal, DAC 2399 of 1955 and DAC 2116 of 1995, (Mag. App. 71/95/01).

Public Affairs Department, Singapore, Singapore Police Force.

Quah, J. (1994) "Crime Prevention: Singapore Style", *Asian Journal of Public Administration*, 14(2): 149-85.

Quah, S. and Quah, J. (1987) *Friends in Blue: The Police and Public in Singapore*, Singapore: Oxford University Press.

Quinney, R. (1975) "Crime Control in Capitalist Society: A Critical Philosophy of Legal Order", in I. Taylor, P. Walton and J. Young (eds) *Critical Criminology*, London: Routledge and Kegan Paul.

Rock, P. (1973) *Deviant Behaviour*, New York: Praeger.

Schur, E. M. (1980) *The Politics of Deviance: Stigma Contests and the Uses of Power*, New Jersey: Prentice-Hall.

Shared Values (1991) Singapore, White Paper, Cmd 1 of 1991.

Singapore SANA News (1974-1999), Singapore: Singapore Anti-Narcotics Association.

Singapore Police Journal (1971-1979), Singapore: Singapore Police Academy.

Singapore Aftercare Association, Proceedings of the Seminar on Crime and Society (1970), Singapore: Singapore Aftercare Association.

Singapore Prison Magazine (1948 – 1999), Singapore: Singapore Prisons Department.

Sykes, M. G. and Matza, D. (1957) "Techniques of Neutralisation: A Theory of Delinquency", *American Sociological Review*, 22: 664-70.

Smart, C. (1977) *Women, Crime and Criminology*, London: Routledge and Kegan Paul.

Smart, C. (1990) "Feminist Approaches to Criminology; or Post-Modern Woman Meets Atavistic Man", in L. Gelsthorpe and A. Morris (eds) *Feminist Perspectives in Criminology*, Buckingham: Open University Press.

Statistical Report on Crime in Singapore (1973-1986), Singapore:, Criminal Investigation Department.

Statutes of the Republic of Singapore, 1985, Singapore: Singapore Government Printers.

The Straits Times 27 March 1971, 6 April 1972, 29 October 1972, 25 June 1973, 16 August 1993, 12 February 1996, 9 July 1996, 11 March 1997, 17 March 1997, 25 May 1997, 13 June 1997, 23 June 1997.

The Sunday Times 16 March 1997.

Suchar, S. C. (1978) *Social Deviance: Perspectives and Prospects*, New York: Holt, Rinehart and Winston.

Sutherland, E. (1947) *Principles of Criminology*, 4th ed., Philadelphia: Lippincott.

Tan L. S. (1979) *A Sociological Study of Transvestism in Singapore*, Unpublished Academic Exercise, Dept. of Sociology, University of Singapore.

Taylor, I. (ed) (1990) *The Social Effects of Free Market Policies*, London: Harvester Wheatsheaf.

Taylor, I., Walton, P. and Young, J. (1973) *The New Criminology*, London: Routledge and Kegan Paul.

Taylor, I., Walton, P. and Young, J. (eds.) (1975) *Critical Criminology*, London: Routledge and Kegan Paul.

Teo, P. H. (1989) *A Study on the Psychosocial Characteristics of Male Inhalant Abusers in Singapore*, Dept. of Social Work and Psychology, National University of Singapore.

Trocki, C. A. (1990) *Opium and Empire: Chinese Society in Colonial Singapore 1800-1910*, Ithaca: Cornell University Press.

Vasoo, S. (1973) "Social Aspects of Drug Abuse Amongst Young People", in S. K. Lee and T. C. Chao (eds) *Drug Misuse in Singapore*, Singapore: Singapore Medical Association.

Wan, P. Y. and Au Yong, H. K. (1973) *Drug Addiction Amongst Youths in Singapore*, Unpublished Academic Exercise, Dept. of Sociology, University of Singapore.

Wee, Y. G. (1985) *Breakdancers: An Exploratory Study*, Unpublished Academic Exercise, Dept. of Sociology, National University of Singapore.

West, D. J. (1982) *Delinquency: Its Roots; Careers and Prospects*, London: Heinemann.

West, D. J. and Farrington, D. P. (1973) *Who Becomes Delinquent?*, London: Heinemann.

West, D., J. and Farrington, D. P. (1977) *The Delinquent Way of Life*, London: Heinemann.

Williams, B. (1958) *The Habitual Offender*, Unpublished Academic Exercise, Dept. of Social Studies, University of Malaya, Singapore.

Wilson, H. (1980) "Parental Supervision: A Neglected Aspect of Delinquency", *British Journal of Criminology*, 20.

Wilson, I. Q. (1975) *Thinking about Crime*, New York: Vintage Books.

Wilson, H. and Herbert, G. (1978) *Parents and Children in the Inner-City*, London: Routledge & Kegan Paul.

Wong, K. S. C. (1985) *Crimes Against Property: A Study of Violent and Non-Violent Offenders*, Unpublished Ph.D. Thesis, Dept. of Sociology, National University of Singapore.

Woon, C. M. (1976) *Drug Abuse Among Female Addicts*, Unpublished Academic Exercise, Dept. of Sociology, University of Singapore.

Wynne, W. L. (1941) *Triad and Tabut*, Singapore: Government Printing Office.

Yahya, Salahuddin Bin C. (1991) *Drug Abuse: A Sociological Study of Malay Drug Addicts in Singapore*, Unpublished Academic Exercise, Dept. of Sociology, National University of Singapore.

Young, J. (1971) "Role of Police as Amplifiers of Deviancy Negotiators of Reality and Translators of Reality: Some Consequences of Our Present System of Drug Control as Seen in Notting Hill", in S. Cohen (ed) *Images of Deviance*, Harmondsworth: Penguin Books.

Young, J. (1979) "Left Realism, Reformism and Beyond", in B. Fine et al. (eds) *Capitalism and the Rule of Law*, London: Hutchinson.

Young, J. (1987) "The Tasks of a Realist Criminology", *Contemporary Crisis*, 11: 337-56.

Young, J. (1992) "Realist Research as a Basis for Local Criminal Justice Policy", in J. Lowman and B.D. MacLean (eds) *Realist Criminology: Crime Control and Policing in the 1990s*, Toronto: University of Toronto Press.

Young, J. (1994) "Incessant Chatter: Recent Paradigms in Criminology", in M. Maguire, R. Morgan and R. Reiner (eds) *The Oxford Handbook of Criminology*, Oxford: Clarendon Press.

Index

ancestor worship, 374, 378-9
anthropology/anthropologists, 81,
    84, 86, 88, 90, 91, 110, 111, 166,
    222, 223, 227, 269, 370, 375,
    380-2, 382-3, 383-4
    disciplinary difference,
        sociology, 84
Arab community, 14, 290, 291
    see also Muslims
Australia, 78, 223, 270
"authoritarian regime", 39-40

British interests
    see Colonial era; Great Britain
Buddhism, 80, 370, 371, 374, 375,
    382-3, 384, 399

Catholic Church, 372, 373, 395
Census data, 81, 102, 106, 114n, 397
Chettiars, 336-7
China, 93, 229, 265, 266, 268, 272
Chinese community, 12-13, 16,
    83-5, 86, 231, 232-3, 247-73
    Babas, 257-8, 261, 267, 272
    biographies, 260
    Christianity, 393
    Diaspora, 232, 254
    economic status, 205-8, 225
    education, 229-31, 264-5, 269,
        270
    family matters, 78, 82-5, 93, 95,
        108-9, 117n
    history in Singapore, 256-70
    identities, 142-3, 229, 231,
        270-3
    Japanese Occupation, 13, 85,
        263-6

Mandarin language, 61, 229,
    230, 269, 324, 355, 361,
    363, 364-5, 365
    numerical majority in
    population, 80, 248
    research studies, 250-4
    schools, 229, 364
    secret societies, 258-9, 414,
    415n, 425, 429
    see also overseas Chinese
Chinese overseas, 254
    see also overseas Chinese
Chinese religion, 16, 370-1, 371-2,
    374-5, 395, 399
    early, 375-82
    recent studies, 382-4
    rituals, 376-7, 383, 399
Christianity, 2, 7, 16, 91, 92, 324,
    370, 371, 372, 373, 378, 393-6,
    399-400
class, 193-213
    characteristics and issues,
        194-6
    crime, 138-9
    development theory, 198-200
    education, 144, 146
    family influence, 134
    future research, 211-13
    human capital theory, 201-2
    inequality, 197-8
    integration, 59
    language, 134, 357-8
    Malay society, 293-4
    middle class, 6-7, 10, 24, 62, 67,
        133, 137, 164-5, 194-5, 196
    segmented labour market
        theory, 202-4

459

working class
 see class
World Bank, 25

Yearbook of Labour Statistics, 156
Yeo, Brigadier General George, 31
young people
 crime/delinquency, 17, 61,
  415, 429-31
 delinquent, 61
 drugs, 17, 415n, 430
 employment, 206
 gangs, 17, 437-8
 housing, 59
 intellectuals, 270
 language, 357
 religion, 378
 music culture, 60-1